Biblical Interpretation in Religious Education

Biblical Interpretation
In Religious Education

A Study of the Kerygmatic Era

MARY C. BOYS

Religious Education Press
Birmingham, Alabama

Library of Congress Cataloging in Publication Data

Boys, Mary C
  Biblical interpretation in religious education.

  Includes bibliographical references and index.
  1. History (Theology)—History of doctrines.
2. Bible—Criticism, interpretation, etc.—History
—20th century.   3. Christian education—History.
I. Title.
BR115.H5B64   220.6   80-10249
ISBN 0-81935-022-5

Religious Education Press, Inc.
1531 Wellington Road
Birmingham, Alabama 35209
10 9 8 7 6 5 4 3 2

*Religious Education Press publishes books and education materials exclusively in
religious education and in areas closely related to religious education. It is commited to
enhancing and professionalizing religious education through the publication of
significant scholarly and popular works.*

PUBLISHER TO THE PROFESSION

Contents

To My Parents, Ruth and M. C. Boys,
In Love and Gratitude

Foreword

Except for a few (but vocal) diehards, in the Roman Catholic church the thesis has won the day that modern biblical insights should be brought over into our theology, our catechesis, our preaching, and our liturgical life. The objection that these insights are human and fallible and should not be trusted falls before the realization that the biblical insights of the past which were also human and fallible were still incorporated into church life.

Nevertheless, the appropriation of biblical knowledge into any area of church life suffers from limitations. On the part of the scholarship appropriated, one must determine which insights among the many are really representative of where most scholars stand; and on the part of church incorporation, one must find the best pedagogy for fruitful assimilation. In the first days of the Catholic appropriation of the "new" biblical insights into catechesis, in the era of Vatican II, inevitably we favored those which least "rocked the boat." *Salvation history,* offering a smooth kind of continuity from Old Testament to Jesus to the church, appealed to many moderates as wholesome and free from provocation. The fact that it was a theory widely espoused by those Protestants to whom Catholics felt an ecumenical closeness helped the cause. What was not realized was that the scientific foundations of such a harmonistic interpretation of the Bible had already been undermined by "hard-nosed" biblical criticism which insisted on diversity, conflict, and pluralism. Moreover, the blandness of these insights meant that they failed to shake up people's lives and to lead them to a change of mind (*metanoia*) which is one of the prime purposes of the biblical message—and this at a time in the 1960s when young people were very much in a mood for shaking up. Thus, the movement for the appropriation into catechesis of the Bible as salvation history failed. To some this has meant the Bible was

1

irrelevant for catechesis. To others it has meant that a better approach to the Bible should be chosen, and a more thought-provoking pedagogy should be adopted both for teacher and for student.

Precisely because this failure has had such diverse interpretations, it is extremely important that the whole era of salvation-history experimentation be carefully chronicled and analyzed. Mary Boys is in a unique position to do this. She taught religion in the most enthusiastic years of the experimentation and personally experienced the possibilities and the limitations of the Bible read as salvation history. Then she did her doctoral studies in New York City at Columbia Teachers College, one of the nation's best schools for careful philosophical analysis of educational theory. At the same time she took a full-scale graduate course in the Bible, including the biblical languages, at Union Theological Seminary. Thus in a way she combined the best of two educations that are offered directly across from each other on Broadway. When she turned her attention to studying the salvation-history experiment in catechesis, she was not a religious educator trying from the outside to fathom the biblical factors. Nor was she a trained exegete trying from the outside to understand the pedagogical problems. Rather she was one who had practical experience in teaching the salvation-history approach, and then had both the biblical and educational training to evaluate the two sides of the experiment *from the inside*. Although I am prejudiced, undoubtedly—for I directed the biblical side of her dissertation—I recommend wholeheartedly her sensitive and perceptive history and analysis as a service to the church. Mary Boys enables us to understand a difficult period as a guide to the future. Many of us insist the Bible must have a dominant role in Christian religious education. Her study offers us a lesson on how that *cannot* be done, which is also a lesson on how it *might* be done. And in her academic career she offers a lesson on how formal biblical studies can be put to pastoral service in the Christian community.

Raymond E. Brown, S.S.
Auburn Professor of Biblical Studies
Union Theological Seminary, New York City

Acknowledgments

During the final months of work on this book, I made a ritual of spending time each evening with the recently published letters of Flannery O'Connor (Sally Fitzgerald, ed., *The Habit of Being* [New York: Farrar, Straus Giroux] 1979). Much buoyed by her wit and insight, I was also instructed by her dedication to the fine art of writing. As I was struggling to rewrite and expand a manuscript that had its genesis as a doctoral dissertation, I found particularly appropriate a wry comment she made to an editor: "When the grim reaper comes to get me, he'll have to give me a few extra hours to revise my last words."

Among the most striking characteristics of Flannery O'Connor's life was her encouragement to less-experienced writers. Her correspondence reveals the loving care she expended on many others; perhaps I could appreciate the value of this attention because I myself have been the recipient of similar care.

First of all, I am deeply indebted to the integrity and scholarship of my mentors, Raymond E. Brown, S.S., of Union Theological Seminary, who has helped me not only through his vast erudition but also through his personal concern and interest; and Dwayne E. Huebner of Teachers College, Columbia University, who both respects and challenges his students in a way that will always serve as a model to me. I am deeply blessed by them both.

A word of thanks is also in order for those who stimulated the development of my work. Robert W. Lynn, formerly of Union Theological Seminary and now of the Lilly Foundation, facilitated the development of the topic and contributed numerous ideas even after leaving Union. Professors Christopher L. Morse (Union Theological Seminary), Vincent M. Novak, S.J. (Fordham Univesity), Gabriel Moran (New York University), James Michael Lee (University of Alabama), and Anthony J.

3

Saldarini (Boston College) read the manuscript in whole or in part. They provided valuable criticism, as did my dissertation committee members, Professors Philip H. Phenix (Teachers College, Columbia University) and Malcolm Warford (Union Theological Seminary).

I am extraordinarily fortunate to teach in the Institute of Religious Education and Pastoral Ministry at Boston College. My colleagues—Richard P. McBrien (Director), Padraic O'Hare, Thomas H. Groome, and Claire E. Lowery, R.S.C.J.—are generous and supportive beyond belief. Their interest in my work has been both immensely instructive and encouraging. I have also been much helped by the administrative services of James M. O'Neill and of Cynthia Ross Lauer and the typing skills of Audrey Mudarri and Carol Klein.

My gratitude extends as well to Nancy M. Malone, O.S.U., whose keen editor's eye caught many imprecisions of thought; and to Judith Ryan, S.N.J.M. and Karen Conlin, S.N.J.M. for much assistance in final preparation of the manuscript.

Finally, I want to thank some special people: my community, the Sisters of the Holy Names of Jesus and Mary, particularly the sisters of the Administration Générale in Pierrefonds, Québec, and the members of my own province of Washington State; my aunt, Catherine Wegner; and Mary Falkenreck. Many others, too numerous to mention by name, have also provided much loving support for which I am deeply grateful. The dedication to my parents expresses my thanks for all they have given me.

Boston College
Chestnut Hill, Massachusetts

Mary C. Boys, S.N.J.M.
8 September 1979

Abbreviations

ALUOS	Annual of Leeds University Oriental Society
ANQ	*Andover Newton Quarterly*
Adv. Haer.	Irenaeus, *Against Heresies*
Adv. Jud.	Tertullian, *Against the Jews*
Adv. Marc.	Tertullian, *Against Marcion*
b. Sabb.	The Babylonian Talmud, tractate Sabbat
BWANT	*Beiträge zur Wissenschaft vom Alten und Neuen Testament*
CBQ	*Catholic Biblical Quarterly*
CTSA	*Proceedings, Catholic Theological Society of America*
DSS	Dead Sea Scrolls
EvT	*Evangelische Theologie*
Frg. Tg.	*Fragmentary Targum*
HTR	*Harvard Theological Review*
IDBSup	*Interpreter's Dictionary of the Bible, Supplementary Volume*
Int	*Interpretation*
JBC	R. E. Brown et al. (eds). *The Jerome Biblical Commentary*
JBL	*Journal of Biblical Literature*
JES	*Journal of Ecumenical Studies*
JR	*Journal of Religion*
LXX	Septuagint
MT	Masoretic Text
NCE	M.R.P. McGuire et al. (eds). *New Catholic Encyclopedia*
NT	New Testament
NTS	*New Testament Studies*
OT	Old Testament
QL	Qumran Literature
RelSRev	*Religious Studies Review*
RSV	Revised Standard Version
SBLDS	Society of Biblical Literature Dissertation Series
SBT	Studies in Biblical Theology
Strom	Clement of Alexandria, *Stromateis* (The Miscellanies)
TBT	*The Bible Today*
TD	*Theology Digest*

Tg.Neof.	*Targum Neofiti* I
TS	*Theological Studies*
TToday	*Theology Today*
USQR	*Union Seminary Quarterly Review*
ZKT	*Zeitschrift für katholische Theologie*

These abbreviations, as well as those used for biblical texts, follow the instructions for contributors to theological and biblical works. See *JBL* 95 (1976) 339–46.

Introduction

In the summer of 1979, the *New York Times Book Review* reported on its request to a number of writers to identify pre- and postwar books they considered among the hundred or so most important works in Western literature.[1] Struck by the scope and diversity of their respective choices, I began to reflect about the enduring power of the classic in a marketplace of printed matter. The written word inundates our lives; while some of it is imaginative, insightful, and prophetic, much is trivial and trendy. The sheer magnitude of it all—books, journals, monographs, magazines—can be overwhelming. Even within a particular specialization, it is impossible to keep abreast of the literature; gone are the days of the renaissance person. In addition, inflated claims of excellence make selection difficult: seemingly every month a new work appears that critics acclaim as a "book of the generation." In desperation, the reader can all too easily become Kierkegaard's "gulper of paragraphs" rather than a reflective critic.

The Bible has, of course, long since manifested its status as a classic. Its narratives and images undergird much of Western literature. But more than a classic, the Bible is also sacred. As the Scriptures of Christians and Jews, it decisively shapes, preserves, and transforms identities (both individual and corporate) when it is used in the common life of those communities. It is a normative source of nurture, criticism, and reform for believers.[2]

Both as a classic and as Scripture, the Bible continues to mean endlessly. Every age has found meaning in its pages, and this meaning has been voiced in a plethora of commentaries, both scholarly and devotional. Not that the same meaning has been found in it. On the one hand, biblical passages have been cited to justify slavery, condone witch hunts, deliver doomsday mes-

7

sages, calculate the number redeemed, announce the end of the world, condemn evolution, and subordinate women to men. Other interpreters find in the Scriptures a mandate for ecclesial involvement in the political and social order, even in some cases to the extent of justification of violent revolution or rapprochement with Marxists. Biblical interpretation as revealed in the secondary literature reflects a tremendous variety of presupposition, method, and conclusion; for that reason, it confuses almost as often as it illumines.

Herein lies the dilemma. For the community of Christian believers, the Bible is a sacred and foundational text. Therefore, "easy access to sacred Scripture should be provided for all the Christian faithful,"[3] in part because, as Jerome admonished his hearers, "ignorance of the Scriptures is ignorance of Christ."[4] Yet the meaning of the Bible is not self-evident, and the conflict of interpretations over the centuries has led many to turn to a new class of highly trained professionals in biblical studies in hopes of finding from them a decisive understanding.

These professionals, most working from the paradigm of the historical-critical method, have made evident the time-conditioned character of the Bible. New understandings of the form and function of literary genre, of the complex process of compilation and revision of traditions, of the influence of the Near Eastern and Graeco-Roman cultures, of philological discoveries, and of the diversity in Judaism and in the early church—all of these have called forth not only a radically different perspective on the Bible as the word of God, but have also engendered a crisis of authority for believers.[5]

One by-product of the new understandings made possible by the historical-critical method is a tremendous proliferation of knowledge in fields relating to biblical theology. This has resulted in an increasing need for specialization; this very proliferation of knowledge is overwhelming even for specialists.

A consequence of this has been an ever-widening gap between, on the one hand, Scripture scholars and, on the other, members of the community whom this Scripture ought to nurture, criticize, and reform. This chasm is deepened by the emotional response (in some cases, near-hysteria) of those who see these scholars as threatening precious and long-standing beliefs —a phenomenon aptly attested to across the spectrum of Christian denominations, and, to a certain extent, within Judaism.[6]

Needed, then, perhaps as never before, are people who will work to bridge the gap between biblical scholars and other community members. It is at this juncture that I understand my own function as a religious educator. Moreover, I see the responsibility for collaboration as pressing with special urgency today, lest the richness of Scripture be lost to a generation either bewildered by the overload of information or ignorant of its layers of meaning.

Undergirding this study, then, is a basic concern that the immense treasury of information and insight provided by biblical scholars be made accessible to the communities of faith for whom the Bible is Scripture. I am equally concerned that the believer's appropriation of Scripture and utilization of scholarly resources in turn inform and affect biblical studies. Religious education is, I believe, the discipline that can by its very nature encompass both concerns; it is the point at which academic and pastoral interests converge.

Accordingly, I have chosen in this book to focus on a particular way of interpreting the Bible that clearly manifests this convergence: the Bible as salvation history. Put in somewhat more technical terms, I have studied the way in which *Heilsgeschichte* (the German term for salvation history or redemptive history, and customarily used among biblical scholars) functions as the overarching hermeneutical principle uniting the Old and New Testaments.[7]

The concept of salvation history was largely Protestant in origin and evolution. First systematically expounded in nineteenth century Germany, it was refined and promulgated in the twentieth century by two leading biblical scholars, Gerhard von Rad and Oscar Cullmann. It came to play a prominent role in the so-called biblical theology movement (ca. 1945–1960), and was evident during this same era in the work of some major Christian educators.

My prime attention, however, has been devoted to its development in Catholicism, where it was no less popular but where it developed later and served quite a different purpose.

It functioned as a linchpin in the kerygmatic renewal movement that swept through Europe and then through North America in the postwar years. Associated particularly with the work of Josef Jungmann and his associate Johannes Hofinger, *Heilsgeschichte* became the leitmotif in the catechetical movement during the period from about 1959 to 1965. Its influence, however, has waned considerably since that era, though salvation history is not without its present-day adherents.

In *Heilsgeschichte,* biblical theology and religious education were intertwined.[8] To my knowledge, no one has inquired at length into the factors involved in the rapid rise and equally sudden demise of this key concept of the kerygmatic era. *Yet, since its dénouement, religious education has not been as readily linked with biblical theology.* Now that salvation history no longer reigns supreme, the two disciplines seem to have grown apart, each developing in isolation from the other. Because I think that such a segregation can have tragic consequences for the church, I have sought to learn from the kerygmatic era whatever might illumine the present state of affairs.

What has been particularly fascinating to me is the extent to which this one hermeneutical principle is inextricably linked with some of the most basic and pertinent theological issues. To study salvation history is necessarily to inquire into the debates over revelation, the relationship between Old and New Testaments, christology, and ecclesiology. These concerns reach to the very core of Christianity, and have serious implications as well for its self-understanding vis-à-vis Judaism.

My focus on *Heilsgeschichte* in religious education has demanded educational as well as theological analysis. Thus I have constructed a typology to order the educational context in which salvation history developed and have then analyzed accordingly the literature of Catholic religious education. By so doing, I have written a brief history of an era, a history which I hope will contribute to foundational studies in religious education.

In a word, I have found salvation history intriguing, primarily because the vital theological and educational issues involved impinge so directly on religious education. *My ultimate concern in this book is with the matter of significance. Of what importance is*

Heilsgeschichte? What does its era of dominance say about Catholic religious education, and about religious education in relationship to biblical theology?

It is not without misgiving that, in a world of specialists, I submit a work directed to both religious educators and biblical scholars. Yet salvation history concerns both, and there is pressing need to discuss the lessons of that era. My hope is that this book will contribute to dialogue, since "all monologue is by nature unkempt. Thanks to dialogue, the soul of others penetrates into our own, as a comb digs its teeth into the tangles of disordered hair. It penetrates it, straightens it out, and tidies it up."[9] Biblical interpretation should be a collaborative venture; salvation history provides a point of entry into some of its most urgent and complex issues.

NOTES

1. "Immortal Nominations," *New York Times Book Review* (3 June 1979) 12–13, 51.

2. See D. H. Kelsey, *The Uses of Scripture in Recent Theology* (Philadelphia: Fortress, 1975) 89 119. On the Bible as a classic, see R. J. Karris ("The Art and Science of Biblical Criticism," *America* 140 [1979] 514.)

3. "Dogmatic Constitution on Divine Revelation," #22 in W. M. Abbott, ed., *The Documents of Vatican II* (New York: America Press, 1966) 125.

4. Jerome, *Commentary on Isaiah*, quoted *Ibid.*, #25.

5. See E. M. Krentz, *The Historical-Critical Method* (Philadelphia: Fortress, 1975).

6. A powerful example of this crisis in Judaism is the novel by C. Potok (*In the Beginning* [New York: Knopf, 1975]).

7. Henceforth I shall use *Heilsgeschichte*, salvation history, and redemptive history interchangeably. I choose to use the German term because of its wide usage among biblical scholars; I will, however, generally utilize the term as both a noun and as an adjective rather than adhering to the German adjectival form, *heilsgeschichtlich*.

8. A brief note regrading terminology: *religious education, catechetics, religious instruction, church education,* and *Christian education* are not synonymous and have precise historical referents. My own preference is for *religious education,* a term I believe most expressive of the ecu-

menical character of the enterprise. When speaking, however, of the religious education component in Catholic kerygmatic renewal, I use the characteristic term of the era, *catechetics*. Similarly, when speaking of the religious education that followed the lines of biblical theology and neo-orthodoxy in Protestantism, I use the characteristic term *Christian education*.

9. E. d'Ors, *Au Grand Saint Christophe*, cited in G. Gusdorf, *Speaking* (Evanston: Northwestern University Press, 1965) 101.

1. *Heilsgeschichte* as a Hermeneutical Principle in Biblical Theology

One of the ironies of the human condition is that hindsight most often provides the clearest vision. That is particularly the case in attempting to account for the emergence of a phenomenon: only in retrospect can the historian discern a pattern.

This chapter assumes that retrospective view in inquiring into the antecedents of the *Heilsgeschichte* hermeneutic that charcterized U. S. Catholic religious education in the 1960s. It will identify some fundamental themes in patristic and early reformed thought, study in some detail nineteenth century formulations, and discuss at length *Heilsgeschichte* as it has been articulated in diverse fashion in this century by Gerhard von Rad and Oscar Cullmann. Finally, it will take note of the linkage between *Heilsgeschichte* and the biblical theology movement.

I. *Antecedents of Nineteenth Century Formulations*

Seeds of a *Heilsgeschichte* theology were undoubtedly sown by Irenaeus of Lyons, whom Robert Grant calls the first Christian theologian to take biblical history seriously.[1] In his late second century defense of Christianity against Gnosticism, *Adversus haereses (Against the Heresies),* the bishop established that God was revealed in both Old and New Testaments, and recounted the preparation in history for the coming of Christ; by means of "types" were God's people called to "realities," by temporal things to eternal things, by the carnal to the spiritual, and by the earthly to the heavenly. The Law of the OT was real and valid in its time, but now entirely superseded in the NT.[2]

This basic understanding reappeared in the early fifth century in the thought of Augustine. His *City of God* offered a brilliant and extended interpretation of the Christian conception of history. But an earlier work, completed shortly after the *Confessions, De catechizandis rudibus,* had established a fundamental principle: one handed on the Christian tradition to the neophyte by narrating the entire story of salvation from creation to the present period of church history.[3]

A more imaginative interpretation of Christian history appeared in the writings of Joachim of Flora (1130–1202), for whom there were three ages or dispensations, corresponding with the three persons of the Trinity. Such a bold schema most likely appealed to the popular imagination, but was highly suspect to church authorities, who officially condemned his works in 1259. Yet Joachim's understanding was not without parallels in later conceptions.[4]

Not, however, until the seventeenth century federal theology of Johannes Cocceius (1603–69) did these notions receive explicit development. In his *Summa doctrinae de foedere et testamento Dei* (1648), this Calvinist laid out a schema in which the covenant of grace—the contrast to a covenant of works—was subdivided into stages.[5] Scripture depicted a historical spectrum, a divine economy without any temporal gaps. Thus God's work as described in Scripture constituted a history of salvation, and Christ became the object of saving faith in both OT and NT, that is, in both dispensations of the covenant of grace. Unlike his predecessor John Calvin, who had accounted for the unity and difference of the two testaments by means of a figural interpretation, Cocceius discerned the unity in progressive stages of the history of salvation. For him, Christ was the manifest theme of the Old Testament; but, after the arrival of the second dispensation, that "old" testament became anachronistic. Furthermore, he hypothesized a unique figural interpretation in which every OT event prefigured one in the New, as well as found fulfillment in the events of post-biblical history, such as in the death of Sweden's "warrior king," Gustavus Adolphus, in Cocceius's day.[6]

Scholarly consensus holds that Cocceius was, in Frei's phrase, the "remote progenitor" of nineteenth century *heilsgeschichtliche* theologians.[7] In him a gradual shift in biblical hermeneutics was initiated in earnest, as the Bible began to be viewed within a larger framework, and the view of the biblical story as an inclusive world in which its readers could locate themselves began to weaken. This ultimately meant a change to a temporal reality other than biblical.

Johann Albrecht Bengel (1687–1752) expanded Cocceius's vision of a periodized salvation history in his *Ordo temporum* (1741) by giving it some sort of future consummation in the thousand-year reign of Christ. Bengel, a Swabian Pietist known primarily for his careful, critical edition of the Greek NT, seemingly gave way in *Ordo temporum* to a more subjective approach, even to fanciful speculation.[8] In a somewhat mystical mode, he expanded upon the "hidden meaning" of the literal sense and assumed that prophecy always referred to future events, so that various numerical schemes from the Bible plotted and ordered the past and future. In discerning a hidden yet accurate reference to future events in biblical accounts, Bengel implicitly claimed that the unity of the Bible lay in the temporal sequence of history depicted by its stories or at least hinted at by them. The Bible reported a reliable sequence of history that was in actuality the divine economy of salvation.[9]

II. *Nineteenth Century Formulations*

But whatever its antecedents in patristic and in reformed thought, *Heilsgeschichte* received its first explicit usage and significant development in German Protestant thought of the nineteenth century. The heritage of pietism, rationalism, and romanticism in this monumental era, a "century" generally considered to extend from Kant (1724–1804) to the outbreak of World War I in 1914, manifested a marked influence on the formation of this hermeneutic.[10]

Heilsgeschichte was associated particularly with the theological faculty at Erlangen University (in what is now West Germany). *Heilsgeschichte*, however, was not so much a creative and unique contribution of this school as it was a logical outgrowth of nineteenth century roots in the thought of Herder, Hegel, and Schleiermacher.

A. Roots of Heilsgeschichte in Herder, Hegel, and Schleiermacher

Johann Gottfried Herder (1744–1803), whom Barth called the "master in the art of circumventing Kant," had established a vital groundwork in his theology of history.[11] Here religion was found within the historical process: "Facts are the basis of all the divine in religion, and religion can only be set forth in history, indeed it must itself continually become living history."[12] The providence of God operated through the direction of history and the foundation of Christianity was provided by facts such as miracles and the fulfillment of OT prophecies. Herder optimistically viewed history as "progressive, development. . . . Great things are in store! . . . the scene of a guiding intention on earth!"[13] Religion being "man's humanity in its highest form," history thus proffered the record and commentary of revelation.[14]

Not only did Herder's understanding of history as the record of progressive revelation serve as a foundation for Erlangen theologians, so also did the classical idealism of Georg Hegel (1770–1831). In continuity with Herder, Hegel saw divine revelation in history in the self-actualization of the absolute spirit. Tillich claimed that Hegel's interpretation of history was the application of the idea of providence in a secularized form.[15] Whereas Hegel's concept of the dialectic in history established the framework for the later work of Ferdinand Christian Baur (1792–1860) and Isaak A. Dorner (1809–1884) in church history, it was his theme of the evolutionary development of history that proved most significant for the Erlangen school. Certainly aspects of his philosophy provided for the apologetic needs of a post-Enlightenment Christianity; Hegel's conviction that Christianity represented both the culmination and fulfillment of history would be a foundation in Erlangen theology as well as in later thought.[16] He acknowledged the contribution of both the Hebrew and Graeco-Roman religions, but valued them as stages in the evolutionary ascent to the absolute revelation of God in Christianity, the final stage in the dialectical process. Such an understanding, of course, meant that the OT was regarded as inferior to the NT, a view reiterated by his contemporary Friederich Schleiermacher and reclaimed by Erlangen theology.

Schleiermacher (1768–1834) considered the OT as a merely historical background for understanding the New; it shared neither its dignity nor status, a view substantially harmonious with the second century claim of Marcion of Pontus and also with the twentieth century contentions of Bultmann.[17] Yet it was not for this understanding alone that Erlangen was indebted to Schleiermacher; far more important was the centrality of experience in his theology. Experience and history were the twin foci of his apologetics; this meant, as Welch has pointed out, that since the time of Schleiermacher, theology had "to start from, to articulate, and to interpret a subjective view of the religious object. . . . That is, any significant speech about God had to be talk in which the self was concerned."[18]

Schleiermacher had once praised Frederick the Great by claiming that "he did not found a school, but an era." Barth in turn applied this tribute to Schleiermacher himself, to whom he granted the first place in a history of contemporary theology.[19] Indeed, Schleiermacher's role in the development of theology can scarcely be overemphasized; numerous studies testify to his significance for hermeneutics, christology, and systematics in general.[20] But of particular pertinence to the development of *Heilsgeschichte* was his dual motif of experience and history that would likewise typify the Erlangen school.

B. *The Heilsgeschichte Theology of Erlangen*

The theology characteristic of Erlangen, emerging against the broad background of reaction to Enlightenment thought and the general upheavals of the 1830s and 1840s, was thus established by its foundation in certain aspects of Herder's historicism, Hegel's idealism, and Schleiermacher's appeal to experience. Of these predecessors, Schleiermacher was the most influential, partly because his work harmonized with the neopietism of the nineteenth century religious revival in Germany and with a rekindled interest in the church.

The dependence upon Herder, Hegel, and Schleiermacher was hardly limited to Erlangen. In fact, Claude Welch establishes an important point in grouping the Erlangen theologians with the Oxford Movement in England and the Mercersburg theology in the United States; all of these were attempts to mediate between modern thought (i.e., post-Enlightenment) and authentic Christianity, and were, therefore, struggles for a better doctrine of the church.[21] The significance of this mediation is twofold: (1) it broadens the impact of Erlangen, for its theology was not some freakish aberration of nineteenth century thought, but, on the contrary, part of a larger attempt to deal with what appeared to many as conflicting claims between Christ and culture; (2) it establishes the dogmatic and apologetic interests implicit in its *Heilsgeschichte*.

Nonetheless, the theology of Erlangen was uniquely Lutheran. Its founder, Gottlieb Adolph von Harless (1806–1879) had been converted while studying at Halle under Friedrich A. Tholuck (1799–1877), genius and father of nineteenth century revivalist theology.[22] As a result, neopietism, with its stress on personal regeneration as a precondition of all theological knowledge, henceforth characterized the thought of Erlangen in its unique intertwining of experience, Scripture, and Lutheran confessionalism.

This theology received its most systematic and classic expression in the writings of Johann Christian Konrad von Hofmann (1810–1877). It is in his work that *Heilsgeschichte* received an extensive, detailed exposition and manifested clearly its grounding in revivalism, Schleiermachian romanticism, and biblicism.

C. J. C. K. von Hofmann and Heilsgeschichte

The *Heilsgeschichte* schema developed by Hofmann was not so much an *a posteriori* result of his biblical exegesis but rather an *a priori* notion rooted in his dogmatics. This suggests the factor of critical significance both in making one's way through the corpus of his works and in isolating his affinity with later usages of

Heilsgeschichte: in Hofmann, biblical theology and dogmatics were closely linked, forming, as Kraus puts it, a doublelayered (*Doppelschichtigkeit*) system.[23]

The cause of such an alliance is not difficult to uncover. Hofmann, a representative par excellence of the mediating theology of Erlangen, faced orthodoxy on the one hand and rationalism on the other. The former, he claimed, had erred in not affirming the historical nature of Scripture. But the latter had likewise erred in its failure to approach Scripture appropriately, that is, to acknowledge the experiential, saving character of its truth. Thus Hofmann proposed salvation history— *Heilsgeschichte*—as a way of recognizing its historical basis and of affirming its relationship with experience; this hermeneutic henceforth provided the principle by which individual texts could be interpreted.

Hofmann's critique of orthodoxy's a-historical approach to Scripture was directed primarily against his colleague in Berlin, Ernst W. Hengstenberg (1802–1869), for whom resistance to historical criticism was a duty of faith. Hengstenberg maintained, in opposition to Schleiermacher, the validity of the Old Testament, and further argued that God's work in history could not be comprehended by law or historical condition: "Who will prescribe for God the rules he is to follow in his revelation? Who will say that what he never does, as a rule, he may do?"[24]

Against such a claim, Hofmann argued in his two-volume work, *Weissagung und Erfüllung im Alten und im Neuen Testament (Prophecy and Fulfillment in the Old and New Testament),* that revelation was indeed the gradual unfolding of God's plan of salvation.[25] There existed an intrinsic connection between prophecy and history; in the unfolding process that is history, each event possessed its roots in the past and its meaning in the present while foreshadowing a further development in the future. God's plan of progressive development was, in Hofmann's perspective, laid out in such a fashion that its extent and character corresponded at every stage with the spiritual development of humanity. Granted this premise, and the further premise that the books of the Bible were composed in the era and order assigned them by tradition, then it followed that it would be possible to trace this historical development and to demonstrate how each stage fitted in at that point and only at that point.

Such a schema was not entirely new, since both Cocceius in his idea of successive covenants and Bengel in his *Ordo temporum* had proposed similar arguments. But Hofmann's christology added a crucial theme that went beyond theirs. He maintained that Christ was the focal point of history: "The self-representation of Christ in the world is the essential content of all history."[26]

Christian Preus has claimed that Hofmann's *Weissagung und Erfüllung* represented the first time in history of biblical interpretation that an organic view of history was applied to the problems of exegesis in a systematic way.[27] As such, Preus argued that it contributed the following to biblical theology: (1) a demonstration that Scripture can and must be interpreted in a historical way, because prophecy has its specific role in the order of salvation history; (2) an example of the fact that the historical perspective—even if it were misused by the Tübingen school—did in fact have a claim upon theology; and (3) a manifestation of the continuity between OT and NT in a way compatible with their content. Concluded Preus, *Weissagung und Erfüllung*

> showed that there is one history of redemption, of which the Bible as a whole is the unique historical monument. Thus for the first time an interpretation of the OT was offered which made sense of its preponderant historical character.[28]

Preus's enthusiasm for Hofmann may not be universally shared nor his claim entirely accurate, as will be made evident in chapter three. But his arguments do serve to highlight the impact Hofmann's first work had on certain circles and to suggest the importance of his labors for future *Heilsgeschichte* theologians. In his polemic with orthodox theologians, Hofmann had established an understanding of the historical character of Scripture that would prove significant for other ages as well. It was no coincidence that Hofmann had been Ranke's pupil.

But his argument with the rationalists was equally formative in the development of his *Heilsgeschichte* hermeneutic, and reveals a dimension not so readily acknowledged by later followers; namely, the extent to which his hermeneutic was determined by his dogmatics.

Hofmann began from the "fact" (*Tatbestand*) of rebirth in Christ—a "certainty" not in the Bible nor in dogma, but in immediate experience—and developed his doctrinal system from this. But the actual laying out of his system was not, as might be expected, in a careful exposition of his doctrinal themes, but contained within scriptural proofs. Hence, his second work, *Der Schriftbeweis,* dealt only cursorily with systematics and instead developed in great depth and "smallest detail" the themes of his previous *Weissagung und Erfüllung.*[29] Of particular note here is the extent to which Hofmann's biblical theology was shaped by his positivistic assumption that the theologian *begins* with an answer, seeing in himself the humanity brought to fulfillment in Christ.[30] Where things went rightly, Hofmann maintained, Scripture and church must offer us precisely what we discover from ourselves;[31] scriptural proof only confirms that the right facts have been correctly ascertained by introspection.[32]

The themes of *Schriftbeweis* were reiterated and his methodology clearly outlined in his 1860 lectures at Erlangen, edited posthumously by one of his pupils as *Biblische Hermeneutik* (1880).[33] Here the principal issue involved the question of what besides scientific exegesis was needed to understand Scripture appropriately. To put it another way: what ought to be added to the general rules of hermeneutics when studying Scripture?

Briefly summarized, Hofmann maintained that there were but two distinguishing features of biblical interpretation. The first concerned the relationship of the theologian to Scripture and the second, the differentiation between the process of salvation and the biblical witness concerning it, a distinction itself resting on two "facts": (1) the historical fact of salvation in Christ had a historical preparation; and (2) the biblical proclamation of salvation originated step by step in the course of salvation history.[34]

These two distinguishing features of biblical interpretation can be best understood in relation to their fuller context in *Biblische Hermeneutik*. Regarding the first, Hofmann contended that, prior to interpreting Scripture according to general laws of hermeneutics, one must have the correct application for it. This assumed the theologian's belief in Scripture as that which Christians already knew to be true through experience. Such a claim countered the rationalists' (e.g., Strauss and Fritsche) assertion that they were guided by no presuppositions whatsoever. Hofmann argued that they, too, were dogmatically determined, and that, in fact, a total lack of presuppositions on the part of the interpreter was "unthinkable":

> It is impossible for the interpreter to be neither Christian nor non-Christian, neither religious nor irreligious, but only the interpreter. As he, whoever he is, approaches the Scriptures, he is not a "tabula rasa" upon which the Scripture inscribes itself.[35]

Supporting this contention was the identification of Hofmann's own departure point in a letter to Franz Delitzsch:

> The point from which I set out is Christ himself, the one who has made me a Christian. And this point is also at the same time a circle, which encloses me and all the world, visible and invisible, present and future.[36]

Likewise, Hofmann declared against the rationalists that faith presupposed the existence of a salvation history in which God dealt with humankind rather than, as they maintained, there being simply a natural order rooted in God.[37] Furthermore, the salvation history presupposed by faith was the realization of the ultimate purpose of God, which had a center toward which it tended and from which it derived completion.[38] That center, of course, was Christ, the subject matter of the whole Scripture and in light of whom every single passage had to be interpreted.[39]

If the development of Hofmann's first distinguishing feature of biblical interpretation reveals once more the close linkage of his dogmatic presuppositions and *Heilsgeschichte* hermeneutic, an unfolding of aspects of the second feature manifests both his nuanced attempt to avoid fundamentalism and to account for the unity of Scripture.

As his disagreement with orthodoxy had shown, Hofmann argued that the Bible itself had a history; it was not an infallible textbook.[40] Besides this, the theologian should not, for example, obscure the Israelitic character of the OT; safeguarding that did not prevent one from evaluating the OT in light of the New. The Israelitic character extended even to the NT, and therefore interpreters ought not to transpose all individual features of the OT directly onto the NT, as had certain allegorical and typological schemas done in the past. Nevertheless, the Christian's certainty of salvation will prompt the exegete to take a distinctive perspective on OT interpretation: the Christian should read and interpret it with spiritual discernment and with historical sense.[42] The spiritual understanding was based on the premise that the OT is inspired by the same Spirit as inspired the NT church, and the historical sense ultimately meant that everything recorded in OT history should be interpreted teleologically.[43]

Two statements regarding the relationship of OT and NT summarize Hofmann's understanding of the unity of Scripture and disclose the outcome of his presuppositions. The first concerns the OT:

> For the Old Testament Scriptures record on the one hand a continuous series of events in which through a reciprocal relationship of God and mankind, the coming of Jesus and the formation of His Church were prepared. On the other hand we find therein statements concerning salvation which gradually realizes itself in those processes and tends toward its full actualization. That is to say, it offers a knowledge of salvation which is completed only in the NT proclamation of present salvation.[44]

The second deals more explicitly with the way the theologian ought to read NT history, for it is not a mere continuation, but rather a "completion" and a "fulfillment":

> One had to notice how the new things which take place therein are molded by the typological connection in which they stand with the

history of the Old Testament and the prophetic word, and also how the fulfillment of the Old Testament history and prophecy is molded by the newness of the Testament history.[45]

Such a review of Hofmann's work sketches something of the legacy given to later theologians. Themes central to his thought—concern for history, progressive revelation, centrality of Christ, and fulfillment of the OT in the New—will reappear in various forms in twentieth century formulations of *Heilsgeschichte*. Less obvious in contemporary work will be the explicit acknowledgment of dogmatic presuppositions.

In Johann C. K. von Hofmann *Heilsgeschichte* received its first extensive development. Other scholars would adapt it, even in ways Hofmann himself would hardly recognize.[46] But whatever twentieth century theologians would do with *Heilsgeschichte*, their work must necessarily be studied from its nineteenth century heritage in Hofmann.[47] That task will be assumed after a brief excursus into one other theologian of Hofmann's era, Martin Kähler.

D. *Martin Kähler and Heilsgeschichte*

To classify Martin Kähler (1835-1912) as a *Heilsgeschichte* theologian is to oversimplify his work and to restrict his influence in the history of theology.[48] Yet he is significant as part of this discussion both because he possessed concerns similar to the Erlangen school and because certain aspects of his thought bear striking resemblance to the later *Heilsgeschichte* theology of Josef Jungmann.

As had Hofmann, Kähler reacted sharply against the rationalists, particularly against the 1835 publication of D. F. Strauss, *Das Leben Jesus, kritisch bearbeitet (The Life of Jesus, Critically Examined)*. Apparently Kähler had even at one point considered studying at Erlangen under Hofmann, whom he knew through *Schriftbeweis*. But he ultimately went instead to Halle, and wrote a dissertation under Tholuck, whose influence had been brought to Erlangen by Harless. Not only did Kähler share these neopietist, revivalist roots with Hofmann, but they both were products of classical German idealism; Kähler knew his Goethe as well as the Bible by heart.[49]

Despite this commonality in background and concerns, Kähler contributed a quite different perspective on the historical character of Scripture. He criticized Schleiermacher for what he termed *Erlebnissubjectivismus,* dissolving the objectivity of revelation into religious "feeling." Kähler further objected that, though Hofmann and the Erlangen school took the concept of historical revelation more seriously than had Schleiermacher, they had not fully avoided the limitation of subjectivism. Since the Bible and the church merely confirmed (and possibly corrected) what Christian theologians had already derived from their own experience, the facts of historical revelation were thus established by faith by means of a kind of "retrojection" into history. The drama of salvation history was reenacted in the inner life of the reborn Christian, who discovered a harmonious parallelism between external history and internal experience via historical research. Kähler considered this coupling of subjectivity and historical objectivity as egocentric.[50] The Erlangen theologians were guilty of their own kind of enthusiasm, and ultimately faith was forced to rely upon itself.

In opposition to this subjectivism of Schleiermacher and Hofmann, as well as in resistance to the objectivism of historicism, orthodoxy, and Roman Catholicism, Kähler formulated his now famous distinction between *Historie* and *Geschichte,* a contrast best understood in the context of his classic study, *Der sogenannte historische Jesus und der geschichtliche, biblische Christus (The So-Called Historical Jesus and the Historic, Biblical Christ).*[51]

The "so-called historical Jesus" was, of course, the Jesus who was the object of critical-historical research. Kähler objected strongly that this view was reductionistic, and contended that it was the antithesis of the Christ of ecclesiastical and apostolic teaching—that is, the "historic, biblical Christ."

This distinction as developed by Kähler has made a remarkable impact upon theology. As Ernst Käsemann wrote in his celebrated essay (1954—"The Problem of the Historical Jesus"—which is generally considered to have inaugurated the "new quest for the historical Jesus"), Kähler's book " . . . is hardly dated and, in spite of many attacks and many possible reservations, has never really been refuted."[52]

Granted Kähler's significance for NT theology, just two of his arguments will be isolated in light of the concerns of this particular study: his understanding of the NT as *Verkündigungsgeschichte* and his distinction between theology and faith.

The NT writers were not preoccupied with the historiographical Jesus, but with the Christ of faith, in whom they already believed. Thus their records were "source-documents of the carrying out of that preaching which established the Church"—a *Verkündigungsgeschichte*.[53] Jesus cannot simply be made an object of historical research, as one does with other figures from the past.[54] No,

> the risen Lord is not the historical Jesus *behind* the Gospels, but the Christ of the apostolic preaching of the *whole* New Testament. . . . This real Christ is the Christ who is preached . . . the Christ of faith.[55]

It is this apostolic proclamation that ought to guide the preaching of the church in its appropriation of the OT.[56] In sum, "our faith is dependent only upon the Christ who encounters us in the picture transmitted to us in the preaching of the apostles."[57]

This distinction permitted Kähler to separate faith from theology. Indeed, he saw himself as a "defense attorney" for the "simple Christian," engaged in the "preservation of the Christian laity from the papacy of scholarship."[58] What was relevant to theology might not be essential to faith; but "what only is present for scholars . . . has no power to awaken and establish faith."[59] Thus, the task of the dogmatician was to "set limits to the learned pontificating of the historians," who "occupy a larger territory than they can maintain," and who fail to observe "the boundary between the concern of the scientific impulse and that of faith in Christ."[60]

Both the stress on apostolic proclamation and the distinction between faith and theology were to become essential components of a later *Heilsgeschichte* theology. Kähler and Hofmann, each with unique perspectives, left an important legacy to those in the twentieth century who would wrestle with the issue of faith and history. As this next section will indicate, their nineteenth century theology provided a significant contribution.

III. *Twentieth Century Formulations*

Just as the nineteenth century would provide the twentieth with a significant formulation of *Heilsgeschichte*, so too on nearly every front of contemporary biblical scholarship has that era figured in a critical way. As James M. Robinson so aptly remarked of the nineteenth century: it was not simply a passage of a hundred years; rather it was a "fulcrum" which basically altered our whole relation to history.[61] The historical-critical method had clearly evolved from the philosophical foundations of the Enlightenment, but it was nineteenth century genius, embodied in such scholars as Julius Wellhausen, F. C. Baur, and Hermann Gunkel, that provided its decisive direction.[62]

A. *Gerhard von Rad: Heilsgeschichte in the Hexateuch*

The great Heidelberg OT scholar, Gerhard von Rad (1901–1971), manifested a unique configuration of this nineteenth century heritage in his theology.[63] Deeply indebted to the pioneering form-critical study of Gunkel (1862–1932), as well as to similar work of August Klostermann (1837–1915) and Hugo Gressman (1877–1927), von Rad developed tradition criticism (*Überlieferungsgeschichte*) rooted in a *Heilsgeschichte* that had a certain continuity with the Erlangen school.[64]

Although von Rad's scholarship has proved extraordinarily important for the renaissance of OT theologies in this century, here our task is simply to describe the function of *Heilsgeschichte* as it was initially articulated in his principal works on the Hexateuch (1938), reiterated in his commentary on Genesis (1949), and developed most fully in his two-volume theology (1957–60).[65] That hermeneutical principle, however, occupied a place of such centrality in his work that it will help to illumine his entire methodology.

It was the 1938 monograph, "Das formgeschichte Problem des Hexateuch" (The Form-Critical Problem of the Hexateuch), that has proved seminal for the rest of von Rad's work and provided the source of his basic assertions regarding *Heilsgeschichte*.[66] The essay, as suggested by the title, rests on the claim that the tradition of the conquest of Canaan, with its conclusion in the Book of Joshua, undergirded the compositional foundation of Genesis through Joshua—hence "Hexateuch" rather than "Pentateuch."[67] In the essay he established by form-critical methods that different traditions were preserved and used in cultic rites over a considerable length of time. This long span inevitably meant that the cult community underwent certain changes and recognized new needs; the traditions were adapted and altered to meet the changes, yet retained the same basic narration of events as their organizing core.

This basic narration proclaimed that the God who created the world called the ancestors of Israel and promised them Canaan. Moses led them to freedom from Egypt, and they received many demonstrations of God's power and grace during their wanderings in the desert before being granted the promised land. Said von Rad in the earliest formulation of his hypothesis:

> Now these statements, which summarize the contents of the Hexateuch, are understood in the source documents to be essentially statements of belief. Doubtless they have been overlaid with much historically "credible" material, yet once the basic facts are enumerated, it is exclusively of the *faith* of Israel that they speak. That which is recounted, from the creation of the world and the call of Abraham to the completion of the conquest under Joshua, is purely and simply a "history of redemption" (*Heilsgeschichte*). We might equally well call it a *creed*, a summary of the principal facts of God's redemptive (*heilsgeschichtliche*) activity.
>
> Let us consider this creed from the point of view of its outward form. It is a truly immense compilation, an arrangement of the most diverse kinds of material which are all brought into relation with one comparatively simple basic idea. At once we see that we have here the end-term of a process, something both final and conclusive. The intricate elaboration of the one basic idea into this

tremendous edifice is no first essay, nor is it something which has grown of its own accord to the proportions of classical maturity. Rather, as we have said, it is something pressed to the ultimate limits of what is possible and of what is readable. It must certainly have passed through earlier stages of development.[68]

Von Rad identified three places in the Hexateuch that re-capitulated this *Heilsgeschichte*. The oldest of these short credenda, he claimed, was Deut. 26: 5b–9, and its usage in cult was made obvious by its context of the presentation of the first-fruits of the soil:

A wandering Aramean was my father; and he went down into Egypt and sojourned there, few in number; and there he became a nation, great, mighty, and populous. And the Egyptians treated us harshly, and afflicted us, and laid upon us hard bondage. Then we cried to the Lord the God of our fathers, and the Lord heard our voice, and saw our affliction, our toil, and our oppression; and the Lord brought us out of Egypt with a mighty hand and an out-stretched arm, with great terror, with signs and wonders; and he brought us into this place and gave us this land, a land flowing with milk and honey. (RSV)

This appears in strikingly similar form in Deut. 6: 20–24, but in a context of instruction. It is embellished with details in Josh. 24: 2b–13, the Hexateuch "in miniature."[69]

These statements of faith, lyrically rendered in 1 Sam. 12:8 and Pss. 78, 105, 135, and 136, served as the fundamental organizing principle for all of the disparate materials and traditions that eventually comprised the Hexateuch. That is to say, for Gerhard von Rad, *Heilsgeschichte*—salvation history as narrated in credenda or kerygma statements—was understood as the primary hermeneutical principle of the Hexateuch.

It, however, ought to be noted that von Rad saw this salvation history primarily in the exodus/conquest tradition, which was, in his view, the "canonical redemptive story" originally distinct from and prior to the Sinai tradition. That latter tradition, first included in Ps. 106 and Neh. 9, gave apodictic law and was first united with and incorporated into the conquest tradition by the Yahwist. Von Rad asserts the significance of the joining of the

two traditions in the following claim made in his commentary
on Genesis:

> The conquest tradition in our credo is a witness to God's gracious
> leading; it is sacred history. The Sinai tradition celebrates God's
> coming to his people, and at its center is the demand of Yahweh's
> lawful will, the revelation of the great sovereign right of God over
> Israel. Without question the simple, soteriological motif of the
> credo receives powerful support from the Sinai tradition. In the
> union of these traditions the two basic elements of all biblical proc-
> lamation are outlined: law and gospel.[70]

Von Rad hypothesized in *Genesis* that the Yahwist worked with
sagas and cultic traditions that had already become separated
from their cultic sphere and that had been undergoing a
"spiritualizing" process (*Spiritualisierung*), and completed this
tendency to subsume these traditions under the simple plan of
the *heilsgeschichtliche* credo.[71]

But it is in his magnum opus, *Old Testament Theology,* that von
Rad's basic argument is laid forth in greatest detail and manifests its fullest significance. The preface to the second volume
offers a particularly enlightening statement of methodology.
Here von Rad argues that, up to this time, conceptions of Old
Testament theology had tended to oscillate between two different possibilities: the approach via Israel's religious ideas
(first evident in Vatke, and apparent in the work of Schultz,
Dillman, Sellin, and Procksch) or via salvation history. This he
traced to J. T. Beck, G. Menken, J. C. K. von Hofmann, F.
Delitzsch, and others. Von Rad clarifies his perspective in relation to the Erlangen school in offering this critique, quoted
here at length because of its significance for the topic under
discussion:

> However, definite contemporary philosophic ideas which, as we
> can see to-day, are not drawn at all from the Old Testament itself,
> contributed even to this way of regarding the subject, especially so in
> the case of Hofmann. In particular, what arouses the greatest mis-
> givings from the theological point of view is these men's interest in
> "objective saving history," for that latter does not derive from the
> Old Testament itself. We certainly find there the greatest possible

interest in various historical data, as well as in the historical developments which follow after them. The crucial thing however is
the way in which the saving data (*objectiven Heilsgeschichte*) are constantly applied to, and made relevant for, contemporary situations.
There is absolutely nothing of that objectification to which this
"saving history" school attached so much weight. In view of all this,
it must be apparent that even today the old question concerning a
theology of the Old Testament is still an open one, and that much
still remains to be done and elucidated before such a theology can
be written as it ought to be.[72]

Von Rad thus divorced himself from the philosophical presuppositions of objectivity as claimed by the Erlangen theologians in regard to *Heilsgeschichte*, but nonetheless allowed room
for his own articulation of it as he saw it manifested in the OT's
reactualization of historical materials. For, as had first become
apparent in his essay on the Hexateuch, *Heilsgeschichte* was von
Rad's term for the way Israel herself had arranged the materials and traditions and was hence the legitimate foundation of
his own theology.

This understanding was elaborated more fully—if not without some imprecision—in a number of assertions regarding the
meaning of *Heilsgeschichte*. Variously described as the series of
events used by Israel to explain her arrival in Canaan[73] or as
"history created by Yahweh"[74] or "with Yahweh"[75] or as "what
took place between Israel and Yahweh,"[76] it was predicated on
the dual assumption that Hebrew thinking was "thinking in
historical traditions" and thus a mode of thought fundamentally distinct from the more metaphysical Greek outlook.[77]

Furthermore, the faith of Israel constructed an account of
history fundamentally different from that created by modern
critical scholarship. That latter picture, rational and objective,
searched for a "critically assured minimum," whereas the
"kerygmatic" picture, confessional in nature, tended toward a
"theological maximum." Von Rad considered the divergence of
these two views as "one of the most serious burdens imposed
today upon Biblical scholarship."[78] This tension remained un-
solved in his theology, particularly since he considered that the
historical-critical picture of Israel's history could not account
for faith or revelation because its methodology did not allow

the hypothesis of divine activity. Furthermore, the saving history confessed by Israel derived in his view from a historical experience of such depth that historical-critical investigations were unable to fathom it. Von Rad therefore questioned whether a consistently applied historical-critical method could do justice to the OT's claim to the truth.[79] Though the precise relation between *Heilsgeschichte* and historical-critical schemas was never entirely clarified in his work, it was apparent that they were generally regarded as polarities.

Its status vis-à-vis modern historical perspectives notwithstanding, *Heilsgeschichte* functioned both as a unifying factor within the OT and as the primary connection between the testaments. This dual function is extraordinarily important, as it both raises the issue of the relationship between his *Überlieferungsgeschichte* (tradition criticism) and *Heilsgeschichte*,[80] and makes manifest the way in which von Rad conceived of the OT as a preparation for the NT, a view not so dissimilar from Hofmann's.

The understanding of *Heilsgeschichte* as the unifying factor of the OT derived from von Rad's distinction (corresponding to the two volumes of his *Old Testament Theology*) between historical traditions and prophetic traditions. During the two *Heilsgeschichte* periods of the historical traditions—patriarchs to conquest, and settlement to exile—past events were reflected upon and interpreted. For the Hexateuch, this resulted in the formation of a linear course of history; for the Deuteronomist and Chronicler, this meant an affirmation of God's steadfastness, despite the obstinacy of Israel. The events of both periods were incorporated into a *Heilsgeschichte*. But the process by which this pattern of saving history was formed could be traced and analyzed by tradition history—thus positing a distinction between *Heilsgeschichte* and *Überlieferungsgeschichte*.

The line of distinction, however, became more blurred in the prophetic period. In the prophets ancient traditions were reactualized (*vergegenwärtigen*) by the selection, combination, and rejection of various components of the tradition, a process summarized in von Rad's now famous phrase, a "charismatic-ecletic process."[81] Basically, what he maintained here was that the prophets placed themselves outside the saving history as understood by Israel up to that point. Their charismatic preaching of judgment and salvation was the means utilized by Yahweh in the inauguration of a new *heilsgeschichtliche* period, and their message itself constituted part of this *Heilsgeschichte*. Prophets and their disciples expounded and reinterpreted traditions so as to make them applicable to their life situations; both the historical development of the tradition and the charismatic-eclectic transmittal process itself were the objects of traditio-historical analysis. It would appear that here von Rad implicitly has equated *Heilsgeschichte* with the history of prophetic traditions.[82]

Something of this merger of *Heilsgeschichte* and *Überlieferungsgeschichte* is likewise evident in his critical section on the relation of OT and NT in the second volume of *Old Testament Theology*—a topic on which *heilsgeschichtliche* theologies manifest a high degree of correlation.

Perhaps a single sentence aptly summarizes von Rad's argument concerning this relation between the testaments: "The Old Testament can only be read as a book of ever increasing anticipation."[83] Within such a hypothesis, *Heilsgeschichte* functions as the unifying principle in three ways.[84] First of all, it provides a promise-fulfillment schema; in the NT the history of Israel "reaches its last hermeneutic modification and its full interpretation"; a law which "determined the whole saving history of the Old Testament comes once again into operation."[85] Secondly, *Heilsgeschichte* is the sphere of revelation: "it is in history that God reveals the secret of his person, a proposition valid for Old and New Testament ideas alike."[86] Thirdly:

> The chief consideration in the correspondence between the two Testaments does not lie primarily in the field of religious terminology, but in that of saving history, for in Jesus Christ we meet once again—and in a more intensified form—with that same interconnexion between divine word and historical acts with which we are already so familiar in the Old Testament.[87]

Heilsgeschichte as the principle of unity in Scripture thus became the fundamental component of von Rad's own perspective on typology by which a specific history, set in motion by God's words and deeds, found its goal in the coming of Christ:[88]

The theological term "prediction" is, after all, simply the discovery that the message of the ancient words holds good right down to the time of Christ and, indeed, that their true message only becomes apparent when they are applied to him. The only difference between ancient exegesis and that of the present day is that the former took as its starting point this final meaning which the ancient words gained in Christ, whereas we, who have a keener eye for history, realise that two possible ways of understanding them are open, the Christian interpretation of the Old Testament and the pre-Christian one.[89]

Given von Rad's explicit acknowledgment of *Heilsgeschichte* as the fundamental hermeneutical principle of the Hexateuch, there can be little doubt of its centrality in his theology, and his name is rightly linked with the development of salvation history.[90] Nevertheless, it would be reductionistic to limit his influence on OT studies to this. One is struck again and again in reading his *Old Testament Theology* by the wealth and power of his insight. Whatever the limitations of his scholarship—von Rad is not without his critics[91]—his tradition criticism has made manifest the vitality and relevance (in the best sense of that much-abused term) of Israel's faith. As Spriggs observed: "Undoubtedly he had the great gift of pointing out the wood as well as the trees, by indicating the main thrust of a traditiion."[92]

Perhaps for that reason von Rad is often more naturally linked with the development of tradition criticism than with *Heilsgeschichte,* though, as the above analysis has shown, salvation history is an essential component of that methodology. But it is his contemporary in the field of NT, Oscar Cullmann, who is more frequently associated with salvation history as it has been formulated in this century. To him we now turn.

B. *Oscar Cullmann: Key Theologian of Heilsgeschichte*

Cullmann expressed great respect for von Rad's work, and the similarities in the overall thrust of their respective *Heilsgeschichte* theologies are evident. *Heilsgeschichte,* in von Rad's perspective, functioned as the key hermeneutical principle in the OT as well as the link between the testaments. So also with

Cullmann, who remarked that he understood *Heilsgeschichte* as the key binding all the biblical texts together.[93] And just as the Heidelberg scholar had rooted his work in the early credenda of Israel, so Cullmann grounded his in the kerygma of the early church; in this sense much of his later theology can be said to be initiated in his 1943 work on *The Earliest Christian Confessions.*[94]

It would be an oversimplification to claim that Cullmann simply did for NT study what von Rad had done for OT study. Despite the basic harmony of their theologies, Cullmann worked out of a different methodological orientation; furthermore, much of his theology must be viewed against the background of his reaction to Barth, Werner, and, above all, Bultmann. In Cullmann *Heilsgeschichte* received its fullest, clearest, and most refined exposition; hence, the importance of a thorough review of his theology.

Two works will serve as the principal focus: *Christ and Time* (1946), in which his basic schema was laid out and which served as a prolegomenon (by his own admission) for the 1965 *Salvation in History*. While the former work seems to be the one most often associated with him, the latter is particularly important for its detailed and careful development of his earlier theses. Cullmann himself commented that, whereas he had set out in *Christ and Time* to develop an outline of NT salvation history, in *Salvation in History* he attempted to discuss every aspect of the content of this history—including its origin, total importance, relation to eschatology, and differences from dominant theological and exegetical currents of the day.[95]

It is apparent, then, that the two works are integrally related, with the second clarifying and sharpening the thrust of the first. But for the sake of showing something of the development of Cullmann's thought over the years, and also as an indication of the chronology of twentieth century formulations of *Heilsgeschichte*, each book will be discussed in turn. Accordingly, the argument of *Christ and Time* will be laid out in a straightforward manner. Following that, some attention will be given to Cullmann's introduction to the third edition, which concisely responds to his critics and provides a natural introduction to *Salvation in History*.

Cullmann made clear both his object and methodology in writing *Christ and Time (Christus und die Zeit)*: to determine what is central in Christian proclamation (xi) by "pure historical study" (29).[96] The connection with his earlier study on Christian confessions was obvious in his contention that the "specifically 'Christian kernel,' as we derive it from all the Primitive Christian sources, really stands or falls with the redemptive history" (29). His argument was further rooted in the assumption that the NT conception of time and history was the basic presupposition of all its theology (26) and also in the equation of biblical history, revelatory history, and redemptive history (27).

Christ and Time is subdivided into four parts, with the first two carrying the burden of the discussion. Part I concerned what Cullmann named the "continuous redemptive line," for which he found the NT notion of *oikonomia* ("plan"—Eph. 3:9; Col. 1:26; Rom. 16:25f; Titus 1:2; 1 Pet. 1:20) an appropriate term (77). He ascribed great significance to NT terminology for time, distinguishing between *kairos,* a point of time having a special place in the carrying out of God's plan of salvation, and *aion,* a period of time or age (39–50):

> The terminology of the New Testament teaches us that, according to the Primitive Christian conception, time in its unending extension as well as in its individual periods and moments is given by God and ruled by him. Therefore all his acting is so inevitably bound up with time that time is not felt to be a problem. It is rather the natural presupposition of all that God causes to occur. This explains the fact that in a great majority of cases the terminology of the Primitive Christian writings has a time reference (50).

This claim concerning the importance of time was developed in his contrast between linear and cyclical conceptions of time. Cullmann, as did many others in his era, found a difference between Judaeo-Christian understandings of time—symbolized in a line—and Hellenistic notions—symbolized in a circle.[97] That distinction was a critical one because it meant that Jews and Christians could envision something being brought to fulfillment, and that a divine plan could *move forward* to complete execution (51–53). Their understanding met opposition in Gnosticism; here Irenaeus figured prominently, for:

> Down to the theologians of the "redemptive history" school in the nineteenth century, Joh. Tobias Beck, Joh. Chr. K. von Hofmann, Carl Aug. Auberlerlen and Martin Kähler, there has scarcely been another theologian who has recognized so clearly as did Irenaeus that the Christian proclamation stands or falls with the redemptive history, that the historical work of Jesus Christ as Redeemer forms the midpoint of a line which leads from the Old Testament to the return of Christ (56–57).

It might be noted here parenthetically that Cullmann explicitly linked himself with Hofmann, that "brilliant representative of the so-called 'theology of redemptive history,'" though he regretted that *Heilsgeschichte* had become far too much a "battle cry" associated with Erlangen (27, n. 10; 184).

Cullmann found that the redemptive-history point of view was indeed present in the OT, but only in a preparatory way, and could be constructed into a straight and complete line only in light of the fulfillment which had taken place in the death-resurrection of Jesus (59).

Another, more vivid way of developing that claim was apparent in his conception of the new division of time. Cullmann argued that, in the primitive Christian view of time, the inherent worth of every epoch was determined by its relation to a central event (68), and that Christ's coming had divided the biblical timeline anew. Whereas Jewish theology saw everything from the perspective of the future, and its twofold division of time ("this age" and "the coming age") had its decisive midpoint in the future with the coming of the Messiah, Christianity envisioned a revolutionary notion. No longer did salvation lie in the future; for the believing Christian after the Easter event, the midpoint had already come in Christ (81).

In Judaism, Israel's history received its meaning from the future coming of the Messiah. But in primitive Christianity, the history of Israel was illuminated from a new christological center; the "decisive incision" had already occurred and time was divided anew. In Christ God's lordship over time had become visible (91).

Cullmann captured this understanding in what has become a well-known metaphor inevitably associated with his *Heilsgeschichte* theology:

> *The decisive battle in a way may already have occurred in a relatively early stage of the war, and the war still continues.* Although the decisive effect of that battle is perhaps not recognized by all, it nevertheless already means victory. But the war must still be carried on for an undefined time, until "Victory Day." Precisely this is the situation of which the New Testament is conscious, as a result of the recognition of the new division of time; the revelation consists precisely in the fact of the proclamation that *that event on the cross, together with the resurrection which followed, was the already concluded decisive battle* (84).

As such, Cullmann's eschatology set itself in opposition to the "consistent eschatology" associated with Albert Schweitzer and Martin Werner (85) and to Bultmann's more metaphysical understanding (92).[98]

Also in contrast to Bultmann, who took the redemptive history framework as dispensable even in his valuable work on demythologizing, Cullmann included both historically verifiable occurrences and things "beyond the reach of historical testing" in his redemptive line.[99] In fact, he maintained that placing history and myth together upon one common line of development in time belonged to the essential core of early Christian understanding of salvation; prophecy was the common bond uniting history and myth. Redemptive history as a whole was "prophecy" (97), and the midpoint was itself "prophetically interpreted history" (100). Only where history and myth were viewed as "thoroughly and essentially bound together" by the common denominators of prophecy and development in time was salvation history correctly understood (106).

Two important notions remain concerning this redemptive line: it is a "Christ-line" and its movement is determined by the theological principles of election and representation. The midpoint was also the starting point, the orientation of the primitive Christian understanding; in Jesus the divine plan of salvation opened up in both a forward and backward direction:

> Thus we see that this is really the line of Christ: Christ the Mediator of the Creation—Christ, God's Suffering Servant as the One who fulfills the election of Israel—Christ the Lord ruling in the present—Christ, the returning Son of Man as the one who completes the entire process and is the Mediator of the new creation. The Pre-existent One, the One who yesterday was crucified, he who today exercises hidden lordship, he who returns at the turn of the ages—they are all one; it is the same Christ but in the execution of his functions in *the successive stages of time in the redemptive history* (109).

The Gospels therefore only reported the life of Christ insofar as it fit into its place in redemptive history (110); the entire NT presupposed a unified conception of the redemptive process (112), and the early confessions confirmed that the redemptive line was the Christ-line (112–114).

The redemptive line, of course, assumed divine revelation and human sin and involved the "election of a minority for the redemption of the whole," that is, "representation." This Cullmann conceived of as a double movement: (1) "progressive reduction" from mankind, Israel, the remnant, one man (suffering servant, Son of Man), and finally to Jesus; and then (2) "progressive advance" from Jesus, those who believed in him, the apostles, the church (the new remnant), redeemed humanity, and ultimately redeemed creation (115–117). Such a dual progression seemed the basis of Gal. 3:6–4:7 and was symbolized in an "astonishingly adequate way" in the manner of reckoning time as B.C. (figuring the years down to Christ's birth) and as A.D. (numbering the years upward from Christ's birth): "We really can find no better schema to illustrate the Primitive Christian conception of time and history" (118).

Part II of *Christ and Time* focused on the unique character of the redemptive epochs, what Cullmann termed the *ephapax,* the "once for all" character of Christ's salvation. Desirous of stressing the unique character of the Christ event, he claimed that it was infinitely easier to believe in redemptive history as long as its midpoint lay in the eschatological future, as in Judaism: "The faith that was asked of the first Christians was something much more difficult than the faith that up until then had been demanded of the Jews" (124). Cullmann saw Docetism as the failure to respect the historically unique character of Christ's redemptive deed, and argued that it remained the "one great Christological heresy down to this day" (128).

Of particular note is Cullmann's understanding of the OT/NT relationship. He rejected as inadequate a view such as that manifested in the Epistle of Barnabas, since there the OT no longer offered a revelation concerning the time before Christ, but gave only a veiled presentation of the events of the life of Jesus himself. To the contrary, the early Christian concept of *fulfillment* had to be taken seriously. The church was justified in preserving the OT because it reflected a *preparation in time* for the Christ-event rather than a parallel presentation of the same truth.

> The recognition that the entire redemptive history of the Old Testament tends toward the goal of the incarnation is the understanding that should now be possible in Christ. This is the correctly understood witness of the Old Testament to Christ, rather than the assumption that the Old and New Testaments are identical in time reference. The Old Testament offers another part of the redemptive history than does the New. It is itself first of all a unique history of what once happened. But its meaning for redemptive history is recognized only when this entire section of time is placed in relation with the unique, once-for-all event of the mid-point, and this relation may be understood only as a relationship, conceived in a strict time sense, between *preparation and fulfillment* (135).

One might say that this view implicitly regarded the Christ-event as a kind of hermeneutical circle, for it both illuminated the OT preparation and was illuminated by that preparation. At any rate, the future now played quite a different role from that which it played in Judaism; eschatology was "dethroned" (139) and the "when" of the *parousia* had lost its importance (142). The present is simply the time between the decisive battle ("D-Day") and "Victory Day." "It is already the time of the end, and yet is not *the* end" (145).

Such an understanding provided Cullmann with an ecclesiology. Against some Protestant views, he maintained the importance of the post-Easter present, that is, the justification of the view that the church continues the redemptive work of Christ. The church is the earthly center from which the full Lordship of Christ becomes visible and its one great task, the missionary preaching of the Gospel: the mission of the church marked redemptive history's intermediate but final phase (158). But against Roman Catholic conceptions, he objected to the "absolutizing" of the period of the church in failing to subject tradition to Scripture (146–147), which meant that Catholics did not sufficiently observe the necessity of constant orientation to the event at midpoint (168–171).

Cullmann's *Heilsgeschichte* theology likewise gave him an outlook on the relation of redemptive history to the general course of world events (Part III) and to individual persons (Part IV). Only a few significant points from these sections need concern us here.

One point addresses the troublesome issue of the relation of salvation history to history in general. Cullmann claimed that the entire creation had been affected by the death-resurrection of Christ, and envisioned what he termed the "narrower" redemptive process as being contained within the universal process. Even the state stood within redemptive history: "nothing exists that stands outside of the redemptive history of Christ" (209).

Secondly, Cullmann held that Christianity immeasurably enhanced the individual person, whereas Judaism tended to consider persons merely in light of their belonging to a people (217). Thus the importance of personal faith as the only way by which the past phase of redemptive history became effectual for the individual (219). Therefore also the NT ethic of indicative-imperative was an ethic of redemptive history (226); in fact, the "indicative of redemptive history" is the foundation of all ethics (158). Finally, in the NT all resurrection hope is founded upon faith in a past fact at the midpoint of the redemptive line—Christ is risen—and in a present fact, the power of the Spirit (242).

As mentioned earlier, the third German edition (1962) of

Christ and Time contained an introduction that revealed Cull-mann's stance vis-à-vis the criticism that had arisen in the interim since its first publication in 1946 (in German, French, English, and Japanese editions); this also provided some indication of what would be developed at length in *Salvation in History* (1965), since that work was first drafted in the course of a 1959 lecture series at Union Theological Seminary, New York City. The introduction is fascinating, not only because it sketches the contours of his response to criticism, but also because it highlights so many of the controversies of recent NT studies. As will be evident, *Heilsgeschichte* offered such a broad basis for Cullmann's theology that is opened up a number of critical NT problems, and the introduction is highly significant because it indicates that so clearly.

Cullmann discussed the theological milieu of consistent eschatology and demythologization out of which *Christ and Time* was written during the war years and from which later came the most trenchant criticism. These streams of thought merged most clearly in Bultmann; Cullmann's *Heilsgeschichte* eschatology of the tension between the present (the "already") and the future (the "not yet")—as imaged so memorably in his D-Day/V-Day metaphor—stood in direct contrast to the *Parousierzögerung* (delay of the *parousia*) theology of Schweitzer and Werner, as well as to the more existential expression of it associated with Bultmann and his school wherein redemptive history was but a mistaken development of the early catholic church.[100] Furthermore, his claim regarding the linear development of the redemptive line and its consequent ecclesiology contrasted with the critique of early catholicism by Bultmann's students Vielhauer and Conzelmann.[101] Conzelmann's work was of particular note, since his *Die Mitte der Zeit* (a title unfortunately not retained in its English translation as *The Theology of St. Luke,* 1954) claimed that salvation history was reflected in the NT only in Luke, and that it was in essence a Lucan distortion so as to remove the scandal of a delayed *parousia.*

Cullmann also responded to Bultmann's critique by refining his notion of "mid-point," which he emphasized implied not two quantitatively equal halves of the time before the *parousia,* but meant rather the decisive incision into that time (4-5). He reacted to Barthian criticism of his concept of linear time, and accused Barth of giving it more significance than he had himself ascribed to it. In answer to Catholic critics, Cullmann made clear that he placed limits on exegesis and set himself apart from more "existentially oriented exegesis," which he found to be a dangerous linkage of dogmatics with Scripture. He emphasized that his work had neither a dogmatic nor philosophic interest in time, but tried only to be an exegetical-historical examination of some specific NT issues. Finally, in an addendum he acknowledged James Barr's recent evaluation of Kittel's *Wörterbuch* and of his own work, and protested that Barr had oversimplified both.

That introduction to the third edition indicated that *Christ and Time* had exploded upon the theological world and stirred up not inconsiderable controversy, bringing response as it did from existential theology (Bultmann, Conzelmann), dialectical theology (Barth), philology (Barr), and Roman Catholic theology (J. Frisque). No wonder Cullmann found it necessary to refine, extend, and develop his arguments in *Salvation in History*.

Given the polemical background from which it was written, that final work must be acknowledged as a major contribution to twentieth century NT studies if for no other reason than its function as a reflection of the varied state of the field in 1965. Nevertheless, here the primary focus remains on its contribution to an understanding of *Heilsgeschichte* as a hermeneutical principle, a focus which cannot account for all of the details of Cullmann's position, but which still does justice to his major thrust.

Several sections of *Salvation in History* need to be highlighted. Attention will be devoted to clarification of terminology and to the relationships of salvation history to history, revelation, and eschatology; some mention will be made as well of Cullmann's views on von Rad, typology, and canonicity. Since the basic argument remains the same as outlined in *Christ and Time*, it will be necessary only to indicate where he has clarified or extended his earlier work.

A clarification regarding "salvation history" (*Heilsgeschichte*) or "economy of salvation" (*Heilsökonomie*) provides the basis for further explorations concerning the relationship of the former term to history and revelation. Cullmann admitted that the term itself was an unhappy one for three reasons. First, his critics have linked his usage of it with its nineteenth century heritage:

> For many the word has something disreputable about it, for in the history of theology it has acquired a pietistic, or even "conservative" (in *malam partem*) apologetic significance. There is a fear that to take a positive stand on salvation history is to fall into bad theological company. In the last century there was a theological school whose adherents, so to speak, wrote the expression *Heilsgeschichte* on their banners, or were given the label *Heilsgeschichtler* by others to designate their theological position.
>
> *It is certainly a welcome thing when people do not wish to approach New Testament exegesis informed by a certain dogmatics,* especially since the school just mentioned was greatly dependent upon the Hegelian philosophy of the time . . . . *There is a temptation to impute ideas held by the earlier theologians to anyone using the term to describe the essence of New Testament faith, even though that person does not represent such views at all* (74–75, emphasis added).

Second, critics have also accused him of imposing a category foreign to the NT. Third, they have claimed that the essential features constituting history are absent in salvation history.

Cullmann nonetheless chose to retain the term. He acknowledged that salvation history was not a biblical term—though the *oikonomia* of the NT and of Irenaeus was very close in meaning—but contended that its usage was justified because it expressed the idea that God carries out his plan in connection with specific, temporal events. Cullmann further argued that his attempts to show what radically distinguished salvation history from all other history would demonstrate that *no philosophy of history* was involved in his usage of *Heilsgeschichte* and would thus distinguish him from the theologians of Erlangen:

> This stressing of the distinction between salvation history and history, which is so important to me, has already indicated how wrong it is to associate my exegetical treatment of New Testament salva-

tion history with the salvation-historical dogmatics of the last century. As a result of its philosophical premises this dogmatism was often, though not always, more interested in how salvation history and history go together than in how they part company (77).

Since Cullmann had set himself apart from nineteenth century *Heilsgeschichte* theologians by his conception of the differences between NT salvation history and history, it is accordingly important to lay out the distinctions as he conceived them.

First of all, the two histories have different origins; though both are based on facts and their interpretations, salvation history was to be distinguished from history by the role played by *revelation:* "The act of revelation as a saving event is always included in salvation history and therefore is included in the narration of salvation history" (152). That, of course, was not to deny certain similarities, even an analogy, between the two. Both histories include a connected series of events, that is, a sequence. In addition, the individual events constituting the historical central portion of salvation history take place entirely within the general historical framework; Cullmann would, therefore, speak of salvation history not as *alongside* history (as his critics had charged) but as *unfolding* in history (152).

But the fundamental distinctions must be recognized. Salvation history, unlike history in general, has remarkable "gaps," in which "isolated events appear differentiated and sorted out of the total historical process" in an arbitrary way (154). Despite the gaps, the events are connected; yet it is not a connection defined according to immanent historical perspectives nor from a philosophy of history but from a progressive divine revelation:

> All biblical salvation history rests upon the tacit presupposition that the selection of events is reached by the decision of God, and that the principle of this selection, that is their being placed in connection with each other, is determined in the *plan of God* (154).

There were not only gaps, but salvation history also meant a "shifting of accent"; for instance, neither the salvation history of Israel nor the description of it was simply isomorphic with the history of Israel as a secular historian would view it. Likewise, many of the events of the NT were "uninteresting" to historians of the time. It was, as Luke-Acts had shown, only a "narrow line within history" (156).

To summarize, the relationship between salvation history and history might be conceived of in a threefold way. The *formal relation* meant that the divine selection of one people and the individual events following upon that selection were not historically conditioned, yet were revealed completely in history and effective in it (159). The *theological relation* confirmed this; since the election of Israel and the appearance of Christ from among the Jews were free choices of God, they cannot be grasped from a historical standpoint. On the other hand, this election by God was toward a goal, the salvation *of all mankind;* there was from the very beginning an intrinsic link between salvation history and history (159–160). Thus the *material relation* might be expressed: salvation history in essence rested upon divine election, on reduction to a narrow line, and this line continues on for the salvation of humanity, ultimately merging secular history with salvation history (and not the reverse).

Two other clarifications of terminology are significant for their indication of the full shape of Cullmann's understanding of *Heilsgeschichte*. One concerns apocalyptic, a topic of heightened discussion since Käsemann's 1960 theological bombshell that "Apocalyptic was the mother of all Christian theology."[102] Such a claim stood in direct contrast to previous understandings of apocalyptic which had tended to regard it in a negative light and which had caricatured apocalyptic as descriptions of the future which "serve as pure speculations merely to satisfy human curiosity, without any actual interest in salvation" (80). Cullmann's decision was that generally it would be "advisable" to drop the derogatory use of apocalyptic and he chose to use it in a neutral sense designating a special literary type meaning "revelation of the final secrets." But caution must be taken that these secrets not be loosed from their total salvation-historical perspective. The derogatory connotation of apocalyptic would be justified when the vision of the future was not anchored in the central Christ-event and became only "pure speculations floating in the air" (83).

Just as apocalyptic became subordinated to salvation history, in Cullmann's clarification, so also did eschatology. Against Bultmann, whom he charged with transforming the term to mean any "situation of decision," he contended that the word has only a temporal significance (79). Hence Cullmann used eschatology and eschatological in their etymological sense of "end time":

> That, of course, does not mean that in the New Testament they are not related to the present. On the contrary, as we shall see later, it is characteristic of the New Testament situation that the end time is *at once* a future and a present. However, the concept of the "end time" is not to be understood in an existential way, but in the temporal sense of "final time." That means that it remains closely bound up with the concept of salvation history. To speak of "final time" only has meaning when it stands in connection with a preceding time (79).

It might be said that eschatology is a fundamental theme of *Salvation in History;* there is without doubt continuity with the way Cullmann had outlined it in *Christ and Time.* But, as the introduction to the third edition had hinted, his views on eschatology were considerably sharpened by the criticism of his initial presentation of *Heilsgeschichte.* One must, in fact, read nearly all of his extensive development of eschatology against the background of his ongoing debate with Bultmann. To discuss all of the contours of this controversy would take this essay too far afield, but it is necessary to sum up the heart of Cullmann's argument and to point to its significance.

To state it simply: Cullmann maintained that there was a distinction between Jesus' expectation of an imminent end and the assumption—which soon prevailed—of a prolonged interval of indefinite length. The connecting factor was the fundamental, *linear salvation history already existing incipiently in Jesus:* "the temporality of the salvation history must not be given up to make way for an existential *kerygma*" (186). What was really new in the "already" and the eschatological understanding of Jesus was the tension between the "already" and the "not yet." It was characteristic of all NT salvation history that between the resurrection of Christ and his *parousia* was an interval which was in essence determined by this tension.

Thus, against both Schweitzer and Bultmann, for whom salvation history was a solution out of embarrassment, Cullmann viewed it as the very *basis* of eschatology. It was the hermeneutical key as well to the extensive exegesis that follows in *Salvation in History*.

A few final comments indicate other pertinent aspects of Cullmann's theology. Of special note to this discussion is the approval he expressed of von Rad's work. In general, he felt that OT scholarship in Germany had been less affected by existentialist interpretation than had NT scholarship and was thus more open to salvation history. He identified von Rad's work as going along the lines of salvation history, though qualified his praise in a note objecting to von Rad's discussion of the NT in the second volume of his *Theology*. He found it over-concerned with demonstrating an analogy between OT and NT rather than showing a further salvation-historical development as was characteristic of the OT (54).

Such a comment raises the issue of typology, which he described as a "parallelism between two figures or phenomena" (132). He agreed with Bultmann that typology stressed analogy and heightening, repetition and consummation, with respect to the two points in contrast; Cullmann remarked that the salvation-historical interest receded to the degree that the stress was placed more strongly on repetition than upon consummation. But the more preponderant were the principle of heightening and the notion of consummation, the more the typology was oriented toward the history of salvation: "All typology, at any rate, presupposes a salvation-historical point of view" (133).

Cullmann noted that this issue was ultimately one of the early Christians' understanding of Scripture. He argued that if one operated from the formal rabbinic understanding of Scripture and its corresponding promise-fulfillment motif, allegory was inevitable. He granted that this rabbinic principle of interpretation was indeed present in the whole NT and especially in Matthew. But he further maintained that there was at bottom in the NT a "deep insight into the plan of God accomplished in *events*" (134); it was this insight into the plan of God which differentiated the NT writers' understanding of Scripture from that of the rabbis. Even though the first Christians borrowed from rabbinic exegesis in reflecting on Scripture, they never lost sight of the total salvation-historical perspective.

Finally, the notion of canon serves to summarize much of Cullmann's position. The canon marked the end of all the preceding history of interpretation and therefore represented the end of the process of revelation and interpretation. "This fusing of both Testaments means nothing less than that here the idea of salvation history is finally *raised to its position as the principle of the whole Bible*" (297). Salvation history must constitute the unity of Scripture because it alone can include all the books of the canon.

This exposition of Cullmann's work from 1946 to 1965 has made evident the extent to which *Heilsgeschichte* underlay his theology. One final citation expresses this succinctly:

> When we wish to interpret some affirmation coming from early Christianity not merely as an isolated phenomenon but as an actual biblical text, as a part belonging to a totality, *we must call upon salvation history as a hermeneutical key, for it is the factor binding all the biblical texts together* (297, emphasis added).

It was thus entirely consistent for Cullmann to conclude that all theological work belonged to the development of salvation history (326). Without doubt, Oscar Cullmann is a *Heilsgeschichte* theologian par excellence.

C. *Heilsgeschichte and the Biblical Theology Movement*

Both as an expositor of salvation history and as its most prestigious proponent, Cullmann stood without equal. Yet the enthusiasm generated in American Protestantism in the 1940s and 1950s for this principle of biblical interpretation transcended a dependence on Cullmann alone.

It was in this era that salvation history became allied with the so-called "biblical theology movement," and was thereby widely promulgated throughout the churches.[103] Though the movement's parameters extended beyond a strictly salvation history approach, the fundamental components of the Hofmann-von Rad-Cullmann tradition played a prominent role.

This harmonious relationship is strikingly evident in the close correspondence between the eight characteristics of the biblical theology movement identified by James Barr and the salient characteristics of salvation history recounted in the preceding pages.[104] Barr first notes the contrast established between biblical thought and philosophical modes of thought; this is especially evident in Cullmann's determination to correct Bultmannian existentialism and in his conviction that his own work involved no philosophy of history.[105] Secondly, Barr observes the movement's opposition to what was perceived as the systematizing tendency of dogmatic theology; this resistance was not as prominent among *Heilsgeschichte* adherents, although perhaps one strain of it is evident in Martin Kähler's distinction between faith and theology.

A third characteristic of the biblical theology movement, the contrast between Hebrew and Greek thought, is also present in von Rad and Cullmann;[106] the fourth characteristic, an emphasis on the unity binding the biblical texts, is evident across the board in the salvation history school. For Hofmann, the OT history was to be understood teleologically; the *telos* and center was Christ. Von Rad expressed the unity between the testaments in typology, and Cullmann in the motif of preparation and fulfillment.

Barr, himself a scholar of Semitic languages, considers the emphasis placed on word studies to be a fifth characteristic. Cullmann's attention to terms such as *kairos* (a point in time), *aion* (a period of time or age), *ephapax* (once for all) and *oikonomia* (economy of salvation) is a prime example. Barr next notes the emphasis in the movement on the distinctiveness of the Bible as against its environment; for Hofmann and his successors, this feature remained largely implicit, as none of the *Heilsgeschichte* theologians concerned himself with extensive comparative studies. In contrast, however, the seventh emphasis of biblical theology, revelation in history, lay at the core of every exposition of *Heilsgeschichte*. Indeed, noted Cullmann, revelation constituted the distinction between history and salvation history.[107]

Finally, Barr reports the interpenetration of biblical study and theological concern, with a particular attention to the renewal of biblical preaching. Kähler manifests this concern most obviously, but so also does von Rad in his uncertainty about how to relate historical-critical methodology to the kerygmatic confessions of faith.

Of particular note is the function the biblical theology movement played in Protestantism. Rising to prominence in the post-World War II years, the movement represented both a rejection of liberal humanism and of fundamentalist categories.[108] It thus provided a biblical and intellectual counterpart for neo-orthodoxy. Moreover, to churches polarized by bitter controversies between fundamentalism and liberalism, the advent of biblical theology provided a unifying force: a way had been found to navigate through the Scylla of liberalism and the Charybdis of fundamentalism. Divine immanence, a motif dear to the liberal heart, was now countered by biblical theology's emphasis on the "mighty acts of God."[109] Similarly, the liberal notion of evolutionary progress was modified by a turning to God's progressive self-revelation. Historical-critical methods, to which the fundamentalists had reacted with such alarm, were embraced by biblical theologians, who simultaneously propounded a strong evangelical spirit derived from their christocentric reading of Scripture.

Thus the biblical theology movement functioned as a mediating theology among Protestants in the 1945–1960 era, just as had the *Heilsgeschichte* theology of Erlangen in the nineteenth century. Consequently, writes Brevard Childs, within a relatively short time the movement "had managed to effect major transformations in several fundamental structures of the Protestant Church."[110]

The themes of biblical theology and of salvation history, insofar as the latter shared common emphases with the former, were widely disseminated through the influential *Christian Faith and Life* curriculum.[111] A product of the Presbyterian Church, U.S.A., and of the leadership of OT scholar James Smart, the curriculum represented not only the "first creative venture in bringing the newer insights of Biblical Theology down to the grass roots of Christian education," but it also "popularized Biblical Theology throughout the entire spectrum of Protestantism."[112]

But the full tale of salvation history as a component of biblical theology in the Christian education curriculum of Protestant churches in the United States must necessarily belong to other narrators. To detail the complete story would take this present work too far afield, since *Heilsgeschichte* had likewise appeared in Catholic education and it is around *that* appearance that this particular study revolves. As will be indicated in the second chapter, salvation history in Catholicism shared a common ancestry with its Protestant forebears but functioned quite differently because of a different historical context.

IV. *Summary*

This historical review of the hermeneutical principle according to which one conceives of the Bible as "salvation history" has established the following points:

1. Though a fully developed understanding of *Heilsgeschichte* did not emerge until the nineteenth century, it had antecedents in the work of Irenaeus and Augustine. In the seventeenth century, Johannes Cocceius formulated a schema with progressive stages of the history of salvation, thus establishing himself as the "remote progenitor" of later theologians.

2. The essence of salvation history theology was established by J. C. K. von Hofmann's nineteenth century contention that God is progressively revealed in history. Though later theologians and religious educators would assume differing perspectives and modify various aspects of Hofmann's work, they followed without substantial deviation these key points:

   2.1 God is revealed *in history*.

   2.2 God's self-revelation in history is *progressive*, that is, it moves through successive stages.

   2.3 The progressive nature of revelation in history is to be seen in the way the NT *fulfills* and *completes* the OT. The Bible records this history of salvation.

   2.4 *Christ* is the *focal point* of God's progressive revelation in history; it is he who fulfills and completes the OT.

3. Another nineteenth century theologian, Martin Kähler, established important components of *Heilsgeschichte* theology in his dual stress on the significance of apostolic

proclamation and on the distinction between faith and theology.

4. Gerhard von Rad, a twentieth century OT scholar, identified certain kerygmatic statements about salvation history that he claimed were the hermeneutical principle for the way Israel arranged the disparate materials and traditions that ultimately came to comprise the Hexateuch. Moreover, von Rad understood *Heilsgeschichte* to function not only as a unifying factor *within* the OT but, even more significantly, as the primary connection *between* the testaments. This view is most aptly summarized in his argument: "The Old Testament can only be read as a book of ever increasing anticipation."

5. It is NT exegete Oscar Cullmann who is most rightly regarded as the *Heilsgeschichte* theologian par excellence; in this contemporary scholar, *Heilsgeschichte* received its fullest, clearest, and most refined exposition. He amplified Hofmann's understanding of the successive stages of salvation by his notion of a "redemptive line" in which Christ was both the midpoint and starting point. His primary departure from Hofmann was his contention that the mission of the church marked the intermediate stage of redemptive history's final phase. By Cullmann's own admission, salvation history was the "hermeneutical key" binding all the biblical texts together.

6. The inclusion of the key points of *Heilsgeschichte* in the biblical theology movement (1945–60) meant a widespread dissemination of the salvation history approach in Protestantism. Of special significance in this regard was the *Christian Faith and Life* curriculum, the most influential means of making the new biblical theology accessible to churchgoers. By its alliance with the biblical theology movement, salvation history again functioned as a mediating theology in Protestantism.

V. Conclusion

This retrospective on *Heilsgeschichte* has served to sketch out its common patterns and varying formulations over the centuries. As the historical survey has manifested, the term itself is far from univocal and its meaning is thus necessarily to be ascertained from its usage in a particular theology. Nonetheless, a definite continuity is evident, especially in the notion of the fulfillment of the OT in the NT according to a progressive divine revelation in which Christ has the central place in history.

It is against this broad biblical background as well as from its own unique historical-theological situation that U.S. Catholic religious education appropriated *Heilsgeschichte*. It is to this situation and to this appropriation that we now turn in the second chapter.

NOTES

1. R. M. Grant, *A Short History of the Interpretation of Scripture* (New York: Macmillan, 1963) 74. This is a revised edition of a volume originally entitled *The Bible in the Church: A Short History of the Interpretation of the Bible* (New York: Macmillan, 1960).

2. *Adv. Haer.* 4: 14, 3. See also A. Bengsch, *Heilsgeschichte und Heilswissen: Eine Untersuchung zur Struktur und Entfaltung des Theologischen Denkens im Werk "Adversus Haereses" des hl. Irenäus von Lyon* (Leipzig: St. Benno, 1957).

3. See trans. of J. P. Christopher (Washington, D.C.: Catholic University, 1946).

4. See H. Bett, *Joachim of Flora* (London: Methuen, 1931).

5. J. Cocceius, cited in H. W. Frei, *The Eclipse of Biblical Narrative: A Study in Eighteenth and Nineteenth Century Hermeneutics* (New Haven: Yale, 1974) 46–50, 173–176.

6. For further commentary on Cocceius, G. Schrenk, *Gottesreich und Bund im alteren Protestantismus, vornehmlich bei Johannes Cocceius* (Gutersloh: Bertelsmann) 82–115. On a modern form of "dispensationalism," see S. E. Ahlstrom (*A Religious History of the American People* [New Haven: Yale, 1972] 808–812). See C. C. Ryrie (*Dispensationalism Today* [Chicago: Moody Press, 1965]) for a sympathetic exposition.

7. Frei, 46.

8. Bengel's 1734 edition of the Greek NT provided an extensive critical apparatus, introducing variant readings. His "lower criticism" provided the raw material from which "higher criticism" would eventually be developed, and he made an imporant breakthrough with his

precept that the more difficult reading was to be preferred to the easier (W. G. Kümmel, *The New Testament: The History of the Investigation of its Problems* [Nashville: Abingdon, 1972] 47–48; also *JBC* 69:127).

9. Frei, 175–179.

10. For discussion of nineteenth century chronology in reference to theological epochs, see C. Welch (*Protestant Thought in the Nineteenth Century* 1: 1799–1870 [New Haven: Yale, 1972] 1–8).

11. K. Barth, *Protestant Theology in the Nineteenth Century* (London: SCM, 1972) 316.

12. J. G. Herder, *Letters Concerning the Study of Theology* 10: 257, cited in Welch, 54.

13. J. G. Herder, *Also a Philosophy*, 144, cited in Barth, 328.

14. Barth, 329.

15. P. Tillich, *A History of Christian Thought* (New York: Simon and Schuster, 1967) 426. Cf. W. H. Walsh, *Philosophy of History* (New York: Harper and Row, 1967) 134–150.

16. Hegel's dialectic was applied to the development of religion in Israel by his disciple Vatke (*The Religion of Israel*, 1835). Here the historical continuum was formed by relating concrete historical facts to eternal truths of reason. From this blend of religion and history resulted a kind of *Heilsgeschichte* (*JBC* 70: 19–20).

17. F. Schleiermacher, *The Christian Faith* (Edinburgh: T. and T. Clark, 1928) 132. Cf. Bultmann's essay, "The Significance of the Old Testament for the Christian Faith" in *The Old Testament and Christian Faith*, ed. B. W. Anderson (New York: Harper and Row, 1963) 8–35: "... *To the Christian faith the Old Testament is no longer revelation* as it has been, and still is, for the Jews. For the person who stands within the Church the history of Israel is a closed chapter. The Christian proclamation cannot and may not remind hearers that God led their fathers out of Egypt, that he once led the people into captivity and brought them back again into the land of the Promise, that he restored Jerusalem and the Temple, and so on. Israel's history is not our history, and in so far as God has shown his grace in that history, such grace is not meant for us. For this very reason it is quite possible, from the Christian viewpoint, to call the Old Testament Law; seen from its own point of view, the Old Testament is both: Law and Gospel. This means, however, that *to us the history of Israel is not history of revelation*" (31). For an appreciative critique of Bultmann by a Jewish scholar, see S. Sandmel, ("Bultmann on Judaism," *The Theology of Rudolf Bultmann*, ed. C. Kegley [New York: Harper and Row, 1966] 211–220).

18. Welch, 60.

19. Barth, 425.

20. See R. R. Niebuhr, *Schleiermacher on Christ and Religion* (New York: Scribner's, 1964); also R. E. Palmer, *Hermeneutics: Interpretation Theory in Schleiermacher, Dilthey, Heidegger and Gadamer* (Evanston, Ill.: Northwestern University Press, 1969) 84–97.

21. Welch, 143–145; 190–240. For an account of the Mercersburg theology, see Ahlstrom, 615–623.

22. See Barth's comparison of Tholuck to Schleiermacher, 511.

23. H. J. Kraus, *Die biblische Theologie: Ihre Geschichte und Problematik* (Neukirchen-Vluyn: Neukirchener-Verlag, 1970) 240. Hofmann's linkage of dogmatics and biblical exegesis was undoubtedly indebted as well to Schleiermacher's contemporary Gottfried Menken (1768–1831) and to his own colleague Johann Tobias Beck (1824–1878). The biblicism of Menken and romantic historicism of Beck bore such relation to Hofmann's work that their names are frequently grouped together in the literature; see Barth, 519–533 and 616–624; Welch, 98; and Kraus, 240–247. Hofmann's theology was more fully developed and hence of greater significance for this survey.

24. Hengstenberg quoted in Welch, 196. An English translation of Hengstenberg's work is the three-volume *Christology of the Old Testament* (Edinburgh: T. and T. Clark, 1856–1858).

25. J. Hofmann, *Weissagung und Erfüllung im Alten und im Neuen Testament* (Nordlingen: C. H. Beck, 1841–1844).

26. Hofmann, 40.

27. C. Preus, "The Contemporary Relevance of Von Hofmann's Hermeneutical Principles," *Int* 4 (1950) 314.

28. *Ibid.*

29. K. G. Steck, *Die Idee der Heilsgeschichte* (Zollikon: Evangelischer Verlag, 1959) 23.

30. J. Hofmann, *Der Schriftbeweis*, 2 vols. (Nordlingen: C. H. Beck, 1857–1860) 15.

31. *Ibid.*, 11.

32. *Ibid.*, 12.

33. Because this is Hofmann's only work in English translation (*Interpreting the Bible* [Minneapolis: Augsburg, 1959]), all references to this work will henceforth be to this edition.

34. *Ibid.*, 236.

35. *Ibid.*, 13. Translation slightly altered.

36. J. Hofmann, *Theologische Briefe der Professoren Delitzsch und v. Hofmann*, ed. W. Volck (Leipzig: J. C. Hinrichs, 1891) 55.

37. Hofmann, *Interpreting the Bible*, 47–48.

38. *Ibid.*, 32.

39. *Ibid.*, 77.

40. *Ibid.*, 64.

41. *Ibid.*, 165 and 5–6.

42. *Ibid.*, 133–134.

43. *Ibid.*, 135.

44. *Ibid.*, 134. See also E. Fleischner, *Judaism in German Christian Theology since 1945: Christianity and Israel Considered in Terms of Mission* (Metuchen, N.J.: Scarecrow Press and the American Theological Library Association, 1975) 44–50.

45. *Ibid.*, 180.

46. The Hofmann who wrote that "we are truly Christians only inasmuch as we are Protestants" and ". . . the Protestant Christian is the only one to have a firm assurance of salvation" would have been surprised that his fundamental themes should find such parallels in later Roman Catholic thought (*Interpreting the Bible*, 27).

47. Hofmann's work also had significance as the beginning of modern Luther research. See Welch, 224.

48. Kähler was an important figure in the development both of form criticism and of dialectical theology.

49. Tillich, 307.

50. This summary of Kähler's critique of Schleiermacher and Hofmann is greatly indebted to C. E. Braaten, "Christ, Faith and History: An Inquiry into the Meaning of Martin Kähler's Distinction Between the Historical Jesus and the Biblical Christ Developed in Its Past and Present Contexts" (Th.D. Dissertation, Harvard University, 1959) 88–98.

51. The importance of this *Historie/Geschichte* distinction, probably first made by Kähler, for later theology suggests repeating here the elaboration by Kähler's pupil Julius Schniewind ("A Reply to Bultmann," in *Kerygma and Myth*, ed. H. W. Bartsch [New York: Harper, 1976] 82): "*Geschichte* means the mutual encounter of persons, *Historie* the casual nexus in the affairs of men. The latter is the subject matter of historical science, which seeks to divest itself of all presuppositions and prejudices and to establish objective facts. *Geschichte*, on the other hand, cannot achieve such impartiality, for the encounter which it implies vitally affects our personal existence: it demands resolve and decision, yes or no, love or hate."

52. E. Käsemann, *Essays on New Testament Themes* (London: SCM, 1964) 16.

53. M. Kähler, *The So-Called Historical Jesus and the Historic Biblical Christ* (Philadelphia: Fortress, 1964) 31.

54. *Ibid.*, 92.

55. *Ibid.*, 65–66.

56. *Ibid.*, 110.

57. *Ibid.*, 101.

58. *Ibid.*, 193.

59. *Ibid.*, 206.

60. *Ibid.*, 73.

61. J. M. Robinson, "Nineteenth Century Theology as Heritage and Fate," *The Drew Gateway* (Winter/Spring 1974) 54–71.

62. For a historical perspective on the relationship between nineteenth and twentieth century biblical scholarship, see Kraus; R. E. Clements, *One Hundred Years of Old Testament Interpretation* (Philadelphia: Westminster, 1976); G. Hasel, *Old Testament Theology: Basic Issues in Current Debate* rev. ed., (Grand Rapids: Wm. Eerdmans, 1975); idem, *New Testament Theology: Basic Issues in the Current Debate* (Grand Rapids: Wm. Eerdmans, 1978).

63. Interestingly enough, von Rad had himself studied at Erlangen, as well as at Tübingen; there is no evidence, however, that suggests he was directly influenced by the Erlangen theology. By the time of his studies, its power had waned, following the passing of Hofmann and his successors, Delitzsch, T. Harnack, and G. von Zezschwitz. But one cannot help but be struck by the "coincidence."

64. J. C. Rylaarsdam makes this distinction: *form criticism* concentrates on the beginnings of the shaping of the traditions; *redaction criticism* on the last stages of editing before the text reached its final form; and *tradition criticism* on all the stages between form and redaction criticism (in the foreword to W. E. Rast, *Tradition History and the Old Testament* [Philadelphia: Fortress, 1972] viii). There are, however, overlapping definitions; for instance, "tradition criticism" tends to be called "form criticism" in NT studies. For clarification, see the entire paperback series, *Guides to Biblical Scholarship* from Fortress Press, which has, in addition to Rast, studies on both OT and NT form criticism and on NT redaction criticism. See also K. Koch, *The Growth of the Biblical Tradition: The Form-Critical Method* (London: Adam and Charles Black, 1969) 3–110. An unusually entertaining and helpful guide is provided by G. Lohfink (*The Bible: Now I Get It! A Form-Criticism Handbook* [New York: Doubleday, 1979]).

65. See *Gerhard von Rad: Seine Bedeutung für die Theologie*, ed. H. W. Wolff (Munich: Chr. Kaiser, 1973).

66. BWANT IV/26, and later appearing in *Gesammelte Studien zum Alten Testament* (Munich: Chr. Kaiser, 1958), translated as *The Problem of the Hexateuch and Other Essays* (New York: McGraw-Hill, 1966). All references to this and to his other essays will be from the English.

67. This constitutes a fundamental difference from the other "father" of tradition criticism, Martin Noth (*A History of Pentateuchal Traditions* [Englewood Cliffs, N.J.: Prentice-Hall, 1972]). The first German edition of Noth's work was in 1948.

68. Von Rad, *The Problem of the Hexateuch*, 2.

69. *Ibid.*

70. Von Rad, *Genesis: A Commentary* (Philadelphia: Westminster, 1972) 20. German original *Das erste Buch Mose, Genesis*, 1949.

71. *Ibid.*, 17–20.

72. Von Rad, *Old Testament Theology* 2 (New York: Harper and Row, 1965) vi (German edition, 1960). But Hofmann's argument against the Rationalists that no interpreter approaches the biblical text without presuppositions (above, 22) suggests von Rad's criticism on this score is not entirely accurate.

73. Von Rad, *Old Testament Theology* 1 (New York: Harper and Row, 1962) 126. First German edition, 1957.

74. *Ibid.*, 70.

75. *Ibid.*, 91.

76. *Ibid.*, 328.

77. *Ibid.*, 116.

78. *Ibid.*, 107–108. Cf. J. M. Robinson, "The Historicality of Biblical Language," *The Old Testament and Christian Faith*, 124–130.

79. Von Rad, *Old Testament Theology* 2, 417. Also, C. E. Braaten, *History and Hermeneutics* (Philadelphia: Westminster, 1966) 110–116.

80. An issue brought to the fore by Kraus (*Die biblische Theologie*, 138, 356) and dealt with at length by D. A. Knight (*Rediscovering the Traditions of Israel*, rev. ed. [SBLDS 9; Missoula, Mont.: Scholars Press, 1975] 133–140).

81. Von Rad, *Old Testament Theology* 2, 324.

82. See Knight, 135–136.

83. *Old Testament Theology*, 2, 319.

84. See D. Spriggs, *Two Old Testament Theologies: A Comparative Evaluation of the Contributions of Eichrodt and von Rad to Our Understanding of the Nature of Old Testament Theology* (London: SCM) 79–81.

85. Von Rad, *Old Testament Theology* 2, 332.

86. *Ibid.*, 338.

87. *Ibid.*, 382.

88. *Ibid.*, 367. See also von Rad, "Typological Interpretation of the Old Testament," in *Essays on Old Testament Hermeneutics*, ed. C. Westermann (Richmond, Va.: John Knox, 1963) 17–39.

89. *Old Testament Theology* 2, 384–385.

90. Hasel, *Old Testament Theology*, 57–76.

91. *Ibid.*, 88-90; See also Knight, 122-141; Clements, 136-137; Kraus, 133-140; Spriggs, 38-59 and 98-102; and W. Eichrodt, *Theology of the Old Testament* 1 (Philadelphia: Westminster, 1961) 512-520.

92. Spriggs, 99.

93. O. Cullmann, *Salvation in History* (New York: Harper and Row, 1967) 297. German edition *Heil als Geschichte*, 1965.

94. O. Cullmann, *The Earliest Christian Confessions* (London: Lutterworth Press, 1949).

95. Cullmann, *Salvation in History*, 14.

96. O. Cullmann, *Christ and Time*, rev. ed. (Philadelphia: Westminster, 1964). Because of the frequency of references in both *Christ and Time* and *Salvation in History* here and in the remainder of this section, citations will be noted by indicating the page number in parentheses rather than in footnotes.

97. For classic formulations of the distinction between Hebrew and Greek ways of thinking, see T. Boman (*Hebrew Thought Compared with Greek* [London: SCM 1960]); J. Macmurray (*The Clue to History* [New York: Harper, 1959]); N. H. Snaith (*The Distinctive Ideas of the Old Testament* [London: Epworth, 1957]).

98. Braaten's section on "Eschatology and History" (*History and Hermeneutics*, 160-174) is helpful background here.

99. Cf. O. Cullmann, "The Connection of Primal Events and End Events with the New Testament Redemptive History," in *The Old Testament and Christian Faith*, 115-123.

100. Of fundamental importance for understanding Cullmann's response to his critics is Bultmann's 1948 review of *Christ and Time* which sharpened the battle lines (translated as "History of Salvation and History," in *Existence and Faith: Shorter Writings of Rudolf Bultmann*, ed. S. M. Ogden [New York: Meridian, 1960] 226-240). The initial portion of Bultmann's essay consists of an excellent summary of Cullmann's position, which the latter notes was a "correct review of its content" (*Christ and Time*, rev. ed.). See also R. D. Newton, "The Method of Biblical Theology in Cullman, Barth and Bultmann" (Ph.D. dissertation, Columbia University, 1960); R. H. Fuller, "Some Further Thoughts on *Heilsgeschichte*," '*USQR* 22 (January 1967) 93-103.

101. P. Vielhauer's essay, "Zum 'Paulinismus' der Apostelgeschichte," (*Evt* 10 [1950-51]) may be found in English in the valuable collection *Studies in Luke-Acts*, ed. L. E. Keck and J. L. Martyn (Nashville: Abingdon, 1966), 33-50. H. Conzelmann, *Die Mitte der Zeit* (Tübingen: Mohr, 1954), translated as *The Theology of St. Luke* (New York: Harper, 1961). The work of both Vielhauer and Conzelmann is

placed into historical perspective in E. Haenchen (*The Acts of the Apostles: A Commentary* [Philadelphia: Westminster, 1971] 14-49). For a new position, see J. Jervell (*Luke and the People of God* [Minneapolis: Augsburg, 1972]).

102. E. Käsemann, *New Testament Questions of Today* (Philadelphia: Fortress, 1969), 102. For a critical perspective on Cullmann's understanding of apocalyptic, see K. Koch (*The Rediscovery of Apocalyptic* SBT 2/22 [London: SCM, 1972] 61); Koch groups Cullmann with theologians who have a superficial understanding of apocalyptic.

103. The distinction is generally made between biblical theology as a movement and as a term referring to significant individual studies in both OT and NT. The rise of the movement has been chronicled most completely by B. Childs (*Biblical Theology in Crisis* [Philadelphia: Westminster, 1970] 13-90). See also J. Barr, "Biblical Theology," *IDB Sup* (Nashville: Abingdon, 1976) 104-111. Childs and Barr disagree on the extent to which the movement was distinctively American; otherwise their accounts are substantially harmonious.

104. Barr, 105.

105. O. Cullmann, *Salvation in History*, 77.

106. Von Rad, *Old Testament Theology* 1, 116; Cullmann, *Christ and Time*, 50.

107. Cullmann, *Ibid.*, 51.

108. For a particularly lucid analysis of this split, see W. R. Hutchison (*The Modernist Impulse in American Protestantism* [Cambridge: Harvard, 1976]). The Presbyterian church was particularly hard hit by the bifurcation; see, for example, C. A. Briggs (*Inaugural Address and Defense 1891/93* [Religion in America, Series 2; New York; Arno Press, 1972]).

109. A phrase made popular by archaeologist G. E. Wright (*God Who Acts: Biblical Theology As Recital* [SBT 1/8; London: SCM, 1952]).

110. Childs, 27.

111. See J. D. Smart, *The Teaching Ministry of the Church* (Philadelphia: Westminster, 1954).

112. Childs, 27.

2. *Heilsgeschichte* as a Hermeneutical Principle in Catholic Religious Education

Twentieth century *Heilsgeschichte* theology differs from its nineteenth century predecessor in one important respect: it is done in a world become a "global village," and in a church painfully aware of its divisions. Cullmann's *Salvation in History*, for instance, is dedicated to the Secretariat of Christian Unity in gratitude for his role as guest and observer to the Second Vatican Council; in the foreword he cites Pope Paul VI's remarks to the non-Catholic observers that a concrete and historical theology centered in *Heilsgeschichte* provided the common ground of ecumenical dialogue.[1]

Thus it is no surprise to discover that *Heilsgeschichte* made its way into Catholic theology and religious education. Council declarations, for instance, speak of God's "plan of revelation" and the "history of salvation." In the fourth chapter of the Dogmatic Constitution on Divine Revelation (*Dei Verbum*), the Council presents the OT in this fashion:

> The principal purpose to which the plan of the Old Covenant was directed was to prepare for the coming both of Christ, the Universal Redeemer, and of the messianic kingdom, to announce this coming by prophecy (cf. Lk. 23:44; Jn. 5:39; 1 Pet. 1:10), and to indicate its meaning through various types (cf. 1 Cor. 10:11). Now the books of the Old Testament, in accordance with the state of mankind before the time of salvation established by Christ, reveal to all men the knowledge of God and of man and the ways in which God, just and merciful, deals with men. These books, though they also contain some things which are incomplete and temporary, nevertheless show us true divine pedagogy. These same books, then, give expression to a lively sense of God, contain a store of sublime teachings about God, sound wisdom about human life and

a wonderful treasury of prayers, and in them the mystery of our salvation is present in a hidden way. Christians should receive them with reverence.[2]

Specifically in regard to religious education, *Sharing the Light of Faith,* an official document intended to provide pastoral standards and guidelines for the catechesis of Roman Catholics in the United States, includes this claim:

> In the covenant of the Old Testament, God announced His plan of salvation prophetically and by means of types revealed the truth about Himself gradually over centuries.
> Now, in the fullness of time when revelation has been consummated in Christ, the Church uses a pedagogy adapted to the final age of salvation history, one in which the message is presented in its entirety while also being expressed according to the circumstances and ability of those being catechized.[3]

In a preceding section, a passage spoke of a revelation of God through Israel and concluded: "Thus the stage was set for a broader and deeper covenant, God's fullest self revelation in Jesus Christ."[4] In a similar spirit are these statements:

> The history of salvation is the story of God's entry into human affairs to save human beings from sin and bring them to Himself.
> In the Old Testament God revealed Himself as the one, true, personal God, creator of heaven and earth (cf. Is 42, 5), who transcends this world. By words and actions God prepared for the ultimate disclosure of Himself as a Trinity: Father, Son and Holy Spirit. (Cf. Mt 3, 16; 28, 19; Jn 14, 23, 26).[5]
> In Jesus Christ the Christian is joined to all history and all human beings. The story of salvation, set in the midst of human history, is no less than the working out of God's plan for humankind: to form His people into the whole Christ, "that perfect man who is Christ come to full stature." (Eph 4, 13)[6]

Such a brief sampling echoes the themes of progressive revelation within the Bible, the centrality of Christ, and the fulfillment of the OT in the NT that had comprised the *Heilsgeschichte* theology of nineteenth and twentieth century Protestant thought. Granted its basic similarity with Protestant thought,

Heilsgeschichte nonetheless developed uniquely in Roman Catholicism; as a fundamental motif in post-modernist kerygmatic renewal in Europe (and ultimately in the United States), it
functioned as a central axis in the configuration of the fledgling.
catechetical, biblical, and liturgical movements.

The task in this chapter is twofold: (1) to indicate the essential
correspondence between Protestant and Catholic formulations
of *Heilsgeschichte;* and (2) to show how *Heilsgeschichte* functioned
uniquely as a hermeneutical principle in twentieth century
Roman Catholic renewal, particularly in catechetics.

In order to fulfill such a task, it is necessary first to turn
briefly to nineteenth century Catholicism, significant not for its
foundational ideas—as it had been in Protestantism—but for
the establishment of a milieu from which and against which
twentieth century renewal must be understood. We will then
focus on the kerygmatic renewal movement in which *Heilsgeschichte* functioned as the principal hermeneutic, especially in
the catechetical theories of Josef Jungmann, Johannes
Hofinger, and of the Lumen Vitae tradition. The final major
section will trace the Jungmann-Hofinger and Lumen Vitae
appropriation of *Heilsgeschichte* in Catholic religious education
in the United States in the 1960s, indicating the amazing consistency with which that hermeneutic was formulated during that
era. Some concluding remarks will highlight the present status
of *Heilsgeschichte* as a hermeneutical principle.

I. Nineteenth Century European Catholicism

In the previous chapter, the first explicit usage and significant development of *Heilsgeschichte* was attributed to nineteenth
century thinkers for whom pietism, romanticism, and rationalism formed an important heritage. The theology of Erlang-
en was found to be broadly similar to that of the ·Oxford
Movement and of Mercersburg. Welch further postulated that
it bore a parallel to the latter portion of the pontificate of Pius
IX—an era characterized by what historians have frequently
termed a "fortress mentality." As he remarked: "The mood of
restoration and recovery, of diastasis and defense, was strong in
mid-nineteenth century Christianity."[7]

A. *Antecedents of the Modernist Crisis*

Yet granted this general spirit of the age, European Roman Catholic theology assumed a posture distinctively defensive.[8] It neither engendered nor encouraged creative, critical scholarship; furthermore, this defensiveness was expressed not so much in a "mediating theology" as at Erlangen, but rather in the form of an increasing concentration of power in the papacy. Thus there was a preoccupation with church-state relations and a tightening of authority even to the extent that scholasticism became the only permissible theological methodology. No *Heilsgeschichte* hermeneutic would come out of this era; and when it did arise in 1936, it was offered precisely as a critique of the arid theology of the previous century.

Nor had the eighteenth century been a particularly fertile era; Herder had observed at the beginning of the nineteenth century that the Church of Rome was like an ancient ruin into which no new life could enter.[9] But the romanticist movement did breathe fresh air into Catholicism, resulting in something of a revival in both Germany and France.

The conversion of poet Friedrich von Schlegel (1772–1829) in 1808 brought one of the leading minds of the romantic movement into German Catholicism; today he is increasingly recognized as one of the most erudite thinkers of that era and acknowledged as a genius who brought a new vitality into the mainstream of Catholic tradition.[10] But it was especially at Tübingen that the romanticist influence was most clearly evident. A Catholic faculty had been founded alongside the Protestant one in 1817 under the leadership of Johann Sebastian von Drey.[11] That very proximity served to remind the Catholics that their thought had of necessity to deal with Kant, Hegel, Lessing, and Schleiermacher; Tübingen, especially in its early years, manifested a dynamic understanding of revelation and a conception of tradition greatly indebted to Schleiermacher.

Drey's student, Johann Adam Möhler, brilliantly represented Tübingen in his 1825 *Die Einheit der Kirche oder das Prinzip der Katholizimus* (The unity of the church or the principle of Catholicism), in which the romantic idea of organic unity was applied to the church, a unity in multiplicity. He viewed doctrinal tradition as governed from within by that same Spirit who inspired the Scriptures, and thus it was not merely a historical phenomenon but also a mystery. His pneumatology led him to see growth in the church as happening by the whole body under the inspiration of the Spirit rather than as an accomplishment of hierarchical authority. And since Christianity is "new divine life given to man and not a dead concept, it is subject to development and elaboration."[12]

Möhler's accent shifted somewhat in his 1832 *Symbolik oder Darstellung der dogmatischen Gegensatze der Katholiken und Protestanten nach ihren offentlichen Bekenntnisschriften*, a comparative study of confessions in which he brought together the church as a community guided by the Spirit with its external structures— and a work which led him into conflict with his Tübingen colleague from the Protestant faculty, F. C. Baur.[13] Dulles notes that Möhler's *Symbolics* marked an "immense step forward in the development of a more irenic type of controversial theology than had been since the Reformation," and that though he argued firmly for Catholic positions, he made a "genuine effort to present the guiding intuitions and inner coherence" of Protestant confessional writings.[14] Such a methodology, however, was a rarity in nineteenth century Catholicism.

Vidler argues that it is not an exaggeration to claim that the Tübingen school "did for Catholic theology what Schleiermacher did, more or less contemporaneously for Protestant theology," and cites two points of comparison.[15] First, the theologians of Tübingen agreed with Schleiermacher in criticism of previous theological systems; the separation between natural and revealed religion was erroneous and led to false supernaturalism and false rationalism. Secondly, both entered a common protest against a forced and static concept of dogma and appealed to religious experience. But in contrast, the Tübingen theologians objected that Schleiermacher had gone too far in his reaction against an intellectualist concept of dogma and they considered his definition of religion as "absolute dependence" an oversimplification, and thus sought an integral definition for themselves.

The theologians of Tübingen, indebted particularly in the foundational years to the romanticist spirit, both appreciated and criticized Schleiermacher, Schelling, Hegel, and scholasticism. Yet for all their attempts to create a new and comprehensive articulation of Catholicism according to their intellectual milieu, their work received little attention and hence could not change the course of nineteenth century Catholicism.

Romanticism, too, was "alive and well" in France, where it inspired the anti-Enlightenment apologetic of François René de Chateaubriand (1768–1848). Something of a foreshadowing of his debt to romanticism as elaborated in his five-volume classic, *Le génie du christianisme; ou, beautés de la religion chrétienne* (The genius of Christianity; or beauties of the Christian religion, 1802), was manifest in the pithy account of his conversion: "I wept, and I believed."[16]

Though Chateaubriand's apologetic could not in any way measure up to the depth of thought evident in the writings of the Tübingen theologians, it at least enjoyed great appeal. Profundity may have eluded Chateaubriand, but so also did "scholarly hairsplitting," which had plagued other apologists. Dulles concludes that by calling attention to the numerous blessings brought to the world by Christianity he helped to restore the morale of a church too long on the defensive and thereby evoked an enthusiastic response from citizens longing for the glories of the *ancien régime.*[17]

But the romantic spirit was not enough to assuage the crisis of French Catholicism in those critical post-revolutionary years. The turmoil in the church engendered by the Revolution of 1789 and by subsequent events is exceedingly important in establishing a historical perspective. One reason for this is aptly articulated by Vidler:

> Thus it is in France that the political impact of the age of revolution upon the Church can best be studied. Not that any stable solution was arrived at there, either in the years succeeding 1789 or at any subsequent time. *Rather, it is the variety, the fluctuations, and the instability of the relations between Church, State and society since 1789 that make French ecclesiastical history a paradigm both of the insecurity and of the survival of Christianity in this age.* What was writ large in France was written in lesser or derivative scripts elsewhere.[18]

Another reason, more directly pertinent to this book, is that post-revolutionary France was the climate in which modern ultramontanism developed, a phenomenon of critical significance for nineteenth century Catholic theology and, ultimately therefore, for twentieth century renewal. A Catholicism that had begun the nineteenth century with a romantic revival, that had by its midpoint become disillusioned, and would by the end be entrenched in its own tight system, was in large measure the product of this upheaval caused by the Revolution.

The church, largely identified with the old order, had, of course, been dealt a severe blow by the Revolution and the later excesses of the Reign of Terror. But Napoleon, astute general that he was, recognized the social utility of religion and thus had restored the external order of the church in his Concordat of 1801. But two aspects of that agreement—the stipend paid by the state to bishops and clergy and the recognition of papal authority over French bishops—planted seeds of ultramontanism ("beyond the mountains," the Alps, to papal supremacy).

During the period of the Restoration (1814–1830), ultramontanism joined forces with liberalism. The official church, aligned with the Bourbons, had become increasingly bound up with Gallicanism. Vidler wryly observes that this "propping of the altar against the worm-eaten throne" was a "suicidal policy," and that the reestablishment of the church might have been as short-lived as that of the legitimist monarchy had it not been for this marriage of ultramontanism with liberalism.[19]

They were strange bedfellows, as a later controversy (ca. 1850) would reveal. But in the early part of the century, ultramontanism was advocated by traditionalist Joseph de Maistre (1754–1821) in his 1817 *Du pape* as an anti-Gallicanism measure, "the sovereign cure for all the ills of Europe."[20] Ultramontanism was envisioned as that basic structure for both a new society and for its religion: dependence on authority was the means to recovery.

Ultramontanism appeared as a doctrine of liberation of the French church in its relationship with a government that could no longer claim to be Christian. Thus did French liberal Félicité de Lamennais (1782–1854) ally himself with it. With his disciples Henri Lacordaire and Charles Montalembert he founded the paper *L'Avenir*. With the motto "God and Liberty," their paper rejected the divine right of kings and urged the papacy to abandon its dependence on temporal power and to build instead a new order by means of its spiritual authority. It advocated separation of church and state, and liberty of conscience, of education, of the press, and of association.

But the reigning pontiff, Gregory XVI, whose papal states were at the time threatened by revolutionary movements, condemned *L'Avenir* in his 1832 encyclical, *Mirari Vos,* and implicitly linked Lamennais with "unbridled license," "contempt for the Church," an ever-approaching "revolutionary abyss of bottomless miseries," and a filthy sewer of "heretical vomit."[21]

But liberal hopes were restored in 1846 with the accession of Pius IX to the papacy, and in the euphoria following the 1848 revolution, the founders of *L'Avenir* began another journal, the *New Era,* which announced that there was no opposition of principle between Catholicism and democracy.

The tide, however, turned quickly, following the revolutionary excesses of 1848, the enforced exile of the pope, and the publication of the *Communist Manifesto* of Marx and Engels. In 1861 Victor Emmanuel was proclaimed king of Italy; thus it was a besieged Pope Pius IX who issued the 1864 encyclical *Quanta Cura* and its supplement, the *Syllabus of Errors.* The encyclical was a sequel to *Mirari Vos,* an expression par excellence of that "fortress mentality," condemning as it did the very notion that the pope should attempt to reconcile himself with progress, liberalism, and modern civilization. Its sweeping propositions condemned rationalism, freemasonry, indifferentism, separation of church and state, and liberty of religion. Socialism, communism, secret societies, biblical societies, and clerico-liberal societies were grouped together and termed "pests of this description."[22]

Just prior to the publication of the *Syllabus* in 1864, Pius IX had announced his intention of convening a Vatican Council, the first ecumenical council since Trent (1545–1563); the members of the Council gathered in 1869. One product of its deliberations, the apostolic constitution *Dei Filius,* reiterated and refined traditional church teaching on reason, revelation, and faith. In affirming the knowability of God's existence by natural reason, the reasonableness of the assent of faith, and the complementary yet distinct roles of faith and reason, the constitution reflected its scholastic influence. Among the more significant ramifications of the constitution's declarations was an encouragement of an Aristotelian, nonhistorical scientific theology. Ultimately this meant a flowering of "conclusion theology," in which theologically certain conclusions were derived from revealed first principles:

> As a result, Catholic "conclusion theology" became a sterile speculative enterprise. Its conclusions became more and more remote from the ordinary Christian's concrete life of prayer and action. Speculative theology ceased to provide the fruitful understanding of the revealed mysteries of which *Dei Filius* spoke. Theology no longer furnished the necessary help to the life of contemplation through which the life of Christian action must be nourished and enlightened. Hence the strong reaction against the pastoral sterility of Catholic speculative theology in the period between the two world wars.[23]

On another front, the dogmatic constitution *Pastor Aeternus* delineated the extent of the pope's jurisdictional primacy and declared him to be infallible on matters of faith and morals. Cut short by the political situation, Vatican I produced a truncated version of the teaching authority of the church by not giving consideration to the role and authority of the episcopacy, an issue not confronted until Vatican II's statements on collegiality in the third chapter of its *Lumen Gentium*.[24]

Vatican I was but a logical outgrowth of the ultramontanist sentiment. A remark made by Pius IX toward the end of his life seems to reveal that even he realized that the "fortress mentality" was too much: "My system and my policy have had their day, but I am too old to change my course. That will be the task of my successor."[25]

Ironically, it was the more accommodating spirit of his successor, Leo XIII, less a liberal than a diplomat, which ultimately precipitated the modernist crisis by restoring the hopes of liberals. His policy was one of moderation and conciliation in contrast to the intransigence of Pius IX; he sought to reconcile the church and the modern world, relieving tension in Germany over Bismarck's *Kulturkampf,* pressing French Catholics to become reconciled to the Republic and encouraging a more progressive social teaching in his famous encyclical *Rerum Novarum*

(1891). He bestowed the cardinal's hat on Newman, whose *Essay on the Development of Christian Doctrine* and *Grammar of Assent* had offended both orthodox theologians and ultramontanists; he opened the Vatican archives for historical research. In short, the style of his tenure created a psychological atmosphere conveying the impression that "after all Catholicism was capable of a fresh orientation, of coming to terms with political democracy and with modern knowledge."[26]

One aspect of great significance for Catholic *Heilsgeschichte* theologians of the twentieth century was Leo's revival of Thomism in the 1879 decree *Aeterni Patris;* scholasticism was enshrined as the *optimus modus philosophandi.* Schoof establishes an important context for this decree when he describes the compatibility of neo-scholasticism with the new objective and analytical thought world toward the end of the century.[27] But *Aeterni Patris* ultimately had less happy consequences:

> What was really ominous, however, was not only that neo-scholasticism was confirmed in theory as *the* theology of the Church, but also that merely to suggest an alternative theology or to question neo-scholasticism became subject to ecclesiastical sanctions.[28]

Other consequences of the encyclical are discussed by McCool, who contends that *Aeterni Patris* reflected the strengths and weaknesses of nineteenth century neo-Thomism.[29] In particular, it failed to recognize the historical context of Thomas and his later commentators. Nineteenth century neo-Thomists had organized a single metaphysical system out of all the scholastic doctors as well as the patristic doctors whom the scholastics had superseded, thus glossing over critical differences in culture, time, and world view. Moreover, the decree clearly preferred objectivity and antiquity over subjectivity and modernity, thereby manifesting a hostility to modern philosophy. Perhaps the deepest irony is that, in its inattention to history, *Aeterni Patris* led to a mistaken interpretation of the philosophical thought of Thomas himself.

Yet McCool also draws attention to the more positive consequences. Among those he considers most important is the significance given to tradition and the necessity of incorporating revelation in Christian philosophy. Without denying the negative effects the encyclical had, he nevertheless contends that, without either the confidence the encyclical's drafters had in the possibilities of Thomas's philosophy and theology or Leo XIII's leadership in Thomistic revival, it is unlikely that the "vast historical scholarship and the remarkable systematic development that characterized the Thomists in the century after *Aeterni Patris* would have taken place."[30] In fact, McCool continues, the "achievements, reverses, and painful conflicts of Thomistic theology's dialectical development" would ultimately become the "leitmotif" of the history of Catholic theology between 1879 and Vatican II.[31]

B. *The Modernist Crisis*

"Ecclesiastical sanctions," as Schoof had written, were indeed to become a frightening reality in the turn-of-the-century modernist crisis, a bitter debate that has left still tender scars in Roman Catholicism. Its complex history, of which only the bare outline will be sketched herein, has not yet been fully untangled, but it is obvious from the narrative of these preceding pages that Catholicism moved toward this crisis with steady step in the nineteenth century: *Mirari Vos* (1832) and *Dei Filius* (1870) and, to a lesser extent, *Aeterni Patris* (1879). Add to that the raised hopes of the liberals during Leo's long pontificate (1878–1903), and one senses the almost inexorable advent of an acrimonious encounter.

This encounter was hastened by the appropriation of historical-critical tools in the Scripture studies of French scholar Alfred Loisy (1857–1940), student of famed ecclesiastical historian Louis Duchesne (1843–1922) at the Institut Catholique in Paris. Loisy considered himself called to use historical criticism to preserve the essence of Christianity from the outdated forms it had assumed in church teaching of the era. This sense of vocation led him to publish a refutation of Adolf von Harnack's "bombshell," *Das Wesen des Christentums* (1902), translated as *What Is Christianity?*[32] Harnack had eruditely argued that the essence of Christianity—the universal fatherhood of God and the infinite value of the human soul—had been lost since the

time of the primitive church, "buried," as it were, under historical accretions. Loisy in reply, *L'Evangile et l'Eglise* (*The Gospel
and the Church,* 1902), countered with the contention that the
gospel of Jesus was *destined* to grow into the church, and so the
church was actually the fulfillment of the biblical message
rather than a distortion of it.

But in the ensuing controversy, Catholic critics soon lost sight
of the nature of Loisy's work as a refutation of Harnack. As
Schoof reminds his readers:

> Looking back now to the beginning of the century, we realize that
> it was hardly to be expected that the Church of that period would
> simply pass benevolently over various comments made by Loisy in
> passing, for example, that the gospels were not historical docu-
> ments, but testimonies of faith, that the later development of the
> Church had not been anticipated by Christ and that constant rein-
> terpretation of the ancient formulae was necessary to the discovery
> of the essence of faith, because the dogmas of the Church "were not
> truths come down to us from heaven and preserved by religious
> tradition in the exact form in which they were first presented to
> us."[33]

His most important writings put on the Index in 1903, Loisy
was excommunicated in 1908.

A similar fate befell Irish Jesuit George Tyrell (1861-1909)
who espoused a dynamic view of revelation and dogma. His
emphasis on the importance of Christian experience over
theological statements and his insistence that theology be responsive to this experience led to his expulsion from the Jesuits
and to condemnation by Pius X.

Two papal documents, the decree of 3 July 1907, *Lamentabili,*
and the encyclical *Pascendi Dominici Gregis* of 8 September 1907,
together with the *motu proprio* of 1 September 1910, *Sacrorum
Antistitum* (which contained the oath against modernism), voiced
the outcry of a church besieged by modern thought.

In its condemnation of sixty-five propositions, *Lamentabili*
denied that the progress of science could require any reformation or modification of Christian doctrine and prohibited
Catholics from free use of historical biblical criticism. Fifty of
these propositions were drawn from Loisy's writings.[34] Several

weeks later the encyclical *Pascendi* appeared, an elaborate sys-
tematization of the modernist "program" that reduced its specific errors to two fundamental philosophical ones: agnosticism
and immanentism.[35] In effect it condemned every effort to
introduce reform of church teaching, and this theoretical de-
nunciation was followed three years later by the *motu proprio*
requiring pastors and professors to take the oath against
modernism—a decree not rescinded until July 1967.

Recent scholarship acknowledges the artificiality of Pius X's
construct, and J. J. Heaney claims that *Pascendi* ought to be
regarded more in the genre of a "theological statement revealing the mind of the magisterium than as an accurate historical
description of any given author."[36]

Nevertheless, the modernist movement was effectively
squelched. Of course, such a reaction was not surprising, given
both the defensive spirit of the times and the severe threat the
modernists posed to neo-Thomism. The modernists had replaced the scholastic metaphysics of being with evolutionary
categories, and had undermined the values of traditional natural
theology with their theory of truth. Scholasticism was inadequate, even an impediment, for understanding Scripture in
the modernist perspective.[37]

Directly contrary to the hopes of the individual scholars who
had sought to mediate between the church and contemporary
modes of thought, it was now virtually impossible for a "loyal"
Catholic to utilize modern critical methods. Scholasticism was
the sole theological methodology. The modernist movement
became, as Vidler observes, as though it had never been, and
the church was more decisively committed to an intransigent
position than it had ever been.[38]

The modernist crisis was, in sum, the crowning tragedy of
nineteenth century Catholicism and the ultimate expression of
the isolation of the church from contemporary thought. As
Walgrave so aptly concludes:

> Its (the spirit of theology's) narrow-minded, one-sided spirit of
> defense, distrust and suspicion, always anxious not to be mixed up
> with modern thought, was as clear a symptom of spiritual and in-
> tellectual weakness as the refusal to take food is a token of illness in
> a living organism.[39]

But the modernist crisis, however devastating and debilitating for the life of the church, did not lead to death. Seeds of renewal were growing in Germany, where modernism had never taken hold.

II. *Twentieth Century Kerygmatic Renewal in Catholicism*

At least two factors seemed to contribute to the lack of impact of modernists in Germany. One was the unique ethos; without Gallicanism, the ultramontanist movement had never gained an extensive hold. Furthermore, the coexistence of Catholic and Protestant faculties in universities such as Tübingen meant that scholasticism did not monopolize the theological scene to the same extent.[40] Secondly, there was the *Reformkatholizimus* movement inspired by the teaching of F. X. Kraus (1840–1901) and H. Schell (1850–1906). This movement shared in the liberal tendencies associated earlier in the century with Tübingen and later with Munich. Bismarck's *Kulturkampf* had heightened the consciousness of many German Catholics; small yet influential groups organized in protest of the "fortress mentality" in Rome, attacking political ultramontanism and demanding freedom in scientific religious work. In short, theology in German-speaking countries was far more open and contemporary than in France or Italy, and there was simply less need to adopt the radical reaction of modernism.

What is more, the heightened consciousness of Catholics following the *Kulturkampf* that had been expressed in the *Reformkatholizimus* came to great fruition in the 1920s, following World War I. That war had, of course, effected a tremendous change in liberal Protestantism, as the rise of dialectical theology associated with Barth, Gogarten, Brunner, and Bultmann revealed. Catholics, too, experienced a change in direction toward the communal aspects of the church and liturgy and a renewed interest in the objective, dogmatic aspect of faith. The Catholic youth movement overflowed into a liturgical movement, a university movement, and a lay movement. Ultimately, these movements engendered a renewal in moral theology, and in theological reflection about the church as the mystical body, about christology, the role of the laity, and about the liturgy as a celebration of mystery. The importance of the work of Romano Guardini and Karl Adam can scarcely be overstressed in the development of this renewed christology and ecclesiology.[41]

But in the decade prior to the outbreak of World War II, the church, increasingly in conflict with National Socialism, became more preoccupied with strictly ecclesiastical matters. As a result, there was a remarkable flowering of liturgical theology, though from two differing perspectives. Benedictine abbot Odo Casel (1886-1948) is perhaps the best known; his 1932 *magnum opus* on the Christian cult mystery, in which he manifested an understanding of liturgy as a renewed presence of Christ's saving action, was clearly at the foundation of Vatican II's Constitution on the Sacred Liturgy (*Sacrosanctum Concilium*).[42]

The second perspective came from Austrian Jesuit Josef Andreas Jungmann (1889-1975). To him full attention must be given, for with his writings *Heilsgeschichte* makes its full entrance into Catholicism.

A. *Josef A. Jungmann: Heilsgeschichte in Kerygmatic Theology*

The contribution of Jungmann to liturgical renewal in Catholicism requires a book in itself; suffice it to acknowledge here the profound effect his writings have had over the years since the 1948 publication of his *magnum opus, Missarum Solemnia*.[43]

Alongside his erudite liturgical work, the prolific Jesuit exercised a leading role in the development of Catholic religious education, likewise a study all its own. Even within the limits of this study, it will be evident that his work inaugurated a new era in this field.

Of particular concern, of course, is Jungmann's understanding of *Heilsgeschichte* as a hermeneutical principle; it functioned as significantly in his theology as it did in the work of Cullmann and von Rad. Briefly stated, the argument is as follows: Jungmann's 1936 publication *Die Frohbotschaft und unsere Glaubensverkündigung* initiated the "kerygmatic movement" in catechetics, a movement that shared also in the liturgical and biblical kerygmatic renewal. Moreover, *Heilsgeschichte* functioned as the the key hermeneutical principle in much of this kerygmatic theology; this was particularly the case in catechetics, to such an extent that it has remained a constant even as catechetics has evolved.

Methodologically, this argument suggests a procedure which, first, identifies and analyzes the *Heilsgeschichte* hermeneutic in Jungmann, and, secondly, traces the extent of its influence. For the sake of imposing some structure to the narrative, the order of tracing the *Heilsgeschichte* hermeneutic that came into Catholic religious education via Jungmann will be examined in turn in (1) the work of Jungmann's student Johannes Hofinger, (2) the tradition of the Lumen Vitae school, and then (3) the United States. Where appropriate, parallels from the biblical and liturgical movements will be cited.

But it is vital to an accurate perception of how *Heilsgeschichte* functioned as the key hermeneutical principle in kerygmatic theology that readers recognize the interconnections and relationships among its various adherents. Philosopher Susanne Langer images this when she writes:

As it is, however, all language has a form which requires us to string out our ideas even though their objects rest one within the other; *as pieces of clothing that are actually worn one over the other have to be strung side by side on the clotheslines.*[44]

So it is with the salvation history hermeneutic in which Jungmann played such a significant role: those figures and institutions that inspired the kerygmatic movement are strikingly interdependent. This interdependence should not be lost sight of even as each of the various elements is traced.

To begin, then, with Jungmann: that he was primarily a liturgist offers insight into both his orientation and his methodology. His historical explorations into early church liturgy had created a keen appreciation for the vitality of the Christianity of that era—"a blossom time of the Christian proclamation"—a vitality he found to be in startling contrast to the lifelessness he witnessed about him in a "conventional

Christianity of traditional external practices and burdensome duties."[45] The remedy appeared to him to lie in an appropriate "proclamation of the faith," a phrase that became the theme of his work. Thus he maintained:

> ... religious teaching today cannot content itself with the mere handing on of hereditary formulas, nor can it assume, as it once did, that the traditional sum of customs, devotions, pious thoughts and practices even intensively used, will avail to hold the faithful firmly in the Church and assure security and nourishment for their religious life. Today religious teaching must lead the faithful to a vital understanding of the content of faith itself, that they may interiorly grasp it, and thus grow to spiritual maturity and proper independence in religious life. It must lead in other words to *the step of Christian formation.* This will demand more than giving the faithful a mere conceptual knowledge of the many individual doctrines of the faith. What is needed is not a knowledge of the "many" but of "the one"—the unity that lies behind the many, the all-embracing salvific plan of God.[46]

This "all-embracing salvific plan of God" is, as one might readily recognize, *Heilsgeschichte;* further exploration of Jungmann's writings will make manifest his understanding of this hermeneutic.

Jungmann's appropriation of *Heilsgeschichte* needs to be read in the context of two historical phenomena. The first and most crucial has already been narrated, namely the nineteenth century developments in Catholicism that had tended to rigidify theology. Much of this is presumed in his distinction between theology and "proclamation of the faith." He questioned whether the proclamation might have lost its cohesive unity and dynamic impact in the "intellectualistic dissection of the great integrated whole of the Christian message," and suggested that scholasticism might have been the "deceptive road" leading to a separation between religious knowledge and religious life.[47]

Jungmann did not deny the need for scientific theology such as scholasticism. He did, however, argue that the development of theology was occasioned by the necessity of giving answers to questions raised by "captious, critical reason"; theology had of necessity, therefore, to be concerned with questions of truth and was thereby involved with distinctions, definitions, proofs, and solutions. It was primarily at the service of knowledge and did not seek to explore the significance of its findings for daily life. On the other hand, the task of proclamation was essentially different from that of scientific theology; it was life-oriented. All that was "mere knowledge" fell outside its purview:

> Basically the proclamation of the faith needs knowledge only about the way which leads to God, about its beginnings and critical turns, about its ramifications and its endings. Its proper subject is and remains the Good News—what was called the *kerygma* in primitive Christianity. Dogma must be known; the *kerygma* must be proclaimed.[48]

Theological analysis, therefore, had only a subservient function with regard to the proclamation of faith. Logically this meant that its method fundamentally differed from that of theology; it was not to be concerned with "reproducing the ontological order" of all things, but with the *economy of salvation*. Thus it preferred the "original, simple modes of expression of Sacred Scripture" to the "sharply defined language of the School."[49]

The second prerequisite for understanding Jungmann is to situate him within the catechetical climate of his day. The first part of the twentieth century had experienced a catechetical renewal emanating from Munich and Vienna, greatly influenced by developments in psychology. This renewal served as a corrective to the excessively rationalistic educational philosophy that had followed the Enlightenment. In Catholic religious education, the catechism had been in vogue since the days of the Counter-Reformation; the methodology of this era was called "text-explanatory," and consisted largely of a dry exegesis of the catechism, followed by mechanical memorization of that text by students. Nineteenth century neo-scholasticism simply reinforced this procedure.[50]

But the emerging science of psychology, particularly the pedagogical steps outlined by Herbart and Ziller, were adapted for the teaching of religion by German catechist Heinrich Stieglitz.[51] Henceforth the topic was developed rather than merely explained, and a fivefold process became the standard pedagogical framework: introduction, presentation, explanation, summary, and application. This school-centered and child-oriented method, the "Munich Method," was adopted by a group of catechetical leaders who had convened a special interest group during the 1912 International Eucharistic Congress in Vienna.

Between the two world wars came another important development in secular education, that of the "activity school," popularized in various modes by Montessori (Italy), Quinet (France), Manjon (Spain), and, of course, John Dewey (United States). The 1928 Catechetical Congress of Vienna gave its approval to these innovations, and found this methodology particularly compatible with learning through liturgy.[52] Both this Congress and its 1912 predecessor conceptualized the catechetical problem as fundamentally a psychological one.

But what Jungmann proposed was far more radical: new content, not merely improved methodology. This content was the proclamation of the faith in which the "economy of salvation" was "above all else" the central theme.[53] Such a theme would transform the objective christocentrism of Catholic doctrine into a "vitally dynamic subjective representation."[54] It would counter those influences that had obfuscated the proper christocentric outlook over the centuries. It would, for instance, emphasize the life-giving mission of Jesus as a corrective to the one-sided emphasis on his divinity that had arisen during periods of christological heresy. It would once again link grace to the totality of Christian doctrine and unite sacramental catechesis with the central core of the economy of salvation.[55] This new content would revolutionize the religious spirit of the age in which:

> everything fits together . . . to give us the image of a strictly logical, soulless, secularized Christendom. Instead of a Savior of the world we find the idea of an appearance of God among men, come to teach and win their love; the Church is the organization for preaching this doctrine; and as for the sacraments, there is the possibility of the remission of sins—and the puzzling assistance of grace for the performance of moral obligations.[56]

And this new content would restore the position of Christ as mediator, a primacy that had been too long obscured in the multiplicity of devotions.

Christocentrism was thus the critical component of Jungmann's conceptualization of the economy of salvation. Christ was the "pivotal point of all God's ways," the "mid-point" and center of all world history.[57] "Instaurare omnia in Christo" ("To restore all things in Christ," the motto of Pope Pius X), with accompanying reference to Eph. 1:10, became the motto of the proclamation of faith.

In an age still suffering the effects of modernism, such proposals were far more earth-shaking than they might appear to present-day readers. In the first review to appear in the American press, liturgist Godfrey Diekmann acclaimed it as the book of the year:

> It is one of those rare masterpieces that coordinates a thousand and one seemingly disjointed facts into one illuminating, logical unity, and which puts in clear terms many a truth which personal study had led one to but vaguely surmise.[58]

Diekmann's editor, Dom Virgil Michel, wrote immediately to the publisher for permission to translate the book.[59]

But permission was not forthcoming; *Die Frohbotschaft* had been withdrawn from circulation. Such reaction may appear as nothing less than hysteria to those accustomed to such phenomena as God-is-dead theologies and Christian-Marxist dialogues. But once again it must be stressed that the book was a startling message when read in its context of ecclesiastical history. Though its reception among European catechists was generally favorable, many theologians were clearly negative. Apparently they were considerably threatened by Jungmann's historical analysis, which had shown that not all developments approved by the church were healthy ones. The chapter on "Guiding Principles for Devotions" was particularly offensive in this regard—a chapter Diekmann had rated as one of the best. These guardians of orthodoxy, mired in a mentality of an earlier era, viewed his study as a criticism of infallibility and consequently exerted considerable pressure to have it condemned.

This, however, was avoided by Jesuit superior general Ladislaus Ledochowski's move to withdraw the book from the market, an action to which the Holy Office responded with gratitude.[60]

Though his friend and colleague Johannes Hofinger reports that Jungmann was deeply hurt by the way in which the entire affair had been handled, he nonetheless continued to teach.[61]. Jungmann likewise continued to publish his highly regarded liturgical writings and served as editor of the *Zeitschrift für katholische Theologie;* he also made frequent contributions to catechetical and liturgical journals. Catholics of the United States, to whom *Die Frohbotschaft* was still unavailable in translation, could follow his thinking in the pages of *Orate Fratres/ Worship,* beginning with a piece in the 1948–49 volume that summarized a lecture he had delivered at the University of Notre Dame summer school of the liturgy.[62] Jungmann published some thirteen articles in that journal between 1948 and 1960, and was listed on the masthead as one of the associate editors between 1954 and 1957. The international journal of religious education, *Lumen Vitae,* contained six articles by Jungmann in its first ten volumes; it will be necessary at a later point in this chapter to discuss in greater detail his influence through the Lumen Vitae tradition.

But it was a 1963 work, *Glaubensverkündigung im Lichte der Frohbotschaft,* that reiterated and redefined many of the arguments he had first put forward in 1936.[63] Jungmann himself noted the controversy that had arisen over that earlier work, and remarked that the present one took up the same theme as that published a quarter of a century ago, and which, because of the "novelty" of some of its arguments, received a very "mixed reception." It is in this work that Jungmann's appropriation of *Heilsgeschichte* stands forth with greatest clarity.

Jungmann reiterated that it was not the separate commandments of God that needed to be placed in the foreground of people's awareness, but rather the divine plan from which the commandments arose; the imperative must proceed from the indicative (15). Thus it was not a case of beginning anew, as if one could create a religious *tabula rasa,* but of fitting the parts properly into the whole, that is, into the picture of a new divine order which was an "unchanging background and fixed framework for the multifarious searchings and struggles that pass across the stage of life" (17).

To describe this totality, Jungmann suggested:

> It is salvation history, begun in the old covenant, reaching its climax in the fullness of time and continuing in the history of the Church until the second coming of our Lord. St. Paul calls it the mystery hidden in God before the beginning of time, but now revealed to his saints. He calls it God's decree, or plan, the purpose of which is to gather together in Christ all things that are in heaven and on earth (Eph. I.10). Elsewhere this totality appears as God's gracious call (κλῆσις Eph. I.18; 4.1, etc.) to the human race, or as the assembly (εκκλησία) of those who have heard and obeyed the call—the holy Church (17).

But whether God's plan is described as "salvation history," as "mystery," or as "call," the person of Christ always stands in the center. He is the "climax of salvation history," the "messenger of the great plan," the "Lord and King of those who are called":

> In this way is the order of religious reality described: it is an objective Christocentricity that is given in divine revelation, quite independently of our minds. That is to say, in the preaching of the faith and in the awareness of the believer not only must separate doctrines and ideas arising from the objective Christian message recur more or less faithfully, but Christ himself must assume his place therein as the centre-point, as the source of light from which all other doctrinal points are brightly illumined (18).

Such had not always been the case with scholasticism; Jungmann granted that scholasticism had made a great contribution, but felt it had also produced a new temptation, that of concentrating on a "multitude of isolated pieces of knowledge" and thereby obscuring the "true message concerning the facts of salvation history" (28). After all, Christianity was "first and foremost a fact," and only secondarily a doctrine. What had happened was that theological science had "overburdened the kerygma" with things of second and third rank (46). Jungmann sought to restore the original and unified power of that *kerygma* as it had been evident in the preaching of the early Church. This meant avoiding all "excessive splitting up of the substance of faith" and all "rank growth around the fringe" (60). Dogmatic theology had its place, but

> amidst all the complexities of distinctions, theses and hypotheses, the *leitmotiv* of salvation-history must be preserved. The kerygmatic climaxes must once more come into their own (62).

This *leitmotiv*, as Jungmann phrased it, would be most apparent when christocentricity was manifest. This was not to be misconstrued as a geometrical concept; it meant that in every separate point of doctrine "the objectively existing reference to the person of Christ should always shine through the exposition" (66). Thus would salvation history form a unity, a "living cosmos," in which the OT was viewed as a schoolmaster to bring all to Christ and the NT seen as the revelation of the shape of God's redemptive purpose (21). Furthermore, in this unified order, the church would be regarded as the assembly of those who belong to Christ, the sacraments as the means by which Christ acts and sanctifies his people, and grace as a sharing in Christ's closeness to the Father. To live a Christian life is to live in Christ.

This plan of salvation must be made evident even in church art. Since the Gothic period there had been a tendency to lose sight of the context of the economy of redemption (82); likewise should the plan of salvation predominate in catechisms and in the liturgy. Especially should devotion to Mary be integrated within the total picture of the Christian order of salvation (90–96). In short, salvation history, that divine plan centered in Jesus Christ, was the *leitmotiv* for the proclamation of the faith and the basis for the kerygmatic renewal.

Jungmann's proposals, as well as those of his followers, have often been categorized under the rubric of "kerygmatic theology." The essence of this is, of course, his focus on the *kerygma*, the core of the Christian proclamation:

> *Kerygma* is a biblical concept meaning "that which is preached." It denotes, therefore, the content of preaching, that is what Christ himself proclaimed and what his apostles proclaimed abroad as his

heralds: that the kingdom of God had entered the world, thus disclosing salvation to mankind. It denotes the original preaching, at first addressed to those who did not yet believe, but which was also intended to provide the core and basis of all subsequent guidance and instruction of believing Christians, and which ought to become all the more clearly sounded in those places where the paths of faith have become overgrown and where a fresh need has arisen for orientation and sign-posting. The *kerygma* is the announcement of facts, above all the facts through which God himself has intervened in human history and uttered his call to mankind (59–60).

There ensued a controversy about whether or not this kerygmatic theology was of itself a separate branch of theology. Shortly after the publication of *Die Frohbotschaft,* several articles appeared in the *Zeitschrift* edited by Jungmann that argued that kerygmatic theology would be sufficient for priests in pastoral ministry, reserving scientific theology for academicians.[64] Jungmann's own view on this was not entirely clear until the clarification of 1955 in the second and third appendices of his *Katechetik* (English translation, *Handing on the Faith,* 1959). Perhaps the most succinct statement of his opinion is this: "the efforts to bring about such a renewal do not imply a special kind of theology but a clear and effective presentation of Christ's messsage itself."[65] Jungmann pressed for more *kerygma* in theology rather than a parallel kerygmatic theology.

That debate, however, is not of itself of great pertinence to the topic at hand except insofar as it indicates something of the background of the term "kerygmatic theology" which would appear with such frequency in the literature of catechetics after Jungmann's time. But what *is* crucial here is to stress the inherent significance of *Heilsgeschichte* for this kerygmatic approach. It is, as the preceding pages have demonstrated, *the* unifying theme, *the leitmotiv* of Jungmann's understanding of kerygmatic renewal.

But what is also obvious is that, though Jungmann's concept of *Heilsgeschichte* certainly shares in the continuity of its basic meaning as a fulfillment of the OT in the NT according to a progressive divine revelation in which Christ has the central place in history, he has nonetheless appropriated it in a quite different fashion from any of the theologians discussed in the first chapter. Two reasons might be suggested in attempting to account for this. The first and more significant is that, as a Roman Catholic, Jungmann worked out a different appropriation of the Christian tradition. Consequently, he began from a different ecclesiological perspective and was necessarily more concerned with doctrinal formulations. Also he wrote in an era just emerging from a bitter theological crisis and before the full flowering of the renaissance of Catholic biblical studies. Secondly, Jungmann came to his understanding of *Heilsgeschichte* from the viewpoint and expertise of a liturgist, rather than as a dogmatic theologian (Hofmann, Kähler) or as a biblical scholar (von Rad, Cullmann). Largely as a consequence of Jungmann's background in liturgy, Catholic *Heilsgeschichte* theologians stressed the mystagogic, whereas Protestants focused more on the historical Christ.

Without denying or reducing the very real difference in emphasis, it is also important to identify some of the affinities between this twentieth century Roman Catholic scholar and the *Heilsgeschichte* theologians Hofmann, Kähler, von Rad, and Cullmann (all Lutherans). Here there is no attempt to prove that any of the four actually influenced Jungmann directly. Indeed, this author could find no reference whatsoever to any of these men in Jungmann's work except for one footnote in *Handing on the Faith* to a Cullmann article on Bultmann.[66] It should be noted, however, that it was rare for a Catholic to be aware of and to cite Protestants during the period in which Jungmann wrote. But the similarities are striking nonetheless.

With Hofmann Jungmann shared a deep concern for doctrinal renewal and a similar starting point: Christ himself. One could certainly speak of biblical theology and dogmatics as forming a doublelayer in Jungmann as in Hofmann. An interesting parallel also exists in the use of the term "fact," for just as Hofmann began from the "fact" (*Tatbestand*) of rebirth in Christ, so Jungmann spoke of Christianity as the message about a fact.[67] "First and foremost," Jungmann argued, "Christianity is a fact" (*Tatsache*); the *kerygma* is the "announcement of facts, above all of the facts through which God himself has intervened in human history."[68]

Both Martin Kähler and Josef Jungmann were drawn by the vitality and significance of the preaching of the early church, and Kähler's understanding of the NT as *Verkündigungsgeschichte* certainly heralded the later theologies of Jungmann, H. Rahner, Kappler, and Grasso (see n. 86) in this respect. Moreover, Jungmann, who so resisted the "dissection of the faith" he sensed in scientific theology, certainly had a precursor in the Halle professor who had claimed that what was present only for scholars had no power to awaken and establish faith. If Kähler envisioned himself as a defense attorney for simple Christians so as to preserve the laity from the "papacy of scholarship," so also Jungmann functioned as a mediator.[69]

The Austrian Jesuit retained something of an ambivalence toward historical-critical biblical scholarship. He found value, for instance, in form criticism because it gave a more exact account of what was actually recorded; yet he thought it also robbed the readers of their "guileless ingenuousness." He had little use for Scripture studies that obscured the christocentric nature:

> There are exegetical publications which seem to consist of nothing but marginal emendations that can be read only with an effort. Our attention is needlessly fixed upon side-issues which do nothing to alter the account as a whole. In the end the figure of Christ stands before us unexplained and inexplicable as always: his incomparable appearance, his self-testimony, his resurrection, and his Church, too, "the sign amongst the nations," remains for ever the same.[70]

Yet one feels such accusations could never justly be levelled at the scholarship of either von Rad or Cullmann. Since Jungmann actually devoted little attention to the OT in itself— it is always seen as preparation for the NT—it is more difficult to compare von Rad and Jungmann. But one might note that von Rad's basic schema of the OT being read as a book of ever-increasing anticipation would readily be in harmony with Jungmann's. It might also be pertinent to indicate that von Rad's derivation of *Heilsgeschichte* from the credenda of Israel bears relation to Jungmann's desire to reconnect the Christian creed with the divine plan of salvation.

Cullmann and Jungmann shared a preoccupation with and profound concern for christocentrism, though Cullmann was, of course, far more exegetically refined in his. In addition, both scholars developed an ecclesiology from their *Heilsgeschichte* formulations; Jungmann's ecclesiology, however, and certainly that of some of his followers, might well have been what Cullmann had in mind when he accused Catholics of absolutizing the age of the church and of not observing the necessity of constant orientation to the Christ event at midpoint. Fascinating, too, is the interest of both men in the early Christian confessions.

Jungmann, then, appropriated the *Heilsgeschichte* hermeneutic in a fashion consistent with both the unique historical-theological situation within which he worked and the basic pattern as established by nineteenth and twentieth century Protestant scholars, even to the point of sharing in some of their individual emphases.

The "kerygmatic renewal" initiated by Jungmann and grounded in *Heilsgeschichte* would intensify, reaching its peak in the United States about 1964. This growth was due not simply to the original inspiration of Jungmann, but especially to his student, the indefatigable and peripatetic missionary, Johannes Hofinger.

B. *Johannes Hofinger: Popularizer of Heilsgeschichte in Kerygmatic Theology*

Fellow Austrian Johannes Hofinger had been Jungmann's amanuensis during his theological studies in Innsbruck and has devoted the substance of his career to the elaboration of his mentor's catechetical insights. That is not to deny that Hofinger has been a leader in his own right; he has indeed considerably influenced the ongoing development of catechetics in his prolific writing and worldwide teaching. But it is nonetheless obvious that Hofinger's fundamental notions are grounded in the kerygmatic theology of Jungmann; suffice it to say that, whereas Jungmann devoted himself primarily to liturgical theology, his student Hofinger developed, expanded, and tirelessly promulgated Jungmann's insights regarding catechetics.

An early article (1947) of Hofinger's makes this clear. Written from his position in Peiping as a professor of dogmatics and catechetics, Hofinger discussed the proper ordering for the presentation of religious truths, and proposed these criteria: (1) the message is an "echo" of divine revelation, and thus ought to show clearly the revealed character of Catholicism; (2) this message is essentially the history of salvation, so it must manifest the historical character in the order of presentation; (3) precisely because the message is the history of *salvation*, it must be made to appear as a series of values and not as a system of burdens and duties; and (4) since the message as the history of salvation is at heart the announcement of the "inexhaustible riches of Christ," the linkage of ideas must always show forth the christocentric character of the message.[71]

Several years later Hofinger made more explicit both his understanding of the OT and his ecclesiology as they related to the history of salvation. Regarding the former he claimed:

> The Old Testament is essentially our "pedagogue in Christ" (Gal. III, 24). We will choose from it the preparation for the "mystery of Christ." We must continually point out the imperfection of the Old Testament. It had to be so, Christ not having come. In elementary teaching for children, it is recommended, after the example of the greatest catechists, to pass immediately from the story of the Fall and the promise of a Savior to the fulfillment of that promise (the Annunciation to Our Lady). If there is sufficient time, one may, in teaching adults (missionary catechesis) deal with some other passages of the OT but always from a Christian angle (Christological).[72]

The church for Hofinger was the "essential work of Christ," the Kingdom of God that he came to found, the "new society of the children of God." Through his church Christ continued to act; as its head he continually vivified it.[73]

Hofinger's affinity with Jungmann is also evident in his contributions to *Worship*, particularly in the mid-1950s. Two of these address specifically the relationship between liturgy and catechesis. In the first, Hofinger maintained that the conscious collaboration of the two movements was not merely a transitory closeness, prompted by extrinsic reasons of expediency; rather it derived from their respective natures: "Each is intrinsically related to the other and can achieve its own purpose only by working together with the other in a well-planned and organic manner."[74] Hofinger saw that the liturgy presented Christian doctrine in intelligible and "prayable" form, not merely in abstractions; it was precisely in active participation in Christian worship that the basic aims of both nascent movements met.[75]

In the second article, Hofinger directly addressed the issue of kerygmatic renewal vis-à-vis both movements. He first offered this important summary regarding the meaning of *kerygma:*

> Since the appearance of Fr. Jungmann's book, the name *kerygma* (a publicly announced message) has come to be attached ever more widely to those parts of revelation which were meant to be explicitly and emphatically proclaimed. The Greek word is found in holy Scripture, and is there repeatedly used by St. Paul in the same sense (e.g., 1 Tim. 2:7; 2 Tim. 1:11; 1 Cor. 1:21; 2:4, cf. esp. 1 Cor. 15). The message which the Apostle as the herald (*keryx*) of the eternal King is to proclaim to a fallen humanity is none other than that bedrock of Christian truths which constitute the essential content of the Christian glad tidings. This message must bring the inner nature and worth of Christianity into as prominent focus as possible. It consists in the incomparable good news of the eternal love of God who through His only-begotten Son has called us to Himself and enables us to reach our true home. In brief, it is the good news of our salvation in Christ.[76]

Hofinger claimed that this kerygmatic renewal had from the outset worked in "closest relationship" with the liturgical revival, and mentions that it was not simply coincidence that Jungmann the liturgist had given the renewal its original impetus. Furthermore, the liturgical movement as it was developing according to the *mysterium* theology of Odo Casel and the monks of Maria Laach had brought the innermost core of the good news into the very center of religious consciousness:

> In this way the contemporary catechetical and liturgical movements have approached each other from within. They belong together of intrinsic necessity. Whoever embraces the one and penetrates into its full meaning, cannot long remain indifferent to the other.[77]

Just as the University of Notre Dame had invited Jungmann to its summer school, so too did they invite Hofinger in the summers of 1954 and 1955; his course was entitled "The Kerygmatic Approach to Christian Doctrine." The substance of that course was later published in his most extensive work, *The Art of Teaching Christian Doctrine: The Good News and Its Proclamation.*[78] Several points from that book highlight his understanding of *Heilsgeschichte.*

Hofinger places his greatest stress on christocentrism, because the mystery of Christ means God's redemptive plan with Christ as its center. Catechists, therefore, should initiate their subjects into this mystery primarily through a biblical-historical catechesis that leads to Christ through the telling of the story of salvation. This was what the apostles themselves had done, and was the principle given by Augustine in his *De catechizandis rudibus.* Theologically, the story of redemption is the essence of Christian revelation; psychologically, the historical-narrative catechesis is the simplest, most adequate, and most effective method of initiation into the Christian religion. Bible history is to be the introduction into the Christian religion.[79]

Hofinger suggested that in basic instruction only the creation, fall, and promise of the redeemer be related from the OT. Where time permitted, more of the OT ought to be given, but always as that "tutor unto Christ," and hence with emphasis on its preparatory and typological nature. He repeated his admonition that catechists should often point out the imperfections of the OT's institutions and individuals precisely because it revealed *only* the time of preparation: "Christ, Who came to perfect all things, had not yet come."[80]

The ecclesiology as detailed in the *Art* likewise echoed his earlier equation of church and kingdom. A further development, however, is his extension of the meaning of christocentricity as the foundation of the hierarchy. Hofinger envisioned each member of the church as partaking in its activity, but claimed that Christ had given special powers to some of its members. Citing John 20:21 ("As the Father has sent me, I also send you"), he saw the continuity of Christ, apostles, bishops, priests and considered this the "christocentric foundation of the hierarchy." He felt, moreover, that those who grasped this fundamental principle would have "no difficulty with the various dogmas that more accurately determine a hierarchical power."[81]

A briefer work coauthored with Sadlier religion editor William Reedy, *The ABC's of Modern Catechetics,* provided a concise summary of these views.[82] Again, *Heilsgeschichte* lies at the heart of his christocentric emphasis:

> What the mystery of Christ really means, then, is this: God has designed a redemptive plan for man with Christ at its center. Once this fundamental fact is grasped it is relatively easy to see in their right order the other fundamental teachings of Christianity as contained in the Creed.[83]

Another way to study Hofinger's appropriation of *Heilsgeschichte* is to survey the six International Study Weeks on Catechetics; Hofinger did not, of course, direct the outcome of these sessions, but he is generally credited with being their initiator and guiding light.[84]

C. Heilsgeschichte in the Catechetical Study Weeks

The first international meeting dealing with the pastoral aspect of missionary work was held in 1959 in Nijmegen, Holland, under the theme of "Liturgy and the Missions." As one participant put it: "In going back to its wellsprings, the liturgy is not just following an archaistic fashion, it is in search of renewed vigour."[85] The inspiration of Hofinger's master was once again evident!

The 1960 session at Eichstätt, Austria, "Catechetics and the Missions," showed both this influence and Hofinger's own touch more forcibly. Eichstätt initiated a new era; there the age of kerygmatic renewal was ushered in. Discussion at this study week focused both on a fuller understanding of the content of the message and on developing an appropriate methodology for its proclamation. Much of the discussion regarding the content follows along lines congruent with what has already been presented in these pages from the writings of Jungmann and Hofinger, though several interesting additions might be noted—one being the subsequent emphasis on the "paschal mystery."

The most significant presentation from the perspective of this study is "The Core of Missionary Preaching" by Domenico Grasso of the Gregorian.[86] Grasso's article served as the primary scholarly analysis of the *kerygma* for study week participants. It is valuable not only for the conclusions he reached, but also for the citations. For instance, he acknowledged at the outset his dependence on C. H. Dodd's classic, *The Apostolic Preaching,* and then proceeded to differentiate *kerygma* (looks to conversion) from catechesis (aims to make conversion more thorough), though Grasso felt the heart of the *kerygma* also to be the heart of NT catechesis.

Grasso's first conclusion was that the core of the *kerygma* is Christ.[87] The second amplifies that: the core of the *kerygma* is not Christ alone, but Christ seen in the story of salvation.[88] And this story has three phases: a preparatory one in the OT, one of achievement in the death-resurrection of Christ, and finally a phase of consummation in the *parousia.*

The third conclusion is of special significance, for in arguing that "Christ is the heart not merely of the *kerygma,* but of New Testament catechesis as well," Grasso manifested his dependence on Cullmann's *Christ and Time*—the first acknowledgment of that dependence by Catholic kerygmatic theologians.[89] This is the section which he had drawn from Cullmann:

> The Pauline concept of mystery lays the groundwork for an authentic theology of history. In the apostle's view history is a thread of events directed by God first to the revelation, then to the dispensation of Christ. In consequence our Lord is the centre of history, the term towards which all that occurred before the incarnation is ordained, and the point from which all that happens after the incarnation derives. Christ gives history its meaning. Precisely because it is designed to communicate the gifts of God, to bring about the union of God with men, history is a *sacred* story, a story of salvation, the story of Christ in whom God saves us. Christ is the centre of the Old Testament (Rom. 4:24; Cor. 9:10; 10:11) and of the era which begins with the New Testament, the "age of the Church," whose aim it is to round out the number of the brothers of Christ (Apoc. 6:11).[99]

This use of Cullmann is extremely important in view of the influence Grasso appears to have had in this phase of the catechetical movement. One ventures the opinion that henceforth this basic idea was accepted in full—it certainly was in harmony with similarly worded understandings—though simply not acknowledged as being rooted in Cullmann's controversial *Christ and Time.*

Cullmann's work on *The Earliest Christian Confessions* underlay much of Grasso's fourth conclusion that Christ in the story of salvation is the center of the preaching and liturgy of the primitive church in their entirety.[91]

A final pertinent point from Grasso is his extensive use of Augustine's *De catechizandis rudibus.* Grasso approved of Augustine's understanding of the OT as simply foretelling the coming of the Lord and being part of a "gradually unfolding plan." He commented that only with the advent of scholasticism did the "reasons" (*rationes*) overcome the "narrative" as a means of catechesis. It was his opinion that preaching concentrated wholly on the story of salvation would result in that synthesis and unity which modern catechesis sought to achieve; the center of that story was none other than Christ.

> When we have come round once more, in the preaching of our faith, to emphasizing the aspect that renders it an encounter with Christ living in the Church, it will have acquired again the distinctive quality of Good News which was so vivid in the early centuries of Christianity and which belongs to its very nature.[92]

Eichstätt participants formulated "four languages" to express this kerygmatic renewal: (1) a biblical language, because the history of salvation is recounted in the Bible; (2) a liturgical language, since the salvation recounted in the Bible finds its expression in the liturgy; (3) an existential language, as the redeeming work of God happens day by day and is borne out by the witness of Christian life; and (4) a doctrinal language, because the history of salvation narrated in the Bible, celebrated in the liturgy, and experienced in daily life progressively utilizes a concrete form in the church.[93] These four languages or "signs" for the proclamation of the faith would be much used in later catechetical literature.[94]

Eichstätt, it has been claimed, brought the kerygmatic renewal to its height. The next four study weeks show something
of a lessening or at least a refocusing of the kerygmatic emphasis. But what is important is that the notion of *Heilsgeschichte*
remains even when other modifications are made.

Briefly then, the next two sessions (Bangkok, 1962, and
Katigondo [Uganda], 1964) stressed the anthropological component and the final two (Manila, 1967, and Medellín [Colom-
bia], 1968) emphasized the political dimensions.

If the *kerygma* was in fashion in 1960 at Eichstätt, "pre-
evangelization" was the word of the week in Bangkok. The
history of salvation included human response as well as divine
revelation; now the discussion moved to "preparing the
ground" and adapting to the special needs and situations of the
various cultures: "The guiding principle of pre-evangelization
is anthropocentric, because we must start with man as he is."[95]
As Alfonso Nebreda asked in the title of his book: is the
Kerygma in Crisis?[96] This was the era in which themes such as
"values," "experience," and "exploration" became predominant
in the literature, above all in the work of Pierre Babin and
Marcel van Caster.

At the Manila study week, the anthropocentric approach
reached its climax, using the categories generated at Bangkok
to rethink the purpose of the mission apostolate. Furthermore,
its concern to deal with the positive values of non-Christian
religions gave some hint of an emerging interest in religious
pluralism and in reappraisal of the social structure. But the
session in 1968 in Medellín would mark a far more significant
shift; henceforth catechetics entered its "political phase."

From the perspective of this study, the Medillín study week
represents a most important development in the understanding
of salvation history as it was to be appropriated in religious
education. The anthropocentric emphasis of earlier congresses
had sensitized partcipants to the necessity of ridding 'salvation'
of its other-worldly connotations; faith was not to be viewed as a
purely spiritual commodity, but as a virtue with social and political aspects.

Such a departure point meant a shift in *Heilsgeschichte;* the
history of salvation and human history were now viewed on one

continuum. God's plan is a unity, and there can be no dichotomy

> between human values and relations with God; between man's planning and God's salvific plan as manifested in Christ; between the human community and the Church; between human experience and God's revelation; between the progressive growth of Christianity in our time, and its eschatological consummation.[97]

This reformulation of the kerygmatic approach was in some measure a result of dissatisfaction with a certain naiveté in the earlier years. There was apparently considerable feeling among the participants that the proclamation of faith was not always the strong antidote to the abstractions of scholasticism that Jungmann had felt it to be, and that a series of ideas merely being replaced by a series of facts could be as boring and meaningless as a profusion of formulae:

> Historico-Biblical systems can be as dangerous as doctrinal systems. In short, the gulf between past and present history was still there despite appearances. There was a gap to be bridged between the history of salvation and modern history, between the content and the subject, between theology and life. It was therefore necessary to build this bridge to join the so-called "sacred" world to the "profane" world.[98]

Medellín therefore represented an attempt to broaden the meaning of revelation. No longer was it enough to repeat or explain the message exactly as found in Scripture, liturgy, church teaching, and Christian witness. Rather "we must increasingly reinterpret the Good News in ways that will complement man's present existence and knowledge."[99]

Medellín marked an extension of the appropriation of *Heilsgeschichte* without transforming its basic meaning. This extension enabled the catechetical world to embrace political theology while at the same time remaining grounded in its fundamental kerygmatic approach. At Medellín a new articulation of Christianity was formulated, with participants viewing Christianity not merely as a religion but as "the historical movement, started by God, towards the liberation of man."[100] Yet at the base was the traditional notion of *Heilsgeschichte*.

A vivid example of this is found in J. L. Segundo's reflection on the documents from the Second Conference of Latin American Bishops also meeting in Medellín in 1968.[101] Building on the presupposition of those documents that there exists a profound relationship between sacred history and human history, Segundo suggests that what God's progressive revelation pointed toward was what might be termed the "salvation of history." At the same time, since this revelation of God, this "salvation of history has been gradual, progressive and spaced out over the unfolding development of humankind, then it should be also termed the 'history of salvation.'"[102]

From this Segundo argued that the presentation of Christianity is adequate only when it moves from the "history of salvation" to the "salvation of history"—that is, to the buildup of history by the humankind God has prepared and commissioned for this task. That movement, says Segundo, is dependent upon three interrelated attitudes: (1) a shift from a particularized history of salvation to the total history of humanity; (2) a turn to interpretation over a mere recounting of events; and (3) a constant reinterpretation of history within the ecclesial community in the face of problems involving human liberation.[103]

His remarks concerning the shift from a "particularist history of salvation" bear further elaboration. Segundo regarded history as being "readymade" at the start of the humanization process, as a "given" to which people reacted. Thus history appeared to be a series of irrelevant, profane, day-to-day events interrupted by decisive happenings which, though small in themselves, were considered divine because of their decisive nature.[104]

But biblical revelation represented a shift from the origins of humanity to the origins of a people in Abraham and his descendants wherein divine history would continue. According to Segundo, the Israelites saw the interventions of God expressed in these happenings rather than an interpretation of the overall human reality. This represented the first, most primitive stage of the history of salvation. Segundo concludes that the events which mark the "history of salvation" in this stage are decisive events which, through the interpretation suggested by God, will help mankind to take charge of history as a whole (not just a limited sacred history) by interpreting it.[105]

The aim and end of the whole of Israel's sacred history was to arrive at the stage where interpretation became dominant and liberative. The Latin American theologian finds the second stage in Pauline theology where salvation is a kind of "political maturity," putting all the elements of the universe in the service of the humanization process. Now the process of divine "education" and the "salvation of history" result in a primacy of interpretation over event. And it is the presence of Christ through his Spirit in the church which means that the "necessary succession of interpretations dealing with salvation right up to the end of time" will not end in relativism or in error, but to the contrary, "in the truth that saves human history step by step."[106]

This summary of Segundo's appropriation of *Heilsgeschichte* highlights the sort of "elasticity" the hermeneutic had acquired. The inclusion of liberation themes certainly represented a profound extension of meaning, but nevertheless the fundamental understanding of *Heilsgeschichte* lay at the base of the expansion, as·the frequent use of the term "progressive revelation" makes clear, albeit with less explicit discussion of the fulfillment of the OT in the NT and of christocentricity.

The attachment of a more sophisticated political connotation to *Heilsgeschichte* in the Medellín era (in both the catechetical and episcopal meetings) was not a repudiation of its earlier meaning as forged in the days of kerygmatic renewal, but rather a kind of "conversion" of its usage—not in the sense of the biblical *metanoia,* but in the sense that one "converts" a furnace from oil to coal. There was, furthermore, no accompanying analysis of the suitability of the fundamental meaning of *Heilsgeschichte* for its expansion into a term for a more politically oriented catechetics and theology.

The "Medellín shift" in which the meaning of *Heilsgeschichte* was extended is also apparent in the work of the Lumen Vitae school. It is especially important to study that tradition because it was largely through Lumen Vitae that kerygmatic catechetics became dominant in the United States in the 1960s.

D. *Heilsgeschichte and Lumen Vitae*

The beginnings of Lumen Vitae go back to 1937 in Louvain where the Jesuit faculty set up a modest catechetical documentary center as an international library for religious education. They moved to Brussels in the early 1940s where, greatly influenced by the work of Emil Mersch, they sought to reshape catechetics along the lines of a christocentric synthesis and with sensitivity to psychological methods.[107] This attention to psychology gave Lumen Vitae a somewhat different configuration from the Jungmann-Hofinger tradition.

In 1946 the Belgian Jesuits established an international journal, *Lumen Vitae,* as a means of disseminating their perspectives. The review as it was originally conceived had a twofold goal: (1) to discover the experiences of contemporaries, both "stepping stones" (*pierres d'attente*) and obstacles in modern society, in a particular mentality of a country, class, or profession, and in the psychology of a period; and (2) to engage in the constructive work of religious education.[108] True to its setting in Brussels, where many cultures met, it has proved a truly international journal from its inception. A sampling of entries in its first volume includes articles on "Russian Piety," "Christianity in French Equatorial Africa," "Apostolate among non-Catholics by the 'Ladies of Bethany,' Holland," "Catechism Face to Face with Chinese Mentality," and "The St. Xavier's Catechetical Institute, Bombay," as well as two contributions from Christopher Dawson on Christian culture. Current entries reflect a similar global concern.

Founding editor George Delcuve acknowledged the formative influence of Jungmann and Hofinger on the journal; in the first decade of publication Jungmann contributed six articles and Hofinger eighteen.

The Jungmann-Hofinger link is most transparent in the journal's 1955 special issue on "The Bible, History of Salvation." As Delcuve expressed the theme: "The Bible is a collection of edifying stories, but it is first and foremost the history of salvation." This theme is reiterated and developed in each succeeding article.

Taken as a whole, the issue established the following understandings of *Heilsgeschichte*. (1) God, acting as a personal being, has a divine plan being unfolded for the sake of humankind's happiness.[109] (2) This plan of salvation is progressively revealed through human history.[110] (3) Christianity is not a philosophical system but a historical fact, and the Bible is the book of the revelation of God that culminates in Christ.[111] (4) The history of salvation is that long preparation needed for discovery of the mystery of Jesus.[112] (5) Thus the OT is but a preparation, a seed which, throughout the centuries, grows and develops until it finally flowers. Its full doctrinal value is manifest only when it is placed in the perspective of the history of salvation.[113] (6) Though the NT texts represent the fulfillment of the divine plan, the history of salvation does not cease with the historical Christ of the Gospel, but is carried on through the presence of Christ in his Church until the *parousia*.[114] (7) The christocentric message by which God achieves his mystery of salvation thus has four fundamental phases: preparation in the OT, realization in Christ, continuation in the church, and achievement in heaven.[115]

These gleanings from the 1955 special issue offer what are by now familiar themes. *Heilsgeschichte* was clearly the hermeneutical principle: God has a divine plan revealed progressively in the Bible; the OT is the preparatory phase of that plan which is in turn fulfilled in Christ's coming and continued until the *parousia* in the church. With the exception of the final point in regard to the understanding of church, that basic schema is clearly in harmony with nineteenth and twentieth century Protestant *Heilsgeschichte* theologians.

Another article in that same issue, "The Bible and Modern Man," distinguished Greek and Hebrew modes of thought, thus paralleling the biblical theology movement's distinction. The Hebrew thought mode was regarded as dynamic, more concerned with the significance of things (rather than with theory), with the rhythmic conception of time (rather than cyclic), and more in search of certitude (rather than impersonal truth); it was also seen as reflecting a trichotomic psychology—body, soul, spirit, rather than a dualist one.[116]

In addition particular note ought to be made of the configuration of the four numbers of *Lumen Vitae* in its tenth volume (1955). The first, summarized above, had focused on "The Bible, History of Salvation." The second and third numbers dealt with "The Liturgy, Re-Presentation of Salvation"; the fourth was entitled "Doctrinal Teaching: Message of Salvation." Or as Lumen Vitae director Delcuve put it:

> The mystery of Salvation, the essential content of catechetics, is related in the Bible, "re-presented" in the liturgy, expressed and systematically proposed in doctrinal formulas, and manifested in the life and witnessing of the Church, the continuation of the Incarnation. The catechist must therefore know how to communicate with the Mystery of Salvation through these four approaches.[117]

Here was, of course, the origin of the "four languages" later promulgated by Eichstätt in 1960.

Several articles in succeeding years fill in the contours of the Lumen Vitae appropriation of *Heilsgeschichte*. Systematic theologian Piet Schoonenberg suggested in a 1956 contribution that both primary and secondary pupils ought to come into contact with the OT in order to be introduced progressively to Christ; he argued for an increasing unity between the religion course and biblical history. Moreover, he found such an approach in accord with the development of faith, for to teach pupils how the people of the OT were prepared for Christ's coming was to demonstrate how "God prepares all the generations and the life of each person for Christ."[118]

In that same volume Walter Croce contended that a christocentric catechesis would unify the complex facts of faith. As a result:

> many difficulties experienced by man, modern man in particular, regarding the Catholic faith fall by the wayside. The Church proclaiming herself the only Ark of salvation (*arca salutis*) outside which there is no salvation, does not provoke scandal, for she appears now, not as a power at the side of Christ, but what she really is, the community of those who believe in Christ and live on His life. A

Christocentric presentation always places man before the fundamental choice: for or against Christ.[119]

Three articles in 1962 manifested various insights regarding *Heilsgeschichte*. The first, entitled "God's Plan," reiterated the notion of the four phases of salvation, and added a new rationale for the concentration on history: persons had become accustomed, partly through the influence of Marxism, to think in historical categories.[120] A second article by Andre Liégé, whose earlier work on evangelization was popularized by his student Alfonso Nebreda, detailed one aspect of this. He contended that all catechesis should be christocentric so as to bring persons back to the initial act of their conversion. Liégé viewed sacred history as the "bearer of a Divine intention which unifies it and manifests the analogy of faith."[121] The third article revealed that the *Lumen Vitae* journal was also a forum for reporting on the catechetical study weeks; Nebreda's summary of the Bangkok session with its discussion of the four languages also appeared in 1962.[122]

Perhaps the most sophisticated—from the point of view of biblical scholarship—study of *Heilsgeschichte* in religious education published in *Lumen Vitae* was Bernhard Grom's 1968 study, "The Catechesis of the Old Testament: Hermeneutical and Theological Bases of Didactic Research."[123] Grom acknowledged that present-day catechists agreed unanimously on one principle entailing numerous consequences: all scriptural pedagogy must integrate the acquisitions of modern exegesis. There is an interesting citation of Bultmann's student Gerhard Ebeling in Grom's identification of the hermeneutical problem: how to enable the Scripture to speak in such a manner that it might activate what Ebeling called the "process of existential transformation due to the Word of God." He recognized a coherent salvation history, beginning with creation, embracing the entire history of Israel and remaining open to the future; this history is constituted by those great literary complexes which were Israel's organization of documents relating to God's interventions, institutions, instructions, and promise. Though one must avoid neglecting the original meaning of the text and an artificially concordant typology, the OT according to Grom's view is best read by beginning from the central message of the NT. A "Christian actualization" of the OT, he concluded, should seek to make manifest past events as the "preparation, the initial realization of God's self-communication in Christ."[124]

In recent years, *Lumen Vitae* articles have dealt less directly with Scripture and devoted greater emphasis to political and pastoral concerns; this represents not so much a shift away from *Heilsgeschichte*—at least not a conscious one—but rather an implicit acceptance of it and a refocusing of energy toward more pressing concerns.[125]

Despite this recent development, there can be little doubt that the Lumen Vitae school has been of the utmost significance in promulgating the more traditional understanding of *Heilsgeschichte* along the Jungmann-Hofinger line. This is particularly apparent on the North American continent in the 1960s; before examining that scene, however, it is first necessary to make a brief excursus. Not only were Jungmann, Hofinger, and catechetical experts in Europe working with *Heilsgeschichte*, but so also were two of the leading theologians, Jean Daniélou and Karl Rahner.

E. Jean Daniélou and Karl Rahner: Heilsgeschichte as a Theological Foundation

Among Catholic scholars, Cullmann considered the *Heilsgeschichte* theology of French Jesuit Jean Daniélou (1905–1974) to be most harmonious with his own views.[126] Study of Daniélou's 1958 *Lord of History* verifies Cullmann's assertions and establishes some counterclaims to Cullmann's ecclesiology as well.[127]

Heilsgeschichte was clearly Daniélou's principal hermeneutic. He understood the Bible as a record of the evidence for certain events (the historical works of God); the Christian outlook was primarily to be determined by tracing a distinct line of development in this series of events.[128] Daniélou's concern was with fashioning a Christian theology of history and his views might most readily be subsumed under four related categories: the relation of sacred to profane history, typology, ecclesiology, and eschatology.

Regarding the first, Daniélou proposed a dual relationship:

Christianity falls within history and, conversely, history falls within Christianity; that is, all secular history is included in sacred history as a part and prolegomenon.[129] As Cullmann had shown in *Christ and Time,* this had been the understanding of Christian philosophy from its earliest days. The Bible insisted that the God of creation was the God of redemption, a point Irenaeus had made against the Gnostics. The history of salvation, furthermore, embraces not only the history of humanity, but the whole of cosmic history.

This religious understanding of history neither conforms to the law of continuous evolutionary progress nor to a Spenglerian evolutionary succession of discontinuous and independent cultures. On the contrary, Daniélou claimed, history should be regarded as a series of *kairoi,* moments of decision. The Christian conception of the structural pattern of history is given in *Heilsgeschichte,* "the temporal succession of works whereby Almighty God, the Creator, proceeds to the building of the eternal city of mankind."[130] Therefore the interpretation of history demands more than comprehension of outward, visible events; it must by its very nature take account of what happens in the hearts of God's people through the Spirit. Sacred history is accomplished through God's creative activity, and consequently stands in contrast with any other kind of history (even Marxist) which humans might fashion for themselves. Christianity is itself the archetype of the historical process, and imposes its own pattern on the development of civilization; hence, it is sacred history which is the key to profane history.

Daniélou devotes a considerable portion of *Lord of History* to typology. In his view, typology was a natural corollary of the "economy of progress" in the Christian outlook on history and also the groundwork of apologetics; furthermore, it was the "very stuff of prophecy, wherein Christian thinkers from the Fathers to Pascal, have seen the essential proof of the truth of our religion."[131] His typological comments open up two components of his *Heilsgeschichte* theology, namely the understanding of the OT and of the centrality of Christ.

Citing Irenaeus's *Commentary on Matthew* (X:9) that everything which belongs to the temporal order must first be imperfect, Daniélou saw that the OT and NT belong to one scheme of things but represent two successive stages of development. Before God gave the "plenitude of revelation to his people," he began familiarizing them gradually with his ways, educating them slowly. Again, Daniélou affirms Irenaeus (*Adv. Haer.* IV: 14, 3):

> Thus he called them from what was secondary to what was essential, from types to realities, from temporal things to eternal, from fleshly to spiritual, from earthly to heavenly.[132]

The typological method of exegesis defined the relationship of the testaments, because it explained both similarities and differences. God, first known through nature, later revealed himself in successive historical events. This meant that later revelations did not destroy the truth of earlier ones, but that later revelations transcended, incorporated, and continued that truth:

> Consequently the nature-symbolism through which men first came to a knowledge of God was adopted into the religion of Abraham and into the religion of Christ, being constantly enriched with new significance. Thus the water of baptism means the waters of the Flood, the divided waters of the Red Sea and the deep waters of death into which Christ went down.[133]

And, Daniélou added, the normal rule of biblical typology is that events recorded in the OT first of all prefigure the mystery of Christ and then are fulfilled in him.[134]

Daniélou's christology, then, flows from his typological framework and also provides the basis for his ecclesiology and eschatology. Christ is the "key and central point of history,"[135] the "point of intersection" of the two OT themes of divine intervention and human response.[136] He is the "culmination of the Old Testament," representing the turning point of history.[137]

Because of Christ, the center of interest in a Christian outlook on history lies neither in the beginning (as it was for the Greeks) nor in the end (as it is in evolutionary theories), but in the middle. In a comment that implicitly states his ecclesiological stance, Daniélou wrote:

> It follows that history differs in kind between B.C. and A.D. History before Christ was a preparation and an awaiting. Once he is come, the essential business is to hand on (παραδοσις) the sacred and now immutable trust delivered once and for all. The idea of tradition thus acquires a real meaning, because the world to come is there already.[138]

Vis-à-vis Protestant presentations of the theology of history, Daniélou stressed that salvation history was not restricted to the contents of the Bible, but was ongoing in the conversion and sanctification of humankind. He faulted the Protestants for making no reference to the church as continuing God's work "through the infallible magisterium and the unfailing efficacy of the sacraments."[139] He found Barth guilty of a sort of post-Christian Gnosticism and acknowledged Cullmann as repudiating this "extreme position." Cullmann affirmed an existing kingdom of Christ and the life of the Spirit in the church, yet objected to the Catholic presentation as overemphasizing the importance of the growing church and the living tradition. But Daniélou countered that the Catholic appreciation of the development of the church did not diminish faith in the unique importance of the resurrection, though it did imply recognition of the positive worth of current history, "constituting the growth of the mystical body through the work of the Spirit."[140]

Daniélou's eschatology carried a kind of implicit "already/not yet" motif à la Cullmann. He asserted that the work of salvation had already been substantially done, that everything essential had already been secured—thus making eschatology incompatible with any evolutionary theory. On the other hand, "this work of Judgment which Christ has substantially completed has not yet produced its due consequences throughout mankind and throughout creation."[141] The paradox of Christianity occurred in the integration of this fulfillment and expectation. Daniélou differs from Cullmann in his emphasis on the epoch of the church as the period of grace given for the acceptance of the judgment, as well as his grounding in typology. Though it is difficult to know for certain, it may well be that Daniélou was the most significant theologian by which the *Heilsgeschichte* theology of Cullmann came into Catholic circles and was modified according to distinct Catholic emphases.

Two essays on salvation history by celebrated systematic theologian Karl Rahner (1904–) reflect substantial agreement with Daniélou.[142] They might be adequately recapitulated by examining his views concerning, first, the relationship of salvation history to profane history and, secondly, the meaning of the OT.

Salvation history, Rahner argued, occurs *within* profane history, yet is *distinct* from it.[143] The two are distinct because salvation history is the result of God's interpreting a particular part of profane history, thereby bestowing upon it a saving or damning character. Rahner accordingly elaborates:

> Hence, whenever profane history is clearly interpreted by the word of God in history as to its saving or damning character—wherever God's actions in general salvation and revelation-history are clearly and certainly objectified by the word of God—and whenever the absolute, unsurpassable and indissoluble unity of God and the world, and its history in Jesus Christ, become historically manifest by Christ's testimony to himself in the form of words—there is found the special, official history of salvation and revelation, immediately differentiated and standing out in relief from profane history.[144]

Salvation history, moreover, *explains* profane history; by setting itself into relief from the world's history it demythologizes and "un-deifies" it. Likewise, salvation history interprets the history of the world as something "antagonistic and veiled," as an "existentially devaluated" history.[145]

This salvation history-profane history distinction is developed when the German theologian applies it to the OT. He considered the OT to be very "fluid" in the dividing line between the two histories. Prophets made only sporadic appearances and, Rahner argued, there did not yet exist an institution "endowed with an absolute discernment of spirits" in distinguishing on every occasion between true and false prophecy. Only with the advent of Christ did divine and human meet in "absolute and indissoluble unity." Only in Christ is salvation history "clearly and permanently" distinguished from all profane history.[146] For Christianity the history of this world is a history to be interpreted in a christocentric sense.[147]

His understanding of the OT is further developed in the *Sacramentum Mundi* discussion of salvation history. Looked at from the perspective of dogmatic theology, the OT is the "phase of the history of revelation and salvation" that had its beginnings in the Abrahamitic covenant, its center in the Exodus and covenant at Sinai, and its fulfillment in the death-resurrection of Jesus.[148]

Rahner maintained that the OT covenant could and did in fact fail, and therefore represents a period in the history of salvation which ought to be interpreted as "not yet eschatological":

> That is to say, God's free, radical and definitive, irrevocable self-revelation and self-communication in his word as victorious grace to the definitively accepted world is not yet seen in such a way that God had already given himself tangibly and irrevocably in the world. OT salvation history was still in suspense between judgment and grace; the dialogue was still open and the conclusion had not yet been reached in the world (i.e. disclosed by an event) that the pardon of God and not man's refusal has the last word.[149]

Consequently, Rahner asserted, the ancient covenant could still be annulled by the unbelief of the human partner; for that reason, an OT sacrament was not an *opus operatum* because "there was no absolute and unconditional promise of grace on God's part." The Law was merely "external legality" and "Levitical sanctification," a "servile bondage to what was other than God."[150]

But the OT was also a "manifest movement, guided by God, towards definitive redemption." Nevertheless, it is a period in the *Heilsgeschichte* which is now fulfilled and ended by its fulfillment. It ought rightly to be interpreted from the standpoint of the NT by which it has been annulled. And now the covenant continues on in the church.[151]

Mention might also fittingly be made here of the moral theology of Bernard Häring.[152] There is little doubt that Häring is the outstanding scholar in the renewal of Catholic moral theology. While it would be vastly reductionistic to categorize him simply as a *Heilsgeschichte* theologian, two points are pertinent: (1) the Biblical basis of his moral theology was grounded in a *Heilsgeschichte* schema; (2) the movement away from casuistic formulations in Häring's moral theology to a much more evangelical sensitivity is in harmony with the "Good News" kerygmatic theology of Jungmann and others. Little surprise, then, that he appears as a visiting professor at Lumen Vitae in 1960.

F. *Heilsgeschichte in Catholic Religious Education in the United States*

The final task is to trace the appropriation of *Heilsgeschichte* in the United States in recent years. Perhaps three phases might be identified: 1948–1958, the early years; 1959–1965, the peak years; and 1966–1976, the years of decline.

One doubts that *Heilsgeschichte* was much in vogue as part of the common parlance of religious educators in the United States during that first period. Nevertheless, certain factors were developing that established the groundwork for its later predominance. The encyclical *Divino Afflante Spiritu* of 1943 had set the biblical renewal underway. *Worship* instituted a regular column on Scripture in 1955 and gave coverage to the work of Jungmann and Hofinger. Daniélou had lectured at Notre Dame in the summer of 1950, and Hofinger in the summers of 1954 and 1955, publishing his lectures in 1957 in *The Art of Teaching Christian Doctrine*.

Another source for examining the state of *Heilsgeschichte* as a hermeneutical principle in this era is the *Proceedings of the 1957 North American Liturgical Week* in Collegeville, Minnesota. There is an article on "Liturgy, the Integrating Principle in Education" by Fuerst (later to be translator of Jungmann's *Katechetik*),[153] and another by Hofinger on "The Holy Mass— Source and Center of Christian Life."[154] Hofinger conducted a special session as well on "Catechetics and the Liturgy." The content of that merely summarized much of what he had already expressed in previous articles in the pages of *Worship,* but one special focus of his is made manifest for the first time in print: the concern for the religious education of students not in Catholic schools in the United States:

> It may seem to some, perhaps, that this kerygmatic renewal is first of all for high schools and for colleges. *Absolutely not!* It is for the poor, the simple, since our Lord's first interest is to make them the children of God . . . never forget that in the United States just half of our youth is going to Catholic schools. We must reach them through the Confraternity of Christian Doctrine, in a very different catechetical situation.[155]

Those comments had already been taken seriously, as Hofinger noted, by a group of sisters in San Francisco, who put out the first textbooks in the United States based on the kerygmatic renewal, the *On Our Way* series for Confraternity of Christian Doctrine (CCD) students. *Heilsgeschichte* in the Jungmann-Hofinger tradition was one of the basic principles of the series; something of that is evident in this remark in a later article by one of the coauthors of the series: "It is the Bible which reveals to us the fundamental outline of the Christian mystery and makes known to us the course of the economy of salvation."[156]

The year 1957 may in some ways represent a rather arbitrary transition point. But it does mark the opening of the Lumen Vitae center as an international school of religious education, and its first years of operation found a number of students from the United States who would shortly thereafter become leaders of the catechetical movement on the homefront: Jesuits Vincent and Joseph Novak, John Nelson, Mark Link, and James DiGiacomo.

The next year was something of a publishing breakthrough, at least from the point of view of kerygmatic renewal and its *Heilsgeschichte* hermeneutic. Jungmann's *Katechetik* appeared in translation as *Handing on the Faith;* this meant that for the first time an in-depth publication by Jungmann on catechetics became available to the English-speaking world. By 1962 when his *Die Frohbotschaft* finally appeared in English, *kerygma* had become a household word—almost!

Only slightly less known is the 1959 article by Canadian NT

scholar David M. Stanley on "The Conception of Our Gospels as Salvation History."[157] Stanley's contribution was significant for two reasons. First, it marked the entry of serious Roman Catholic biblical scholarship from North America into the kerygmatic renewal-*Heilsgeschichte* thought world. Secondly, it provided yet another forum in which the viewpoint of Cullmann was disseminated to Catholic readers.

In an earlier number of *Theological Studies*, Stanley had extensively reviewed the 1957 German original of Cullmann's study of NT christology, remarking that he wished he had written it himself.[158] Stanley noted with approval that the basic quality of the NT christology is its *heilsgeschichtliche* character "which differentiates it so radically from anything like myth."[159]

The Canadian's study of the gospels as salvation history both reflects his debt to Cullmann and manifests his own approaches. The initial section of the article provides a sort of modern Scripture scholar's *apologia pro vita sua* and was of the sort to be very helpful to initiates in the world of "new" biblical scholarship.[160]

In the second and lengthier section of the essay, Stanley examines the meaning of the historical character of the gospels, grappling with the issue of how the biblical conception of history might differ from the modern understanding of that term. His solution is worth citing at length:

The biblical notion of history rests upon the belief that God has, in the past, revealed Himself in a special way within the cadre of human affairs. Through specific events, personalities, and human utterances, God has intervened in the world of man. From this point of view, it is clear that the intelligibility to be seen in the biblical narratives is essentially that of a divine, not a human, pattern. It is best described as a "mystery," in the Pauline and Johannine sense, viz., as God's revelation, in time, to men of His eternal plan for the world's salvation. This Mystery was disclosed to mankind in two stages: one incomplete and rudimentary to God's chosen people in the OT; the second, complete and definitive through His only Son, Jesus Christ, to the Church of the NT. *This genre of history, which we call salvation-history or Heilsgeschichte, is the story of God's self-revelation to us; and its aim is obviously very different from that modern scientific history which is written without reference to the divine point of view.*[161]

Stanley further offered the opinion that *Heilsgeschichte* differs from the *Weltanschauung* of people of our own era, since it reflects the ancient Semitic mentality rather than that of the Greek culture, so formative for moderns.[162]

As Stanley saw it, *Heilsgeschichte* functioned not simply as a key hermeneutical principle, but also as a way of educating people away from fundamentalism. His article was oriented toward explaining that the gospel accounts are not intended to be straightforward, biographical records; rather they narrate the history of salvation and thereby offer insight into the meaning of the mystery of Christ. *Heilsgeschichte*, furthermore, permitted one to discern other literary forms—genealogy, eyewitness account, midrash, popular tradition—which "aid us in grasping the meaning of the Gospels' historical character." Stanley continued:

> The problem posed by the presence of certain literary forms in our Gospels is in no sense to be regarded as one of reconciling the "history" with the Christology. Once we grant the supreme truth of the Incarnation, with all its consequences, the Christology *is* the history.[163]

This article was published with some minor revision in 1965 as part of a collection of essays on *The Apostolic Church in the New Testament,* and enjoyed a fairly wide circulation in those early post-Vatican II years among Catholics interested in biblical studies relating to the early church.[164]

A Stanley essay from that anthology appeared in 1964 in another collection, *Studies in Salvation History,* which was aimed at making the work of leading biblical scholars—R. A. F. MacKenzie, Bruce Vawter, Carroll Stuhlmueller, John McKenzie, Myles Bourke, Barnabas Ahern—accessible to a wider audience.[165] Most of the essays were of the type presented at workshops, conferences, and conventions, and one could presume they reached large audiences. The articles differ in quality (perhaps a reflection of the varying audiences to whom they were given) and emphasis. For the purposes of this survey of *Heilsgeschichte* in the United States in the first half of the 1960s, it is particularly helpful to look to the introductory essay by editor C. Luke Salm:

> Salvation history has become the unifying theme that dominates biblical studies today. Sacred scripture, in fact, is itself sacred history or salvation history. In the articles that comprise this collection the expression occurs often, sometimes in connection with the German *Heilsgeschichte* which it translates. Salvation history is a special sort of history; it records the "mighty works of God rather than of men."[166]

Salm reiterates what by now were ideas repeated with amazing consistency in the days since Jungmann. God has a plan for human salvation, instructing his people in the details of that plan "little by little." In Jesus God's plan for salvation works because the man Jesus who works it is personally God. And this plan of God for salvation is communicated to all humankind through the community, the church; although this plan is essentially complete in the salvation events accomplished in Christ, there are "details" that still remain to be worked out until the *parousia*.[167]

It is important to recall that many of those to whom these essays were directed were religious educators relatively unfamiliar with the Bible, and perhaps even somewhat bewildered at the magnitude of approaching this formidable piece of literature, "word of God" or not. Hence, the significance of a piece such as Thomas Barrosse's "How to Approach the Bible"; to the initiates, Barrosse taught:

> The Bible, then, is substantially a record of successive divine interventions that gradually formed Old Testament Judaism and Christianity. It is history, sacred history, or—to use a term that has become more or less technical—salvation history. If we are to present what the Bible has to say—the Bible's message, if you will—how else can we do it than historically?[168]

Barrosse recalls, citing Jungmann, that such an approach had already been "tested and tried," for it was the church's own way, used throughout the patristic period (chiefly the *De catechizandis rudibus* of Augustine), and, of course, the way of the apostles and first missionaries as evidenced in Acts.[169]

The other essays in the volume are more biblically sophisticated and represent in some cases highly nuanced understandings of history and theology. Stanley is foremost among the biblical scholars in discussing *Heilsgeschichte*, but it ought to be pointed out that, though his conclusions were certainly in harmony with the kerygmatics (Jungmann, Hofinger, *et al.*,), methodologically he was far closer to Cullmann.

Studies in Salvation History helps to establish the point that, by the middle of the 1960s, *Heilsgeschichte* was becoming the *leitmotif* of religious education in Catholic circles. Other examples will corroborate this observation.

For instance, a symposium on "Kerygmatic Catechetics" had appeared in the *Religious Education* journal in late 1962;[170] the introduction by the editors noted:

> We can see the fruits of a revolution in religious education within the Roman Catholic Church. The development has been coming on us for some time, but the fruits are just beginning to show. Partly it is a change in educational theory and methods, but chiefly it is a new emphasis on the place of *kerygma* or proclamation in teaching. This insistence on *kerygma* may also be found among Protestant educators.[171]

Gerard Sloyan provided the lead article for that symposium, "The Use of Sacred Scripture in Catechetics." He identified the basic problem: the "clear lineaments" of biblical and Catholic faith had been "blurred" by certain "unintended omissions" and stresses on the accidental; human language had been substituted for the "divine speech of the Scriptures." Hence the return to the core, the *kerygma*. To this end Sloyan proposed a fourfold practice: (1) seek the form in which the apostles preached faith in Jesus as found in the Acts; (2) study the Pauline formulations in regard to the plan of God and becoming a new person in Christ; (3) focus on the places in the gospels where Jesus describes himself as fulfilling all prophecy; (4) then read the sacred history itself, for the two testaments go together, the Old concealed in the New and the New revealed in the Old (Augustine's phrase):

> The Old Testament is like a great tapestry that waits to be woven, its myriad strands lying around the weaver's shop. Then Jesus comes, and with his hands weaves the image which is he himself, and we come to know all that was meant by the "shadowing promise" in that clear fulfillment which is the saving person of Jesus Christ.[172]

Despite Sloyan's rather clear affirmation of the kerygmatics as evidenced in this article and by the choice of contributors— Jungmann, Hofinger, Delcuve, among others—to a 1958 collection of essays he had edited,[173] Sloyan eventually developed something of an ambivalence toward this movement. In an address to over one hundred participants in the summer of 1964 at the Grailville, Ohio, "Catechetical Crossroads," the chairman of Catholic University's religious education department humorously recounted his experiences with the sudden resurgence of interest in catechetics:

> People approach you nowadays with puckered brows and say "I've read Father Hofinger's book and Jungmann's and (lamely) oh, of course, yours—and we've got this new approach going pretty strong in River City" . . . Then they say "new approach," "kerygmatic" and "new interpretations of Scripture" about six times in the next three minutes, and you're supposed to get the idea that they're *really* in the club.[174]

Sloyan took issue with the faddism, the fear of long and in-depth study, and the claims of newness. *Heilsgeschichte* reflected this; it had become something of a "cure-all" and there was a:

> growing tendency to conceive all catechizing in simple, biblicist terms. We have discovered "salvation history," which all too often means neither more nor less than Bible history on new and better terms. It is scholarly. It is enlightened. But it is mere Bible history which saves no one.[175]

Sloyan charged that students were losing all sense of immediacy, that religious educators were "retreating" from the real work of catechetics because it proved so satisfactory to give biblical lectures after so many years of giving theological lectures. He reminded his audience that they had discovered the Bible recently, and were rushing impetuously to share their treasure "without taking time to do with it what the church has always done: teach Christ from it."[176]

Sloyan's ambivalence was further evidenced in a 1966 book "roundup" in *Worship* magazine.[177] He provided a history of the term *kerygma* in NT literature and commented that the practical effect of it all was an attempt by catechists everywhere to replace the analytic and noetic, "even nominalist, schema based on the articles of the creed, the decalogue and the commandments of the church and sacraments and prayer" with a "Christ-*kerygma* culminating in the 'glory of the Father.'"[178]

But, continued Sloyan, in its most popularly available form, this mode of presenting the mystery of salvation was "almost Marcionite" in its disregard of the OT. Similarly, critical words were reserved for the appearance of Jungmann's *Die Frohbotschaft* in its 1962 translation:

> On balance the book may be said to have great power as a demolisher and rubble-remover of certain faulty doctrinal and devotional emphases which have been gathering in strata since the Arian challenge of the fourth century; at the same time, the author calls nostalgically for a world which might have been retrievable in 1936 but is not to be recovered three decades later. The impression is given by both Jungmann and Hofinger that a telling of the story of God's love in biblical categories will achieve the desired results. Both ask for adaptation to the hearer but neither engages to any notable degree.[179]

Other challenges to the kerygmatics and their *Heilsgeschichte* hermeneutic would soon be forthcoming, most notably in Sloyan's student Gabriel Moran; these shall be considered in later analysis. But what is apparent in reading between the lines of Sloyan's 1964 and 1966 criticisms is the extent to which *kerygma* and its *Heilsgeschichte* hermeneutic had assumed such prominence on the catechetical scene in the United States within a relatively brief period of time. The critique by Sloyan was essentially a reaction to the oversimplification and naiveté of many of the adherents of the kerygmatic approach: it was not a questioning of *Heilsgeschichte* as a hermeneutical principle per se. Suffice it to say that in this respect, Sloyan was a harbinger of future criticism.

It would be appropriate at this point to return to that 1962 symposium for a closer look at William J. Reedy's contribution, "About the Kerygma." As religion editor of the W. H. Sadlier textbook company, Reedy had collaborated with Hofinger in producing the above-mentioned *ABC's of Modern Catechetics*.[180] That brief (120 pages) work must be regarded as extremely important for the formation of catechists if one applies the principle of "progressive reduction" (to borrow a term from Cullmann): the more basic and popularized an idea, the greater its circulation. One might venture the opinion that *ABC's* had a wider readership than either the *Good News* or the *Art*, though these latter works certainly would have been in the hands of professionals.

Reedy's symposium article is essentially an outline of *ABC's*, and thus provides a clear view of its structure. Of chief concern here is his presentation of *Heilsgeschichte*. Reedy begins by listing the components of the "Good News" brought by Christ: the invitation by the Father to divine life through Jesus, Jesus as the core of the message and central figure in God's plan for human salvation, and the unity of all individual Christian doctrines in light of this. In explaining the *kerygma* (the "substance of the Christian Good News upon which detailed doctrine is built," classically found in the catechesis of Peter's speeches in Acts), Reedy stressed that its first great concept in regard to the teaching of religion is the internal unity of content seen in the formula *to God through Christ*.[181] *Kerygma*, Reedy emphasized, is not so much a body of doctrine as it is a person, Jesus, who is the way to the Father. Jesus is the central figure in the history of salvation, which has three phases: OT preparation, achievement in the death-resurrection of Jesus, and consummation in the glorious return of Jesus:

> Many today use the term "salvation history" in presenting the full view of God's plan for us. With St. Paul they speak of the "mystery of Christ," which means that God has designed a redemptive plan

for man with Christ as its center. Once this fact is grasped it is relatively easy to see, in their right order, the other fundamental teachings of Christianity. Our knowledge of the mystery of salvation is made known to us by God through Christ.[182]

Reedy ends by recounting the fourfold presentation of the one message of Good News in a biblical-narrative style of presentation, a liturgical orientation, a systematic catechesis, and a direction of the student to Christian life in the world as a witness to Christ.

If the Hofinger-Reedy recension of kerygmatic catechesis and its *Heilsgeschichte* hermeneutic influenced thousands of teachers, particularly CCD teachers, another work, the *Lord and King* series generated by Lumen Vitae school alumnus (1959) Vincent M. Novak, effectively took over the religion curriculum in Catholic secondary schools in the mid-1960s.

Novak, a student at Lumen Vitae in 1958–59, returned to New York City to pioneer this approach at Fordham Preparatory School, and from this pilot project resulted the series. Novak reported to the participants of the 1963 North American Liturgical Week on his attempt (in collaboration with his brother Joseph and John Nelson, who did the senior and junior year texts respectively) to construct a salvation history program for high schools which retained its basic structure as "God's plan for me," yet began each year with a fresh point of view.[183]

What the Lumen Vitae alumni produced was a first-year book, *Lord of History*, which featured the biblical-historical approach to the mystery of Christ, proportionately integrating the liturgical, doctrinal, and witness approaches. The second year, *Jesus Christ Our Life and Worship*, contained a strong liturgical-mystagogical emphasis; the other three signs were subordinated in complementary roles. The third-year text, *The Church: People of God*, featured the doctrinal sign, and the fourth year, *Christian Witness: Response to Christ*, the sign of witness, integrated the other signs under their respective emphases.[184]

Textual analysis would reveal numerous examples of *Heilsgeschichte* as a hermeneutical principle in the four books. Suffice it here to indicate merely the basic orientation of *Lord of History*. Novak writes in the teacher's manual that there are three key ideas in the text itself. (1) Jesus Christ is the center of God's plan for man's salvation; all history prior to the incarnation looked forward to his coming, and all history since takes its significance from reference to him, and will do so till the end of time. (2) Christ reigns in glory here and now, sharing with each of us today the graces of his paschal victory. (3) Each of us is involved in the plan of God; our vocations in life will determine the contributions each of us will make.[185]

The text summarizes the first-year religion course in four stages: Christ promised, Christ on earth, Christ living on in the church, and Christ triumphant. Regarding the first stage, from the creation to the incarnation, Novak wrote:

> The promise to Adam of a redeemer was the first plank in a vast bridge of prophecy that spanned what we call the Old Testament. Christ is coming, but no one knows exactly how or when. Adam, Abraham, Moses, David and the prophets wait in hope.[186]

The *Lord and King* series not only was used in nearly sixty-five percent of Catholic secondary schools in the United States in the mid-1960s, but, it should also be emphasized, provided a means by which many teachers learned OT *alongside* their students. Teachers by and large had minimal competence in biblical theology, and whatever interest they had was largely centered in NT studies. Hence, though frustration would later be voiced about the difficulty of teaching salvation history, it was not generally a reflection of disagreement with the content: teachers at that point simply did not generally have the theological resources to criticize *Heilsgeschichte* as integrated into the four signs of revelation, but they did have the capability based on their daily classroom experiences to judge pragmatically whether or not it "worked."

Several publications that would have had wide appeal to such teachers appeared at this point and served to reinforce the approach of the *Lord and King* series. Fellow Lumen Vitae alumnus Mark Link edited a collection of essays that had earlier appeared in that school's journal. The three headings by which Link organized the articles made apparent his harmony with the Novaks.[187] The first, "God Meets Man," is subdivided into four sections—the biblical, liturgical, doctrinal, and witness signs—and includes contributions from, among others, Jungmann, Häring, and Delcuve. The second division, "Man Meets God" (the sexist-language critique was not yet prevalent!) contained two articles on faith; the third, "Transmitting God's Message," incorporated articles by Liégé and Nebreda as well as Grasso and Hofinger.

Paralleling Link's work was a book edited by Johannes Hofinger and Theodore C. Stone which "happened" to contain precisely the same organizational headings.[188] In the first section on the biblical sign, an article by Richard Sneed, "The Biblical Renewal and Its Bearing on Catechetics," repeats what had by this point become the standard introduction to *Heilsgeschichte* as "the narrative of the continuity of God's dealings with man and on behalf of man." Sneed noted that modern biblical scholarship gave new emphasis to the Bible as the "narrative of the progressive saving encounters of God with man," as a "continuous series," a "unity revealing a progressive plan culminating in the definitive encounter of God and man in Jesus Christ."[189]

... And so forth. In surveying the writings of this era, one comes to the conclusion that the religion teacher, particularly in a Catholic school, who did not accept *Heilsgeschichte* as a hermeneutical principle either never prepared the religion lesson or was "stiff necked and uncircumcised of heart." It was, as these pages have detailed, absolutely pervasive. In lectures, summer schools, textbooks, anthologies, teacher guides, liturgical meetings: *Heilsgeschichte* was the "password."

One further example of the extensive usage of *Heilsgeschichte* completes the picture, and provides a point of transition. Emerging at this point as one of the worldwide leaders in catechetical renewal was Lumen Vitae professor Marcel van Caster; it was largely his influence that turned the kerygmatics in a more anthropocentric direction following the 1962 Catechetical Study Week in Bangkok. His analyses, appearing in English in 1965 and 1966, proved valuable for teachers sensitive to the personal lives of their students; and his formulation of the triple task of catechesis (instruction, formation, and initiation) provided the groundwork for terms such as "encounter," "experience," and "values" that soon came into prominence.[190]

But, it must be pointed out, if van Caster helped to lead into a new era which was more experience-centered, he was still firmly rooted in the *Heilsgeschichte* hermeneutic. The "economy of salvation was progressively realized and revealed" throughout the history of salvation, and had three stages: preparation, realization, and continuation.[191]

From 1966 onward, however, *Heilsgeschichte* rapidly assumed a lesser role in religious education. In some cases it went "underground," that is, was generally assumed but simply was not as significant as it once was. The emergence of *Heilsgeschichte* from time to time in official documents, such as the National Catechetical Directory and occasional articles, reflects this. In other cases, it fell victim to alternatives; after 1965, kerygmatic renewal work did not control religious education books to the same extent it once did, and new religion series incorporated more "existential" emphases. Finally, in some cases, it was expressly repudiated, though nearly always as part of a larger critique. The most vivid example is Gabriel Moran's attempt to reformulate an understanding of revelation begun in his two-volume *Theology of Revelation* and *Catechesis of Revelation* in 1966 and continued in his recent *The Present Revelation*.[192]

But whatever the status of *Heilsgeschichte* today, it is important to highlight the functions it played as the key linchpin in twentieth century Catholic kerygmatic renewal. Salvation history provided a corrective to the sterility of "conclusion theology" and an amplification for the rigid categories of the catechism. Jungmann's insistence that focus on God's "all-embracing salvific plan" would lead to a renewal of Christian life remained a characteristic claim: *Heilsgeschichte* was clearly envisioned as an understanding with the *power to renew the church*. Whereas the biblical theology movement had played a certain *mediational role in Protestantism,* kerygmatic renewal served as a *progressive force in Catholicism.*

Secondly, this hermeneutical principle functioned both as *an invitation and introduction to biblical study.* The excesses of post-Reformation polemics had meant the removal of the Bible from the heart of Catholic life, and, as a consequence, most Catholics knew the Scripture only at second remove (or in liturgical usage) and as a proof text for ecclesiastical doctrine. Biblical renewal had been fostered by the 1943 encyclical, *Divino Afflante Spiritu,* and the "good news" of salvation history provided a guiding principle of interpretation to facilitate the "neophyte's" comprehension of, and appreciation for, the word of God. The educational and pastoral function of *Heilsgeschichte* ought not to be underestimated; it encouraged and enabled many Catholics to open a book that had long lain closed. The genuine enthusiasm with which salvation history was greeted in many Catholic circles had its basis in this phenomenon: without *Heilsgeschichte,* biblical renewal in Catholicism would have had a very different beginning.

Thirdly, salvation history proved a *unifying factor;* as the centripetal force in biblical studies, liturgy, and catechetics, it offered scholars and nonspecialists alike common ground for dialogue. The interdisciplinary character of the kerygmatic renewal is remarkable when looked at from the vantage point of the present, highly specialized era.

III. *Summary*

Though it had been primarily through Protestant theologians and biblical scholars that salvation history rose to prominence, *Heilsgeschichte* also functioned as a linchpin in the catechetical, biblical, and liturgical movements of twentieth century Catholicism. In this second chapter the Catholic appropriation of salvation history—particularly in catechetics—has been both compared and contrasted with its antecedent usage in Protestantism.

1. Whereas the nineteenth century had been an especially fertile era for Protestant theology, the opposite was the case for Catholic theology. A markedly defensive posture had developed in which official Catholicism both saw itself apart from and condemned contemporary (i.e., post-Enlightenment) thought. Scholasticism was enthroned as the sole theological methodology, and Scripture scholars

were denied the usage of historical-critical methodologies. The nineteenth century constituted a fundamentally different matrix for the emergence of the *Heilsgeschichte* hermeneutic in Catholicism.

2. The intransigence of nineteenth century Catholicism, most apparent in the condemnation of the excesses of the modernists at the turn of the century, gradually gave way under the impetus of fledgling liturgical, biblical and catechetical movements. These interdependent movements shared an emphasis on biblical rather than philosophical categories and were particularly characterized by usage of the term *kerygma,* derived from the proclamation of salvation found in the NT. *To the extent that this so-called kerygmatic movement "rediscovered" the Bible for Catholics and insisted on the revolutionary character of its good news for ecclesiastical life, it utilized the salvation history approach. Indeed, Heilsgeschichte, the "all-embracing salvific plan of God" (Jungmann), was the single most important hermeneutical principle of biblical interpretation in the kerygmatic movement.*

3. Josef Jungmann's book, *Die Frohbotschaft und unsere Glaubensverkündigung* (1936), is the seminal work in the kerygmatic renewal in catechetics. He argued for a proclamation of the faith in which a christocentric "economy of salvation" would be the central theme. *Heilsgeschichte* was the *leitmotiv* of Jungmann's understanding of kerygmatic renewal.

   3.1 Jungmann criticized scholastic theology for obfuscating the *kerygma* with "things of second and third rank"; likewise, he criticized the devotional mind-set that had permitted a multiplicity of devotions to obscure the centrality of Christ as mediator. In both cases what was needed was focus on salvation history.

   3.2 In contrast to his Protestant predecessors, Jungmann as a Catholic and as a liturgist wrote from a different ecclesiological perspective and emphasized the mystagogic rather than historical Christ.

   3.3 Differences notwithstanding, Jungmann shared with Hofmann an interest in doctrinal renewal; with

Kähler, emphasis on the preaching of the early church and a concern for the pastoral responsibility of the theologian; and with Cullmann, a preoccupation with christocentrism, as well as acknowledgment of the church's place in the plan of salvation.

4. Jungmann's student, Johannes Hofinger, popularized and promulgated the kerygmatic theology of his mentor. Hofinger is primarily responsible for dissemination of Jungmann's catechetical theories and did not himself differ substantially with his work. Concerned particularly with the preparation of religion teachers at all levels, Hofinger made Jungmann's work accessible in numerous articles and popular books.

   4.1 Because of the overwhelming significance of Christ in the history of salvation, Hofinger urged teachers to point out the "imperfection" of the Old Testament.

   4.2 Hofinger extended Jungmann's ecclesiology by equating the church with the kingdom of God and identifying the continuity of Christ, apostles, bishops, and priests as the "christocentric foundation of the hierarchy."

5. The international catechetical study weeks, initiated by Hofinger, provided yet another perspective on the way Catholics appropriated *Heilsgeschichte*.

   5.1 The 1960 meeting at Eichstätt sparked global usage of the "languages" of kerygmatic theology: *biblical* (recounting the history of salvation), *liturgical* (dramatizing the salvation story), *doctrinal* (enfleshing God's plan in the life of the church), and *existential* (witness to salvation). Eichstätt represents the high point of kerygmatic renewal.

   5.2 The 1962 meeting in Bangkok and the 1964 session in Katigondo shifted the emphasis slightly by examining the anthropological ground of salvation history. The optimism manifest in the Eichstätt meeting was no longer evident, as one of the participants suggested by titling his book, *Kerygma in Crisis?*

   5.3 The 1967 study week in Manila and the 1968 gathering in Medellín considerably extended the anthropological interest. Particularly at Medellín was a major reconsideration of kerygmatic theology evident: the history of salvation and human history must be seen on the same continuum so as to insure that God's redemptive plan would mean liberation in the political and social realm. This "Medellín shift" is significant primarily because of its legitimation of the political obligations of the church, but it is also important because it represents an expansion of the usage of *Heilsgeschichte* without examination or repudiation of its fundamental tenets.

6. The Belgian catechetical school, Lumen Vitae—and its international journal of the same name—contributed greatly to kerygmatic renewal. Its contribution to the promulgation of salvation history is most striking in a 1955 special issue of its journal, "The Bible, History of Salvation"; reiterated here are the foundational understandings: a divine plan of salvation revealed progressively in history, prefigured in the OT, fulfilled in the coming of Christ, and continued in the church until the *parousia. Lumen Vitae* had been the source of the "four languages" of Eichstätt; moreover, the school was the place where a number of leading American religious educators studied.

7. Theologians Jean Daniélou and Karl Rahner each contributed to the Catholic appropriation of *Heilsgeschichte,* the former by a theology of history rich in typology, and the latter by his contention that the OT covenant had failed and thus ought to be interpreted from the standpoint of the NT.

8. The salvation history school made an entrance into Catholic religious education in the United States in three phases.

   8.1 In the period from 1948 to 1958, the ground was being prepared, so to speak: the biblical and liturgical renewals were underway, articles by Jungmann and Hofinger appeared in *Worship,* and Notre Dame had Daniélou, Jungmann, and Hofinger lecture to summer school students.

   8.2 The second era (1959–1965) marked the high point of salvation history as the key hermeneutical principle. *Lumen Vitae* alumni published widely dissemi-

nated textbooks and teacher manuals; scores of articles, workshops, and symposia for religion teachers
"introduced" the Bible as the history of salvation (a
clear contrast to the catechism). In short, "salvation
history" was pervasive.

8.3 In the third phase (1966–1976), however, salvation
history faded from prominence. Among the earliest
critics was Gerard Sloyan. Also felt were the "shock
waves" from the International Catechetical Study
Weeks with the new interest in anthropology.
Heilsgeschichte has now receded from prominence;
while more "existential" concerns dominate the contemporary scene, this hermeneutic is often still assumed.

9. Salvation history, as the centripetal force in the kerygmatic movement in twentieth century Catholicism, functioned
to renew church life, to invite and to introduce people
to the study of Scripture, and to draw together the biblical, liturgical, and catechetical movements.

IV. *Conclusion*

The significant function of *Heilsgeschichte* suggests the importance of engaging in a serious and sustained examination of its
demise and then reflecting on the meaning of its "rise and fall"
for the field of religious education. It is to those analytic and
reflective tasks that we now turn. The third chapter will include
four interrelated areas for analysis: (1) theological—the prob-
lematics inherent in *Heilsgeschichte*, namely its christology and
ecclesiology, and its understanding of revelation as well as its
conception of the relation between OT and NT; (2) cultural—
the "after shocks" of Vatican II within Catholicism and the
concomitant "cultural revolution" in the United States as a
whole in the late 1960s; (3) educational—the emergence of a
new era of progressivism and romanticism in general education
which affected religious education as well; (4) religious
educational—the evolution of religious education, including the
flowering of greater pluralism and the emergence of new emphases. Perhaps only a combination of all of these can account

for the dénouement, though the first three factors will be dealt with in greater detail. The fourth and final chapter, an inquiry into the significance of this for religious education, will focus particularly on a reconsideration of the relationship of biblical scholarship and religious education in light of what the *Heilsgeschichte* hermeneutic phenomenon has meant.

NOTES

1. O. Cullmann, *Heil als Geschichte* (Tübingen: Mohr, 1965) v.

2. Given 18 November 1965; in W. M. Abbot, ed. *The Documents of Vatican II* (New York: America Press, 1966) #15; cf. #2 and the Dogmatic Constitution on the Church (*Lumen Gentium*) #9.

3. *Sharing the Light of Faith: National Catechetical Directory for Catholics of the United States* (Washington, D.C.: United States Catholic Conference, 1979) #176. This formulation of national guidelines follows the 1971 *General Catechetical Directory*, issued from Rome, and the 1973 *Basic Teachings for Catholic Religious Education*, issued by the bishops of the United States. The NCD is particularly interesting in view of the unique consultation process that has characterized its composition; see W. Paradis ("Update on the National Catechetical Directory," *The Living Light* 12 [1975] 412–421).

4. *Sharing the Light of Faith* #53.

5. *Ibid.*, #83.

6. *Ibid.*, #88. See also #47: "First and foremost, catechesis is trinitarian and christocentric in scope and spirit, consciously emphasizing the mystery of God and the plan of salvation, which leads to the Father, through the Son, in the Holy Spirit. (Cf. Eph 1, 3–14) Catechesis is centered on the mystery of Christ. The center of the message should be Christ, true God and true man."

7. C. Welch, *Protestant Thought in the Nineteenth Century 1: 1799– 1870* (New Haven: Yale, 1972) 190.

8. Recent discussion has called attention to the fact that for years "European Roman Catholic theology" was taken for granted as *the* Roman Catholic theology. Europe, regarded as the font of learning and culture, controlled theological paradigms. Hence, the attempt here to delineate more accurately that nineteenth century theology in Catholicism was formulated from a European perspective; there is not an "objective, non-ideological theology."

9. J. G. Herder in A. R. Vidler, *The Church in an Age of Revolution*, rev. ed. (Harmondsworth U.K.: Penguin, 1971) 31.

10. For a summary of his thought and an assessment of his contributions, see J. Walgrave (*Unfolding Revelation* [Philadelphia:
Westminster, 1972] 282–284). It is appropriate here to note also that
these were the years of the "triumph of romanticism" in English literature; one thinks of Wordsworth (1770–1850), Shelley (1792–1822),
Byron (1788–1824), Keats (1795–1821), Coleridge (1772–1834), Scott
(d. 1832), and Austen (1775–1817); somewhat later in this century
came the great romantic period in American literature associated with
Bryant, Emerson, Lowell, Thoreau, Hawthorne, Melville. On Coleridge, see Welch, 108–126, who considers him as important for
British and American thought as were Schleiermacher and Hegel.

11. For analysis of Drey's work and an evaluation of his significance,
see G. A. McCool (*Catholic Theology in the Nineteenth Century: The Quest
for a Unitary Method* [New York: Seabury, 1977] 67–81).

12. J. Möhler in Walgrave, 289. Cf. McCool, 67.

13. See J. R. Geiselmann, *Die katholische Tübinger Schule* (Freiburg:
Herder, 1964).

14. A. Dulles, *A History of Apologetics* (London: Hutchinson, 1971)
181.

15. A. R. Vidler, *The Modernist Movement in the Roman Church* (Cambridge: University Press, 1934) 33–35. For an assessment of contemporary Tübingen theology, see McCool, 263–264.

16. Chateaubriand in Dulles, *A History of Apologetics,* 172.

17. *Ibid.,* 173–174.

18. Vidler, *The Church in an Age of Revolution,* 11–12. Emphasis
added.

19. Vidler, *The Modernist Movement in the Roman Church,* 20.

20. *Ibid.,* 21.

21. C. L. Manschreck, *A History of Christianity 2* (Englewood Cliffs,
N.J.: Prentice-Hall, 1964) 366.

22. Cf. the text of the *Syllabus* in Manschreck, 372–80, and commentary in K. S. Latourette, *A History of Christianity 2,* rev. ed. (New
York: Harper and Row, 1975) 1099–1101. Pius IX was the same pope
of whom two members of the Oxford Movement, R. Wilberforce and
J. B. Mozley, had written in 1848: "A pretty state we are in altogether,
with a radical pope teaching all Europe rebellion" (quoted in Vidler,
Church in an Age of Revolution, 148).

23. G. A. McCool, *Catholic Theology in the Nineteenth Century,* 225.

24. See B. Cooke's concise evaluation of papal authority from Vatican I to the present (*Ministry to Word and Sacraments* [Phildelphia:
Fortress, 1976] 504–507). For an assessment of the practical consequences of the ecclesiology of Vatican I, see R. P. McBrien (*The Re-

making of the Church [New York: Harper and Row, 1973] 28–34, 91–92). On the infallibility issue, see H. Küng (*Infallible? An Inquiry* [New York: Doubleday, 1971]; J. Kirvan, ed. (*The Infallibility Debate* [New York: Paulist, 1971]); and P. Chirico (*Infallibility: The Crossroads of Doctrine* [Kansas City: Sheed, Andrews and McMeel, 1977]).

25. T. M. Schoof, *A Survey of Catholic Theology 1800–1970* (New York: Paulist, 1970) 57.

26. Vidler, *The Modernist Movement in the Roman Church*, 63.

27. Schoof, 33–36.

28. *Ibid.*, 68.

29. McCool, *Catholic Theology in the Nineteenth Century*, 234.

30. *Ibid.*, 236. McCool is, of course, referring to theologians of the stature of Gilson, Maritain, Garrigou-Lagrange, deLubac, Bouillard, K. Rahner, and Lonergan.

31. *Ibid.*

32. See W. G. Kümmel, *The New Testament: The History of the Investigation of its Problems* (Nashville: Abingdon, 1972) 178–183 and 299–301. Loisy's work is now available in paperback in a "Lives of Jesus" Series edited by Leander Keck and published by Fortress (Philadelphia: 1976).

33. Schoof, 61. For a perspective more sympathetic to Rome, yet in support of historical-critical scholarship, see F. M. Braun (*The Work of Père Lagrange* [Milwaukee: Bruce, 1963] 66–100).

34. See Manschreck, 370 and the text of *Lamentabili*, in Manschreck, 372–375.

35. R. Aubert, "Modernism," in K. Rahner, ed., *Encyclopedia of Theology: The Concise Sacramentum Mundi* (New York: Seabury, 1975) 973.

36. *NCE Supplement*, s.v. "Modernism."

37. See McCool, *Catholic Theology in the Nineteenth Century*, 247–249.

38. Vidler, *The Modernist Movement*, 223. But cf. B. Cooke, 502–503, who places this crisis in the context of difficulties in other denominations. For an account, see W. R. Hutchinson, *The Modernist Impulse in American Protestantism* (Cambridge: Harvard, 1976).

39. Walgrave, *Unfolding Revelation*, 157.

40. When the antimodernist oath was required, there was on the whole general acceptance of it; apparently only forty priests worldwide refused to take it. When Tyrell's friend Maude Petre held out against taking it, she was denied the sacraments. But in Germany, the situation was altered by the coexistence of Catholics with Protestants in the universities; theology professors who exercised no pastoral ministry were dispensed from taking the oath.

41. R. Guardini, *The Lord* (Chicago: H. Regenery, 1954) and K. Adam, *The Spirit of Catholicism*, rev. ed. (New York: Macmillan, 1941).

42. *NCE*, s.v. "Odo Casel." See B. Neunheuser, ed., *The Mystery of Christian Worship* (Westminster, Md.: Newman, 1962); M. C. Bryce, "Mystery, Cult, and Catechesis According to Dom Odo Casel," *The Living Light* 15 (1978) 455-468.

43. J. Jungmann, *The Mass of the Roman Rite*. Abridged trans. (New York: Benzinger, 1951).

44. S. Langer, *Philosophy in a New Key* (Cambridge: Harvard, 1963) 66. Emphasis added.

45. This reference is from the English translation of *Die Froh-botschaft, The Good News Yesterday and Today*, ed. W. A. Huesman and J. Hofinger (New York: Sadlier, 1962) 3. All other references to Jungmann's writings, unless otherwise noted, will be to this edition, which also contains essays by Hofinger, P. Brunner, D. Grasso, and G. Sloyan appraising Jungmann's contribution.

46. *Ibid.*, 7.

47. *Ibid.*, 28.

48. *Ibid.*, 33-34.

49. *Ibid.*, 35.

50. See Jungmann's discussion of this in *Handing on the Faith* (New York: Herder and Herder, 1959) 33-37.

51. See A. Friesen's essay on Herbart, *A History of Religious Educators*, ed. E. L. Towns (Grand Rapids: Baker, 1975) 249-263. Cf. H. Burgess, *An Invitation to Religious Education* (Mishawaka, Ind.: Religious Education, 1975) 22-25; 45-47 and J. Goldbrunner, "Catechetical Method," in *New Catechetical Methods*, ed. J. Goldbrunner (Notre Dame: University Press, 1965) 39-55.

52. On Dewey, see M. S. Dworkin's introduction and commentary (*Dewey on Education: Selections* [Classics in Education Series, No. 3: New York: Teachers College Press, 1959]) and the essay of D. H. Roper, "John Dewey" (Towns, ed., *A History of Religious Educators*, 310-336). On the impact of the activity school on catechetics, see F. Kopp, "Basic Principles of the Activity School" (Goldbrunner, ed., *New Catechetical Methods*, 56-82); also, Sloyan's comments on American educator T. E. Shields in "The Catechetical Scene in the United States" (Huesman and Hofinger, eds., *The Good News Yesterday and Today*, 214-215). For an example of its impact on liturgy, see L. Dworschak, "Learning by Doing" (*Education and the Liturgy: Proceedings of the 1957 North American Liturgical Week* [Elsberry, Mo.: The Liturgical Conference, 1958] 28-33).

53. *The Good News*, 34.

54. *Ibid.*, 11.

55. *Ibid.*, 51.

56. *Ibid.*, 55.

57. *Ibid.*, 79.

58. G. Diekmann, "Review of *Die Frohbotschaft und Unsere Glaubens-verkündigung*," *Orate Fratres* 11 (January 1937) 142.

59. J. Hall, "The American Liturgical Movement: The Early Years," *Worship* 50 (1976) 483. Hall's article is also valuable for its insight into the concern for religious education by the liturgical movement in the States from its earliest years; she recounts the development of the elementary textbooks, the *Christ-Life* series, as the first attempt to relate liturgy and catechesis correctly. See also L. M. Lazio, "Jane Marie Murray," *Living Light* 12 (1975) 270–275. Note especially the recent article by M. C. Bryce, "The Inter-Relationship of Liturgy and Catechesis" (*American Benedictine Review* [1977] 1–29) for a significant attempt to confront the two.

60. J. Hofinger," J. A. Jungmann (1889–1975): In Memoriam" *The Living Light* 13 (1976) 354–356.

61. *Ibid.*, 356.

62. J. Jungmann, "Pastoral Effect of the Liturgy," *Worship* 23 (1948–49) 481–491.

63. (Innsbruck: Tyrolia, 1963); the English translation (from which the references are henceforth taken), *Announcing the Word of God* (London: Burns and Oats, 1967). Because of the frequency of references to this work in the next few pages, page numbers will simply be cited in parentheses.

64. The articles were by F. Lakner, "Das Zentralobjekt der Theologie" (*ZKT* 62 [1938] 1–36) and J. B. Lotz, "Wissenschraft und Verkündigung" (*ZKT* 62 [1938] 465–501). Also important for its relationship in the work of his Innsbruck colleague was H. Rahner's *Eine Theologie der Verkündigung* (Freiburg im Breisgau [Verlag Herder KG, 1939]); it appeared in English in 1968 as *A Theology of Proclamation* (New York: Herder and Herder). H. Rahner's work bears notable parallels to Jungmann on this topic. Also see E. Kappler (*Die Verküngdigungtheologie* [Freiburg im der Schweiz: Paulusverlag, 1949]7), who traces his work to Jungmann.

65. *Handing on the Faith,* 398. Cf. P. O'Hare, "Religious Education: Neo-Orthodox Influence and Empirical Corrective," *Religious Education* 73 (1978) 627–639.

66. O. Cullmann, "Rudolf Bultmann's Concept of Myth and the New Testament," *Theology Digest* 4 (1956) 140–145. Cited in Jungmann, *Handing on the Faith,* 402.

67. *Announcing the Word,* 20.

68. *Ibid.,* 60. Cf. the German original: "Das *Kerygma* ist Kunde von Tatsachen, vor allem von den Tatsachen, mit denen Gott selbst in die Geschichte der Menschheit eingegriffen und die Menschheit gerufen hat," 60.

69. A. Dulles, "Contemporary Approaches to Christology," *Living Light* 13 (1976) 119-144. Dulles traces the biblical-kerygmatic approach of Jungmann *et al.* to Kähler.

70. *Announcing the Word,* 172.

71. J. Hofinger, "Die Rechte Gliederung des katholischen Lehrstoffes," *Lumen Vitae* 2 (1947) 719-744.

72. J. Hofinger, "Our Message," *Lumen Vitae* 5 (1950) 265.

73. *Ibid.,* 270.

74. J. Hofinger, "Catechetics and Liturgy," *Worship* 29 (1954-55) 90.

75. Note here the implicit linkage to the "activity school." See above, n. 52.

76. J. Hofinger, "Teaching Good News," *Worship* 29 (1954-55) 130.

77. *Ibid.,* 135.

78. J. Hofinger, *The Art of Teaching Christian Doctrine: The Good News and Its Proclamation* (Notre Dame: University Press, 1957). Note the striking similarity in the subtitle to Jungmann's work.

79. *Ibid.,* 23-32.

80. *Ibid.,* 105-106.

81. *Ibid.,* 122.

82. J. Hofinger and W. Reedy, *The ABC's of Modern Catechetics* (New York: Sadlier, 1962).

83. *Ibid.,* 20.

84. The foregoing analysis is dependent particularly on L. Erdozain ("The Evolution of Catechetics," *Lumen Vitae* 25 [1970] 7-31). For a historical perspective, see B. L. Marthaler ("The Modern Catechetical Movement in Roman Catholicism," *Religious Education* 73 [Special Edition 1978] S - 77-90).

85. G. Delcuve, "International Session: 'Missions and Liturgy,'" *Lumen Vitae* 15 (1960) 155.

86. D. Grasso, "The Core of Missionary Preaching," in *Teaching All Nations,* ed. J. Hofinger (New York [Herder and Herder, 1961] 39-58). Grasso was V. Novak's mentor at the Gregorian; on Novak, see n. 185-186.

87. *Ibid.,* 43.

88. *Ibid.,* 44.

89. *Ibid.,* 47.

90. *Ibid.,* 46.

91. *Ibid.,* 50.

92. *Ibid.,* 58. See his *Proclaiming God's Message: A Study in the Theology of Preaching* (Notre Dame: University Press, 1965).

93. "Basic Principles of Modern Catechetics X" (*Teaching All Nations,* 398–99), one of twelve conclusions from the study week. Note this description of the biblical sign: "The Bible is the basis of the Church's proclamation and thus also of her catechesis. We use the Bible to follow the history of salvation in the way God himself made it known. These sacred books take us from the creation of the world to its end and show us how Christ is the fulfillment of all" (399). Cf. also the third principle: "Catechesis is Christ-centered, reflecting the fulfillment in and through Christ of the Father's loving design" (395). These principles are also listed as an appendix in Hofinger, *The Art,* rev. ed., 266–271.

94. See *Sharing the Light of Faith* #60. Cf. B. L. Marthaler, *Catechetics in Context: Notes and Commentary on the General Catechetical Directory Issued by the Sacred Congregation for the Clergy* (Huntington, Ind.: Our Sunday Visitor, 1974) 69–70.

95. A. M. Nebreda, "East Asian Study Week at Bangkok," *Lumen Vitae* 17 (1962) 724.

96. A. Nebreda, *Kerygma in Crisis?* (Chicago: Loyola, 1965), a summary of lectures in the United States in 1963, represented a reflection on the need to "condition" people for faith, that is, to "pre"-evangelize. As a student of A. Liégé, whose 1954 article distinguishing evangelization and catechesis had become classic, Nebreda's career as a missionary in Japan led him to value the importance of personal contact with one being evangelized. See also Liégé, "The Ministry of the Word: From Kerygma to Catechesis," *Lumen Vitae* 17 (1962) 21–36; M. Warren, "Evangelization: A Catechetical Concern," *Living Light* 10 (Winter 1973) 487–496. Also of interest is Hofinger's latest work, *Evangelization and Catechesis* (New York: Paulist, 1976), in which he claims it has become difficult to maintain the distinction between the two.

97. General Conclusion, No. 12 from the International Catechetical Week in Medellín 11–17 August 1968, reprinted in *Lumen Vitae* 24 (1969) 346. Cf. M. van Caster's background report (*Lumen Vitae* 24 [1969] 142–146). See also J. Hofinger and T. J. Sheridan, eds., *The Medellín Papers* (Manila: East Asian Pastoral Institute, 1969).

98. Erdozain, 26.

99. General Conclusion, No. 12 from Medellín, 347.

100. From the conclusion of the study group of Medellín on "The

Present Course of Catechetics," cited in Erdozain, 27. Excerpts from the Latin American Episcopal Conference in Medellín in 1968 are available in an excellent anthology by Joseph Gremillion, ed. (*The Gospel of Peace and Justice: Catholic Social Teaching since Pope John* [Maryknoll, N.Y.: Orbis, 1976]).

101. J. L. Segundo, *Our Idea of God: Theology for Artisans of a New Humanity* 3 (Maryknoll, N. Y.: Orbis, 1974).

102. *Ibid.*, 37.

103. *Ibid.*

104. *Ibid.*, 37–38.

105. *Ibid.*, 39. See also his citation of André Scrima, p. 53: "I tell myself now and again that the notion 'history of salvation,' traced out on its fullest horizon which is that defined by the relationship between *oikonomia* ('economy' in the sense of 'plan' or 'dispensation') and *theologia,* differs markedly from the 'local' and restricted use that is made of it by a certain occidental theology which is too greatly stamped with a specific cultural problematic (now somewhat out of date). The *oikonomia* does not lend itself to ready identification with the merely 'historical' aspect, as the latter is understood by those who maintain this line of thought. What I would like to see in the not too distant future is the cosmological emphasis gaining the upper hand, within a total Christological perspective, over the historicism that now dominates."

106. *Ibid.*, 39–42. See Segundo's remarks in his n. 19 on liturgy: ". . . any plan for liturgical renewal must pass through the stages that mark the transition from 'history of salvation' to 'salvation of history.' It must pass from the history lived in the liturgical sign to history as a whole. It must gradually give priority to the interpretation of the liturgical sign rather than to the quantity, invariability, and validity of the commemorative rite" (54–55).

107. See E. Mersch, whose work *The Theology of the Mystical Body* (St. Louis: Herder, 1951) became widely known through the great interest following the 1943 encyclical of Pius XII, *Mystici Corporis*.

108. "Editorial," *Lumen Vitae* 1 (1946) 14–15. Early volumes contained articles in French, German, and English; since that time the journal has contained both French and English versions simultaneously.

109. Cf. J. Dheilly, "The History of Salvation in the Bible," *Lumen Vitae* 10 (1955) 37: "There is a Divine plan which is unfolding towards an end easy to discern: God is carrying out this plan for the sake of man's happiness."

110. A. Dreze and J. Bongler, "Why Teach the Old Testament?" *Lumen Vitae* 10 (1955) 107: "The mystery of salvation unrolls little by little, in its true meaning throughout the historical events, for it is truly integrated in the historical process."

111. Dheilly, 43: "The history of salvation is therefore not a collection of events which leads through an abstract activity to a philosophical idea."

112. Cf. Dreze, 107, 113. Also M. van Caster, "The Substance of the Christian Message: The Mystery of Salvation," *Lumen Vitae* 10 (1955) 498: "The substance of catechesis does not therefore consist in a series of truths and practices, following one another. Its subdivisions are more like the spokes of a wheel of which Christ is the center. The Christian message is christocentric as regards the means by which God achieves His mystery of salvation."

113. I. De La Potterrie, "The Efficacy of the Word of God," *Lumen Vitae* 10 (1955) 48: "The New Testament texts represent the last stage in the revelation of the divine plan." Cf. also J. Jungmann, "Norms for an Elementary Textbook of Sacred History," *Lumen Vitae* 10 (1955) 117–118: "Christianity did not enter the world as a philosophical system, but as an historical fact; the divine plan develops by a progressive unveiling in the vast expanse of time."

114. Dreze, 107: "The mystery of salvation does not only terminate with the historical Christ of the Gospel, but through Him and the Church which continues Him in time, it will expand in the Mystical total Christ and the beatitudes of Heaven."

115. Cf. M. van Caster, 498.

116. C. Moeller, "The Bible and Modern Man," *Lumen Vitae* 10 (1955) 51–64.

117. G. Delcuve. Cited in E. A. Lawrence, "The Spirit of Lumen Vitae," *Worship* 25 (1960–61) 217.

118. P. Schoonenberg, "Christ in the Old Testament," *Lumen Vitae* 11 (1956) 391–400.

119. W. Croce, "Contents of Catechesis, the Message of Salvation," *Lumen Vitae* 11 (1956) 603.

120. H. Oster, "God's Plan," *Lumen Vitae* 17 (1962) 37.

121. Liégé, "The Ministry of the Word," 21.

122. Nebreda, "East Asian Study Week," 724.

123. B. Grom, "The Catechesis of the Old Testament," *Lumen Vitae* 23 (1968) 319–342.

124. *Ibid.*, 337.

125. See the decennial tables, 1966–1975 and index of articles in

Lumen Vitae 30 (1975) 477–487. Cf. *Lumen Vitae* 33 (1978), an issue devoted to "reading texts and events"; now structuralism rather than salvation history is the focus.

126. Cullmann, *Heil als Geschichte*, 45. (English translation, 63).

127. J. Daniélou, *Lord of History* (Chicago: Henry Regnery, 1958). French original, *Essai sur le Mystere de l'Histoire*, 1953.

128. *Ibid.*, 1. Against Bultmann and the existentialists, Daniélou held that these events had meaning in and of themselves.

129. *Ibid.*, 24.

130. *Ibid.*, 80–81.

131. *Ibid.*, 140.

132. *Ibid.*, 5–6. See J. Daniélou, *From Shadows to Reality: Studies in the Biblical Typology of the Fathers* (London: Burns and Oats, 1960), which had preceded *Lord of History* (French, *Sacramentum Futuri*, 1950). For an extensive analysis of *Heilsgeschichte* in Irenaeus, see J. Daniélou, *Gospel Message and Hellenistic Culture* (Philadelphia: Westminster, 1973) 166–183 and 221–229.

133. *Lord of History*, 145.

134. *Ibid.*, 254. On typology, see J. N. D. Kelly (*Early Christian Doctrines*, rev. ed. [New York: Harper and Row, 1978] 69–75).

135. *Lord of History*, 185.

136. *Ibid.*, 190.

137. *Ibid.*, 195.

138. *Ibid.*, 7–8. This also means that Daniélou saw Judaism as "anachronistic survival" (*Ibid.*, 17, n. 1). For an elaboration, see his *Dialogue with Israel* (Baltimore: Helicon, 1968), which includes a response as well from Rabbi J. B. Agus.

139. *Lord of History*, 10.

140. *Ibid.*

141. *Ibid.*, 276.

142. Rahner's prodigious output of theological and pastoral work (more than three thousand published pieces) is indicated in a remark made to an interviewer: "Some days I write nothing" (*American Ecclesiastical Review* 153 [1965] 221), and cited in Schoof, *A Survey of Catholic Theology*, 156.

143. K. Rahner, "History of the World and Salvation History," *Theological Investigations* 5 (Baltimore: Helicon, 1966) 100.

144. *Ibid.*, 107.

145. *Ibid.*, 110–112.

146. *Ibid.*, 108–109.

147. *Ibid.*, 114.

148. K. Rahner, "History of Salvation," *Encyclopedia of Theology: The*

Concise Sacramentum Mundi (New York: Seabury, 1975) 1512. This article contrasts notably with Klaus Berger's preceding entry on "History of Salvation" from the perspective of a theological analysis which is more characterized by a tradition-history approach.

149. *Ibid.,* 1515.

150. *Ibid.*

151. *Ibid.,* 1517. These claims are developed and refined in Rahner's recent compendium (*Foundations of Christian Faith* [New York: Seabury, 1978] 138–175). To summarize briefly, Rahner maintains that the history of salvation and revelation are "coextensive" with the whole of human history; within this universal, transcendental revelation exists a special, categorical revelation which is a "self-interpretation of the revelatory and transcendental experience of God" (p. 152). This is not merely to be equated with the history of revelation in the OT and NT, but within it exists a "special 'official' history of revelation" identical with Old and New Testaments. Nonetheless, Rahner argues, "Not until the full and unsurpassable event of the historical self-objectification of God's self-communication to the world in Jesus Christ do we have an event which, as an eschatological event, fundamentally and absolutely precludes any historical corruption or any distorted interpretation in the further history of categorical revelation and of false religion" (p. 157).

152. B. Häring, *The Law of Christ* 3 vols. (Westminster: Newman, 1961–66). In vol. 2 Häring writes: "And yet the Old Testament was no more than the period of promise. It was not the perfect fulfillment, but rather only its anticipation . . ." (xxix).

153. A. Fuerst, "Liturgy, the Integrating Principle in Education," *Education and the Liturgy, Proceedings of the 1957 North American Liturgical Week.* 87–112.

154. J. Hofinger, "The Holy Mass—Source and Center of Christian Life," *Ibid.,* 113–116.

155. *Ibid.,* 129, 134.

156. M. de la Cruz Aymes-Coucke, "Teaching the Very Young 'in Spirit and in Truth,'" *Modern Catechetics,* ed. G. S. Sloyan (New York: Macmillan, 1960) 107. B. L. Marthaler ("The Modern Catechetical Movement in Roman Catholicism," S-86) speaks of the *On Our Way* series as the "prototype" of today's religion texts; later editions, now entitled *The New Life Series,* have versions both for parochial schools and CCD programs.

157. D. M. Stanley, "The Conception of Our Gospels as Salvation History," *TS* 20 (December 1959) 561–589.

158. D. M. Stanley, "Cullmann's New Testament Christology: An

Appraisal," *TS* 20 (September 1959) 409. See O. Cullmann, *The Christology of the New Testament* (Philadelphia: Westminster, 1959).

159. Stanley, 420.

160. See also J. L. McKenzie, "Problems of Hermeneutics in Roman Catholic Exegesis," *JBL* 77 (1958) 197-204.

161. D. M. Stanley, "The Conception of our Gospels as Salvation History," 573.

162. *Ibid.,* 574.

163. *Ibid.,* 584.

164. D. M. Stanley, *The Apostolic Church in the New Testament* (Westminster, Md: Newman, 1965) 238-278. Cf. also these essays in the same volume: "Salvation in the Primitive Preaching," 38-66; "Liturgical Influences on the Formation of the Gospels," 119-139; and "Salvation in the Synoptic Gospels," 214-237.

165. D. M. Stanley, "The Concept of Biblical Inspiration," in C. Luke Salm, ed., *Studies in Salvation History* (Englewood Cliffs, N.J.: Prentice-Hall, 1964) 9-28.

166. C. Luke Salm, "Introduction to Salvation History," *Studies in Salvation History*, xiii.

167. *Ibid.,* xiii-xvii.

168. *Ibid.,* 3.

169. *Ibid.,* 4-5.

170. *Religious Education* 57 (Sept.-Oct. 1962) 329-362. Contributors to the symposium were G. S. Sloyan, "The Use of Sacred Scriptures in Catechetics," 329-334; M. M. Isomura, "The New Approach to Catechetics," 334-339; F. Schreibmayr, "The Faith of the Church and Formal Doctrinal Instruction," 340-349; W. J. Reedy, "About the Kerygma," 349-355; and L. E. Sheneman, "A Protestant Response," 355-361.

171. *Religious Education* 57 (1962) 329.

172. Sloyan, "The Use of Sacred Scripture in Catechetics," 334.

173. G. Sloyan, *Shaping the Christian Message* (New York: Macmillan, 1958).

174. G. Sloyan, "Catechetical Crossroads," *Religious Education* 59 (March-April 1964) 146. This article is now reprinted in J. Westerhoff, ed., *Who Are We: The Quest for a Religious Education* (Birmingham, Ala.: Religious Education Press, 1978) 123-132.

175. *Ibid.,* 148.

176. *Ibid.,* 149.

177. G. Sloyan, "Books on Religious Education 1955-65," *Worship* 40 (1966) 209-217.

178. *Ibid.,* 212.

179. *Ibid.*, 213–214. The accusation of being "almost Marcionite" was levelled against the Hofinger-Reedy *ABC's of Modern Catechetics.*
180. Cf. another work in which Reedy collaborated, G. E. Carter, *The Modern Challenge to Religious Education* (New York: Sadlier, 1961). Also, G. E. Carter, "Head and Heart: Catechisms with a Modern Heart," *America* 109 (13 July 1963) 40–43.
181. W. Reedy, "About the Kerygma," *Religious Education* 57, 353.
182. *Ibid.*, 354.
183. "The Mystery of Christ and Curriculum Construction," *The Renewal of Christian Education: Proceedings of the Twenty-Fourth North American Liturgical Week* (Washington, D.C.: The Liturgical Conference, 1964), 83–91. See also V. M. Novak, "Teaching Salvation History," *TBT* 1 (1962) 115–119, and "Teaching the Old Testament," *TBT* 1 (1963) 368–372. Cf. E. Kevane, "Sacred Scripture in the Catholic High School," *CBQ* 17 (1955) 136–153.
184. Lumen Vitae director George Delcuve wrote the foreword to each.
185. V. M. Novak, *Teachers Guide, Lord of History* (New York: Holt, Rinehart and Winston, 1966) 27. For one user's evaluation, see the review by J. E. Kraus, *Living Light* 2 (1965–66) 170.
186. V. Novak, *Lord of History* (New York: Holt, Rinehart and Winston, 1964) 7.
187. Mark Link, ed., *Faith and Commitment* (Chicago: Loyola University, 1964).
188. J. Hofinger and T. Stone, eds., *Pastoral Catechetics* (New York: Herder and Herder, 1964).
189. *Ibid.*, 17.
190. M. van Caster, *The Structure of Catechetics,* 2nd ed. (New York: Herder and Herder, 1965) and *God's Word Today* (New York: Benzinger, 1966).
191. *The Structure of Catechetics,* 32–33.
192. G. Moran, *Theology of Revelation* (New York: Herder and Herder, 1966); idem, *Catechesis of Revelation* (New York: Herder and Herder, 1966); idem, *The Present Revelation* (New York: Herder and Herder, 1972).

3. The Dénouement of *Heilsgeschichte* as a Hermeneutical Principle

As recounted in the narrative of the previous chapter, *Heilsgeschichte* functioned as the key hermeneutical principle in Catholic religious education in the early 1960s in the United States, and then declined rather precipitately. Inquiry into the various factors that seem, in retrospect, to have contributed to its dénouement is the focus of the present chapter.

In sorting out the factors and in subsuming them under four categories—theology, culture, education, and religious education—one risks fragmenting the analysis. Nevertheless, each category includes such significant developments that it is important that each be given its due consideration. Only then will it be appropriate to survey the whole and to theorize about its significance.

A further methodological note is in order before proceeding. In identifying the factors that seem to account for the demise of *Heilsgeschichte* as a hermeneutical principle, it will be possible within the limitations of this study to indicate merely the parameters and fundamental meaning of each development; the notes will serve to direct the reader to sources that deal in greater detail with the issue at hand.

I. *Theological Perspectives*

As one examines the claims common to the *Heilsgeschichte* theologians discussed in this study—Hofmann, von Rad, Cullmann, Jungmann—it becomes evident that a number of their fundamental contentions have become problematic within recent years. Specifically, their basic assertion that God reveals himself in history according to a plan of progressive revelation of which Christ is the center and the NT the fulfillment of the OT is now called into question on nearly every front. Contemporary efforts at reconceptualizing revelation, christology, the relation of OT and NT, and ecclesiology cast heavy shadows on the *Heilsgeschichte* theology that was once so illuminating in Christian thought. Thus must these new theological perspectives be scrutinized in turn.

A. Revelation

The pairing of revelation with history is, as Braaten points out, an omnipresent feature of modern theology; as a result, there has occurred a certain "inflation of revelation as an answer to the hypersensitive epistemological consciousness of modern theology."[1] The question of revelation has, perhaps more than any other area, encompassed some of the most pressing theological concerns; consequently, theology has witnessed a "fallout" of studies on revelation in the past fifteen years.[2]

Two levels of discussion on revelation touch directly on the *Heilsgeschichte* issue. The first deals with the notion of revelation in history and the second with the meaning of revelation itself.

1. *Revelation in History (Gilkey, Barr, Frei).* Systematic theologian Langdon B. Gilkey initiated the critique of the juxtaposition of revelation and history by questioning the philosophical premises of biblical theology.[3] Gilkey contended that biblical scholars were operating with contradicting categories: on the one hand they accepted the contemporary, secular understanding of spatio-temporal world process; but on the other, they retained the traditional understanding of God as the one whose "mighty acts" (a term popularized by G. Ernest Wright) made him sovereign Lord of history. In brief, their cosmology was modern and liberal and their theological language biblical and orthodox.

The underlying cause of the situation, as Gilkey viewed it, was the partial acceptance by biblical scholars of the liberals' repudiation of orthodoxy. Liberals had rejected the notion of special revelation, of God actually intervening in human history (*Heilsgeschichte*) for two reasons: (1) acceptance of a literal understanding of God's deeds and words represented a primitive, prescientific view of religion; and (2) special revelation denied the universality of religious truth. Thus, in liberal theology, revelation was reduced to subjective human insight into immanent divine activity. But such contentions were rejected by biblical theology (now identified with neo-orthodoxy). Revelation was not, as liberals had claimed, merely a universal human experience but in fact a manifestation of a God who shared himself in special events. Yet while repudiating the liberals' reductionistic conception of revelation, biblical scholars accepted the post-Enlightment, Western notion of causal order.

What Gilkey rightly perceived was that modern biblical theology had grown more sophisticated; rather than viewing the Bible as a book describing God's actual deeds and words, it regarded Scripture as a book containing the theological beliefs of the Hebrew religion. But such a perspective, he contended, confused two types of language: theological and scientific. When Wright (*Book of the Acts of God*) and Anderson (*Understanding the Old Testament*), for example, spoke theologically about revelation, they centered on the objective event and spoke in orthodox terms of a God who speaks and acts, revealing himself through his mighty deeds in history. But when they spoke scientifically as archaeologists concerned with what really happened, they then proceeded to discuss those same events in purely naturalistic terms; thus they repudiated the concrete elements in the biblical account which had made the event unique and had given content to their theological notion of the divine action. "Mighty acts," therefore, were not the actual deeds of a God intervening in history, but his "inward incitement" of a religious response to an ordinary event within the space-time continuum.

Such a contradiction, Gilkey held, reduced the understanding of revelation to a meaningless term:

> When we are asked about what actually happened, and how revelation actually occurred, all we can say is that in the continuum of the natural order an unusual event rescued the Hebrews from a sad

fate; from this they concluded that somewhere there must be a great God who loved them; thus they interpreted their own past in terms of his dealings with them and created all the familiar characteristics of Hebrew religion: covenant, law and prophecy. This understanding of Hebrew religion is strictly "liberal": it pictures reality as a consistent world order and religious truth as a human interpretation based on religious experience. And yet at the same time having castigated the liberals, who at least knew what their fundamental theological categories were, we proclaim that our real categories are orthodox: God acts, God speaks, and God reveals. Furthermore, we dodge all criticism by insisting that, because Biblical and Christian ideas of God are "revealed," they are, unlike the assumptions and hypotheses of culture and of other religions, beyond inspection by the philosophical and moral criteria of man's general experience.[4]

As a result, biblical theology had a set of theological abstractions ultimately more abstract than the dogmas of scholasticism. The biblical point of view had been stripped of all its "wonders and voices"; by falling back upon liberal assumptions the categories of divine deeds and divine revelation had been emptied of any significance.[5]

To Gilkey this state of affairs demanded a theological ontology "that will put intelligible and credible meanings into our analogical categories of divine deeds and of divine self-manifestation through events." Such has apparently been the agenda of his own life work, to which his *Naming the Whirlwind*[6] and *Reaping the Whirlwind*[7] give ample testimony.

Meanwhile, on another front, British biblical scholar James Barr likewise began to cast doubt upon the notion of revelation in history. In his inaugural address at Princeton, Barr questioned whether the biblical evidence, particularly that of the Old Testament, fitted with and supported the assertion that history was the "absolutely supreme milieu" of God's revelation.[8] At the time (1962) Barr maintained there was no single principle more powerful in dealing with Scripture than the belief in history as the medium of divine revelation. This formula he saw both as a response to nineteenth century apologetics and as the unifying factor in modern theology. Yet Barr could no longer grant it such importance. He had become convinced that, for some important areas of the Old Testament, the notion of the centrality of revelation through history could not be applied without doing violence to the texts.

He identified three major areas of difficulty. First, substantial areas of the Old Testament, such as the wisdom literature and a number of psalms, simply did not fit in with the fundamental motif of revelation through history. Secondly, the notion of history was a non-biblical category, and to attribute to it a revelatory character having priority over divine communication with particular people was to do violence to the way in which the biblical traditions themselves spoke. Finally, the insistence on "history" as the aptest category by which one organized biblical material was to split that material apart. History simply could not be applied uniformly to the creation, flood, exodus, and the destruction of Jerusalem by Nebuchadnezzar.

In the same lecture, Barr called attention to the apologetic interests served by the concept of salvation history. It had succeeded in making the Bible "intelligible and accessible" to a generation troubled by problems of historical challenges to faith. Barr even granted that the concept itself was a "fair expression" of a very important element in the Bible. There really was, he claimed, a *Heilsgeschichte,* a series of events set within the plan of human life in historical sequence through which God revealed himself and which served as the central theme of the Bible, and as the main link between Old and New Testaments.

But, Barr warned, there were other equally pervasive and important axes through the biblical material; these, however, might prove much less comforting apologetically. One axis was that of direct verbal communication between God and particular people on particular occasions, which he saw as "infinitely more scandalous." Too often the revelation through history motif had permitted the difficulty of elements such as this one to be mitigated. And since a new apologetic situation had arisen, Barr concluded that the question about *Heilsgeschichte* should remain an open one.

In a work also published in 1962, Barr had taken issue with another dimension of the *Heilsgeschichte* hermeneutic by challenging some of the lexical methods fundamental to Oscar Cullmann's *Christ and Time.*[9] By questioning the semantic contentions of the salvation history scholars (among others) who, for instance, claimed distinctions between *kairos* and *aion*, and who exalted Hebrew modes of thought over Greek categories, Barr contributed both to the development of a refined exegetical methodology and brought under doubt some of the *Heilsgeschichte* premises. As Barr claimed: "In so far as Cullmann's arguments elsewhere in his book depend on the terminological examination, they are likely to be faulty."[10]

The appearance of his *Old and New in Interpretation* in 1966 reiterated and developed both his previous stance on the relationship between Hebrew and Greek modes of thought and on the concepts of history and revelation.[11] He repeated his earlier assertion that history, when used as an organizing and classifying bracket, is not a biblical category, and asked that the Old Testament's nearness to history not be exaggerated.

In this work Barr also has some important comments about the linkage between revelation and history. He argued that the notion of salvation history, when taken as a mandatory concept for theology, seemed to lead to the idea of revelation. Conversely, the concept of revelation as a central and normative concept might ultimately prove harmful to general theology, and lead as well to an "obfuscating and disturbing influence" on the more empirical analysis of biblical evidence. He concluded by suggesting that the refusal to seek a unitary concept of history as theologically regulative would in the end do more justice to history. It would give a more positive place to the history of religions, allow historical criticism to become a discriminating element in theological interpretations, and provide greater theological function for the history of traditions.

Barr's debt to the history-of-religions approach was manifest in a 1973 paper to the Fifth International Congress on Biblical Studies.[12] Here was explicit citation of Bertil Albrektson's research, which showed that the gods of other nations also "acted in history": the Old Testament idea of historical events as divine revelation "must be counted among the similarities, not among the distinctive traits: it is part of the common theology of the ancient Near East."[13] Such research obviously damaged that older theological stance which claimed divine action in history was unique to Israel.

A further significant point in this address was Barr's contention that, rather than there being a single organizational principle of unity (e.g., salvation history), there are compelling reasons to accept that a:

> "plurality" of centers may exist for a work as complex as the Old Testament: in the expression of biblical theology the variety of possibilities is a creative opportunity. Where there is one landscape, many different pictures may nevertheless be painted. And this comparison is not a chance one: to me biblical theology, at least at some levels, partakes of the nature of an art, rather than of that of a science.[14]

Barr's most recent essay on this topic serves to summarize his writings on *Heilsgeschichte* from 1962 to 1976 and suggests an alternative hermeneutical principle. In view of the long narrative corpus of the Old Testament, Barr considered the notion of "story" to be rich with possibility. It is unitary and cumulative, set into a chronological frame, sometimes constitutes a fairly reliable source of historical evidence, and even at times approaches in certain respects actual historical writings. Moreover, story moves back and forth between human and divine causation, history and myth, human viewpoint and divine intervention. As Barr noted, the ability to mingle styles is the mark of the genius of the literature, but it is also an indication that history was not the primary governing factor in the selection and presentation of the material.[15]

Barr's critique of revelation in history and his subsequent turn toward story is paralleled by Yale scholar Hans W. Frei, who nonetheless brings *Heilsgeschichte* under question from a quite unique perspective in his 1974 publication, *The Eclipse of Biblical Narrative: A Study in Eighteenth and Nineteenth Century Hermeneutics.*[16]

Frei's position on salvation history is embedded in the course of his complex and sometimes obscure argument that critical interpretation "eclipsed" the story element of scriptural narratives in its preoccupation with historical truth. As a result, biblical interpretation became a matter of "fitting the biblical story into another world with another story," and this, he maintained, was a drastic and devastating change from the era of precritical interpretation when the world of the biblical narratives was the one and only real world—and thus the reader's world. Frei accuses the nineteenth century *heilsgeschichtliche Schule* of being among the prime causes of that dichotomy.

Johannes Cocceius (1603–1699) had acted as a "remote progenitor" in his formulation of a "federal" theology, in which he took a traditional reformed concept of a covenant between God and humankind and worked it into a notion of distinctive temporal stages operative in the history portrayed in Scripture. Here the literal and historical had begun to come apart: no longer did the story render the reality of the history it depicted. A shift in hermeneutical principle was underway.

This shift was completed when salvation history became the meaning of the Bible. No longer did the biblical story by itself and its own right depict the world and allow readers to locate themselves and their times in the real world rendered by the depiction. Scripture itself now did not, in Frei's terminology, "render" events; it "referred" to them. Thus there was a change to the sense of another temporal reality than the biblical.

Frei located the emergence of the *heilsgeschichtliche Schule* in the quest for a unitary meaning of Scripture.[18] This school of thought held the unitary theme or meaning of the Bible to be inseparable from its arrangement into a cumulative account. In effect, this view claimed that Scripture's unity lay in the temporal sequence of world history depicted by the stories or hinted at by the text; the unity did not lie in a logical identity between the depiction and the reality rendered by it. The historical critic, therefore, assumed the task of explaining the "real" meaning of a passage.

Frei considered this move a "strenuous effort" to discover a substitute for figuration as the unifying principle of the canon. But the attempt resulted not only in ultimately divorcing meaning from narrative but also in obscuring the relation of the biblical sequence to ordinary historical events. In a confused sort of way, the saving facts were real and historical, yet not in an ordinary way verifiable by religiously neutral scrutiny. This ambiguity has never been satisfactorily clarified, according to Frei.

So the Bible had become a witness to history rather than a

narrative text. The history of salvation—defined by Frei as "an overarching reality or world which encompasses a self's present relations and the factual occurrences in which it was embodied, as witnessed by the Bible"—led to an overriding interest in reconstructing the context to which the text "really" referred.[19] Allegory and myth, once so important to typology (a natural extension of literal interpretation in precritical days), were now relegated to technical categories of literary classification.

Frei commented that one result of this preoccupation with salvation history was a failure to take the realistic elements of narrative seriously. He called attention to the parallels between realistic narrative and historical account. Frei remarked, moreover, that he could not account for the failure of the tradition of literary realism that had arisen in the eighteenth century to be applied to the technical task of biblical interpretation. Literary realism might have proved a corrective to the excessive preoccupation with historical fact. But in actuality the historian's interests prevailed. From the eighteenth century to the present day, "the historical critic does something other than narrative interpretation with a narrative" because "he looks for what the narrative refers to or what reconstructed historical context outside itself explains it."[20]

Frei shared Barr's conviction that, while this historical concern is not entirely wrong, it misses the richness of the narrative; there are many elements that may enter into the way a story makes sense. The two scholars seem agreed that the narrative shape is an important and distinctive one that ought not to be confused with others. Frei then moved beyond Barr in contending that renewed attention to the biblical narratives precisely as narratives would help to restore that immediacy of encounter with Scripture possible in days before the advent of historical criticism. He enfleshed this thesis in a complementary volume, *The Identity of Jesus Christ,* in which he operated by an exegetical method characterized by its attentiveness to what the story says.[21]

Frei's work has not been uncritically received; despite, however, the number of questions and objections from his critics, there does seem to be a consensus that he has provoked a new line of thought and offered a thorough and penetrating analysis.[22] What is more, no disagreement has apparently been registered with his critique of *Heilsgeschichte*.

But not only had the notion of revelation in history become problematic; so too had the very concept of revelation itself. Of particular significance in relation to this study is the work of Catholic religious educator Gabriel Moran.

2. *Revelation under Doubt (Moran)*.   Moran's best known study, the dual volume *Theology of Revelation* and *Catechesis of Revelation*, appeared simultaneously with the early waning of *Heilsgeschichte* in the United States and may indeed have been an important contributing factor to its sudden demise.[23] Thus the need here to scrutinize Moran's theses in light of their possible impact on adherents of the salvation history hermeneutic.

Moran's early writings on revelation need to be viewed in the context of Vatican II's momentous document *Dei Verbum*, which represented a veritable revolution in the understanding of revelation, especially in regard to the relationship of Scripture and tradition. To his analysis of revelation, Moran brought not only his theological and catechetical interests, but his philosophical concerns for language and symbolism as well—factors even more evident in his later works. Moran acknowledged the pioneering work of Jungmann and the kerygmatic theologians who preceded him; indeed, it provided the departure point for his own articulation. But, as he envisioned it, his function was to "push back" to the foundational issue of revelation and to press for the implication of their work:

> On the surface, Jungmann was merely asking for a reorientation of pastoral efforts and a greater emphasis upon Scripture and liturgy. Implicit in these proposals, however, was a challenge to theology, a challenging of the fundamental content, framework and methodology of modern theology. It was, in short, a questioning of whether modern theology had really come to grips with the nature of revelation.[24]

In brief, Moran considered the kerygmatic movement as implicitly calling for " not a non-scientific study of revelation," but one that was "so deeply scientific that it would become pastoral, practical and relevant."[25] Thus in *TR* Moran accepted this implicit challenge, and argued that studies of revelation must give due consideration to the human persons who were themselves within revelation, not outside it. Such had not been the case with the salvation-history approach, which he criticized as being preoccupied with past events and remaining simply at the level of abstraction and conceptualization.[26] Moran proposed instead that revelation be viewed as a continuing process and that its communal nature be acknowledged. Or as he defined it: "Revelation is a personal union in knowledge between God and a participating subject in the revelational history of a community."[27] Such a description meant that revelation could not be confined to or equated with any text, because it was what happened in the living experience of people. Its meaning was not exhausted by its "objective content": "Revelation is what happens between persons, and exists only as a personal reality. If there is revelation anywhere in the Church today, it can only be in the conscious experience of people."[28]

Although Moran made no claim that a new theology of revelation could in itself assuage catechetical dilemmas, he did argue that the catechetical problem could become intelligible "only through a continuing study of revelation." Moran, convinced that the questions were more complex than the "kerygmatic enthusiasts" were willing to admit, was fearful that the catechetical movement had "hovered on the brink of trivialization" from its inception. As he perceived it, the great crisis was not the dying catechism and theological manual but

> the still rising hope that the education of hundreds of millions of people in an incredibly complex world can be carried out with a bit of Scripture and liturgy and much sincerity and good will. This simply is not enough. There is need for patient inquiry, deep understanding and detailed knowledge.[29]

In much the same vein as his mentor Gerard Sloyan, Moran remarked that not all questions were resolved simply by saying that God used history to teach and therefore Christians were to do the same. Rather, teachers desirous of leading their students into the history of salvation needed to commit themselves to the time, patience, and effort involved in examining their own understanding of revelation and history, "lest they patch up old concepts with new words, and thus show that they fail to see the real significance of history in catechizing."[30] Furthermore, Moran's understanding of revelation involved a recognition of the life situation of the student:

> To learn of God's revelation means to discover God and man together, not an abstract humanity but the present person in the self-awareness of his own historical existence. Each person recommences with fundamental and unpredictable newness the dialogue with God. . . . A catechist who refuses to work with the actual history of the student's life cannot be of much help in mediating God's revelation.[31]

Such a position logically meant that teaching on Christian revelation must be united with humanistic study and scientific technology in "reciprocally illuminating relationships." Otherwise one had only an abstractly conceived sacred history totally irrelevant to moderns or an "exaggerated optimism or pessimism" about human life in the future. Moran concluded: "But a sacred history that would really emerge out of the Christian life in the contemporary world would be far from outdated or irrelevant."[32]

That latter claim provides, it might be argued, something of a key to Moran's initial writings on revelation. Somewhat analogously to the progression of the catechetical study weeks from kerygma to anthropology to the political/social sphere, Moran placed in doubt both the theological and educational naiveté of the kerygmatic movement characterized by the *Heilsgeschichte* hermeneutic while at the same time retaining some of its fundamental categories. That continuity is evident in his comments about the OT and the centrality of Christ.

Moran had commented earlier (*TR*, 31) that modern biblical scholarship had been the primary factor influencing the development of a deeper understanding of revelation. That assertion is developed at greater length in *CR* (76–89); of particular note, however, is his assertion:

> The most important single principle for organizing Old Testament teaching is its relation to the person of Christ. Although some pro-

gression from the state of slavery to that of sonship perdures in the Christian life, a fundamental and irreversible newness has been introduced with Christ. As Vatican II has pointed out, the Christian always reads the Old Testament through the prism of its fulfillment and conclusion with Christ.[33]

Pedagogically, this entailed teaching the OT only after establishing the prior relation of Christ; whatever is taught, the OT formed the "ever present background" and the NT within the church the "foreground." And, in what appeared to be an implicit challenge to the Novak *Lord and King* series, Moran continued:

> On the basis of this principle I would strongly question the value of new programs in high schools and colleges that devote the first year almost exclusively to the Old Testament and follow this with a year of New Testament exegesis. I see no justification for these programs either psychologically or theologically. Many places are already reaching the point of diminishing returns on the newness aspect. Surely there are more imaginative approaches than ploughing through the books of the Bible one after the other.[34]

At this point in the development of his thought, Moran chose to speak of Jesus as the one in whom God's revelation had reached a high point; revelation was "recapitulated" in Christ, and he was the "participating subject" who had first received the Christian revelation.[35] While Moran had added a new dimension to the articulation of kerygmatic christology in his use of the notion "participating subject," he was still in fundamental harmony with the christocentricity of the *Heilsgeschichte* theologians.

Moran's critique of the kerygmatics, however, was far more transparent than his continuity; perhaps, as will be evident in later discussion in this chapter, this was as much due to the era in which he wrote as to his own point of view. Moran had provided Catholic religious educators with a theological and catechetical basis for replacing the salvation history-oriented approaches that had achieved such dominance in the early sixties.

But, as his later work would soon make evident, Moran was

himself in the throes of a more radical break with the kerygmatic formulations about revelation. With a bit of whimsy, Moran recently described his attempt to use revelation as a link between catechetics and theology, and to open it in such a manner that theology would find the need for education:

> Given my intention, the title TOR (*Theology of Revelation*) was wholly inadequate. I was placing the word revelation within theology though I was trying to get the word revelation out from under theology's control. Having a "theology of revelation" link theology and catechetics was comparable to having B'nai B'rith mediate the Jewish-Arab conflict. At the time I was surprised how well the book was received but I shouldn't have been. I was challenging the premise of theology in the language of theology. The book became a textbook in seminaries.[36]

The foundational piece for Moran's departure from his earlier understanding of revelation was his 1971 publication, *Design for Religion*.[37] This relatively brief work occupies a significant place in the corpus of Moran's writings since it signals a fundamental shift in his thinking. Here Moran attempted to present a new framework for religious education or, as he now preferred to call it, "ecumenical education." He envisioned an ecumenical theology as having the power to break the hold of the preaching model inherent in kerygmatic formulations. Specifically in regard to revelation, Moran now spoke of three developmental stages: (1) the "primitive religious" stage in which "religion has a revelation"; (2) the "narrow Christian" stage in which one spoke of a "specifically Christian revelation"; and (3) the stage of "ecumenical religion/Christianity" in which the terms "revealed truths" and "Christian revelation" no longer made sense.[38] This third stage meant that revelation was a concept that needed to be "filled in" from the phenomenology of human relationships and the comparison of religions. It involved Christianity relinquishing what he termed its "ecclesio-central world"; "in the stage of ecumenical religion/Christianity the final norm of truth is human experience."[39]

The third stage usage of revelation included both an expanded understanding of education—"The aim of ecumenical education is the same as education itself, namely the lived truth of a humanized world"[40]—and a more restricted function for theology, now intended to "designate that a person, after a long personal development and some comparison, has chosen to get on the inside of a tradition and to understand and live on its own terms."[41]

Design for Religion included an important enlargement and refinement of the category "experience." Moran took care to establish the term as including both rational and nonrational elements. Experience referred to the "totality of human interaction within the environment," and subsumed both understanding (the "assimilation of experience in a specifically human way") and intelligence (the "ability to deal with experience in a way that leads to understanding").[42] It was a key term in the States, having provided direction for philosophical, psychological, social, and political theory, and having dominated educational discussion primarily through Dewey's influence. What "experience" immediately connoted for Moran was the *relational*. He saw experience as the fundamental mode of being that undercut the split between subject and object as well as comprehended both theory and practice. Parallel to his three-stage schema of revelation, Moran identified three levels of experience: (1) a primitive kind of "involvement in action," a sort of "direct, unreflective, sensed encounter with the world"; (2) reason in which the "subjective power of control arises," but in which the possibility also exists for ideas that become a substitute for action; and (3) experience that is intellectual understanding, a "transcending of reason possible only by discipline and communion."[43]

The educational anthropology and movement toward ecumenism that characterized *DR* and marked the shift from *TR* and *CR* laid the conceptual framework for his most extensive exploration of revelation in 1972, *The Present Revelation*.[44] Moran described this as an attempt to fill out the religious part of *DR*,[45] and to "reconnòiter a position somewhere between phenomenology and theology."[46] *PR* represented his most nuanced and radical critique of the revelational theology of the kerygmatics and even of his own earlier positions. As he recounted, initially he had set out from the texts of Vatican II and traditional theology to show that biblical and church sources would themselves lead to a much broader meaning for the word revelation. But meanwhile he had been confronted by a nagging methodological problem: how a theology that presupposed a revelation could also establish its meaning. Thus his desire to establish a new paradigm beginning from a universal meaning of revelation and only then moving toward specificity.

Moran maintained that Christian theology had to face the possibility that there was no "Christian revelation," and argued that unless the term revelation could be "established on its own as a non-Christian and even non-religious word, it would always pose an insoluble problem in Christian theology"(31).

Moran's grounding in *DR* is immediately apparent in his new usage of the term "revelation":

> Revelation is relation qualified by the fact that the poles of the relation initiate activity toward the other. Thus, revelation in its primary sense is capable of being as extensive as all reality. The only words more fundamental would be words like being, relation or activity.... Revelation refers to the relational character of being.... Revelation is relationship in which the relata really relate (36).

In light of this, Moran now rejected the expressions "Christian revelation," "biblical revelation," and "historical revelation" as inadequate ways of speaking, since they implied a set of data external to faith (38–39). Moran preferred to develop the distinction between universal and particular as a more accurate way of articulating the relationship between revelation and Christianity.

What Moran sought to establish was a base for religion that was *relational, social,* and *practical;* this category was revelation. This broadened notion led him to criticize sharply what he perceived as a sort of Christian arrogance in preempting the term and to advocate the widest possible experiential base for discussions of revelation. As a result, he made a number of startling assertions that were quite logical in view of his total argument but which inevitably provoked the cry of "heretic" from those who either took his statements out of context or who were unfamiliar with the development of his thought since 1966.

Some of these claims indicate how completely Moran had broken with the understanding of revelation in kerygmatic theology. For instance, he wrote:

> None of the statements, including those of the bible or church councils, is God's revelation. Of nothing formulable into human words can it be said: You must "believe that" that is true because God has revealed it (46).

Or, in a line bound to anger or startle many, Moran declared: "The heart of the problem with 'Christian revelation' is not *what* is there but *that* it is there" (51). And in a dictum that heralded his further journey as evidenced now in *Religious Body* and some recent articles, Moran announced his departure from the theological perspective:

> Theology which presupposes a "Christian revelation" can never, no matter how hard it works, eliminate the concept of a "Christian revelation." Only by stepping outside of the theological circle can one begin to reconstruct some understanding of a religious and revelationai way of living (52).[47]

Human experience was the "site" for grasping "anything that can be grasped about revelation." Revelation, correlatively, was the category he deemed most helpful in making sense of human existence; to demand a divine revelation outside of or above human experience was a search for idols (77–82).

Consequently, Moran devoted the second chapter of *PR* to an exploration of the human aspects of revelation; he identified these as "experience and relation," "one and all," "power," "subject/object," "temporality," and "language." In a third chapter, Moran extended his analysis of human experience to explore religious traditions and phenomena in an explicit way. It is an important development of his thesis, a creative appropriation of the phenomenological approach to religion, particularly of Rudolf Otto and Mircea Eliade. What is of particular significance in this study of *Heilsgeschichte* is Moran's final chapter, "Jewish and Christian Experience." Herein are the implications of his argument most evident and his break from the kerygmatics most apparent.

"The Christian attitude toward the contemporary Jewish community," declared Moran, "is the key test for the adequacy of the Christian understanding of revelation" (238); indeed, only as the notion of "Christian revelation" disappears will Christian anti-Semitism dissolve (239). Accordingly, Moran proposed to show how the existence of Judaism shed light on the meaning of revelation.

Moran's initial observation was that Judaism, an "extraordinary embodiment of the religious meaning of revelation" (259), is testimony to the religious life as an intersection of God's total otherness and his intimate involvement with humanity (241). Secondly, its claim to being a "chosen people" Moran found especially harmonious with and illustrative of his earlier universal/particular distinction: chosen "signifies that mysterious paradox of human life that we all must be chosen in the particular" (247). As he expanded the meaning in a closely reasoned paragraph:

> The choice of Israel, therefore, is not an exclusive but an inclusive one. She is chosen because all are being chosen. So that the chosenness of all may become evident, the least must be the most dramatically chosen of all. In the choice which excludes, the chosen one is given something to possess as his own because he has merited it. In the choice which includes, the chosen is moved to receive and thereby to share what is the birthright of all. The failure to clarify the word revelation has consistently blocked understanding of this distinction. Revelation is not something one is given; revelation is a relation in which one participates. The Jews do not claim to have revelation but they do claim to dramatize by their lives the relationship to the one God to whom all are called (248).[48]

By being "chosen people," Jews embody what God is doing everywhere. Likewise does the experience of Israel illuminate the meaning of "revelation in history." Moran made the distinction that the Jews did not discover one kind of revelation called historical, but that they understood revelation as historical: "They did not discover a tract of history called sacred; instead they helped to discover history" (250). He saw in Jewish life an extension of the meaning of history; the discovery that revelation was historical was "concomitant with the discovery that human life is historical" (251). Such a discovery was not without painful consequences, for the impetus in most religious traditions was to escape the limitations of time and matter:

> But what distinguished Israel was the awareness that the process of human life, the total pattern of history, is revelational of God. A God who revealed himself from time to time and then retired to the heavens above would be a God not really involved with history. Such "revelations" would be unhistorical, that is, they would be things deposited into history but not of history. Israel came to see that although some moments may be strikingly revelational it should not be concluded that other moments are not revelational at all (253–254).

Thus it might be concluded that Moran saw in the Jewish experience a legitimate usage of "revelation in history" but that it was redefined in such a manner as to differ sharply from the kerygmatic formulations.

Similarly, Moran's study of Judaism led him to a more nuanced christology. In struggling to articulate the centrality of Christ, Moran first assumed a critical posture toward those whose forms of Christ-centeredness had led them to abstract themselves from the historical and social matrix of humankind and who therefore had an individualistic concept of revelation extrinsically related to social situations (265). He proposed, rather, that the centrality of Christ be seen as being directed toward God; the alternative to christocentrism would be some other thing, such as church organization or written texts. But Moran found a paradox in a religion centered in Jesus Christ, namely that "it might not speak much about Jesus Christ," since the great teachers and prophets do not proclaim, "Go out and quote me and speak endlessly of my accomplishments." Rather:

> The reason for the centrality of Jesus Christ, therefore, is not that he is a substitute for human struggle but that he is a constant reminder that there are no substitutes. No thing could serve that purpose; a thing becomes the exclusive possession of some group. No ordinary person is capable of turning back power and life to all those who are afraid to assume it. It requires a most extraordinary human being to lead men by refusing to accept what leadership seems to

mean, to teach men by saying that his message is not his own but belongs to all who can hear, and who is willing though not anxious to lay down his life in the cause of trying to get all people to recognize their sister/brotherhood (267).

Moran used his category of "chosen" as another way of expressing the role of Christ. Jesus was the "chosen one" who affirmed the historical character of revelation; in him "the divine pole of revelation emerged in the concreteness and ambiguity of a single life" (268). Moran rejected the formulation that he was the one mediator between God and humanity, but advanced the position that Jesus was the man who "brought mediation to a personal peak" (269). Similarly with the term "incarnation," Moran preferred to speak of it as happening in everyone's life, reaching a climactic stage with the appearance of Jesus, and continuing on into the present (269–270).

While Moran accepted the formulation of Jesus as the "revelation of God," insofar as that was meant to convey that "in Jesus the receptivity of the human for the divine reached a high point" (272), he retained some ambivalence about the discussion of Christ as "unique." Once again it is necessary to pay heed to Moran's nuanced articulation.

Moran distinguished the adjective "unique" as being descriptive of both things and persons, but maintained that it made full sense only when used with the latter. Each human being is an "unrepeatable original," and to the extent that one's human integrity is developed, one's uniqueness is more apparent. By this logic, the claim that "Jesus is the [most] unique revelation of God would mean that his receptivity for divine communion was the greatest known to men" (273). But in fact the usage of the term "unique" in regard to revelation has resulted not so much in speech about a Jesus who is unique but of Christianity as unique, an application of the term that obscures the meaning and leads to either intolerance or indifference. In summary:

If . . . the person is receptive to other beings he or she will become more and more a unique self. Complete uniqueness for a person would imply a similarity to every being in the universe. A unique revelation would be a divine-human relation capable of being filled

out by all that is human and divine. The significance of the figure
of Jesus is that he should be the continual reminder that all claims
to an exclusively unique revelation are false in principle because
they reduce revelation to a thing. In reference to revelation, Jesus'
person excludes only the claim to exclusion; it affirms that all reality
is revelational (274–275).

As one might suspect in view of this appropriation of the term
"unique," Moran concluded that it would be preferable to
eliminate the term, given its difficulties.

In surveying the corpus of Moran's studies on revelation, one
is struck by both continuity and development. Certainly his *TR*
and *CR,* which enjoyed such popularity among religious
educators, contained the seeds of his later work. Yet, as prefigured in *DR* and detailed in *PR,* Moran increasingly expanded
the meaning of revelation in hopes of establishing a foundational category. In so doing, he inevitably placed in doubt the
very heart of the *Heilsgeschichte* hermeneutic in which the concept of Christian revelation was so fundamental.

3. The Revelation Debate: An Evaluation.   What is one to make
of this recent theological furor over revelation? Certainly Gilkey's contention that biblical scholars have operated out of con-
tradictory categories highlights the dogmatic interests of neo-
orthodox claims to revelation in history. He raises at least two
issues that demand serious consideration: (1) Did something
actually happen in God's dealings with Israel, or was it a matter
of "inward incitement"? (2) To what extent must biblical
theologians be accountable to the systematicians in grounding
their work philosophically?

The former issue is of great pertinence to the salvation history question. It would seem to this writer that, if the experience of Israel was primarily that of "inward incitement" rather
than that of actual liberation, or, analogously, if the experience
of the early church was primarily that of an evolution in consciousness rather than that of an actual encounter with the risen
Jesus, then, however loudly it is asserted that God is revealed in
history, it is a strange God and a truncated history. But perhaps
Gilkey too simplistically establishes a polarity whereas, in real-

ity, there are at least four ways of conceptualizing the understanding of God's acts as described in the Bible. The first position, in simple fidelity to the biblical narratives, holds that God
visibly intervened in history; thus in the exodus he actually
drove back the waters of the sea for the Israelites and also told
them the meaning of his deed. A second position represents a
more nuanced fidelity to the Bible; in the exodus, for instance,
ordinary historical factors were at work in the Israelites' escape
from the Egyptians, but God inspired certain "spokesmen" to
understand that his steadfast love was present through the
medium of those factors. Another view is present in a third
position: ordinary historical factors were operative in the actual
event of liberation which pious Israelites naively attributed to
God. The fourth position, at the opposite end of the spectrum
from the first, would hold that there was no escape from Egypt
and the entire exodus was merely a reconstruction of theology.

The second position, it would appear, is that most compatible
with a more sophisticated idea of revelation, and highlights
Barr's contention that there is a "scandal" in the Judaeo-
Christian tradition insofar as it speaks of God communicating
with humankind, and those who want *only* to make the Bible
"intelligible and accessible" may well have done injustice to the
magnitude of its claims.

Barr's suggestion, furthermore, that a "plurality" of centers
may be appropriate for the complexity of the OT implicitly
allows for a de-emphasis of the revelation debate. His regard
for "story" as an alternative to history is compellingly amplified
by Frei. There is little doubt that *The Eclipse of Biblical Narrative*
is a provocative work, and its challenge to attend to the narrative dimensions may further serve to relieve the inflated importance given to revelation in history. What seems problematic in
Frei is whether historical criticism need necessarily "eclipse" the
narrative, and his implicit call for a return to modes of interpretation from the "precritical" era appears highly questionable.

Gilkey, Barr, and Frei have shaped a critical turn in the revelation debate and offered an agenda for further study. Moran's
contribution is more difficult to assess.[49] What would happen,
for instance, if he were to grapple with Gilkey's theses? In his
attempt to reconceptualize revelation by grounding it anthro-

pologically—a refreshingly creative move—Moran may be caught in liberalism, or at least in a certain "fuzziness." It is unclear to this student of his works how he conceives the relationship between human experience and divine action. Does God actually act?

Two other troublesome areas emerge in Moran's writings. One is his highly nuanced christology, which seems to pass far too quickly over the process by which the Jesus who himself preached the kingdom of God came to be proclaimed and believed in as the Christ who ushered in the kingdom. The other is Moran's admonition to his critics that *PR* represents an attempt to step out of the theological circle: granted the anthropological stance he has assumed since *DR,* it is unclear how or whether he has actually succeeded in stepping out of it. Moreover, his understanding of theology is not developed in his later works, and it is at times puzzling why he feels compelled to divorce himself from the theological enterprise.

These are substantial reservations. Nonetheless, there is a clarity about Moran's concern to broaden the notion of revelation which is especially manifest when his works are studied in chronological order. Particularly welcome in view of the concerns of the present study is his contention that an understanding of Judaism is the "litmus test" for Christian revelation. Moran has thereby highlighted the intrinsic linkage between *Heilsgeschichte* and Christian dogmatic interests. But whether his position as detailed in *PR* adequately addresses the complexity of the topic is a question which deserves more thorough treatment elsewhere; ironically, it would appear to stand in need of greater theological depth.

4. The Significance of the Revelation Debate. If, as John Macquarrie contends, revelation is the primary source of theology and a basic category in theological thinking, then the recent debate about its meaning has crucial significance for contemporary theology.[50] The creation of new formulations in such a foundational area as revelation obviously will entail reworking corollary notions.

Specifically in regard to the *Heilsgeschichte* hermeneutic, it may be hypothesized that the debate about revelation as reflected in the studies discussed here challenged its most fundamental assumption, that of a progressive divine revelation in history, and hence its ancillary understandings as well. In assessing the import of that challenge, it appears obvious that, *at the very least, a critical element had become problematic,* and, as a result, *Heilsgeschichte* was cast under the shadow of doubt. Consequently, the term receded more and more from the foreground of theological literature as the debate about the meaning of revelation intensified. Simply put, the more sophisticated the theology of revelation, the less *Heilsgeschichte* functioned as an operative term.

The pattern is a bit more complex when one assesses the religious education scene in the United States among Roman Catholics. It is highly probable that the critique of both Gilkey and Barr would have had a negligible influence for several reasons: (1) there was as yet little dialogue between Catholics and those of other denominations; (2) the Gilkey-Barr arguments were not generally accessible to the majority of religious educators, having appeared in technical theological journals; (3) neither Gilkey nor Barr directly alluded to the appropriation of the *Heilsgeschichte* hermeneutic by Catholics from Jungmann to Novak. Furthermore, the penetrating study by Frei is of such recent origin and obfuscated in such ponderous prose that its significance in the demise of the *Heilsgeschichte* hermeneutic in the late sixties and early seventies must be entirely discounted.

That, however, is not the case with Gabriel Moran's writings. As has been observed earlier, the appearance of his dual study on revelation in 1966 (*TR* and *CR*) provided both a theological and catechetical legitimation for questioning the salvation history approach. It might be noted as well that by this point many religious educators had been using that approach for several years and knew first hand of its naiveté. In conjunction with the romanticist trends in general educational circles, with the cultural upheavals in the States, and with the euphoria of the early post-Vatican II church, Moran's *Theology of Revelation* and *Catechesis of Revelation* functioned as a veritable catalyst in the downfall of *Heilsgeschichte*.

These other factors deserve their own analysis, and will be

discussed at a later point in this chapter. But note must be made at this juncture that Moran's later writings (from the 1971 *DR* through the 1974 *Religious Body*), despite their more radical critique of *Heilsgeschichte,* particularly in *The Present Revelation,* appear to have contributed little to its dénouement. Two explanations for this might be suggested: (1) in shifting away from a theological preoccupation, Moran alienated himself from theologians; (2) his highly nuanced and broadly grounded arguments were unclear to those who did not follow carefully the development of his ideas, and they surpassed the interest and education of most religious educators. As a result, Moran has had an exceedingly limited community of discourse with which to dialogue. The irony is that, whereas the theory of revelation Moran proposed in *The Present Revelation* dealt a devastating blow to kerygmatic theology, his much milder criticism in *Theology of Revelation* and *Catechesis of Revelation* had, in league with the other factors enumerated above, already contributed to its rapid demise.

Not only had the fundamental assumption of *Heilsgeschichte* become problematic, so also had its schema of the relation of Old and New Testaments.

B. *Relationship of OT and NT*

As has been strikingly apparent in the survey of the various appropriations of *Heilsgeschichte,* one of its basic tenets is the fulfillment of the OT in the NT, albeit a claim made with varying degrees of sophistication from von Rad's more nuanced understanding of the OT as a book of "ever increasing anticipation," to the Marcion-like position of Hofinger and Reedy. Despite theological differences present within a spectrum of *Heilsgeschichte* views, it is nevertheless obvious that the incompleteness of the OT and its subsequent fulfillment in the NT is an essential component of salvation history.

That is not to claim that *Heilsgeschichte* is the only hermeneutical principle which viewed the OT as inferior. On the contrary, the history of Christian theology is filled with many such claims; witness, among others, Augustine's "Reply to Faustus the Manichean,"[51] Hegel and Vatke's conception of Christianity as the culmination of the developmental process and final state of the dialectic,[52] Vischer's christological reading of the OT,[53] the Bultmannian-Lutheran law-gospel distinction,[54] and even the early Moran. Indeed, *Heilsgeschichte* is not unique in this respect, and, in fact, actually represents a well-attested point of view in Christian theology over the years. The claim here, however, is that recent theological developments on the question of the relationship between the testaments give evidence that this issue is far more complex than the *Heilsgeschichte schema permits one to think.*[55] *At best the relationship between OT and NT in Heilsgeschichte theologies is insufficiently nuanced; at worst, it is a distorted and harmful view which served to denigrate Judaism while legitimating Christian ideologies.*

Such a complexity inevitably means that it will not be possible to do full justice within the limits of this study to the scope and depth of the current theological debates. Rather the focus in this section will be to draw attention to some of the most pertinent developments regarding the relationship between the testaments that make the *Heilsgeschichte* formulation problematic. What will also become evident is the significance of this issue for christology, and ultimately for ecclesiology.

1. Intertestamental Pluralism. Undoubtedly the single most critical factor operative in recent biblical-theological reconsideration on the relationship between the testaments is the attention being devoted to the way the writers of the NT appropriated the OT, a topic reflecting the heightened interest in the intertestamental period engendered particularly by the discovery of the Dead Sea Scrolls (DSS) in 1947, as well as by the Nag Hammadi texts and the additional Targumic materials.

The importance of this period is a major point in James Barr's *Old and New in Interpretation.*[56] In refusing to accept that a central motif can function as a single hermeneutical key in the process of understanding Scripture, Barr preferred to speak of the "multiplex" nature of the OT. The intertestamental period contributed greatly to the complexity, because during that time a significant change in perspective took place in the transition from OT to NT. In Barr's terminology, the OT tradition was "soteriologically functional," that is, certain situations were produced through the development of the traditions of the OT which "set the stage," as it were, for the coming of Christ. The OT traditions not only testified to the acts of God in the past, but also formed the framework within which the events of the life of Jesus had meaning, either positively or negatively. It was the religion of "late Judaism" that set the religious framework for the NT: it defined the questions of centrality and eliminated others.[57] The intertestamental period was that "time of ripening," the formation of the "matrix for the coming divine acts and the impulse for their very occurrence."[58]

In detailing the changes of perspective which took place historically between the testaments, Barr remarked that the shift and reorientation of elements may be viewed as either an obedient response or disobedient response to the OT situation, depending, of course, on one's point of view as a Jew or a Christian. The first of these shifts as identified by Barr was the substantial increase of messianic interest, discussion, and expectation. As a consequence of this expansion of messianism, Jesus came into a world where, to use a phrase from Reinhold Niebuhr's *The Nature and Destiny of Man,* "a Christ is expected." Moreover, messianism was not a univocal term; during the intertestamental era, variant images coexisted: Davidic king, prophet like Moses, priest, judge, and leader of the eschatological war against Satan and evil people. The NT writers appropriated aspects of these different images in proclaiming Jesus to be the "Messiah."[59]

A second change in perspective was the greatly heightened emphasis on the predictive side of prophecy. Prophetic prediction (in which the prophet under divine guidance gave some kind of verbal statement that was expected to bear sufficient similarity to an event which, when it happened, could be identified as having been foretold by or related to the preaching of the prophet) was among the various aspects attributed to the office of prophet by Israelite consciousness. It was not, however, the only aspect nor a universally held one; modern historical criticism, furthermore, has tended to de-emphasize this dimension of prophecy and to highlight instead the ethical function. But the predictive element in prophecy was greatly magnified in later interpretative consciousness:

In the New Testament, for example, the attention to prediction as the milieu in which the prophets were creative is so great as almost to swamp any attention to such other elements as their social consciousness. As the prophets died out, they came to be seen more and more as men who had spoken words which referred to times to come. This in turn provided an interpretative principle for the study of them. For the whole problem of connecting the past with the future, nothing was better adapted than a word spoken in the past which had reference to the future.[60]

Barr added that, though moderns see the prophets fundamentally as servants of their own time and generation, later Judaism did not always so view them; as an instance, he cites the NT writer who declared that it was "not for themselves, but unto us" that the prophets ministered (1 Pet. 1:12). By the first century A.D. it was a widespread belief in certain circles that the prophets were eschatological predictors, even when this meant including prophetic passages not intended to be predictive in their original setting; one obvious example is Hos. 11:1 ("Out of Egypt have I called my son") which clearly refers to the past (the exodus) but is used in Matt. 2:15 as predictive.[61]

This notion of predictive prophecy was linked as well to a third shift. The rise of apocalyptic encouraged the eschatological application of prophetic passages:

it [apocalyptic] had already experimented with the corresponding interpretative devices, such as numerical schemes, mysterious words, and detailed pondering on scriptural phrases; it could foster the development of Messianic concepts; and it created an atmosphere in which reformist sects were encouraged to see themselves, along with their own constitutions, practices, leaders, vicissitudes, enemies and persecutors, as representing a final stage in the great world drama which could, under apocalyptic conditions, be surveyed from beginning to end.[62]

Still another change in perspective was what Barr termed the "strongly emphatic" development of the "law"; these legal concepts of late Judaism were natural outgrowths of movements from within the OT itself. Finally, all the tendencies— messianism, predictive prophecy, apocalyptic, and legal developments—were significantly connected with another great process: the move of the OT itself from the status of a living folk literature to the status of "scripture."[63]

Accordingly, Barr maintained that when the question of the relationship of the testaments is asked, it is first necessary to attend to the way they related themselves historically, asking: "What situations were produced through the development of traditions on the basis of the Old Testament, and how does the New Testament express itself in relation to the Old within the terms of that situation?"[64] What Barr sought to emphasize through his discussion of the changes in perspective during the intertestamental times is that the men of the NT did not simply import a "homogeneous package" of OT ideas and backgrounds, but rather that they, along with other Jewish sects, engaged in a mixture of emphases in which the OT materials were used, reorganized, and revalued. Moreover, the way the writers of the NT exegeted OT texts differs greatly from contemporary exegesis.

In characterizing the relationship of OT to NT as "extremely complex," Barr identified several levels at which the OT operates in relation to the NT. One, obviously, was the religion of early Judaism, which set the religious framework for the NT and which illustrated both the continuity and discontinuity between OT and NT; secondly, there was the existence of the text, which simply by being keeps open the possibility of a challenge to accepted interpretations.[65] A third level was the self-understanding of Jesus, which, though notoriously difficult to describe with reliability, nevertheless was clearly rooted in biblical patterns and which starkly contrasted with a quietist and passive approach to the biblical text. Fourthly, there was the understanding of the apostles in their coming to understand the Christ and in what sense Jesus might be this Christ, as well as in their use of the OT for preaching and discussion.

It is common to claim that the apostles saw the Christ as the "key" to the OT. Barr, however, would turn this equation around:

> In the minds of the apostles, we may suggest, the relation was the opposite: the problem was not how to understand the Old Testament but how to understand Christ . . . . The problem is to identify

the Christ, to form reciprocal relations between Jesus and that which is the Messianic vocation, to demonstrate this to the Jews and also to the Greeks, and to clarify and illustrate what it means in the eyes of Christians to be the Christ promised by God, and to follow after him.[66]

Barr's argument, therefore, was that trying to assuage people's uncertainty about the OT by taking Christ as the "key" assumes too readily that they know what and who the Christ is. On the contrary, he claimed, the failure to know who the Christ is causes the lack of clarity about the OT. The OT, in Barr's view, is a source of elucidation of what it means to be the Christ. Thus he asserts:

The proper strategy in the Church, then, is not to take Christ as the given and argue from him to the authority or meaning of the OT; it is, rather, taking the Old Testament as something which we have in the Church, to ask in what ways the guidance it affords helps us to understand and discern and obey the Christ more truly . . . . Practically the execution of it means the placing of our knowledge and conceptions of Christ in a hypothetical status. Do we really understand Christ? If we study him as he seems to be when reference to the Old Testament is constantly made, what differences do we find and which concept is the more illuminating?[67]

Perhaps the point which most significantly sums up Barr's thought is his comment that, *if we are to speak of a "history of salvation" as a sequence of the acts of God, we must also speak of the sequence of the "history of biblical interpretation."* Indeed, the latter is as much a source of continuity as is the former. Israel had provided the "mental, traditional, religious and verbal matrix" in which the Christ came to be born.[68] Clearly, the NT is to be viewed as an interpretation of the OT; its characteristic christological interpretation is founded not on historical-critical methods, but on a theological assertion: the God of Israel is the one God and Father of the Lord Jesus Christ. The direction of thought is from God to Christ, from Father to Son, and not from Christ to God. Barr noted that this allows one to proceed to a christological interpretation, but doubted the wisdom of beginning from the christological.[69]

Barr, then, has assigned a positive role to the growth of the

Jewish tradition after the OT. He has highlighted the theological significance of the intertestamental era by pointing out the shift in perspective that undergirded the NT point of view.

2. Christian and Jewish Exegesis. This theologically significant interval has been studied in greater detail in relationship to the Qumran literature (QL); of particular pertinence to this study is the essay by J. Fitzmyer, "The Use of Explicit Old Testament Quotations in Qumran Literature and in the New Testament,"[70] and a recent study by R. Longenecker, *Biblical Exegesis in the Apostolic Period.*[71]

Fitzmyer analyzes forty-two passages in the QL which contain OT citations and subsumes them under four generic patterns: literal or historical, modernized, accommodated, and eschatological. These patterns are also illustrated by the way the NT handles OT quotations, though the categories do not exhaust the uses of the OT in the NT. What is of special note here is his conclusion that the exegetical practices of the NT writers parallel those of their Jewish contemporaries, as illustrated by the QL. Yet, despite similarities in exegetical practices, there were numerous differences in theologies; while both depended on the OT and cited it in generally common ways, each had a different set of presuppositions in light of which they read the OT. These presuppositions were the source of the distinction between the two groups.

The similarity of exegetical procedure, yet difference in presupposition, also provides a way of discussing the ways both Jews and Christians might appropriate the OT. In an extensive note, Fitzmyer writes:

> ... As far as I am concerned, the interpretation of any Old Testament text should be one that a Jew and a Christian could work out and agree on from the standpoint of philology, exegesis, and Old Testament biblical theology. I see no reason why a Jewish synthesis of Old Testament theology would be *radically* different from a Christian synthesis. To admit this is not to deny the "harmony of the Testaments," nor to abandon one's Christian heritage. Nor is it said merely to be irenic. The Christian interpretation of the Old Testament must begin with that which a Jewish interpreter, writing with the empathy of his own heritage and a recognition of the value of modern historical, critical interpretation of the Bible, would set

forth. The difference between the Jewish and the Christian interpretation of the Old Testament lies not in the primary literal
sense of the Old Testament text (arrived at with the same philological, historical, and literary-critical means), but in the plus value that
the Old Testament takes on when it becomes part of the Christian
Bible. One may call this a fuller dimension that the Hebrew Scriptures have because of their relation to the book of the Christian
community. This fuller sense is one which a Christian interpreter
would not expect a Jewish reader to accept. . . .[72]

Fitzmyer's discussion about the similarity in exegetical practices is underscored by Jewish scholar Geza Vermes:

> In inter-testamental Judaism there existed a fundamental unity of
> exegetical tradition. This tradition, the basis of religious faith and
> life, was adopted and modified by its constituent groups, the
> Pharisees, the Qumran sectaries and the Judeo-Christians. We
> have, as a result, three cognate schools of exegesis of the one mes-
> sage recorded in the Bible, and it is the duty of the historian to
> emphasize that none of them can properly be understood inde-
> pendently of the others.[73]

Vermes's contention is in turn developed by Longenecker,
who attempts to analyze NT exegesis in light of first century
Jewish hermeneutics. Of particular values is his demonstration
of the interplay of Jewish presuppositions and practices, on the
one hand, with Christian commitments and perspectives on the
other, which joined together to fashion a distinctive interpretation of the OT from a christocentric perspective. Longenecker
concludes these three main points regarding the nature of NT
exegesis: (1) the earliest Christians employed many of the
exegetical presuppositions (corporate solidarity, redemptive
correspondences in history) and practices (such as the Hillelian
exegetical principles of *qal waḥomer* and *gezerah shawah*) common within the various branches of the Judaism of the day;[74]
(2) they looked to Jesus' own use of the OT as the source and
paradigm for their own employment of Scripture; and (3) they
believed themselves to be guided by the exalted Christ through
the inspiration of the Spirit. He argues:

> What we have in the preaching and writing of the early apostolic
> band indicates that the apostles were not so much interested in

commentaries on the biblical texts or the application of principles to issues of the day as they were in demonstrating redemptive fulfillment in Jesus of Nazareth. Accepting the Messiahship and Lordship of Jesus, and believing that in his teaching and person was expressed the fullness of revelation, they took a prophetic stance upon a revelatory basis and treated the Old Testament more charismatically than scholastically.[75]

This "charismatic" treatment of the OT by the NT writers is articulated most compellingly by James A. Sanders.[76] Sanders examines Torah from a canonical perspective, and views it as a "balanced intermingling of story and law."[77] He lays out its dual character: on the one hand Torah is *muthos,* gospel, story, identity, *haggadah;* on the other, it is *ethos,* laws, ethics, life style, *halachah.* Whereas the Judaism of the Second Temple was pluralistic, only two denominations survived after 70 A.D.: the rabbinic Judaism of the Pharisees and Christianity of the early church. Sanders argues that these two differing directions are best understood in the particular emphasis that each showed: rabbinic Judaism stressed the *ethos* or *halachah* aspect of Torah; Christianity, on the contrary, stressed the *muthos* or *haggadah* aspect, though in neither instance was one emphasized to the exclusion of the other. In addition, Christianity was highly eschatological, even more so than were the Essenes. It was, in Sanders's view, this eschatological faith and the *haggadic* view of Torah which distinguished early Christianity from rabbinic Judaism. But to the Jews, it appeared that these early Christians overstressed the gospel aspect of Torah as a story of the deeds of God and replaced the Torah with Christ as a new identity symbol; hence their denial of the validity of Christian claims.

Sanders establishes a critical point in his argument that the reason the Jews did not accept the Christ is that they did not read the OT story as did Paul and the early Christians:

The frustration for Paul did not stem so much from a lack of affirmation of Christ by the majority of Jews of his day, as that he could *not* get them to read the Torah and the Prophets correctly, that is, in the way he read them. For he was certain that if they would review the Torah story with him in the way he viewed it, they would then accept the Christ.[78]

Accordingly, Sanders suggests that it is necessary to read most of the NT as a midrash of the Torah and the Prophets. When, for instance, in Rom. 10:4 Paul speaks of Christ as the *telos* of the Torah who brings righteousness for all who have faith, he means not simply Christ as the "end," but also as the "climax" and "main purpose" of the Torah. The righteousness of God made manifest in Christ is like the exodus event or the conquest event, but it is different in that "it brought all those chapters of the Torah story to completion, fulfillment and made sense of them all."[79] Paul's contention is that if all Jews would read the Torah concentrating primarily on the acts of God they would then be able to see the "Christ is the climax of the Torah for all who believe in the righteousness of God."

The value of such an analysis is that it highlights the magnitude and audacity of the Christian claim. The basic Torah story had ended with the farewell of Moses; no one, whether it be Jeremiah, Ezekiel, or the Chronicler, had succeeded in adding to it:

> Now what we can see from the point of view of the divine odyssey is that the New Testament really makes this quite bold and scandalous claim that in Christ God committed another salvation or righteousness and that it should be added to the Torah story as a climax or the ultimate chapter of the whole story or odyssey.[80]

As Sanders argues, Paul saw that, if specific points of the law were overstressed or absolutized, then the Torah story about God's righteousness was obscured. Thus Paul distinguished between focusing on the sort of righteousness of which humankind is capable and the righteousness of God that is constitutive of the Torah story; it is this that he is saying in Romans and Galatians when it appears on a superficial reading that he is antilegalistic. Where the church and Christianity have gone so wrong, Sanders claims, is in thinking that *all* Judaism was therefore legalistic. Every Pharisee realized that the Torah was fundamentally about the righteousness of God; but it was the special calling of Pharisaism to try to find ways, in the light of the specific expression of God's will on Sinai as codified in the legal texts of the OT, to discern the will of God for first century

Judaism.[81] Given that point of view on Torah, no Pharisee and "very few really good Jews knowledgeable in Torah" would accept the argument of the early church and of Paul that the life, death, and destiny of Jesus constituted the same sort of mighty acts as the exodus from Egypt.[82]

Like Barr, Sanders reminds his readers that one knows the righteousness of God prior to Christ, even as one comes to know the righteousness of God in Christ: "It is not so much that Christ reveals God as it is that God revealed Christ."[83] It is the Gentiles who enter Israel through Christ.

The fact that the church has turned this around and viewed itself as gospel and grace over against law and self-righteousness is, in the opinion of R. Ruether, derived from an ideological need to provide an *apologia pro vita sua.* She sees the anti-Judaic thinking in the Christian tradition as the negative side of its christological hermeneutic.[84] Identifying the crux of the conflict in the church's erection of messianic midrash into a new principle of salvation, Ruether argues that the anti-Judaic tradition grew as a "negative and alienated expression of a need to legitimate its revelation in Jewish terms."[85] Furthermore the differences evolved from matters of biblical hermeneutics and theology into law and social policy when Christianity became the religion of the Graeco-Roman empire in the fourth century. Thus Christianity fused the universalism of messianic hope with the "ideological universalism of the ecumenical empire," and thereby insured that humanity had but one society for salvation, the church.[86] By historicizing the eschatological:

> the "two eras"— the historical world and the messianic age to come—became the Christian historical era, over against Judaism as the type of unredeemed humanity. The line between history and eschatology is imported into history as though it were a line dividing history at the time of Jesus, into a premessianic and a post-messianic era (B.C. and A.D.). Judaism (and all that is not Christian) not only then but now becomes the unredeemed, "carnal" mankind over against the Christian "eschatological" man. The common use of B.C.E. and C.E. by both Christians and Jews would be one way of overcoming this tradition.[87]

Ruether's total argument, including her remarks about the psychopathology represented by Christian anti-Judaism, is beyond the scope of this study. It ought to be indicated, however, that her scholarship has engendered considerable controversy, most notably provoking the ire of John M. Oesterreicher, director of Seton Hall's Institute of Judaeo-Christian studies.[88]

But of special significance here are three points: (1) Ruether's insight into the ease with which Christianity moved from the radicalness of its messianic midrash into an establishment position; (2) the close correlation between christology and the way Christians conceptualize Judaism; and (3) the fact that, with Ruether's proposal for universal usage of B.C.E. and C.E., one has moved full circle from Cullmann's insistence that the B.C. and A.D. schema was an "astonishingly adequate way" of conceptualizing *Heilsgeschichte*.

It is obvious that the *Heilsgeschichte* schema makes Christianity, the later stage, superior to Judaism. But such a view, argues K. Stendahl, means that Christians ought logically to take the emergence of Islam far more seriously, for that is a tradition which makes the "reasonable claim of having superseded both Judaism and Christianity, and doing so according to the will and plan of God."[89] Stendahl's point notwithstanding, no *Heilsgeschichte* theologian has done this. Hans Küng, furthermore, speaks of a "pseudo-theology" which:

> falsely interpreted the Old Testament salvation history of the Jewish people as a New Testament history of divine condemnation and overlooked the continuing choice of the Jewish people accepted by the New Testament and referred to itself exclusively as the "New Israel."[90]

In Küng's view, *Heilsgeschichte* has falsified the way the early Christians read the OT, and has helped to legitimate that nearly two-thousand-year-long history of Christian anti-Judaism culminating in the Nazi atrocities, the work of "godless anti-Christian criminals."

The *Heilsgeschichte* hermeneutic, however, functions more positively in Samuel Terrien's recent attempt to demonstrate that the Hebraic theology of presence binds the testaments. Not unmindful of a Christian arrogance and anti-Semitism that has confused "eschatological hope with real-estate appropriation, promise with earthly possession, and vocation with presumed prerogative,"[91] Terrien nevertheless maintains that the results of both *Heilsgeschichte* interpretation and the myth and ritual school are necessary for an inquiry into the theology of presence. The salvation history school, he maintains, had rightly emphasized the significance of covenant in OT religion; furthermore, scholars such as Eichrodt, von Rad, and Cullmann had offered a platform for further research.

Despite this importance, Terrien argues compellingly that the covenant motif inherent in *Heilsgeschichte* must necessarily be subordinated to the motif of presence. After all, there was really no such entity as *the* Hebrew covenant as a single, homogeneous rite or ideology; at least two distinct but complementary traditions of covenant exist in the OT: the Mosaic and the Davidic.[92] Indeed, as important as were the covenant traditions, they did not dominate the OT; the sapiential literature, in particular, did not assign a major role to the ideology of covenant. Even the prophets, for whom the covenant obligations of Israel were central, discovered their "religious passion" and interpretation of history elsewhere; namely, in the experience of being grasped by Yahweh. The notion of the covenant was of little importance in the Apocrypha and Pseudepigrapha and DSS, "hardly mentioned" in rabbinical literature, and absent from the synoptic traditions of the teachings of Jesus (except for the textual variant in Luke 22:20). For Terrien, the covenant motif could not account for the multifaceted complexity of Hebrew religion; the uniqueness of Israel lay in the theology of presence rather than that of covenant. Hence the rite and ideology of covenant were dependent upon the prior reality of presence.[93]

Having thereby asserted that the theology of presence is the primary motif and is thus the principle of continuity for the biblical texts, Terrien then proceeds to trace the theme of *Deus absconditus atque praesens* in Hebrew experience: the patriarchal epiphanies, theophanies at Sinai, presence in the temple, prophetic visions, "psalmody of presence," and "play of Wisdom." In the postexilic years when Judaism emerged, God's "elusive presence" was ritually celebrated on the Day of the Sabbath and on the Day of Atonement, and sought for on the Day of the Lord.[94]

Christians were similarly rooted in the Hebraic theology of presence. Terrien sees the gospel accounts as crystallized in three "pivotal moments"—annunciation, transfiguration, and resurrection—which, by interrelating the motifs of theophany, temple, and final epiphany, thus interpreted Jesus in the context of divine presence. The cultic presence, as exemplified in the Last Supper, brought together the liturgical memory of the "mighty acts of God" with the anticipation of the Day of the Lord. The church began not primarily because of its reinterpretation of messiahship but because of its appropriation of the temple ideology in the context of the risen Lord.

Therefore Terrien claims:

It is the Hebraic theology of presence, not the covenant ceremonial, that constitutes the field of forces which links—across the biblical centuries—the fathers of Israel, the reforming prophets, the priests of Jerusalem, the psalmists of Zion, the Jobian poet, and the bearers of the gospel. The history of biblical religion hinges upon the growth and transformation of the Hebraic theology of presence.[95]

Terrien conceives of his work as a "prolegomenon" to a new biblical theology which will in turn be a servant of the *oikoumene*. It is his desire to contribute to an ecumenical theology that takes the OT seriously. His contention that the theme of God's presence will be more fruitful than other motifs in offering a "unifying yet dynamic principle" that accounts "not only for the homogeneity of the Old Testament literature in its totality," but also for the "historical and thematic continuity which unites Hebraism and large aspects of Judaism with nascent Christianity," demands careful reflection. While an evaluation of Terrien's contribution lies beyond the scope of this work, one must acknowledge gratefully his massive erudition and poetic insight. *The Elusive Presence* may well represent the most balanced scholarly and artistic contribution to date regarding the complex issue of the relationship between the testaments. Its subordination of *Heilsgeschichte* to the motif of presence offers a note of hope that the story of salvation might be told with greater nuance and in a fuller context.

3. The Relationship of the Testaments: An Evaluation of the Discussion. Christianity's lack of ease with the OT is manifest throughout its history, as numerous points in this study have attested. But perhaps it is not an exaggeration to claim that recent studies provide the most hopeful note in this long and, at times, vitriolic, debate. The discovery of the Dead Sea Scrolls and deepened attention to intertestamental literature, above all, have enabled scholars to attain a fresh perspective and to assume a posture less determined by dogmatic concerns. As a consequence, there presently exists opportunity for real dialogue on this critical issue.

That is not to suggest that the issue is settled or that arguments will not be laden with polemics (as the Ruether-Oesterreicher exchange indicates). It is, however, to claim that the conditions are now ripe for Christians to understand their identity vis-à-vis Judaism in a way hitherto impossible. Furthermore, it is to proffer the opinion that defining the relationship between the testaments is one of the most significant tasks before Christian biblical scholars, and that this task has been well begun by Barr and by Sanders and Terrien, in particular.

4. The Significance of the Discussion of the OT/NT Relationship. Taken in sum, the scholarship of Barr, Fitzmyer, Longenecker, Sanders, Terrien, and, to a lesser extent, that of Ruether, Stendahl, and Küng, places the *Heilsgeschichte* view of the relation between OT and NT under severe doubt. It establishes the pluralism of the intertestamental world, analyzes the continuity of the early Christians with Jewish exegetical practices, and manifests the distinctiveness of those Christians in their messianic-eschatological reading of the OT.

To say that the OT is a "preparation" for the NT is not altogether untrue if one understands this in a highly nuanced way, cognizant of the boldness, even scandal, of that interpretation. But far more often, viewing the OT as "preparation" is a reflection of dogmatic concerns beyond the Scriptures.

A case in point is the view of Vatican II in the fourth chapter of *Dei Verbum* which is concerned with showing that the OT as salvation history is a historical and theological record of God's saving action. As R. E. Brown has criticized it:

. . . One must constantly explain away the mentality of the Constitution. It is not a scriptural mentality; it is a mentality that has been directed by dogmatic concerns, as I think Professor Minear pointed out more eloquently than I could ever do ["A Protestant Point of View"]. I do not believe that these documents concerning the Old and New Testaments would have been written by an exegete in this way. They were written in view of a dogmatic concern that is extraneous to the Scriptures themselves. One could read the Old Testament and find the tremendous value there, without ever suspecting that the primary purpose of this whole book was the New Testament.[96]

Such a critique makes apparent the scriptural naiveté of the recent catechetical statements in the United States as they continue to speak of the OT as the history of salvation, and illustrates the pitfalls of insufficient exegesis.

It would seem, in conclusion, that the recent theological reconsiderations regarding the relationship between the testaments mean that any *Heilsgeschichte* schema simplistically viewing the fulfillment of the OT in the NT does not do justice to what is known about early Christian exegesis in its Jewish context. Thus another of the fundamental elements of salvation history has become theologically problematic; such is also the case with its christocentrism, as will be elaborated in the next section.

C. *Christology*

The reconceptualization of the relationship between the testaments speaks as well to the contemporary interest in refashioning christology, and in some cases provides the foundation point for these newer emphases. Perhaps more than any other single issue, the complexities of the christological controversies and formulations reflect the struggles of the followers of Jesus to come to terms (however haltingly and inadequately) with his meaning and significance in every age.[97]

The *Heilsgeschichte* theologians were no exception; indeed, christocentrism might well be regarded as the heart of their hermeneutics. Not only is it common to all of the salvation history adherents, but christocentrism is the key term and primary point from which all else is understood. A sustained examination of the theologies of *Heilsgeschichte,* furthermore, reveals the apologetic interests lying at the base of each. For instance, against the rationalists, Hofmann argued that Christ's self-representation was the essential content of all history and that, since no interpreter could pretend to be a *tabula rasa,* his own departure point was Christ. Against Bultmann, Cullmann contended that Christ had not somehow "risen into the kerygma," but that he was both the midpoint and starting point, the orientation of all history. Against the excessively intellectualist and casuistic tendencies of nineteenth century Catholicism, Jungmann-Hofinger and the Lumen Vitae school posed christocentrism as a powerful critique and corrective. The "restoration of all things in Christ" was a way of cleansing the accretions that had been gathering for centuries and which had metastasized during the modernist crisis.

Whatever else, *Heilsgeschichte* was a Christian hermeneutic; no Jewish scholar could agree with its fundamental tenets. Such an obvious statement makes evident the dogmatic presuppositions upon which it rests.

This exclusively Christian character notwithstanding, it would be arrogant not to acknowledge the power of the kerygmatic and christocentric emphases of *Heilsgeschichte* over against the inadequacies of rationalism, liberalism, scholasticism, and legalism. Nevertheless, it must still be asked whether christocentrism as understood in this hermeneutic can withstand more recent theological probings. In particular, two areas of development, occasioned by the increased attention of Christians to world religions and, in particular, to Judaism, make the *Heilsgeschichte* schema problematic. Ecumenical interests, it would appear, have now made exclusive christocentrism an inadequate departure point.

1. Christianity and World Religions.   To deal first with the relationship between Christianity and the world religions, it is necessary to acknowledge the fundamental fact of pluralism: how is it possible to maintain the centrality and universality of Christ in a world of such vastly different religious traditions? It may have once been possible to imagine a world evangelized completely, wherein all confessed explicitly that "Jesus is Lord," but no longer can such a vision be considered realistic.

At least in contemporary Catholic theology, Karl Rahner's essay on "Anonymous Christians" has become something of a *locus classicus* for wrestling with this issue. Given his assumption that all grace is the grace of Christ, Rahner maintains:

> In the acceptance of himself man is accepting Christ as the absolute perfection and guarantee of his own anonymous movement toward God by grace, and the acceptance of this belief is again not an act of man alone but the work of God's grace which is the grace of Christ, and this means in its turn the grace of his Church which is only the continuation of the mystery of Christ, his permanent visible presence in our history. . . . Therefore no matter what a man states in his conceptual, theoretical and religious reflection, anyone who does not say in his heart, "there is no God" (like the "fool" in the psalm) but testifies to him by the radical acceptance of his being, is a believer. But if in this way he believes in deed and in truth in the holy mystery of God, if he does not suppress this truth but leaves it free play, then the grace of this truth by which he allows himself to be led is always already the grace of the Father in his Son. And anyone who has let himself be taken hold of by this grace can be called with every right an "anonymous Christian."[98]

Another articulation of the issue comes from Charles Davis who, while arguing that the universality and finality of Christ cannot be denied without emptying the Christian tradition of meaning, nonetheless establishes a number of points indicating what faith in the centrality of Christ does *not* imply. The confession of the lordship of Jesus does not imply for Davis: (1) any denial of genuine religious faith, meaningful religious symbols, and prophetic revelation outside the Christian tradition; (2) that Christians have nothing to learn religiously from other traditions; or that (3) other religions no longer have a function in God's providential ordering of history. Davis places under doubt whether we ought to consider the elimination of religious plurality within history as an essential part of God's plan, and, consequently, as an essential goal of the Christian church. He suggests, rather, that the mission of Christianity might best be viewed as "representation" involving both service and redemptive suffering. He concludes that the unique role of Christians in forming the community of those acknowledging the Christ ought not to lead to a denial of the persisting function of other religious traditions in God's ordering of history or to a devaluing of the positive aspects of religious pluralism.[99]

The work of Davis has provided an important foundation for a recent essay which seeks to open up the possibilities of belief in the risen Jesus as a basis of developing a transcultural faith.[100] Here an effort is made to avoid both "believing in the Lord at the expense of a genuine encounter of the religions"— which betrays an insensitivity to the historical nature of humanity—and "encountering the religions at the expense of belief in the Lord"—which tends to "undercut the absolute."[101]

William Thompson grounds his theses in two phenomena: the post-Enlightenment historical consciousness that has functioned as a critical factor in bringing about religious pluralism and "planetization," that process of world unification that provides a hitherto unknown possibility of transcultural enrichment. The latter is not without inherent danger, for it has given rise to loss of identity, confusion, and "universalization of doubt"; yet Thompson proffers the hope that planetization provides the potential for a "fundamental maturing of the contemporary Christian's consciousness," as is illustrated in the works of John Dunne and the late Thomas Merton. Building upon an interpretation of the resurrection as the event through which Jesus became the "finally integrated man" (Merton's phrase), he concludes with three theses: (1) contemporary transcultural experience is teaching Christians that faith in the risen Lord needs to be understood in a transcultural manner; (2) the Christian response to transcultural experience must also result in a new self-understanding; and (3) transcultural experience is teaching Christians that their belief in the risen Lord is not a hindrance to encounter with the world religions, but, on the contrary, is a catalyst to such a dialogue:

> The more a belief in the risen Lord becomes the center of Christianity, the more that belief itself should universalize the Christian consciousness—the more, that is, the Christian himself should participate in that paschal mystery of death to one's narrow and com-

promising horizons and resurrection to wider and more universal horizons.[102]

Each of these efforts rather substantially expands the discussion about the centrality of Christ, seeking to broaden its context. They reflect but three among numerous efforts to wrestle with this complex problem; perhaps particularly illuminating is a recent typology that establishes the parameters of the discussion.[103]

J. Peter Schineller's synthesis, amazing in its clarity and conciseness, is obviously not done full justice when merely summarized. But it is crucial to the discussion here to lay out his views of Christ and church because they reflect so accurately the present divergence and complexities and manifest the link between christology and ecclesiology.

In Schineller's first type or model, Jesus Christ is the exclusive mediator between God and humankind, the kingdom of God is viewed as coextensive with the church, other religions are absolutely false, and all must be brought into the church in order to be saved. The second type, perhaps most identifiable with mainline Christian views such as exemplified by Vatican II, is the position of an "inclusive, constitutive christology." Here the kingdom is present for all through Christ, other religions are seen as only relatively false; that is, ultimately the non-Christian world is interpreted in terms of Christian categories (as is the case with Rahner's "anonymous Christian"). The mission of the church is to point all to Christ in order that what is implicit in the hearts of many might someday be made explicit. The third position on the spectrum Schineller classifies as "theocentric, normative christology"; meaning that the kingdom is manifest most fully in Christ, but that Christianity represents the "extraordinary" way of salvation: God's love, though revealed most clearly in the person and work of Jesus, is not mediated only through him. Thus Christians, while witnessing to Christ as normative, engage in genuine and open dialogue with other religions. Finally, there is a fourth type reflecting a "theocentric universe and non-normative christology"; Jesus is one of many ways of salvation, and judgments about claims to uniqueness or normativity are unverifiable and therefore without basis. Ecclesiologically, there are many communities of salvation, and no way of differentiating the value of one way over another.

In sum, what Rahner, Davis, Thompson, and Schineller are involved in is the attempt to push back the meaning of the centrality of Christ. Their efforts involve fundamental philosophical and theological positions, as the christological debate between Catholic theologians Avery Dulles and David Tracy so vividly illustrates.[104] Against this complexity and pluralism, the *Heilsgeschichte* proponents, particularly as exemplified by religious educators such as Hofinger, appear quite simplistic in their assertion that "the mystery of Christ is the fundamental theme and unifying principle of all Christian religious instruction."[105]

It is not so much that this claim is in error as that it is unnuanced and glosses over the heart of the matter. There is more to the gospel than "proclaiming the Good News"—a statement with which the kerygmatics would undoubtedly agree, but which was unfortunately all too often belied in their continual repetition of the same phrases without a sufficiently critical perspective.

2. *Christianity and Judaism.*   A premise often implicit in Christian theology in general and in the *Heilsgeschichte* school in particular is that postexilic Judaism was legalistic and, hence, in sharp contrast to early Christianity. From Daniélou's contention that Judaism was "anachronistic survival" (the distinctive error in Judaism being a "refusal to die and rise again or a failure to grow up") to the continual proclamation among salvation history adherents that the OT covenant was provisional, preparatory, and imperfect, Christian theologians and educators generally fostered the understanding that Christianity replaced and superseded Judaism.[106] Typically they honored Abraham, Moses, David, and the prophets, but portrayed the period after the exile as an era of decline and of sterile legalism. In teaching the NT, they tended to establish a firm distinction between Jesus' ethic of love and the harsh legalism of the Pharisees and the later rabbis; moreover, they regarded the OT as a "manual of Messianic predictions em-

bedded within a repository of legal requirements of a racially and ritually particularistic nature."[107]

Among the kerygmatics, the problem arose principally because of a desire to emphasize the centrality of Christ. As a consequence, assertions that the OT was characterized by "desperate inadequacy," "naive pettiness," and "sickening brutality" not only manifested an inadequate understanding of the relationship between the testaments (as demonstrated in the previous section) but also obviated any appreciation for the perduring existence of Judaism.[108] For instance, a British scholar offered this observation to religious educators:

> The Christian cannot pretend to see God's plan in any of the Old Testament themes, whatever they may be—the temple, the monarchy, the passover, even original sin itself—except in the light of Christ. It is precisely the Christian belief that Christ is the person who explains each of these themes.[109]

Such an argument implicitly suggests that Judaism had a validity only until the coming of Christ.

A more sophisticated version of this viewpoint is represented in the scholarly works of Ferdinand Weber (*Jüdische Theologie auf Grund des Talmud und verwandter Schriften*, 1897), Wilhelm Bousset (*Die Religion des Judentums im späthellenistischen Zeitalter*, 1925), Paul Billerbeck and Herman Strack (*Kommentar zum Neuen Testament aus Talmud und Midrasch*, 1924–31; English translation, *Introduction to the Talmud and Midrash*), and Emil Schürer (*Geschichte des Judischen Volkes im Zeitalter Jesu Christi*, 1886–1890; English translation, *The History of the Jewish People in the Age of Jesus Christ*). Weber's understanding of Judaism as a legalistic religion in which the individual must earn salvation and in which God was remote and inaccessible was generally accepted; it remained influential largely because of Bousset's dependence upon his theory. Bousset, in turn, was widely disseminated by Rudolf Bultmann, and thereby became a prime source for NT students. Strack and Billerbeck, compilers of rabbinic parallels to the NT, likewise portrayed Judaism as a religion of self-redemption with no need for a savior; their collection of parallels has proved immensely influential by virtue of the fact it has provided virtually the only contact with rabbinic literature for theological students unable to work directly with the Hebrew text. Similarly, Schürer's massive, five-volume history, in which rabbinic Judaism is portrayed as a failure to understand truly religious faith, has been regarded as a prime authority.

The widespread influence of the Weber-Bousset-Schürer-Billerbeck line of thought has been amply documented in a recent work detailing the manner and extent to which Judaism has been denigrated in Christian scholarship.[110] Author Charlotte Klein compiles example after example from leading continental biblical scholars and theologians to illustrate the sixfold shape of the Christian misunderstanding of Judaism: (1) Judaism has been superseded and replaced by Christianity; (2) as a consequence (at least implicitly), Judaism has "scarcely any right to continue to exist"; (3) regardless, its teaching and ethical values are inferior to those of Christianity; (4) Christian theologians continue to assume they have the right to pass judgment on Judaism; (5) only a few specialists in departments of Judaica make "fresh examination of authentically Jewish sources," since, for the most part, others simply appropriate material collected in certain works about the turn-of-the-century (i.e., Weber, Bousset, Schürer); (6) often the same author, when expressly speaking of Judaism in an ecumenical context, assumes a "strikingly different" approach from that adopted when dealing mainly with the Christian religion and only incidentally with Judaism.[111]

By exposing the inadequacy and distortion of Weber, Bousset, Schürer, and their multitude of followers, Klein has continued the line of critique inititated by George Foot Moore in an earlier essay.[112] Her work, moreover, is of particular value to religious educators; not only does she summarize and critique a stubbornly entrenched scholarly tradition not readily available to a nonspecialist (Weber is out of print, Bousset is available only in German, only the first volume of Schürer is still in print in English), but she offers as well some sobering reflections about education. Klein traces the genesis of her book to reading the final papers for her lecture course at a German university

(1970–71); her students (most of whom would become pastors or teachers of religion) submitted papers with negative and derogatory portrayals of first century Judaism that virtually ignored and contradicted the entire content of her own presentations. In their research, the students had simply returned to the standard works on Judaism; the greater their reading, the stronger grew their negative judgment. Klein's realization— "Lectures by individual teachers with different opinions are of little or no avail against these fixed ideas"—generated this book which ruthlessly traces the anti-Judaic bias of much German and French biblical scholarship.[113] Her exposé invites Old and New Testament scholars to "examine afresh" their own attitudes and *objectively* to present Jewish teaching and the Jewish way of life in the period between the testaments from their study of *original* sources.[114] It also provides religious educators with a valuable source book for reexamining their own teaching.

Klein's mandate to scholars is admirably fulfilled in an erudite volume by E. P. Sanders, *Paul and Palestinian Judaism: A Comparison of Patterns of Religion.*[115] As does Klein, Sanders utilizes the Moore article (cited above) as a point of departure. Arguing that Bousset, Billerbeck, and Schürer are "completely untrustworthy" insofar as they deal with rabbinic literature,[116] Sanders sets out himself to work directly from the primary source material: Tannaitic literature (rabbinic literature from approximately 70 c.e. to 200 c.e.), the Dead Sea Scrolls, and the Apocrypha and Pseudepigrapha.

Accordingly, Sanders seeks to determine the basic pattern (i.e., how one moves from a logical starting point of a religion to its logical end) of rabbinic religion; by so doing, he is searching for a pattern that would account for the foundational motivating forces of the religious life and how individuals perceived religion to function.[117] Contending that *covenantal nomism*— "the view that one's place in God's plan is established on the basis of the covenant and that the covenant requires as the proper response of man his obedience to its commandments, while providing means of atonement for transgression"—[118] constitutes the essence of Judaism, Sanders argues that the purpose of law (*halakah*) was to determine how to obey the God who chose Israel and gave it commandments. His reading of the literature of Palestinian Judaism has convinced him that obedience to laws simply *maintained* one's position in the covenant; it did not *earn* God's grace—an oftmade accusation reflecting a retrojection of the Reformation debate.[119]

Sanders leaves no doubt that his reading of the evidence "destroys" the Weberian view which had such a tenacious grasp on NT scholarship. He sees a twofold purpose in *halakah:* (1) definition of law; and (2) help for the observant Jew in determining when it had been fulfilled. Of central significance was the covenant; in seeking after the religious motives that drove the rabbis to detailed and minute investigations of the biblical commandments, Sanders infers:

> The bulk of the halakic material deals with the elaboration and definition of Israel's obligation to God under the covenant. This is what accounts for the halakic material in general.... The only reason for elaborating and defining man's obligation under the covenant is that God's faithfulness and justice in keeping his side are beyond question.[120]

Rabbinic formulations were not animated by the question, "Who can be saved?" but by the concern, "How can we obey God who redeemed us and to whom we are committed?" The ultimate goal of the religious quest was not in becoming righteous, as Christian scholars had wrongly judged, but to live in fidelity to the covenant offered at Sinai and, hence, to the commandments which made operative God's kingship.[121]

As Sanders later summarizes, the basic pattern of covenantal nomism in Palestinian Judaism flows like this: God has chosen Israel and given Israel the law. Law implies both God's promise to maintain the election and the requirements to obey. Furthermore, God rewards obedience and punishes transgression; it is law that provides the means for atonement. Atonement, in turn, results in the maintenance or reestablishment of the convenantal relationship. All who are maintained in the covenant by obedience, atonement, and God's mercy belong to the group which will be saved; election and salvation are considered to be by God's mercy rather than by human achievement.[122]

Contrary, then, to the common view in Christian scholarship

that there was a degeneration of the biblical view in postbiblical Judaism, Sanders maintains that in all the literature surveyed (with the exception of Ben Sirach), obedience to God is shown to be related to living one's covenantal relationship rather than a legalistic means of earning grace.[123]

Similarly, in regard to the literature of the intertestamental period, Sanders concluded that pre-70 c.e. Judaism kept grace and works in the proper perspective, did not trivialize God's commandments, and was not unduly characterized by hypocrisy. Sanders grants no credibility whatsoever to the frequent Christian charge that Judaism "necessarily tends toward petty legalism, self-serving and self-deceiving casuistry, and a mixture of arrogance and lack of confidence in God."[124] Rather, the Christian scholar maintains that "the surviving Jewish literature is as free of these characteristics as any I have ever read." He continues:

> By consistently maintaining the basic framework of covenantal nomism, the gift and demand of God were kept in a healthy relationship with each other, the minutiae of the law were observed on the basis of the large principles of religion and because of commitment to God, and humility before the God who chose and would ultimately redeem Israel was encouraged.[125]

This monumental work by E. P. Sanders provides an exhaustively researched basis for Christian scholars to do a fundamental revision of their understanding of Judaism. *Paul and Palestinian Judaism,* while not without its controversial points, as its reviewers have indicated,[126] represents nonetheless a new landmark in articulating the relationship between Christianity and Judaism.

Christological reassessments have been engendered as well by the continuing existence of Judaism. Vis-à-vis the Jewish presence, Christian claims that Jesus is the center of all history are placed under doubt; the proclamation that the messiah has come and salvation has taken place sounds arrogant when juxtaposed against the Jewish protest that the world does not appear to be redeemed:

> The Jew has a keen sense of the world's lack of redemption, and within this absence of redemption he recognizes no enclaves of

redemption. The idea of a redeemed soul within an unredeemed world is essentially, basically alien to him; the primordial ground of his existence makes it inadmissable. This is the heart of Jesus' rejection by Israel, not in a merely external, merely national understanding of messianism.[127]

The criticism that in the history of Christianity a realistic messianic hope has all too readily been replaced by an individualized and spiritualized notion of salvation has been most sharply and fully articulated by Christian ("post-Roman Catholic," by her own description) theologian Rosemary Radford Ruether.[128] But, lest this criticism be dismissed because of her controversial stance, it is significant to take note here of the growing number of studies addressing the issue in similar terms. Of special value in demonstrating this is Michael B. McGarry's study, *Christology after Auschwitz.*[129]

McGarry adopts the schema proposed by A. Roy Eckardt to analyze the theologies dealing with the relationship between Judaism and Christianity—theologies obviously grounded in a particular conceptualization of the relationship between the testaments and in a particular christology.[130] The first set of theologies is grouped under the rubric of "theology of discontinuity"; taken as a whole, these theologies tend to stress the uniqueness and finality of Christ. They speak of Jesus as the messiah who fulfilled the hopes of the Jewish people and OT prophecies; he is the absolute fulfillment of Judaism. The rejection by the Jews is a mystery, though the merciful God is still faithful to them despite their rejection of his son. Christianity, furthermore, is the successor to Judaism, which prepared its way; Christians are the new chosen people and are missioned to preach Christ to all, including the Jews.[131]

McGarry includes J. Daniélou in this category, and the *Heilsgeschichte* theologians surveyed here in Chapters 1 and 2 ought certainly to be likewise categorized, though Cullmann is actually the only one to have explicitly attended to the implications of salvation history for the relationship of Christianity and Judaism.[132]

But pertinent to this critique, McGarry identifies a substantial number of theologians who attempt to profess Christianity

while simultaneously maintaining the continued validity of
Judaism. Grouping these as "christologies of continuity," he
characterizes these nonsupersessionist views as generally stressing the relativity of Christ and the proleptic nature of his messiahship. From the perspective of continuity, messianic times
are viewed as being not fully realized, and Christ as but the
partial fulfillment of the Jewish faith and Scripture. A positive
evaluation of the Jewish rejection of Jesus as the Christ is made
possible by the understanding that they were responding faith-
fully to their covenant and to their understanding of messianic
fulfillment. Thus these theologies hold the continuing validity
of Judaism *alongside* Christianity; Judaism is not merely preparatory for Christianity. Christians have an obligation to witness
to their belief in Christ, but no exigency to convert Jews; conversion, rather, involves the call of all persons to fidelity within
the revelation granted them by God.[133]

Gregory Baum has articulated much of this position in his
introduction to Ruether's *Faith and Fratricide*.[134] He argues, on
the one hand, that when a church that became culturally dominant proclaimed Jesus as the one mediator and regarded him as
the way to salvation invalidating all other ways, it created a
"symbolic imperialism that no amount of personal love and
generosity can prevent in the long run from being translated
into social and political realities."[135] On the other hand, Baum
notes that if Christian teaching is merely proposed as one truth
among many, all powers of discernment are lost; if the gospel is
true only for Christians, then they have nothing to say to others
and no relevance to the liberation of people from personal and
social oppression. Thus he proposes a "responsible relativizing
of Jesus."

This would mean, as McGarry lines up Baum's theses, eight
mandates for the church. First, its self-understanding must be
other than that of the successor to an obsolete Israel. Second,
the church must acknowledge Judaism's validity beyond mere
preparation for Christianity. The church, third, must recognize
that its christological reading of the Scriptures is not the only
way they might be interpreted, and it must, fourth, reinterpret
its claim that Jesus is the one mediator without whom there is
no salvation. Fifth, the church must go beyond a Logos-

christology viewing the Jews as anonymous Christians and it must, sixth, understand the absolute and universal significance of Jesus as a critique applicable to all religions (including itself) rather than as an invalidation of non-Christian religion. Seventh, the church's proclamation of Jesus should speak of him not as the one who has already fulfilled all the promises of God but as the "guarantee" of God's final victory. Finally, it ought to proclaim the redemption now existing in Christ as "unfulfilled messianism," as that divine grace empowering believers to pray and struggle for the coming of the kingdom in full glory.[136]

In an article which includes a survey of many of the same theologians, whom McGarry categorizes under the "christologies of continuity," J.T. Pawlikowski writes:

> But what the theologians we have just looked at are saying, despite their many differences, is that Christianity must look anew at its contention that the Messianic age, the time of fulfillment, far more crucial to Judaism than the notion of a personal Messiah, took place with the coming of Christ. However we may eventually come to explicate the uniqueness and mystery of the Christ event, it has become obvious to them and to me that we can no longer simply assert that the Jewish notion of the Messianic age was realized in the Death-Resurrection of Christ. Such a conclusion does not imply a total discarding of traditional christology, but it does demand a significant restatement and clarification.[137]

A related point is established by Jürgen Moltmann who, in arguing that no new convergence between Christianity and Judaism can result without a revision of Christology, contends:

> Christology can only treat Jesus as the confirmation and fulfillment of the messianic hope if it discovers within this person the messianic future of God himself. Only when it recognizes the difference and the connection between the rule of the Son of Man and the rule of God himself can it recognize its own eschatological impermanence. The Pauline idea that the Son will hand over rule to the Father, so that God may be all in all (1 Cor. 15:28) points in this direction on the theological level. If it is taken seriously it means the end of Christian absolutism. The Church will see itself as provisionally

final and hope, with the Jews and for the poor, for the completion of the kingdom in the history of God.[138]

3. The Christology Discussion: An Evaluation. This discussion obviously picks up themes from the revelation debate (especially from Moran's *PR*) and from the reconsideration of the relationship between OT and NT; it leads as well to ecclesiological implications. What seems especially important is that Christian theologians are (1) aware of the arrogance too easily linked with christological assertions, yet responsible as well for articulating the primacy of Christ in their tradition; (2) in acknowledgment of the political and social ramifications of a christological proclamation allied with cultural predominance; and (3) sensitive to the "not yet" dimension of the kingdom of God and to Jesus as a proleptic figure.

From this author's vantage, Baum's eight mandates for the church seem to offer the most succinct and significant agenda for further study. Yet there is puzzlement about his stance in relationship to that of his colleague Rosemary Ruether, whose *Faith and Fratricide* does not sufficiently value Christian traditions. His third point (recognition that the church's christological reading of Scripture is not the only possible interpretation) underscores the importance of the essay by J. A. Sanders discussed in the previous section and provides a task in which biblical theologians and religious educators might fittingly collaborate.

4. The Significance of the Discussion of Christology. The common elements in these various theologies of continuity is the critique of the perennial tendency in Christianity to equate the lordship of Jesus with the arrival of the messianic age. Such a reconsideration demands that Christians hear as well the cries of the survivors of Auschwitz who rightly ask:

> But what kind of a messiah
> Is a messiah
> Who demands
> Six million dead
> Before he reveals himself.[139]

In short, the christological reconsiderations revolve largely around the question of eschatology, an area superficially and simplistically treated by Catholic salvation-history proponents and to which only Cullmann among the *Heilsgeschichte* theologians explicitly attends at length. His assertions regarding eschatology provide a natural linkage between christology and ecclesiology.

D. *Ecclesiology*

Cullmann's refutation of the *Parousierzögerung* (delay of the *parousia*) theology of Schweitzer and Werner had established the basis of his ecclesiology: the interval between preparation and fulfillment, the time of the "already" and the "not yet," was the age of the church. Unlike Bultmann and his disciples Conzelmann and Vielhauer, Cullmann granted significance to post-Easter developments and viewed the church as the continuation of Christ's redemptive work. Obviously his theological stance in this regard established an important linkage with Catholic pre-Vatican II ecclesiology. In distinction, however, from the latter, he held for the subjection of the church to the Christ of the Scriptures.[140] In addition, Cullmann did not conceive of the church as God's kingdom but as the point at which the kingdom of Christ is made visible.[141]

The Catholic *Heilsgeschichte* theologians did in fact manifest a different understanding of church, although Cullmann's criticism did not adequately account for the difference. Basically theirs was a kerygmatic point of view in which the church's mission was understood almost exclusively in terms of proclamation. Furthermore, it was a church seen as coextensive with the kingdom of God; the usual formulation was that what was begun in the OT came to a climax in the NT in the death-resurrection of Jesus and was continued in the church. Hofinger's 1950 statement that the church was the "essential work of Christ," the "new society of the children of God," the "Kingdom of God he had come to found," illustrates this equation.[142] Moreover, he carried it to its most simplistic extreme in later asserting that christocentrism provided the foundation for the

hierarchy and thereby legitimated the various dogmas determining hierarchical power.[143]

Hofinger's excesses aside, the Catholic *Heilsgeschichte* theologians were, nonetheless, merely reflecting the general tenor of
a long entrenched ecclesiology. From the later Middle Ages to
the twentieth century, Catholic ecclesiology had focused almost
exclusively on the institutional character of the church. Accordingly, ecclesiology tended to be reduced to "hierarchology."[144]
As Avery Dulles notes, an unfortunate consequence of this
juridicizing of ecclesiology was a concomitant individualizing of
eschatology.[145] Because the social aspects of salvation were
thereby obscured, virtually no attention was directed toward
the relationship between the church and the eschaton.

Thus Cullmann's explicit treatment of the linkage of eschatology and ecclesiology exercised a corrective function for
Catholic thought. Jürgen Moltmann, in spite of his opinion that
the idea of salvation history was "philosophically anachronistic
and theologically deistic," observed more positively that
Heilsgeschichte functioned to "preserve the question of the eschatological future outlook which the Christian revelation
holds for a world involved in history."[146] By being insufficiently
attentive to eschatology, Catholic kerygmatics inadvertently
promulgated a distorted understanding of the church.

1. Ecclesiology and Eschatology.   Dulles contends that one's
viewpoint regarding the status and mission of the church depends on the way one conceives the relationship between the
partially and finally realized eschaton.[147] A similar understanding is cogently laid out by Richard McBrien, who proposed the
thesis that the present spectrum of viewpoints on the church
results from a threefold pluralism of theological methodology.[148] The first theological method he classifies as "doctrinal";
this positivistic, nonhistorical method is characterized by a generally uncritical attitude toward history, a fundamentalist
understanding of the commission of Christ to the apostles regarding the founding of church, and a notion of church as the
means of dissemination, exposition, and defense of whatever
God has revealed to humans for the sake of their salvation
through Scripture and official church statements. One might

see McBrien's doctrinal method as being in substantial harmony with Schineller's first type (ecclesiocentric universe, exclusivist christology) and with the nineteenth century "siege mentality" in Catholicism.

The second method, the "kerygmatic," McBrien likewise classifies as positivistic and nonhistorical; it considers revelation to have been completed in the words and deeds of Jesus and regards theology as essentially evangelical. Accordingly, such a point of view equates the mission of the church with that of proclamation of God's word to the world. Thus, in the kerygmatic method:

> the Church is essentially a kerygmatic community which holds aloft, through the preached Word, the wonderful deeds of God in past history, particularly his mighty act in Jesus Christ. The community itself happens wherever the Spirit breathes, wherever the Word is proclaimed and accepted in faith. The Church is event, a point of encounter with God.[149] .

McBrien rightly associates this kerygmatic method with the great Karl Barth, but it is also evident in view of the work surveyed in the second chapter of this study that the Catholic *Heilsgeschichte* theologians certainly ought to be classified here. Thus it is of significance that McBrien rejects both the doctrinal and kerygmatic methods as providing too narrow a base for an adequate view of the church, and contends that when the limitations of those two methods are unacknowledged, they lead to "certain selective perceptions of the church. And selective perception in theology means 'heresy.'"[150] Specifically, he faults both for not accepting *diakonia* (service) as an essential task of the church.

McBrien proposes that the third fundamental focus be categorized as "eschatological theology," which utilizes a correlative rather than a positivistic method. It is, however, important to his argument to recognize his differentiation of five variations within this method. The first three variations ("consistent" eschatology [Schweitzer, Weiss, Werner, Buri], "realized" eschatology [Dodd], and "existentialist" eschatology [Bultmann, and to a certain extent, Bornkamm, Käsemann, Ebeling, Fuchs, and Conzelmann]) he rejects for the same reasons as he has the doctrinal and kerygmatic methods. He suggests, however, that both "salvation history" eschatology (Cullmann, Jeremias, Schnackenburg, Kümmel) and the "proleptic" eschatology associated with Moltmann, Pannenberg, Metz, and later writings of Schillebeeckx and Rahner offer the best possibilities for grappling with the mission of the church in the post-Vatican II era.

In fact, the salvation history and proleptic eschatologies are actually regarded in McBrien's view as being substantially harmonious, with the latter perhaps being a variation of the former but placing greater emphasis on the future. Most crucial to his critique is that neither of these eschatologies permits the simple equation of church with kingdom. Indeed, the central thrust in the corpus of McBrien's work on ecclesiology is that the kingdom of God ought not to be reduced to the church.[151] Just as Baum has proposed a "responsible relativizing of Jesus," so McBrien contends that the church must be relativized for the sake of the reign of God.

Reconsideration of the threefold mission of the church thus entails that primary emphasis be given to the kingdom of God. In light of *kerygma*, the church is indeed called to proclaim in word and sacrament the definitive arrival of the kingdom, but this must not be done in an uncritical and naive manner; everything is placed under God's reign, even (or especially) the church. (Nor is progress inevitable; though McBrien does not recognize this, the salvation history schema is predicated upon a developmental presupposition in which evolution is equated with progress.) The church, furthermore, is missioned to be a sign of the kingdom; this means existing as a community (*koinonia*) marked not only by faith, hope, and love but also by the pursuit of truth. Thirdly, by its character of service (*diakonia*), the church is called to "realize and extend the reign of God through service in the sociopolitical order."[153] No longer can the activities of the church for human rights and social justice, for instance, be merely regarded as "pre-evangelization." Thus:

> The Church must offer itself as one of the principal agents whereby the human community is made to stand under the judgment of the enduring values of the Gospel of Jesus Christ and to

see itself against the horizon of its eschatological expectation: the time of freedom, justice, righteousness, peace, charity, compassion, reconciliation. The Church must be a place where all those forces, personal and political, which challenge and undermine these values in the future are themselves effectively exposed, prophetically denounced, and through the instrumentality of moral rather than material force, initially disarmed and dismantled.[154]

This tripartite division of the mission of the church has become relatively commonplace, particularly among Catholics.[155] Certainly the last decade has witnessed a remarkably deepened consciousness of the social nature of salvation; among the clearest articulations of this in Catholicism is the 1971 document from the Second General Assembly of the Synod of Bishops. It affirms:

> Action on behalf of justice and participation in the transformation of the world fully appear to us as a constitutive dimension of the preaching of the Gospel, or, in other words, of the Church's mission for the redemption of the human race and its liberation from every oppressive situation.[156]

This theme, of course, also dominates the literature of the various theologies of liberation; of special note here is that the now familiar refrain about the social and political mission of the church is rooted in an eschatological outlook which subordinates the church to the kingdom of God.

The recovery of the eschatological dimension of ecclesiology corresponds to five major needs of modern times, according to Dulles.[157] First of all, it reminds members that the church is a pilgrim and wayfarer subject to trials and weakened by human sinfulness. Second, an eschatological view of the church, by positioning the fullness at the end of history, liberates its members from the "tyranny" of the past:

> The eschatological vision, by focussing one's faith on the absolute future, generates a certain critical liberty with regard to the value of ecclesiastical structures, even those that have served well over many centuries. This outlook is therefore favorable to the current demands for institutional reform within the Church. It harmonizes

with our modern sense of responsibility for shaping the institutions of the societies to which we belong.[158]

Third, the attention to eschatology facilitates a turning away from a purely individualistic notion of salvation; moreover, by fostering an understanding of the church primarily as a community of grace rather than as an institution, it makes possible more humanly satisfying ways for people to relate to the church. Fourth, the renewed eschatology "relativizes every historical realization of the Church, including that which obtains in one's own confession"; thus the ecumenical implications are significant. Finally, Dulles argues that, because of its recognition that the new creation will be the ultimate future of the entire world, insofar as it stands under God's salvific will, "its horizons are as wide as the whole inhabited world (*oikoumene*) and indeed as wide as the cosmos itself."[159]

2. The Ecclesiological Discussion: An Evaluation.   Attention to eschatology as an essential component of ecclesiology, particularly as analyzed by McBrien and Dulles, has made evident the deficiencies of Catholic *Heilsgeschichte* theologians; their ecclesiology appears very weak indeed, particularly in terms of expressing the fullness of the church's mission. In their zeal for proclaiming the "good news," they regarded the church uncritically. Their salvation history hermeneutic also provided a means by which the "new" (since the 1943 *magna carta* for Catholic biblical scholarship, *Divino Afflante Spiritu*) biblical theology legitimated the identification of church and kingdom. Unlike liberal Protestantism, in which the kingdom was heralded by the progressive spiritual and moral development of humankind, Catholicism had continually made evident the profound interrelationship of divine and human. But, as McBrien clearly lays out, it had failed to subordinate *ekklesia* (church) to *basilea* (kingdom), and had thus permitted triumphalism and insufficiently grounded its political and social obligations.[160]

Obviously, this discussion of the ecclesiological implications of *Heilsgeschichte* is rooted in the previous critique of its christology and is, hence, a derivative matter. Nonetheless, the ecclesiological deficiencies vividly illustrate the compatibility of that hermeneutical principle with an uncritical self-understanding of Catholicism. Salvation history had thereby, on the one hand, eased the entrance of renewed biblical studies, but, on the other, hindered the development of a more nuanced and complexified self-understanding to which more trenchant biblical criticism would inevitably lead. By examining the linkage between eschatology and ecclesiology, the dogmatic interests inherent in *Heilsgeschichte* are made transparent.

3. The Significance of the Discussion of Ecclesiology.   One implication of an insufficiently eschatological ecclesiology for religious education is that texts of the salvation history era taught a simplistic understanding of the church. Students consequently were provided with few tools of discernment to aid them in making judgments during the post-Vatican II years of crisis. In fact the crises of that period fill out the context of the demise of *Heilsgeschichte* as a hermeneutical principle in Catholic religious education in the United States, as will be presented in the following section.

Another, perhaps potentially more significant, implication has been generally overlooked. Because of their deficient ecclesiology, Catholic kerygmatics could not provide the basis for a well-grounded development of the constitutive political and social character of the church. Yet recent publications, such as the National Catechetical Directory, *Sharing the Light of Faith,* [161] merely juxtapose kerygmatic and political emphases without paying heed to a certain gap between the two—a lack of analysis strikingly similar to the "conversion" of kerygmatic categories to political categories at the 1968 Medellín Catechetical Study week.[162]

The ecclesiological inadequacies of the Catholic *Heilsgeschichte* theologians were, of course, in large measure a sharing of the distorted ecclesiology which characterized the pre-Vatican II church. But what is of significance from the perspective of this study is that the eschatological emphasis in recent theology has exposed another vulnerability in the kerygmatic position.

At this juncture, it may be helpful to draw together the elements of salvation history which theological developments have made problematic. Intensified analysis of revelation placed under doubt the simple assertion that God has been revealed in history to Israel and in Jesus to the church. Secondly, attention to the literature of the intertestamental period has provided significant refinements in understanding the relationship between OT and NT; consequently, the assumption that the former is but a preparation for the latter could no longer be taken for granted. Expanding apologetic interests, moreover, on the part of Christians vis-à-vis other world religions (particularly vis-à-vis Judaism) engendered christological reconsideration, which in turn made questionable the unnuanced christocentrism of *Heilsgeschichte*. And sustained examination of eschatology has made manifest the relation between the kingdom of God and the church, thus revealing the inadequacy of the kerygmatic equation of the two.

Whatever the disagreements among scholars in each of these areas, the broad consensus is clear: the theological tenets of *Heilsgeschichte* had become inadequate.

However much theological reconsiderations had caused the *Heilsgeschichte* hermeneutic to become problematic, they are in themselves insufficient in accounting for its rapid demise. Indeed, it is difficult to assess precisely what effect the theological critiques had. On the one hand, during the course of the latter 1960s, there appeared a heightened interest in "updating," as evidenced in numerous renewal programs and a spate of master's programs. On the other hand, though Moran's *TR* and *CR* made accessible to many the new theology of revelation, developments in christology and in the relationship of the testaments were not as readily available to religious educators. In general the more traditional formulations of Vatican II predominated in these areas, as they likewise did in ecclesiological issues. Perhaps one might conclude that, to the extent that the theological critiques were accessible to less-specialized religious educators, they would have challenged the kerygmatic stress on salvation history as the primary hermeneutical principle.

Without denigrating the significance of theology, it is nevertheless of critical importance to point out that one must assume a broader horizon in seeking to account for the lessened force of *Heilsgeschichte* in Catholic religious education in the United States in the late sixties. *Hence the following hypothesis is proposed: In the latter 1960s, Catholic religious education assimilated various aspects of certain cultural and educational developments. The resulting pluralism in religious education meant that salvation history lost its force as a motif of singular importance. The kerygma no longer had hegemony.* Such a claim suggests an analysis proceeding in the following sequence: (1) cultural cataclysm; (2) general educational movements; and (3) pluralism in religious education.

II. *A Cultural Perspective*

According to Talmudic legend, the ingenuity and perseverance of Hananiah ben Hezekiah, who enclosed himself in his study with food and three hundred jars of oil until he harmonized the difficulties of the book of Ezekiel, saved that prophetic work from suppression by rabbis unable to reconcile its details on temple restoration with the prescriptions from the Pentateuch.[163] While his dedication remains an inspiration even until the present, such solitary scholarship will not suffice to account for the contradiction and complexities of recent years. The definitive history of the sixties and early seventies is yet to be written; it requires not only considerably more distance than is presently possible, but also a discerning eye for differentiating revolution from rebellion, authenticity from faddism, and true prophecy from false. It calls, furthermore, for that poetic sense of which Ibsen spoke when he wrote that "to be a poet is to preside as judge over oneself,"[164] as well as for an analytic rigor in distinguishing the "sacred paradigm from its copies and secular counterfeits."[165] In short, the task of interpreting the recent past is a Herculean hermeneutic endeavor!

But if no one person can presently sort out the kaleidoscopic visions and dissonant voices of that era, it is nonetheless incumbent upon this writer to sketch in broad outline *one* perspective on it insofar as it is the environment in which critical shifts in both general and religious education occurred. To that end, it may be helpful to view the period in terms of "outer space," "inner space," and "landscape."

A. *"Outer Space"*

The space age brought a hitherto unrealized sense of the universe. The photograph of planet earth from the moon starkly imaged McLuhan's notion of the "global village," while philosopher-scientist Pierre Teilhard de Chardin's vision of the noösphere provided a poetic and spiritual narrative.[166] But the same technology that had enabled the moon landing also offered the possibility of global holocaust, and perhaps for the first time, one realized that the divine command to subdue the earth (Gen. 1:28) was fraught with danger.

B. *"Inner Space"*

Simultaneously there appeared an intense interest in "inner space," resulting in what that chronicler of the counterculture Theodore Roszak has termed the "Age of Therapy." It was an era of "expanded consciousness" ("Consciousness III," in Charles Reich's categories), of apocalyptic imagery, of deep interest in the esoteric and mystical, of an a-historic focus on the "now," and of unparalleled emphasis on "human potential" and "liberation."[167]

C. *"Landscape"*

Meanwhile, "terra firma" was a "landscape of nightmare." Twenty-five thousand civil rights marchers in Selma, Alabama, in 1965 confronted the South with its racism, while rioters in the ghettos of New York, Jersey City, Rochester, and Detroit served notice that the oppression of blacks and the poor was a national and not a regional cancer. But more than any other event, the war in Vietnam manifested the depths of disillusionment and divisiveness that characterized the late sixties. It represented the curse of technology, the disease of a defense economy, the Machiavellian machinations of the politicians, and a grotesque perversion of the "American way." Students revolted in demonstrations at Berkeley, Columbia, Kent State, and campuses across the nation; their antiwar chants which had at first sounded so strident to the majority of the country soon took on the ring of truth. One thinks of C. D. Bryan's *Friendly Fire,* the narrative of the radicalization of an Iowa farm couple, as one of the most powerful testimonies to the pathos and despair brought by the war.[168]

The war heightened the religious unrest that had been simmering since Gabriel Vahanian's 1961 publication, *The Death of God: The Culture of Our Post-Christian Era,* and the ensuing controversy.[169] The advances of mass communications systems had meant that:

> our electronic global nervous system relentlessly transmits the anger, fears, and hopes of every emerging nation and pent up ghetto to the sleepless mind of the radio listener . . . he lies pathetically enmeshed in the network of "constant contact news" and has no hour of the day, no sabbath rest, when he is not made to be a sharer in the abrading or engulfing sensations of other men.[170]

One significant result was that doubt became a spiritual mark of the age, "one of the threads in the ever more complex web binding the individual into his generation," attesting to the "pervasiveness with which the saeculum is present in the individual."[171]

The familiar religious categories no longer held; theologians proclaimed that God was dead while the Beatles extolled themselves as being more popular than Jesus. The Augustinian distinction between the City of God and the City of Man gave way to Cox's *Secular City.* The traditional understanding of respect for authority ("Render to Caesar . . .") and its corollary separation of religion and politics now clashed with civil disobedience in deeds such as the Berrigan brothers' destruction of Selective Service records of May 1968. Resistance and dissent were legitimated by religious ideals—"The times are rude and descend like a guillotine," wrote Jesuit poet Daniel Berrigan—and the "nation with the soul of a church" plunged into a spiritual abyss.[172]

As historian David O'Brien analyzed it:

> The war made a mockery of a Christian identity forged around service to fellow man through American institutions. Indeed, the Viet Nam war and the events accompanying it destroyed for many

the moral authority and credibility of almost every institution that could provide a context for finding meaning, identity and useful work. The government, once the apparent agent of democratic progress, now seems the purveyor of massive oppression, which in the form of the draft immediately impinges on the young. The churches seem so compromised by their respectability or so internally divided that they can provide no locus for meaningful commitment. The university's service to the nation has made it an agent of the government's no longer beneficent purposes. Even social services agencies that work for the poor seem simply to put Band-Aids on the cancers of American Society. Where is one to turn in this situation, to find community, to serve one's fellow men, to worship God with others?[173]

The war in Vietnam precipitated one of the gravest crises ever experienced by this nation. Perhaps Irish poet William Butler Yeats has provided the aptest metaphor: "things fall apart; the center cannot hold;/mere anarchy is loosed upon the world."[174]

III. *An Educational Perspective*

In subsuming major educational movements within the tripartite paradigm established above, one obviously risks the danger of oversimplification. Accordingly, several *caveats* are appropriate: (1) The typology being laid out here is primarily for heuristic purposes, as even the poetic language of "outer space," "inner space," and "landscape" suggests. Hence readers ought to recognize a certain fluidity to the categorization and allow for a continuum of variation within each construct. (2) At present no consensus exists among educators as to a single, overarching construct which would provide a conceptual organization of educational activity. One interpretation of this diversity and confusion is to claim that, given the elusiveness of the human quest for knowledge, such a chaotic state is inevitable. A less kind reading of the situation is that curriculum theory is "moribund."[175] At any rate, the inevitable result is that every typology must be regarded as tentative, as a hypothesis rather than as a statement of reality.

A. *"Outer Space"*

Not unsurprisingly, the educational trends of the sixties mirrored the turbulence and complexity of the era. The "outer space" metaphor suggests that one stream of educational activity reflected an interest in what has been variously termed "instrumental reason" or "technological rationality" or "technocracy"; as a broad category, it encompassed two related but distinguishable approaches to curriculum. The first, which might be called the "production-oriented curriculum," is especially indebted to theorist Ralph Tyler and is manifest in a number of derivative movements such as systems analysis, competency-based teacher education, and behavioral objectives. The second approach, the "structural curriculum," rests on an interest in epistemology through the language of psychology; included within this subdivision would be both those who view curriculum through the disciplines of knowledge and those who view it from the developmental perspectives of genetic epistemologist Jean Piaget. Obviously, the production-oriented curriculum and the structural curriculum reflect rather different emphases. Yet their commonality lies in their grounding in the "technological," that is, in their concern for and application of the scientific method to educational activity.

The production-oriented curriculum had its antecedents in the scientific management theories promulgated by Frederick W. Taylor.[176] Their appeal to a populace engulfed in the post-Civil War chaos and lured by the attractions of industrialization was understandable; in Taylor's view, productivity was the central concern, and the individual was simply an element in the total system. Job satisfaction and physical comfort at the work site could be subordinated to the primary motivational factor: money. Efficiency became a predominant value.

Two educators drew from Taylor's scientific management theories. The first (whose rather memorable name has been popularized in a volume whimsically entitled *The Wonderful World of Ellwood Patterson Cubberly*) rather crassly claimed in 1916: "Our schools are, in a sense, factories in which the raw products (children) are to be shaped and fashioned into products to meet the various demands of life."[177] With about the

same subtlety, J. Franklin Bobbitt extrapolated Taylor's principles into the curriculum, thus inaugurating the "efficiency
movement" in education. Cost accounting and maximum utilization of school plants were priorities in Bobbitt's view; so also
was efficient "handling" of students:

> Work up the raw material into the finished product for which it is
> best adopted. Applied to education this means: Educate the indi-
> vidual according to his capabilities. This requires that the materials
> of the curriculum be sufficiently various to meet the needs of every
> class of individuals in the community; and the course of training
> and study be sufficiently flexible that the individual can be given
> just the things he needs.[178]

An obvious correlate to the principle of educating children
according to their capacities is the "measurement movement,"
associated particularly with the work of Edward L. Thorndike
in psychological testing.[179] Moreover, Bobbitt, in collaboration
with Werrett W. Charters, proposed that curriculum makers
"particularize" their educational objectives; their methodology
called for scientific analysis of human activities from which
were derived specific objectives for the classroom.[180] In so doing, Bobbitt and Charters broadened the scope of the curriculum into the "boundless domain" of human activity; they
are credited with infusing a "dynamic dimension" into curriculum and establishing that endeavor as a professional activity.[181]

By the end of the 1920s, Bobbitt's earlier notions of efficiency
and social control no longer predominated. His concern, however, for "particularizing" objectives, has had a longer lasting
effect, due above all to Ralph Tyler's role in expanding and
developing Bobbitt's scientific view of the curriculum.

Tyler's rationale represents the apotheosis of the production-
oriented curriculum; his immense influence suggests the perduring nature of the production model:

> The power and impact of the Tyler model cannot be overstated.
> Virtually every person who has even been in a teacher education
> program has been introduced to this model. It has become
> synonymous with curriculum work at all levels. Teachers, cur-

riculum committees, and curriculum theorists have perceived the asking and answering of Tyler's four questions as their main task.[182]

The four questions form the central axis of his classic study, *Basic Principles of Curriculum and Instruction*.[183] Tyler first asks about *what educational purposes* the school should seek to attain. Underlying this inquiry is Tyler's contention that the purpose of education is to bring about significant changes in the behavior of students. Thus a statement of objectives for a school should be formulated in terms of changes that will take place in students; the threefold sources of these objectives are learners, contemporary life, and subject matter specialists. Philosophy and psychology are used simply as "screens" through which one judges the consistency of the objectives.

Secondly, Tyler proposes that educators ask *how learning experiences can be selected* that will, in all probability, be useful in attaining the articulated objectives. The logical result of this query is his third: *how can learning experiences be organized* for effective instruction? Here Tyler argues that there are three criteria for effective organization: continuity, sequence, and integration. Moreover, in working out the organizational plan, it is incumbent upon the educator to discover the "organizing thread"; in mathematics, for example, concepts and skills are typical organizing elements. Finally, Tyler poses a fourth question: *how can the effectiveness of learning experiences be evaluated?* At stake here is whether or not the specified objectives have been realized. He suggests a twofold analysis: (1) appraising the behavioral change in the students; and (2) making multiple appraisals (rather than a single evaluation).

Two major theorists, Hilda Taba and John Goodlad, reflect a marked debt to Tyler. Taba, who sought to improve teaching by developing and applying concepts for classroom behavior derived from cognitive development theories, also manifests a linkage to the discipline-centered theorists.[184] By developing specific teaching strategies to match what she identified as three cognitive operations—concept formation, inference, and application of principles—Taba became well known for her challenge to teachers to draw forth the "higher level" thinking abilities of her students, such as problem analysis, prediction, and application of logic. Taba popularized the term "teaching strategy" and is of particular importance because her work represents one of the few attempts in which research on teaching has been utilized in curriculum theory. In addition, she manifests an obvious relationship with both the Tylerian production-oriented approach and with the structural-disciplines approach (to be discussed below).

Likewise significant is John Goodlad, whose influence has been widely disseminated through the Institute for the Development of Educational Activities in Los Angeles and the Center for the Study of Instruction in Washington, D.C. As does his mentor Ralph Tyler, Goodlad views curriculum as a set of intended learnings; he suggests that the fundamental question revolves around the kinds of persons the schools ought to produce. Goodlad, however, is critical of Tyler's "screen" of philosophy and psychology, and maintains that values must be clearly identified before specifying objectives.[185]

The "Tyler rationale," then, has been amplified and refined in the work of Taba and Goodlad. Other logical outgrowths of this rationale include behavioral objectives, systems analysis, and competency-based teacher education and certification. Each of these is related to the other by virtue of its grounding in the behavioral sciences. Behavioral objectives (variously termed "instructional" or "performance" objectives) are the articulation of goals in terms of an observable and measurable change in learner behavior; though their widespread usage in the educational world is relatively recent, they are essentially a refinement of Bobbitt's call to "particularize" and a popular application of Tyler's summons to state objectives in terms of a change in student behavior.[186] One critic charges:

> About all we have done on the question of the role of objectives in curriculum development since Bobbitt's day is, through some verbal flim-flam, convert Bobbitt's "ability to" into what are called behavioral or operational terms and to enshrine the whole process into what is known as the "Tyler rationale."[187]

Systems analysis, an outgrowth of engineering and of the biological and physical sciences, is an educational means of dealing with the overflow of information.[188] Essentially it is a way of processing and managing information, and, while there are many varying models, a typical systems analysis might be charted something like this:

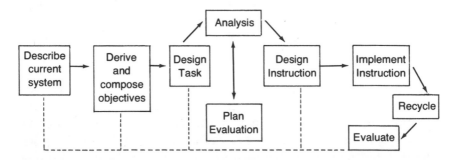

As is evident, the fourfold curricular question of Tyler lies at the base of this.

The competency movement has similar roots; as an approach to curriculum that is systematic, process oriented, and situationally based, it delineates teacher activities in precise, measurable behaviors.[189] As a proposal for teacher education, it is a clear alternative to a previous preparation that specified a certain combination of courses and credits. As a licensing criterion, the competency movement represents the contention that good teachers are those who possess and practice identifiable skills. In many respects, the competency movement in teacher education and certification is a hybrid of behavioral objectives and systems analysis.

While the widespread influence of Tyler can be traced in the work of Taba and Goodlad and in the related movements of behavioral objectives, systems analysis, and teacher competency, it is not possible to locate antecedents of B. F. Skinner's operant conditioning in the Tyler rationale.[190] Clearly Skinner comes out of stimulus-response psychology; yet his emphasis on behavioral change as learning bears relation with the Tyler rationale.

Skinnerian behavior modification, based on the assumption that humans behave according to certain psychological laws and are subject to certain variables, considers behavioral change to result from the change of conditions. Usage of this technique increases efficiency in arranging conditions for learning; the educator's role is to control the learning environment. One of the better known embodiments of Skinner's work is programmed instruction, perhaps the most highly refined application of learning theory in a typical school setting.

Kliebard notes that one reason for the success of the Tylerian paradigm is its rationality:

> In one sense, the Tyler rationale is imperishable. In some form it will always stand as the model of curriculum development for those who conceive of the curriculum as a complex machinery for transforming the crude raw material that children bring with them to school into a finished and useful product. By definition, the production model of curriculum and instruction begins with a blueprint for how the student will turn out once we get through with him.[191]

In the 1960s, however, another understanding of curriculum grew up alongside the Tyler rationale. Much of this came via the scientific community, particularly in the post-Sputnik (1957) years. Prior to that, however, was the work of Jerrold Zacharias and his Physical Science Study Committee (PSSC) during the decade 1955–1965. Sharing in the optimism of those early years when Kennedy's "New Frontier" seemed but a brief journey, Zacharias felt in 1960 that he could work a revolution in the quality of United States education with $100 million per annum for curriculum development. His wry comment five years later that it was easier to put humans on the moon than to reform public schools reflected something of the rapid disintegration of Johnson's hopes for a "Great Society."[192]

Because curriculum endeavor since Bobbitt and Charters had tended to focus on the student's "ability to," little attention had been devoted to the manner in which a student could be trained to grasp the deep structure or significance of complex knowledge. Furthermore, the testing of recruits during World War II had revealed the inadequacies of their science and mathematics backgrounds, a lack made all the more evident by the Soviet space triumph in 1957. As a consequence, thirty-five scholars gathered in Woods Hole (on Cape Cod), Massachusetts, in 1959 to discuss how science education might be improved. The sponsoring agencies which provided funding and assistance in planning included: the National Science Foundation, Air Force, Rand Corporation, U.S. Office of Education, American Association for the Advancement of Science, and Carnegie Corporation—a clear testimony to the technological interests that lay at the heart of the agenda.[193] The major outcome of this conference was the contention that students would learn the substance and method of science by examining its fundamental processes. To learn the structure was to see how things were related; henceforth was promulgated the "disciplines of knowledge" approach to the curriculum.

Harvard psychologist Jerome Bruner collated the results of the meeting in a volume, *The Process of Education,* which provided a "manifesto" for educational reform.[194] Four major themes predominate: (1) the significance of understanding structure as a basis for deeper comprehension and transfer of learning; (2) attention to "readiness for learning" according to the dictum that "any subject can be taught effectively in some intellectually honest form to any child at any stage of development";[195] (3) the necessity for both intuitive and analytic thinking; and (4) motives for learning.

Fundamental to the Woods Hole Conference and to subsequent discussion was the organization of curriculum along the lines of the constructs of the various disciplines. Academicians proposed that secondary and elementary school educators could hold together both content and method by designing curricula in accord with the fundamental principles, concepts, and generalizations of disciplinary knowledge.

The two most refined expositions and development of this approach appeared shortly after Bruner's *Process of Education.* Philip Phenix proposed in his *Realms of Meaning* that knowledge could be organized in six complementary realms: symbolic (ordinary language, mathematics, nondiscursive symbolic forms), empirics (physical science, biology, psychology, social science), esthetics (music, visual arts, arts of movement, literature), synnoetics (personal knowledge), ethics (moral knowledge), and synoptics (history, religion, philosophy).[196] In his erudite integration, Phenix argues that the controlling ideas of education ought to emerge from epistemology; the human way of knowing is the experience of meaning. Thus education is a search for meaning (a means of counteracting skepticism, depersonalization, fragmentation, overabundance, and transience), and curriculum, the analysis of meaning as it emerges from the six distinctive modes of knowing.[197]

Phenix, then, presented a comprehensive schema by which all curricular content could be drawn from the disciplines; a variant on his notion was propounded by Arthur King and John Brownell in *The Curriculum and the Disciplines of Knowledge*.[198]

King and Brownell identify five views of the human person that have been translated into persistent curricular claims. When the claim of the "occupational man" predominates, curricular control and definition inevitably move to the consumers of manpower; on the other hand, when that of the "political man" attains primacy, certain power groups utilize schooling for their own interests. If the "social man" controls curriculum, then schooling becomes reducible to socialization, behavior becomes an organizing "idiom" as an organizing principle for curriculum, and the structures of knowledge are replaced by methods and "educational experiences" which will produce the desired behaviors. In contrast are the claims of the "religious man," which, when in control, offer synoptic disciplines of knowledge for all students and a strong defense of tradition, but which may not make an unconditional commitment to the intellectual realm. Hence King and Brownell assert that the claims of the "intellectual man" should predominate, thereby making the disciplines of knowledge central to the curriculum.

While not drawn directly from the disciplines of knowledge approach, the taxonomies of educational objectives developed by Benjamin Bloom and his associates offer an obvious correlate.[199] As classifications of cognitive, affective, and psychomotor processes, the hierarchical ordering of the three taxonomies reveals an attempt to get at the structure of knowing. Moreover, Bloom as a student of Ralph Tyler, reflects a marked dependence on his mentor in his penchant for objectives framed in behavioral terms. An application of the Bloom *et al.* taxonomy for the cognitive domain is Norris M. Sanders's *Classroom Questions,* which details appropriate questioning strategies for each of the categories (knowledge, comprehension, application, analysis, synthesis, evaluation).[200]

Finally, it is appropriate to mention the work of Swiss genetic epistemologist Jean Piaget under the rubric of "outer space" insofar as he attends to the inner capacity humans bring to the process of knowledge. In looking at how persons interact with, assimilate, and accommodate their environment, Piaget has identified four constant, hierarchical, and sequential stages: sensory motor (up to age two), preoperational (ages two to seven), concrete operations (ages seven to twelve), and formal operations (ages twelve to fifteen).[201]

As with Bruner, Piaget is concerned with readiness for learning. Nonetheless, his developmental stages lead to at least one very basic difference. While Bruner maintained that the intellectual activity of the child and of the adult differed only in degree, Piaget's research indicates that they differ in kind. Because for Piaget the child's maturation process is inextricably linked with his or her intellectual development, educators ought not to regard children as small adults. Indeed, Bruner's thesis that "intellectual activity anywhere is the same" leads Piaget to retort: "I never understood Jerome Bruner and I don't think he ever understood me."[202]

As such remarks indicate, significant differences exist among the educators grouped under the "outer space" metaphor. In addition, a number of the educators discussed in this section have somewhat modified their views in recent years. Consequently, one must acknowledge a fluid relationship among the members categorized herein.

There remains, nevertheless, a fundamental substratum of emphasis on the rational and empirical which distinguishes these educators from colleagues who work out of more romanticist or revisionist notions. Discussion of the educational analogues to "inner space" and to "landscape" will make this evident.

B. *"Inner Space"*

Much of the human potential movement spilled over into educational reforms intensely concerned with the child's experience, feelings, and goals; these contrasted sharply with the academic reformers à la Bruner for whom structure and methodology were primary. Psychologists became the precursors in the trend toward humanizing education. Educators created a "Gestalt" via Perls, Hefferline, and Goodman[203] and sought Abraham Maslow's "self-actualization."[204] William Glasser campaigned for "schools without failure" made possible by his "reality therapy" (to be succeeded a few years later by Thomas Harriss's "transactional analysis").[205] The Lewinian group dynamics and principles of organizational psychology experienced by so many educators in "T-groups" at the Bethel (Maine) National Training Laboratory (NTL) were now amplified by encounter group exercises at the Esalen Institute in Big Sur, California.[206]

Thus it is no coincidence that in the "Age of Therapy" the psychological theories of Carl Rogers assumed paramount importance.[207] Perhaps more than any other single source, Rogers' work became a rationale and a legitimation for "humanizing" the schools. His conception of the counseling relationship as applied to the teaching-learning process became prescriptive for the way many teachers sought to organize and manage their classrooms; it also established the pattern for the mode of their interaction with students. In Rogerian theory, the teacher became the counselor.

The basic assumption underlying Rogers's work is that individuals can handle their own life situations in constructive ways; as a consequence, the counselor ought to facilitate that competence by creating an interpersonal relationship of trust. In terms of the classroom, the Rogerian premise is:

> You can trust the student. You can trust him to desire to learn in every way which will maintain or enhance the self; you can trust him to make use of resources which will serve this end; you can trust him to evaluate himself in ways which will make for self progress; you can trust him to grow providing that atmosphere for growth is available to him.[208]

Thus counselors (teachers) were to assume a "non-directive approach," in which they sought to adopt the clients' frame of reference and to clarify their clients' attitudes. From the perspective of the classroom, this meant that the teachers were to place the students' feelings and problems at the heart of the teaching process while muting their own. In short, teachers were to aim at developing an atmosphere of growth.

Such premises led Rogers to develop some principles and hypotheses in regard to teaching. These constituted the basis of his "student-centered teaching":

> We cannot teach another person directly; we can only facilitate his learning. . . . A person learns significantly only those things he perceives as being involved in the maintenance of, or enhancement of, the structure of self. . . . Experience which, if assimilated, would involve a change in the organization of self tends to be resisted through denial or distortion of symbolization. The structure and organization of self appears to become more rigid under threat; to relax its boundaries when completely free from threat. Experience which is perceived as inconsistent with the self can only be assimilated if the current organization of self is relaxed and expanded to include it.[209]

Rogers concluded that the educational situations which most effectively promoted significant learning were those in which threat to the self of the learner was at a minimum and in which a differentiated perception of the field of experience was facilitated.

Correlatively, an atmosphere of freedom ought to characterize this student-centered teaching. A primary goal was the development of students as individuals:

—who are able to take self-initiated action to be responsible for those actions;

—who are capable of intelligent choice and self-direction;

—who are critical learners, able to evaluate the contributions made by others;

—who have acquired knowledge relevant to the solution of problems;

—who, even more importantly, are able to adapt flexibly and intelligently to new problem situations;

—who have internalized an adaptive mode of approach to problems utilizing all pertinent experience freely and creatively;

—who are able to cooperate effectively with others in these various activities;
—who work, not for the approval of others, but in terms of their own socialized purposes.[210]

Such a philosophy fit quite naturally with another current in humanizing education, that of "open" education. Influenced as well by the English primary schools, reformers across the nation called for the establishment of "alternative schools," of "schools without walls," or at least for "open classrooms."[211] Though there exist comparatively few measurable criteria for determining precisely what constituted an "open classroom," in general these were characterized by (1) a more flexible provisioning of the learning environment (for instance, learning centers rather than desks); (2) more student self-determination in scheduling of learning activities; and (3) a new understanding of the teacher role as "facilitator" or "resource person." Often implicit in "open" education was a judgment on the traditional way of structuring learning as rigid, authoritarian, and incongruent with humanization.

A negative assessment of traditional modes of schooling likewise characterizes other theorists who, despite their differences, nevertheless may be grouped under the umbrella term of "neo-romantics." Best known is the work of Sidney Simon and his colleagues on "values education," and the acerbic criticism of John Holt, Paul Goodman, and Edgar Friedenberg.[212] Of lesser impact, yet representative of one point of view among these neo-romantics, is the writing of George B. Leonard, former vice-president of the Esalen Institute.[213]

Critical of the competitive, consumerist society, Leonard charges that its way of life elicits a "high shallow breathing," which in turn "serves to reduce the flow of feeling and thus perpetuate this way of living."[214] Echoing the themes of "Consciousness III," Leonard claims that moderns, in the terminology of Willis Harman, are in the midst of a "New Copernican Revolution," which "by no means excludes objective observation and replicable verification, only their tyranny."[215] Accordingly, dichotomies will be overcome: "To view the universe anew is to change in feeling and being. Just as there is no mind without body, no spirit without matter, there is no cognition without affect, no observation without personal change, no unmoved mover."[216] The key term in this changed perspective is "awareness"; in fact, "Awareness more than any other single thing *is* the Transformation."[217] Education, therefore, must break out of tired modes and awaken people to the beauty of their feelings so that repression will end and "all of life will become erotic and what is erotic will become commonplace."[218]

Leonard recognizes that this quest for a new education shares a common basis with the quest for new organizational modes, new living patterns, new religions, and new consciousness; and that all are rooted in deeper transforming forces at work in the entire culture. His resistance to Cartesian dualities and sense of changed perspective is echoed by proponents of "confluent education," who seek to modify instructional practice with Gestalt therapy.

Leadership in this confluent education movement likewise has a linkage to Esalen; in joint sponsorship with the Ford Foundation, the Institute provided the setting for initial explorations in 1967 led by George Brown.[219] Key to "confluent" education is the coming together or "confluence" of the cognitive and affective domains of learning and of intrapersonal, interpersonal, and impersonal processes. As might be suspected, its *leitmotif* is "integration"; specifically, the basic premise holds: "emotional life can be integrated with intellectual life . . . when this happens, learning happens more quickly, involves the whole child and is significant."[220] As such an assertion unfolds, its linkage with Gestalt therapy is readily apparent.

Confluent education shares four foundational values with Gestalt: (1) *holism,* that is, "the relationship between intellect and affect is indestructively symbiotic";[221] (2) *responsibility,* the emphasis devoted to the individual's accountability for psychological growth: (3) *homeostasis,* which involves the recognition, expression, and satisfaction of needs so that persons can maintain health and balance even amidst change; and (4) *contact and contact boundary,* that is, the passage through one's own "ego boundary" through awareness of one's projections and the ability to differentiate between self and others.

Given these values, the objectives of confluent education are obviously derivative. Mark Phillips identifies six goals: the development of persons who are whole, integrated, responsible, aware, nonmanipulative, and able to focus attention on the "here and now."[222] These goals, in turn, comprise the basis of teacher education and curriculum. The various confluent education programs focus particularly on the development of *awareness* in its graduates; teachers are helped to come to a sense of personal responsibility (a sense of "existential mastery"): "a greater focus on the immediate and present... a realistic awareness of abilities and limitations, and an overriding sense of control, ... which is freely responsive to a changing environment." Somewhat more specifically, desirable teacher skills include the ability to differentiate between one's own needs and concerns and those of the student; to diagnose what is happening with a student at a given moment (the "Now"); to utilize correct "ego language" reflective of personal, direct and responsible communication; and to create an accepting environment in the classroom for the expression of feelings.[223]

If teacher preparation in confluent education focuses on teacher personality and teacher skills, then the written curriculum utilizes those skills through application of Gestalt learning experiences in both traditional and nontraditional content, as well as in personal growth goals. Brown reports, for instance, a teacher leading a projective fantasy so as to increase the "personal relevance" of *Lord of the Flies:* students imagined themselves to be animals in a forest encountering individuals for whom they had high regard or antipathy.[224]

Confluent education, like Rogerian educational theory, represents the wedding of psychology with educational practice; its differences from the Rogerian client-centered approach lie primarily in its appropriation of Gestalt techniques. Differences in psychological theory notwithstanding, certain "code words" appear with consistency among proponents of this "inner space" paradigm: freedom, self-directedness, becoming, trust, wholeness. Many phrases spawned in this broad movement remain in current colloquial usage: being "in touch" with oneself, knowing where a person is "at" or "coming from," "getting it together," and living in the "here and now."

The rhetoric of the humanistic educators exists side by side with the outcries of the "back to the basics" advocates of the mid-1970s. To use a phrase dear to Gestaltists, the categories of outer space and inner space "interface." And into this cohabitation of technological and humanist enters a third category: the "landscape" of the educational "revisionists."

C. *"Landscape"*

"Revisionism" is not a univocal term and its multiple variants mean that any definition necessarily must remain loose. *In the context of this study, educational revisionism is construed as that sharing in the disillusionment of the sixties manifested particularly in an attentiveness to the "worldly" or political dimension of education.* One might view it in terms of a critique of both the technological and neo-romantic trends; as such, it is grounded primarily not in the empirical sciences nor in humanistic psychology, but in sociology and philosophy.

To date, revisionism is more manifest in its negative assessment of education than in any programmatic directives. The preponderance of criticism over program makes classification difficult, but it may be helpful to sort out two rather distinct emphases within this category.

The first group is linked by the common contention that schools reproduce and legitimize the social inequality of society. Just as the neo-romantics looked at reality through the perspective of Rousseau's sense of the innate goodness of human nature, these revisionists tend to view reality through the lens of class conflict.[225] Hence their judgments are generally rooted in traditional Marxist class analysis.

The second revisionist perspective differs from the first primarily (though not exclusively) in its usage of the critical theory associated particularly with the so-called Frankfurt School.[226] Critical theorists, of whom Max Horkheimer is the "father" and Jürgen Habermas the most notable contemporary figure, are fundamentally antimetaphysical and antipositivistic; thus, their concerns center around unmasking ideologies for the sake of the development of emancipative *praxis*. Educational revisionists grounded in critical theory seek to lay bare the structures of human relationships not simply by analysis of the social controls and political activities of education, but also by attending to the basic philosophical questions hidden by more recent emphases on learning theory and developmental psychology. This second group of revisionists might appropriately be termed "reconceptualists," as a way of differentiating them from the former group.

The contours of the two revisionist postures become clearer when attention is focused upon their respective theorists. Though, on the whole, the visibility of revisionist works has been relatively low (not surprising in light of their questioning of long-accepted and nearly sacred assumptions), one rather notable exception has given prominence to aspects of the first viewpoint: Ivan Illich.

The controversial Illich has long been a gadfly to the Western establishment in the Catholic church, in education and, more recently, in medicine. His 1970 tract, *Deschooling Society,* sharply condemned the schools as vehicles of social control, and proposed the radical alternative of ridding society of its schools and the accompanying myth of equal educational opportunity.[227] Illich and his colleague Everett Reimer at the Center for Inter-Cultural Documentation (CIDOC) in Cuernavaca, Mexico, argued that schools reinforced the position of the upper class, rigidified class structure, and reduced the expansiveness of educational experience to the narrowness of the classroom. In their perspective, it was the poor who, by believing that social and economic conditions might be changed through education, suffered most extensively from the mythology of schooling.

Schooling, in the Illich-Reimer view, has exercised a virtual monopoly on education and conveyed the message that those with more schooling are therefore better people. Critics who desire only to reform the school system are trapped by their own inability to imagine education without schooling. As Illich puts it:

> Once the child becomes viscerally aware that he has been socially conceived in the school-womb, he demands to suck at the breasts of

mother school forever. He perceives the unity of mankind as the result of common gestation by Alma Mater. He can no longer imagine a society without one organ, one institution, which monopolizes the social reproduction called education.[228]

That the school system presently exists as strongly as ever in the United States is ample testimony that the strident outcry of Illich and Reimer was not fully heeded. Nonetheless, their critique was heard sympathetically by a number of educational reformers, among them a disciple of Illich and a self-declared anarchist, Joel Spring.

Spring's position is most starkly stated in the introduction to a volume jointly authored with Clarence Karier and Paul Violas. They lay out their starting point:

> If one starts with the assumption that this society is in fact racist, fundamentally materialistic, and institutionally structured to protect vested interests, the past takes on vastly different meanings. The authors of these essays write from such a conception of the present, which shapes their own view of the past. Given these assumptions, new material long ago passed over as unimportant takes on significance as indeed older data requires fresh interpretation.[229]

Their conclusions are consistent with their point of departure. Karier contends that twentieth century schools in the United States are instruments of the economic and political elites who manage the American corporate state;[230] that the liberal faith in science and technology has led to social control;[231] and that the testing movement, financed by corporations, has played a key role in fashioning a peculiar American meritocracy.[232] Educational historian Violas accuses Jane Addams of being the principal architect of a new liberalism that "moved the nation toward the acceptance of a compulsory corporate state in which the individual would be simply a part of the greater collective unity."[233] Spring extends Illich's call for deschooling; he argues that the quest for social control has turned the school into a "custodial institution to maintain the social order," and thus that the school is but an "inexpensive form of police."[234]

The work of Spring and his colleagues has been roundly attacked in a work by Diane Ravitch that takes issue with the revisionist stance.[235] Ravitch's book is particularly useful here in that it draws together the principal revisionist works and thereby provides an overview of their basic line of argumentation. Her critique, however, though insightful and at times devastatingly perceptive, is flawed by her own inability to grapple with the conditions of inequality that do indeed plague American education.[236] Nevertheless, Ratvitch's work is extremely useful in filling in the outline of the revisionist position.

In addition to the aforementioned Spring, Violas, and Karier, Ravitch places in the revisionist camp Michael Katz, Colin Greer, Walter Feinberg, Samuel Bowles, and Herbert Gintis.[237] Despite substantial differences in their various perspectives, Ravitch locates the common thread of their thought in their shared opinion that "American schools have been an *intentional, purposeful* failure and an integral part of the larger failure of American society."[238] They have, furthermore, assigned the responsibility for this failure to liberals, progressives, and reformers.

In sharpening her definition of revisionism, Ravitch utilizes a distinction by Marvin Lazerson between liberal and radical historians of education that is also illuminating here. As Lazerson sees it, liberals describe educational failures as the result of errors or as good intentions gone awry, whereas radicals are convinced:

> that our educational failures are neither accidental nor mindless, but endemic, built into the system as part of its raison d'être. For these historians, schools in America have acted to retain the class structure by molding the less favored to the dominant social order. They are designed to repress blacks and other non-white minorities while enhancing the growth of a professional establishment. These aims, the radical critics and historians believe, have been achieved through the construction of elaborate administrative bureaucracies impervious to reform by parents and students, by the development of ostensibly scientific criteria for selecting out a meritocracy, and by creating an ideology of equality of opportunity that masks the public school's real functions.[239]

In agreement with Lazerson, Ravitch next proceeds to identify three analytical devices frequently employed by the revisionist historians. She first notes a social and economic determinism, in which "conclusions about people, events, and institutions are attributed to the assumed imperatives of social class."[240] Ravitch, while not rejecting connections between education and social class, herself finds the revisionist usage insufficiently nuanced. Secondly, she sees at the base of revisionist analysis a one-to-one correspondence between the ultimate effect of a policy and the intentions of its creators—a type of "sociological functionalism, in which inferences are loosely made about people's motives or about the hidden purposes of school or society."[241] Thirdly, the revisionists tend to work from the notion that the structure of an institution determines its purpose; such an analytical device suffers, in Ravitch's opinion, from an oversimplified perspective on the public's response to schooling.[242]

Ravitch also suggests the major motifs of revisionist thought. One is the contention that public schools are instruments of "coercive assimilation, designed to strip minority children of their culture and to mold them to serve the needs of capitalism."[243] Another is the assertion that the schools have not, contrary to the popular myth, fostered social and economic mobility.[244] A third is that the inequality of opportunity resulting from the exclusion of certain groups is a "systematic, structural defect in American society," which the schools either are partially responsible for or are powerless to change.[245]

Ravitch's work not only brings together the difficult questions about class, race, and the educational bureaucracy on the revisionist agenda, but especially manifests their proclivity to "write a deterministic history in which elites and vast historic forces always pipe the tune."[246]

In contrast, a rather different revisionist perspective is offered by Brazilian educator Paulo Freire.[247] Though his critique of the Western establishment has been as sharp as Illich's and as preoccupied with inequality as the revisionist historians, Freire has been more widely received. One may speculate that his popularity may be due to a certain selective reading; his conviction that education must be "dialogical" in nature has an obvious correlation with Rogerian language, and thereby might lull indiscriminating readers into subsuming him into humanist/romanticist categories, and thus of effectively absorbing his criticism and of ultimately desiccating it. To the contrary, Freire questions the origins of a system in which certain groups possess language about the world which they in turn impose upon others. His illuminating metaphor of "banking education" (education as an act of depositing, in which students are depositories and teachers depositors) and his summons to engage in "problem-posing education for critical consciousness" provide challenges by which educators can assume a critical political stance vis-à-vis the status quo:

> Banking education (for obvious reasons) attempts, by mythicizing reality, to conceal certain facts which explain the way men exist in the world; problem-posing education sets itself the task of demythologizing. Banking education resists dialogue; problem-posing education regards dialogue as indispensable to the act of cognition which unveils reality. Banking education inhibits creativity and domesticates (although it cannot completely destroy) the *intentionality* of consciousness by isolating consciousness from the world, thereby denying men their ontological and historical vocation of becoming more fully human. Problem-posing education bases itself on creativity and stimulates true reflection and action upon reality, thereby responding to the vocation of men as beings who are authentic only when engaged in inquiry and creative transformation. In sum: banking theory and practice, as immobilizing and fixating forces, fail to acknowledge men as historical beings; problem-posing theory and practice take man's historicity as their starting point.[248]

Freire, it may be noted, differs from the first group of revisionists by virtue of his efforts to create alternative means of education. He is most justly famous for his program in which illiterate peasants are engaged in an educational process of naming the world, and thereby learning to read. Freire perhaps may be seen as a transition figure between revisionists and reconceptualists insofar as his concerns are directed toward an emancipative *praxis.*

In examining the reconceptualist position, one finds few

clearly delineated standpoints; as James Macdonald has commented regarding his own attempts to classify, "the curriculum field may be likened to all growing persons, eventually the shoes or the categories pinch."[249] Certainly this is the case with the reconceptualists, who, though sympathetic to much of the revisionist critique, are nevertheless obviously preoccupied with different aspects of the same general concerns. Reconceptualist questions tend to revolve around certain fundamental issues such as language, liberation, power and work, knowledge and human interest, theory and practice. William Pinar, editor of two collections of reconceptualist thought, claims that they represent somewhere from three to five percent of curricular theorists and that the function of their work appears to lie in understanding rather than in offering any guide for practitioners. Reconceptualists, as Pinar has named them,

> tend to concern themselves with the internal existential experience of the public world. They tend to study not "change in behavior" or "decision-making in the classroom," but matters of temporality, transcendence, consciousness, and politics. In brief, the reconceptualist attempts to understand the nature of educational experience.[250]

Pinar's volumes contain a rather broad spectrum of reconceptualist views, from John Steven Mann ("The only way a teacher can work against exploitation and oppression is to attack the root cause of it, which is capitalism,")[251] to Philip Phenix ("The thinker I find most congenial in the effort to gain a comprehensive and integral outlook on life is A. N. Whitehead, whose union of the mathematical and scientific outlook is a model of the human quest for wholeness and humaneness.")[252] These substantial variations notwithstanding, the reconceptualist perspective seems most fully articulated by James Macdonald and Dwayne Huebner.

Macdonald has drawn well the distinction between the revisionist and reconceptualist views. He contends that the most satisfying analysis of curriculum is Marxist in orientation. Out of this context, the radical (revisionist) curriculum thinker might ask questions such as "How are the patterns of human relationships found in the broader society revealed in schools?"

"Why is there unequal opportunity to learn in the schools, at least in terms of race and social class?" "Do schools provide for unequal access to knowledge by the way they operate?"[253]

But, Macdonald continues, his problem with the radical view of curriculum is not in its level of analysis or in the questions it asks. Rather, Macdonald's sense is that revisionist questions are one step behind the world. The radicals leave him, as McLuhan once said, with the feeling of traveling down a superhighway at faster and faster speeds looking out the rearview mirror.[254] Macdonald finds their materialistic focus to be limiting, because it is essentially a reading of the nineteenth century rather than of the contemporary world. He concludes that the radical-political perspective is a hierarchical-historical view that has outlived its usefulness: it has neither allowed adequately for the tacit dimension of culture nor been sufficiently aware of the realities of technology.

Another Macdonald essay makes plain the reconceptualist usage of critical theory.[255] Drawing upon Habermas's thesis that all knowledge is grounded in human interest, Macdonald establishes two propositions. The first is that the basic phenomenon undergirding curriculum theory and design is the existence of human interest. The second proposition follows: the three basic cognitive interests identified by Habermas (control, consensus, and emancipation) provide the basic sources of value differences in curriculum. The technical interest in control underlying the empirical-analytical approach is manifest in the production-oriented curriculum of Bobbitt, Tyler, and Goodlad. The practical interest in consensus underlying the hermeneutical-historical approach is found in theorists such as Maxine Greene or Joseph Schwab.[256] The critical interest in emancipation underlying the self-reflective approach undergirds the work of Paulo Freire and the reconceptualist view.

While Macdonald uses Habermas primarily to illumine the differing interests underlying curriculum theory, Dwayne Huebner draws upon critical theory to call in question educational usage of the language of socialization and of learning. A critical-theorist perspective on socialization unmasks it as a term coming from a "dominating relationship between the adult and the child, perhaps an oppressive one, clearly one of the power-

ful over the powerless."[257] The language of socialization hides
the domination of one group (children and young people) by
another group (adults); Huebner instead calls for the "mutuality of power," which is not a power *over* individuals but a power
for the making of the common world. Similarly, the language of
the psychology of learning is reductionistic, because its focus on
behavioral change is grounded in a form of controlling
power.[258] Learning theory, as it is typically understood, is directed toward explaining how patterning and conditioning occur; it tends to focus upon abstraction and generalization, thus
pulling human beings out of their collective environments and
freezing them at a stage in their own biographical evolution.[259]
In contrast, education should be talked about as the "concern
for the evolving biography of the person and the evolving history of societies or communities."[260]

The dual concern for the individual and for the community
is a leitmotif of Huebner's work. This theme is particularly
evident in his rejoinder to Tyler's fourfold curricular question.
In his concern to direct attention to the historical dialectics of
curriculum so that the relationships among objects, ideas, and
ideals might be more readily seen, Huebner proposes an alternative fourfold question: (1) What educative content (2) can be
made present (3) to what educatees (4) within what social-
political arrangement to govern and adjudicate the distribution
of power between educator and educatee?[261]

Each aspect of this question needs to be unfolded. The
"educative content" refers to the "stock of knowledge" as embodied in goods and services; another way of talking about this
is to speak of the conservation of the past in traditions,
memories, and artifacts. Huebner's choice of "to make present"
reveals his attention to what he has termed the "thingness" of
educational content, that is, the materiality or objective nature
of content. Such a verb emphasizes that the educator's task is to
construct an environment that embodies the content (as a sign
in a fabric store puts it, to "materialize your ideas"). The question about what content should be made present "to what
educatees" reflects Huebner's intention to negate the language
of learning; of special concern to him is the way language about
the "slow learner" or the "unmotivated learner" hides the in-

adequacies of educational materials and educator skills. Finally, the question about social-political governance reflects Huebner's attempt to raise the so-called "hidden curriculum" to the surface and to provide a forum for making explicit the political structures that guide, legitimate, and adjudicate the educator's diverse uses of power.[262]

As a reconceptualist Huebner is preoccupied with developing alternative ways of talking about education and, in particular, with calling attention to the political dimension of curriculum. His concerns are with an accurate naming of educational activity and with asking questions about how content is selected, made accessible, distributed, and controlled; how educational goods and services are to be reformed and developed; and how to empower people to reclaim their past and project their future.

Freire, Macdonald, and Huebner all share a reverence for the transcendental ground of education. The dialogue which Freire regards as the basis of problem-posing education "cannot exist . . . in the absence of a profound love for the world and for men."[263] Macdonald makes explicit two fundamental value questions which he thinks should underlie curriculum talk and work: what is the meaning of human life and how shall we live together?[264] Huebner speaks of education as a pilgrimage: the story of where human beings have been, the projection of where they are going, the memories to nourish their journey, and the tools and symbols necessary to keep moving. In his perspective, to teach is to be a "guardian and servant of language";[265] to educate is to assume, tacitly, a religious ground:

> Education is, for me, care for the finite transcendence of men, for the forms life takes between birth and death, for the emerging biography of others. . . . The man who would educate another, using finite norms, i.e. already established ways of being, can, without a second thought, control the formation of another's life; he can unreflectively and uncritically accept his own ways of being in and about the world.[266]

The reconceptualists are first and foremost critics. They question what they regard as the positivism of technological rationality as well as the individualism and utopianism of neo-romantic approaches to curriculum. Revisionism is seen as incomplete and too simplistic; as C. A. Bowers has written, "the revisionist educators promised the millennium through subordinating science and technology to the centralized control of the dictatorship of the proletariat." [267] Yet the reconceptualists also exercise a positive function in their attempt to rethink curricular theory insofar as their attempt to unmask ideologies and to lay bare structures establishes a foundation for new work.

Having surveyed the landscape of revisionism, this educational typology may be regarded as complete. In summary form, it can be diagrammed as follows:

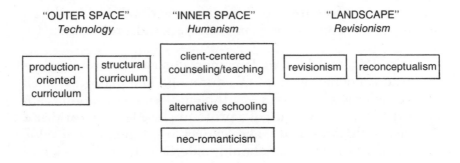

Again, it needs to be emphasized that these categories are not absolute; there is great fluidity and overlap. Nonetheless, the outer/inner/landscape schema, which has its educational analogues in technologism, humanism, and revisionism, established a partial but fundamental context out of which a pluralism in United States Catholic religious education emerged in the late sixties. In fact, these same categories may be employed in identifying the streams of that pluralism.

IV. A Perspective on Religious Education

Previous to the mid-sixties, post-Reformation Catholic religious education was characterized by an amazing homogeneity, particularly when one considers the vast cultural and social variations within Catholicism. The transition to a literate culture made possible by the printing press meant that the largely oral handing on of religious traditions became linked with the printed word. One implication of this is that both Protestantism and Catholicism moved from "catechesis" to "catechism," as witnessed in the catechisms of Luther (1529), Canisius (1555), Bellarmine (1598), and the Council of Trent (1566).

In nineteenth century Catholicism, this phenomenon was evident in the demand for a universal catechism which would insure uniformity in articulation of the tradition. A lesser known outcome of Vatican I was its legislation in January of 1870 mandating this catechism; the mandate, the *Schema Constitutionis de parvo catechismo,* was never set in motion.[268]

But in the United States, the Third Plenary Council of Baltimore responded to this mandate as well as to the 1829 proposal of the Provincial Council of Baltimore for a national catechism, by issuing in April 1885, its own composition, *A Catechism of Christian Doctrine, Prepared and Enjoined by the Third Plenary Council of Baltimore,* widely known as the "Baltimore Catechism," revised in 1941 and still in print.[269] From the earliest days following its publication, there were some rather strongly worded criticisms of this catechism, and there were also extant a considerable number of alternative catechisms; yet the literary genre "catechism" with its question and answer format held a virtual monopoly on religious education. Moreover, the Baltimore Catechism, composed during the waning of the nineteenth century, provided a natural channel for the promulgation of the decrees of Vatican I and was obviously compatible with the mentality of that unfortunate era.

The power of the kerygmatic renewal is further evidenced in the suddenness and completeness with which its approaches substituted for the catechism. As narrated in the preceding chapter, it replaced the monopoly of the catechism in the early sixties with a monopoly of its own.[270] But from about 1965 until the present, the scene in the United States reflects a diversity of approaches. That heterogeneity is best explained in terms of the categories employed in the previous sections on culture and education.

A. *"Outer Space"*

The kerygmatics and their *Heilsgeschichte* hermeneutic came under criticism from James Michael Lee, whose social science approach to religious instruction is a correlate of the "technological" trends in general education.[271] In seeking to establish an overarching theory, Lee has sought to develop a comprehensive and systematic foundation for religious education in a trilogy delineating a social science approach.

The focus of each work in the trilogy reveals the major structures of Lee's architectonic system. *The Shape of Religious Instruction* (1971) establishes his basic rationale of religious education and religious instruction as a social science. A second volume, *The Flow of Religious Instruction* (1973), centers on teaching (instructional practice), and thereby establishes what Lee regards as the "structural content" of religious instruction. *The Content of Religious Instruction* (in preparation) completes the trilogy by delineating and developing eight major categories of "substantive content": product content, process content, cognitive content, affective content, verbal content, nonverbal content, unconscious content, and lifestyle content.[272]

Looked at from the vantage point of the trilogy, the content of religious instruction is precisely the religious instruction act itself. Its two dimensions—structural content (instructional practice) and substantive content (religion [not theology])—are distinct yet interrelated.

The fusion of structural content and substantive content in the religious instruction act is the fundamental motif of the Lee corpus and will provide a paradigm from which to assume a panoramic view of his stance vis-à-vis the kerygmatics. But before surveying the landscape of his vision on this matter, it is first appropriate to trace the individual elements.

The trilogy had been preceded by a 1970 essay presenting an extensive articulation of Lee's thesis that the teaching of religion is grounded in the social sciences rather than in theology. In this Lee argued that the "transmission theory" of the kerygmatics, based as it was on a preaching model rather than on a teaching model, was inadequate for five reasons: (1) it posited a univocity of learning; (2) it assumed a materialistic view of the person in that it assumed knowledge, attitudes, and values could be transfused from one to another as blood was; (3) it took the learner out of the center of the teaching-learning process and replaced him or her with the teaching; (4) it confined teaching within overly narrow parameters (verbal, conceptual, and product); and (5) it unduly restricted the freedom of the learner to explore and to experience, since the teacher rather than the student became both the *terminus a quo* and the *terminus ad quem*.[273]

In sum, Lee maintained that the transmission theory of the kerygmatics imaged the classroom as a broadcast studio: the teacher-transmitter directed a message to the student-recipient. In sharp contrast was Lee's description: the classroom as a learning laboratory in which students "act, interact, and react toward the development of personalized and meaningful learning outcomes."[274] At the basis of this was his own structuring theory which, unlike the transmission theory, encompassed affective, cognitive, and lifestyle domains. Moreover, the transmission theory was experiential, student-centered, and process-oriented.

Concerned by the dominant, "imperialistic" role of theology, Lee's fundamental contention since 1967 has been that social science is more properly the domain of religious instruction. Indeed, he "radicates" catechetics in the teaching-learning process: religious instruction as approached via the social sciences is a "conscious and deliberative facilitation of specified behavioral goals."[275] The religion teacher, therefore, is fundamentally a "professional specialist in the modification of student behavior as it affects his religious life."[276] This demands a "technical competence or process expertness," and exacts a sensitivity to the "laws of learning."[277] Note the application of the "Tyler rationale" in the following assertion:

> Teaching religion, then, must be radicated in concrete specific behavioral goals in terms of the students' lives. To structure the learning situation means nothing more than to carefully and systematically architect the lesson and, indeed, the entire course to insure that specific behavioral outcomes are achieved. To do this effectively is not to erect—as has been done ad nauseam—general statements of aims or goals of the religion class, but *to delineate with some measure of precision just what particularized behavioral outcomes are to be worked for* (emphasis added).[278]

Lee lays out his basic principles in *The Shape of Religious Instruction*. Though they are too rich in detail to be recounted extensively herein, his work has been summarized elsewhere.[279]

Nonetheless, it is especially important to note the manner in which his rather thorough critique of the kerygmatics is part and parcel of the total nexus of his argument. Thus, in focusing on a particular aspect of his thought—his view of the kerygmatic school—one glimpses accurately the overall structure of Lee's premises.

It is possible to subsume Lee's perspective on the kerygmatics under three topics: (1) the focus of religious instruction; (2) religious instruction as social science; and (3) approaches to teaching. In regard to the first topic, Lee identifies six "focal points" of religious instruction: Christian living, experience, "nowness," socialization, kerygma, and person.[280] Of obvious pertinence in this study is his appropriation of kerygma, which he identifies as the initial phase of a three-stage teaching cycle: after the *kerygma* (proclamation of the glad tidings of salvation) followed *catechesis* (oral instruction for neophytes) and, ultimately, *didascalia* (more extensive instruction). All stages encompass behavioral ramifications, and do not merely indicate intellectual assent.

Lee distinguishes three complementary usages of kerygma: the *product content* of religious instruction (the gospel); the *process content* of religious instruction (the formative dimension of becoming Christlike); and the act of *proclamation itself* (teaching).[281] The distinction between product and process is of particular importance, since it functions prominently in Lee's total argument that authentic religious instruction necessarily focuses as much on the dynamic of educational practice (process content) as on the more tangible subject matter (product content).[282] The emphasis is underscored by his insistence that process content is one of the eight modes of substantive content.

The significance of the distinctions lies in Lee's contention that kerygma represents a pedagogical *approach* rather than a particular teaching method; kerygma is personalistic, christocentric, joyous, zestful, and existential. Thus, precisely as approach, as process, it permeates the three stages of the cycle; Lee even speaks of the "kerygmatic approach to life."[283] He summarizes:

> The kerygma is basically a process, the process of Christification, of the flowing of Jesus into the teaching act and into the lives of both

learner and teacher in a continuing ongoing revelation which is educative and salvific. Kerygma is, above all, a process approach to, and a process outcome of, the enterprise of religious instruction.[284]

Lee has thereby incorporated the salvation history school's kerygmatic emphasis into his own schema, albeit in a manner reflective of interest in the technological. His understanding of religious instruction as a social science clarifies further both his overall stance and his view of the *Heilsgeschichte* adherents.

Jungmann and Hofinger had, in Lee's understanding, appropriated kerygma from a theological approach rather than from a social science perspective.[285] Consequently, they tended to make claims based on *a priori* assumptions; in contrast, religion teachers working in the mode of the social sciences would have been concerned with gathering data to verify their hypotheses. This was, in fact, what Jesus had done; Lee asserts that Jesus made frequent use of "empirical verifiers to confirm the truth and validity of his teachings for those to whom he was giving religious instruction."[286] Lee cites Mark 2:1-12 (healing of the paralytic at Capernaum) as an example.

At the core of such an argument is Lee's contention that religion teachers need hard empirical data and empirically derived laws, so as to be able to predict the variables that will most effectively achieve the learning of desired outcomes under given conditions—a procedure proper to social science and not to theological science.[287]

This argument is continued and extended in a chapter of *The Flow of Religious Instruction* entitled "Theoretical Approaches to the Teaching of Religion"; here Lee has laid out the strengths and weaknesses of seven theories, contrasting each in turn with his own "teaching" theory.[288] That latter, he claimed, included all of the various strengths, but was most complete in that it provided for effective modification of the religious behavior of learners as it happened in the explanation and prediction of variables. On the other hand, the kerygmatic approach might be described under the rubric of both the "witness" theory (the religion teacher as a witness to the Christian message through words, deeds, and lifestyle) and especially under the category of the 'proclamation" theory, wherein the teacher proclaimed to the students the Good News of salvation. The witness theory had the advantage of highlighting the importance of modeling behavior, but it led to a devaluation of the teaching-learning process by implying that holiness was the supreme criterion for the religion teacher rather than skill. Proclamation theorists, including Jungmann, Hofinger, Goldbrunner, and van Caster, had their strong points, conceded Lee. They had usually devised well-thought-out product and cognitive objectives to be acquired by the learner, and also advocated a highly structured instructional process with a minimum of vagueness. In addition, their pedagogical practice (the lecture and its derivatives) formed the easiest and simplest pedagogical technique for the religion teacher to use.

Despite these advantages, Lee argued forcefully that the proclamation theory was inadequate as a "macrotheory" upon which to build an entire religious instruction practice. It was not multidimensional, since it focused only on teacher behavior and subject content, while ignoring learner behavior and environmental variables. Furthermore, it ignored and negated the "wide variety of available and empirically demonstrated effective teacher behaviors, confining teacher activity to deployment of the transmission strategy and the lecture technique."[289] Its major weakness was its stipulation for the inactivity of the learner during the lesson, which conflicted with the data Lee had amassed to attest to the desirability of experiential student involvement in as many phases of the learning situation as possible. Lee hypothesized three reasons for the kerygmatic stress on teacher control and student passivity. First, proclamation theorists emphasized the religion teacher's absolute fidelity to the message. Secondly, they accentuated the religious, intellectual, and social authority of the teacher; and thirdly, they concentrated on technological content rather than on the dynamics of the teaching-learning process. As a consequence, their theory was rooted in a cognitive rather than in a lifestyle orientation.

Of particular note is Lee's assertion that the kerygmatic theory made an "inappropriate if not an incorrect use of scripture as its foundation." Citing the statement of the participants of the Eichstätt congress that "catechesis follows God's method of proclaiming the Glad Tidings of salvation," he challenged:

But it is a commonly accepted hermeneutical principle that the Bible is not a textbook for natural science or for engineering or for instructional practice. Hence to indicate that Jesus or one of the Old Testament prophets used such and such an instructional practice does not mean that this practice has the force of revelation, or even the force of optimum pedagogy. Even if the instructional practices used by Jesus were optimum pedagogy, still the arguments of the proclamation theorists on behalf of the lecture or other heralding techniques are very weak. As I note at length elsewhere, the instructional practices of Jesus as narrated in the New Testament unmistakably indicate that Jesus made use of the structured learning situation strategy as a matter of course. Jesus did not frequently lecture except when circumstances forced him to, such as when addressing a very large crowd. In such cases Jesus often used the parable, which is a verbal representation of a structured learning situation. Whenever possible, Jesus placed what learning and proclaiming he did within the context of a structured learning situation, for example, the Last Supper (John 13:17).[290]

Other religious educators, most notably Gerard Sloyan, had also criticized the kerygmatic appropriation of Scripture. Nonetheless, there is a uniqueness in Lee's critique: in his view the kerygmatics had failed to utilize the implicitly social science-based pedagogy of Jesus. Contemporary biblical scholarship, looking at the redactional level of gospel composition, would not support Lee's point here; nevertheless, his fundamental contention—that the early Christian teaching was embodied in a rich context—would hold even when more sophisticated methodology is used in Scripture study.[291]

At this point it may be helpful to review Lee's line of argumentation against the kerygmatics by situating it in terms of his distinction between structural content and substantive content.

As structural content, the kerygmatic method exemplified simply a variant on a theological approach, which itself suffers from the limitations of being unable to generate, explain, or verify modes of instructional practice as can the social science approach. Because the kerygmatics could neither generate nor explain pedagogical practice, they were reduced to utilizing a practice that seemed compatible with the kerygma. Thus they were "trapped" in a cognitive, verbal, and transmissive pedagogy.

In regard to substantive content, Lee viewed the kerygmatic movement as a valuable contribution to religious instruction. It reawakened and refocused the centrality of Jesus; it also rekindled a sense of the "good news," thereby touching the affective level. But while indispensable to religious instruction, the kerygmatic approach ought not to have been made the entire substantive content, as Lee objects some theologians had done.

Lee's objections here are twofold. First, by advocating a theological approach, the kerygmatics had ignored the learner. Lee's criticism thus is not directed at their theology, but at the possibility that their theology might not be suitable for a particular learner's religious life. (At the root of this critique, of course, is Lee's contention that theology is an objective, cognitive science in contrast with religion as a subjective, personally lived reality.) His second stricture is that those "who claim to proclaim salvation history are themselves unmindful of the historical roots and ecology of the substantive content they advocate."[292] At issue here is the failure of the kerygmatic theorists to insert their content into the overall *kerygma-catechesis-didascalia* cycle of the early church.

In many respects, Lee's extensive questioning of the kerygmatics was both one of the most severe criticisms of their work and yet simply a single aspect of his entire *apologia* for the social science approach. In regard to the typology suggested in these pages, Lee's theses on behalf of the social science approach place him rather squarely in the technological, "outer space" analogue particularly insofar as he works out of a framework sympathetic to Tyler. The impact of his arguments against the kerygmatics would necessarily need to be measured vis-à-vis the impact of his overall position. Lee's critique of the kerygmatics is clearly consistent with the totality of his schema.

In general the reaction to his work has been mixed. Burgess and Piveteau and Dillon have written sympathetically and positively of the social science approach.[293] In contrast, other critics have raised less affirmative voices.[294] It should be clear from the typology in use here that a dissenting school of educators would question Lee's understanding and usage of social science, particularly his contention that it is value free.[295] Whatever the present status of Lee's work, it is evident that another "volley" had been fired at the kerygmatics, and that the shot came from the "technological" camp.

B. *"Inner Space"*

The significance of the humanistic dimension is of critical importance in accounting for the rapid dissolution of the kerygmatic movement, particularly when it is viewed in relationship to the 1966 writings of Gabriel Moran on revelation. It was this humanistic influence that legitimated and disseminated the latter's premises concerning experience and relationship, even to the point of distortion. To borrow a term from Kraus *the humanistic approach combined with the Moran of 1966 on revelation to form a double-layered system ("Doppelschichtigkeit") that appears, from the present vantage point to be the single factor most responsible for the demise of Heilsgeschichte as a hermeneutical principle.*

It is the attentiveness to "inner space" that characterized the shift from kerygmatic catechetics to experiential catechetics, or from the "preaching" model to the "relating" model. This shift is apparent in the work of Lumen Vitae theorists Marcel van Caster and Pierre Babin as well as in numerous publications in the United States.

French Oblate Pierre Babin, influenced by the Freudian orientation of priest-psychiatrist Marc Oraison and by the theological anthropology of Karl Rahner and Marcel van Caster, maintained that there could be no such thing as a revelation of God if persons were not also revealed to themselves. He criticized religious education that indoctrinated rather than vivified, and proposed that teachers aim to lead adolescents to recreate and to invent their own vision of faith. Such would be, in his terms, a "pedagogy of invention" rather than one of "transmission," since it invited students to search for meaning.[296] Babin helped to make the "crisis of faith" a permissible stage, and to make adolescent psychology accessible to religious educators. His *Friendship* series, coauthored with Nancy Hennessy, Carol White, and Joan Lark, offered them a tool by which the psychological approach with its emphasis on the relational could be integrated into the religion program. Salvation history receded to the background.[297]

His colleague Marcel van Caster likewise exerted great influence in similar emphases. His work might best be summed up as an extended reflection on the fourth sign, that of witness. Van Caster suggested, in view of his anthropological categories, that the task of catechesis was to initiate one into an "encounter" which engendered a "participation in the supernatural relationship that God started when speaking to man."[298] This resulted in the formation of a Christian mentality that implied a scale of values based on the gospel; the importance of the term "value" for van Caster is evident in the development of his works from 1965 to 1970 and is especially significant when one considers the attention to values then arising in the United States in general education in the work of Sidney Simon, Louis Raths, and Merril Harmin.[299]

Van Caster formulated three rules of catechesis: (1) fidelity to the word of God; (2) fidelity to this word as it is addressed to persons; and (3) fidelity to the dialogue that this establishes between God who speaks and the person who replies. As has been noted earlier, van Caster retained the fundamental *Heilsgeschichte* schema, but led the way in providing a more anthropological appropriation of it. His theory was key in legitimizing stress on the personal, dialogical, relational, and present aspects of revelation, and bore an obvious correlation to the 1966 work of Moran on revelation. Most importantly, the anthropological categories of the European catechists harmonized easily with the humanistic concerns shared by both general and religious education in the United States.

The religion textbook market, once dominated by the *Baltimore Catechism* and its derivative approaches, now reflected the pluralism of approaches. Salvation history texts remained on the market, primarily the Benziger series for elementary school children and the Novak *Lord and King* series for secondary students. In addition, St. Mary's College Press published a high school series incorporating the more existential and personalist motifs; the junior year text, for instance, began with the text of *West Side Story*.[300] Paulist Press issued its popular *Discovery* series in which students used film, drama, newspapers, advertising, song, art, slides, posters, and literature to "discover" revelation in their midst:

> The authors are certain that in probing the truth, meaning, and significance of these many and various media, the adolescents will be led back into their own personal and social experience of the world in a new and revealing way. As Thomas E. Clark, S.J., has put it: ". . . the word is inescapably religious and Christian" (*America*, May 29, 1965, p. 802). Accordingly the Discovery materials are so designed as to maximize the student's possibilities of finding the religious and Christian dimension of the world.
>
> Some may ask at this point whether this is really theology. The authors say, with Gregory Baum, that this is indeed theology, albeit a new and growing sense of theology: ". . . theology is a special dimension of any inquiry whatever into human life."[301]

In a similar vein, a teachers' manual from Argus Communications prefaced its *Choose Life* series with this comment:

> . . . revelation happens in the student's experience. . . . The materials meet the young person where he is. They draw upon everyday experiences of ordinary life: the spoken word, the newspaper headline, the Madison Avenue gimmick, the sophisticated catch phrase, the tongue-in-cheek editorial, the serious scholar's report, the sights and sounds that are all around us—the world of the "now" generation.[302]

The transition from kerygmatic to experiential with its appropriation of humanistic educational trends is most apparent in the three manuals prepared by Paulist Press for its *Discovery* series. For instance, the second book, *Patterns of Dynamics and Strategies*, includes articles on "Group Sensitivity" (William Schutz), "The Dialogical Teacher" (Ruel Howe), "Clearing a Space for Honesty, Openness and Self-Awareness" (John Holt), "A Theory of Values" (Raths, Harmin and Simon), "The Personalist Approach" (Nebreda), and "Relevance in Religious

Education" (Cooke). Particularly valuable in demonstrating the shift is Carl Pfeiffer's article, "Religious Education and Life in the Sixties."[303]

Pfeiffer initiated his essay with these remarks of students: "Who cares about Abraham and Moses?" "We've heard all that before!" "What does it have to do with my life and problems?" He maintained that the resistance of students, as reflected in questions such as these, the consequent frustration of teachers, and the experts' reflection on the dilemma all pointed to the importance of the person of the religious educator. Pfeiffer concluded that there existed an "increasingly clear concensus (sic) in theory and practice that there is no one method universally applicable, nor is there one predetermined sequence of content."[304]

In reflecting on the principles underlying this consensus, Pfeiffer argued:

> The basic insight that grounds modern religious educational theory is the conviction that God reveals his love and communicates his life not so much through words as through events—this is what is referred to as salvation history. He is actively, creatively present in both nature and history, telling us tangibly of his love, and sharing with us his life. He is met not in doctrinal formulations or abstract truths; rather he is met in the experiences of life. *If salvation history means anything, it means that God is revealing his love and communicating his life to men today, in the events of our history and in the phenomena of our world. . . .*
>
> If this is true, it is necessary to reflect more deeply on another commonly agreed upon premise. Book after book repeats that Christian education draws its message from four sources or signs: Bible, Liturgy, Doctrine and Witness. From these sources comes the true content which is then applied to the lives of the students. This is perhaps a true and valid procedure, but is not the only one, *for according to the very principles of salvation history, if salvation and revelation happen now, today, then the most fundamental source or sign is life itself today* (emphasis added).[305]

Pfeiffer then suggested that, rather than teachers viewing themselves as heralds proclaiming the Good News of Salvation (the typical kerygmatic role), they might better understand their roles in terms of being prophets. Prophets attended to the present situation of their people, listened to God's word in the ordinary events of the day, and then interpreted for their people the deeper meanings of the happenings. Teachers as prophets would be able to help students discern God's word within the "confused noises of modern living." The catechist-prophet who, like Jesus, would cast "light on life through love," needed to appreciate life, because "only to the extent that one appreciates human and secular values can one understand the Scriptures."[306] Life, in short, was the most immediate sign of revelation.

That this tended to trivialize the meaning of prophecy and to lead to a preoccupation with educational relevance (what literary critic Francine du Plessix Gray has called the "Women's Wear Daily of reality, a hem-like notion that changes every year according to the fluctuating stamina of educators")[307] is obvious. What ought to be equally obvious is that the fundamental categories of the kerygmatics still stood; they were merely expanded to incorporate the anthropological and experiential emphases. Ironically, the humanist influence on religious education made salvation history passé while proceeding from its premises.

The humanistic trends in general education, likewise shared by religious education in the United States, fit, as has been noted, the anthropological emphases coming from European theologians and catechists. That the shift from kerygma to anthropology to politics apparent in the catechetical study weeks from 1960 through 1968 characterized the situation in the United States as well is more strikingly evident in the revised draft of the National Catechetical Directory, *Sharing the Light of Faith.*[308]

This document begins on an anthropological note, describing the cultural and religious characteristics affecting catechesis in the United States: the racial, ethnic, religious, and theological diversity, the importance of science and technology, and the changes in family life and structure. Its rootedness in kerygmatic categories is immediately evident: evangelism (#35), pre-evangelization (#34), and the sources of catechesis, that is the "four signs" (#42–46). The OT is viewed as the "setting of the stage" for the "broader and deeper convenant, God's fullest self-revelation in Jesus Christ" (#53; cf. #176). Because Jesus, the "center of all God's saving works," joins Christians to all history and to all human beings (#88), catechesis is "trinitarian and Christocentric in scope and spirit" (#47). The political shift is attended to in the seventh chapter, "Catechesis for Social Ministry," which details the development of Catholic social teaching, analyzes some contemporary social issues, and suggests some catechetical guidelines for justice and peace.

Such a document arising from a broad consultative process will undoubtedly assume a normativity for some time to come; thus it seems likely that the kerygmatic-anthropological-political mélange will dominate religious education (or, in the terms of the document, "catechetics") in the United States. If the roots of this mainstream approach lie in the attentiveness to "inner space" manifested in the shift from kerygmatic to experiential catechetics, it is crucial to note that the fundamentals of kerygma lie embedded in its "heart."

However much the National Catechetical Directory will assume priority in the considerations of Catholics in the field, there are, nonetheless, dissenting voices; these might be broadly grouped under the category of revisionist-reconceptualists. They are, like their "revisionist" colleagues in general education, different from one another. Yet their common linkage is apparent in their rejection of the kerygmatic schema.

C. "Landscape"

Foremost among these revisionists is, of course, Gabriel Moran, whose efforts to reconceptualize the field revolve around expansion of the term "revelation." As traced earlier in this chapter, Moran's fundamental shift in thinking was signalled in his 1971 *Design for Religion,* in which he rejected the preaching model inherent in kerygmatic formulations in favor of "ecumenical theology." Particularly key in indicating Moran's differing assumptions is the third chapter in that work, "An Educational Anthropology"; it is an anthropology vastly different from that of van Caster. It is, first of all, much less susceptible to the humanistic and personalistic trends:

A complete authropology would be one that is concerned with all of the social relationships that structure human life. . . . The social structure is not what one talks about in school; it is the reality within which the schooling happens.

A related failure in educational writing is to assume that in the final analysis the question of education is the relating of the teacher to the student. One can hardly over-estimate the importance of the personal relationship between teacher and student. The writing in religious education throughout the last few decades has rightfully dwelt on this theme. Nevertheless, it must still be insisted upon that American education includes many other questions than the I-thou attitude of teachers. An anthropological understanding that neglects the political, social and economic elements will eventually make personalistic attitudes of teachers more difficult and less effective.[309]

Secondly, a complete anthropology is concerned not only with human freedom, but also with social organization. Thirdly, it is an anthropology that refuses to split the mind from its larger context; intelligence refers to persons perceiving, symbolizing, understanding, and directing experience: "Intelligence is man's capacity to deal with life as a whole."[310]

Moran's *Religious Body* (1974) develops these notions.[311] Moran's focus has now turned to the primary words "religion," "community," and "education." He rejects the definition of religious education as "officials of a church indoctrinating children to obey an official church," and lays claim instead to this definition: "The whole religious community educates the whole religious community to make free and intelligent religious decisions vis-à-vis the whole world."[312] It is this he calls "ecumenical religious education," in contradistinction from "catechetics" (a Catholic term) or "Christian education" (a Protestant one):

I see no way in which either of these terms can be the basis of a reform of religious education. The term "Christian education" arose in Protestantism largely as an escape out of the educational mainstream. Neo-orthodox theology insisted that Christianity is based upon a "revealed word": a pure message which can be distinguished from human experience and religion. The educational application of that theology is "Christian education," whose main task is "proclaiming a message of salvation." All the educational techniques and educational psychology that are put in the service of that message do not make the undertaking an educational one. . . .

The catechetical movement in the Catholic church was part of the same movement away from the risks of education. . . . For a time in the 1950s and 1960s it appeared to be a force that could change the Roman Catholic church. As with the liturgical movement, the official church solved the problem by embracing the movement and further exaggerating its rhetoric. In 1960 the word catechetical was considered subversive; by 1970 it was an in-house slogan. Also, like the liturgical movement, the catechetical movement was never as radical as it might have seemed. An educational movement in the church cannot be successful unless it does away with the distinction between clerical and lay.[313]

The "later Moran," then, rejects catechetical language in favor of educational language largely because he wants to free religious education from its exclusively ecclesiastical moorage: "Religious education is larger than the Christian church, a fact not even vaguely suspected in official pronouncements."[314] By broadening his definition, Moran seeks the synthesis of "what is best in education and what is richest in religion."[315]

An article published in the spring of 1977 provides more clarity on this issue, as Moran suggests the possibility of differentiating two languages of religious education.[316] The first language, ecclesiastical and educational, is governed by the relation of theology to catechetics (or Christian education), a relationship largely dominated by theological discourse. The second language, that of education (the "systematic planning of experience for growth in human understanding") Moran would keep in tension with religion. He identifies three aspects of education in religion: (1) the study of a specific religion from within; (2) the study of religion from a position of some distance; and (3) the practice of religious life.[317] He concludes that, though the first language need not be abandoned, the second has the advantage of extending religious education beyond the parochial and ecclesiastical. The language of education opens the dialogue to religious people not identified with the church and facilitates the dialogue lest education "prematurely close its accounts with reality" or religion become irrational.[318]

Moran's concern for language, his attentiveness to the social and political dimensions of religious education, and his desire to discuss it outside of ecclesiastical settings place him in the "revisionist" stream. And, most pertinent to this study, his work substantially modifies the kerygmatic foundation common to the mainstream of Catholic religious education in the United States. To the extent that Moran's work is accepted, *Heilsgeschichte* will no longer even implicitly be an operative hermeneutical principle.

Yet even as the reconceptualist par excellence of religious education, Moran ought not to be rigidly classified. He has, for instance, reviewed appreciatively the National Catholic Directory, noting its advances over previous Roman Catholic documents.[319] But there can be little doubt that Moran's concerns vary significantly from the "establishment" position, in large measure because he is interested in speaking to a wider society beyond the church. Moran appears to see himself standing against the church in the name of education, as his comments in his most recent book, *Education toward Adulthood,* suggest:

> The professional educator's commitment is not 100% to the existing church. The church educator precisely for the good of the church has to stand against the church in the name of education. This stance, too, should not be sharply abrasive, but it should be crystal clear. The way educators can contribute to the Church is to resist ecclesiastical language and not allow the institution to swallow them. The swallowing is done with the best of intentions and it does relieve the tension, but the Church will have lost a crucial lever for its own advance.[320]

Moran, it should also be noted, is not the only Catholic religious educator whose work aims at reconceptualizing the field and hence builds from nonkerygmatic foundations. For example, the "shared praxis" approach of Thomas H. Groome marks a new attempt to ground religious education in critical reflection on Christian action.[321] With Moran, Groome shares a concern for language and for political implications. He differs most sharply in his attention to *praxis* theology and to critical theory. In this respect, Groome's work manifests some rather

clear parallels with the reconceptualist school in general education.

It is obviously beyond the scope of this study to examine in
detail these reconceptualizations of religious education. *But
what is of vital significance is that certain dissenting voices in the field
are speaking from a nonkerygmatic foundation, and therefore do not
accept the hermeneutics of Heilsgeschichte.*

V. Summary

Whereas the twofold task of the previous chapter was the
description of the rapid rise of *Heilsgeschichte* as a hermeneutical principle in Catholic religious education and the tracing of
its equally rapid demise, the task of this third chapter has been
speculation on the factors contributing to the dénouement.
Four sets of contributing factors were identified and developed
in turn: theological, cultural, educational, and religious educational.

1. *Theological.* Scrutiny was given to developments which
    made problematic the basic assertion of the *Heilsgeschichte*
    schema; namely, that God is revealed in history according
    to a plan of progressive revelation in which Christ is the
    center and the NT is the fulfillment of the OT. Accord-
    ingly, four specific and interrelated issues were examined.
    1.1 Revelation: An intense focus on the revelation ques-
        tion has surfaced on nearly every theological front,
        thereby uncovering the naiveté of the claim that God
        is revealed in history. Gilkey called attention to cer-
        tain philosophical contradictions; Barr pointed to the
        inadequacy of the insistence on history; and Frei to
        the misreading of the biblical narratives. While one
        may presume that these critics would have exercised
        little influence over Catholic religious educators, the
        widely read work of Gabriel Moran on revelation in
        1966 *(Theology of Revelation* and *Catechesis of Revela-
        tion)* called attention to another aspect of the issue.
        Furthermore, his insistence in his later works *(The
        Present Revelation* and *Religious Body)* that revelation is

a far broader concept than most Christians are willing to admit placed under doubt their very usage of the term, and summoned them to a basic reconstruction of the matter.

1.2 Relationship of OT and NT: Recent developments in biblical studies, particularly in the area of intertestamental studies and in exegetical practice, have manifested the inadequacy of the assumption that the OT is "fulfilled" in the NT. Such a view, in the opinion of numerous contemporary scholars, devalues the OT, denigrates Judaism, and reflects the dogmatic bias of Christianity.

1.3 Christology: "Christocentrism" functioned as a fundamental tenet of *Heilsgeschichte;* yet increased attention given to the relationship of Christianity to world religions, particularly its relationship with Judaism, indicates a need for reconsideration of this focus. A number of theologians contend that Christian claims of the past have dealt inadequately with the contributions of other religious traditions, have too often been allied with cultural predominance, and have reflected an insensitivity to the eschatological nature of the kingdom of God.

1.4 Ecclesiology: As *Heilsgeschichte* had been appropriated by many Catholic theologians and religious educators, the church's mission was equated with proclamation and its nature viewed as coextensive with the kingdom of God. But recent ecclesiology suggests that the church must be regarded more critically; most particularly, it suggests that church must be subordinated to kingdom. *Heilsgeschichte,* especially as used in Catholic religious education, had an ecclesiology insufficiently grounded in eschatology.

2. *Cultural.* Yet, however much theological reconsiderations had made problematic the *Heilsgeschichte* hermeneutic, they were in themselves insufficient to explain totally its rapid demise, especially because many of the theological developments were not readily accessible to religious educators, for whom factors in both general and religious

education had more direct bearing. Thus it is necessary to look further to account for the dénouement. Scrutiny of the educational scene of the 1960s (both general and religious) reveals an immense variety of presuppositions and practices. This pluralism is best understood when placed in the context of a *cultural* cataclysm, that is, an environment of great upheaval in the social order. Three metaphors suggest the contours of that upheaval: "outer space," "inner space," and "landscape."

2.1 "Outer space": The moon landing represented the apotheosis of human technical knowledge; technology, however, not only had made possible that "giant leap of mankind," but it also had brought closer the threat of nuclear holocaust.

2.2 "Inner space": Alongside the interest in technology was an inward focus on human growth; the "Space Age" coexisted with the "Age of Therapy." Terms such as "human potential," "freedom," and "relevance" typified an introspective, even narcissistic, turn in the culture.

2.3 "Landscape of nightmare": Despite the advances (and dangers) of technological development, despite the rhetoric of human potential movements, much of the nation was torn by strife. Particularly in the latter part of the 1960s had unrest over civil rights and involvement in the war in Vietnam divided the country, undermined respect for authority and placed traditional religious categories in doubt. For many this was also an "Age of Crisis," when moral and spiritual questions called for a revolution in thought and action.

3. *Educational.* These cultural metaphors have educational analogues also.

3.1 "Outer space": Educational interest in the "technological" was reflected in the attention to reform of science education; in the design of curricula to reflect the basic structures of knowledge; in the development of behavioral objectives, systems analysis, competency-based teacher education, and in behavioral psychology.

3.2 "Inner space": Much of the human potential movement was reflected in educational concerns over the
child's experience, feelings, and goals. Great attention
was devoted to "humanizing" education. Open
classrooms and alternative schools offered new structures. The therapeutic age was brought to education
via client-centered counseling/teaching and Gestalt
theory.

3.3 "Landscape of nightmare": Still another educational
thread can be discerned in a number of dissenting
voices for whom neither technologism nor humanism
appeared as a sufficient solution. These revisionist
and reconceptualist voices, while not univocal in their
message, called attention to the political nature of
education, criticized the way in which schooling in the
Western world tended to maintain the status quo, and
suggested that more critical eyes be focused on education from a sociological and philosophical vantage
point.

4. *Religious Educational.* The three metaphors may also be
used as analogues to describe the situation in Catholic
religious education in the United States, which has become
increasingly pluralistic since 1965.

4.1 "Outer space": In religious education, the social science approach of James Michael Lee correlates with
the trends in general education that emphasized the
empirical and behavioral.

4.2 "Inner space": The shift from kerygmatic catechetics
to experiential catechetics reflects the inclusion of
the humanistic dimension into religious education.
Textbooks incorporated more personalist and existentialist motifs. Of prime importance was the emphasis that revelation happened in the here and now
of the student's life. Such a contention bore obvious
relationship with the 1966 work of Moran; indeed,
many of the texts and writings of this era legitimized,
disseminated, and popularized the early Moran (but
often inadequately and inaccurately). Such a

"double-layered system" seems, in retrospect, to have been the factor most responsible for the demise of *Heilsgeschichte* as a hermeneutical principle. Of special significance is the fact that this layering of the early Moran with humanistic trends did not represent a repudiation of the fundamental categories of the kerygmatics, but merely an emphasis on their existential import.

4.3 "Landscape of nightmare": The work of the later Moran, in particular, represents an attempt to work from a nonkerygmatic foundation. His most recent work, as well as that of Thomas Groome, represents a clearly dissenting and reconceptualist perspective on religious education.

VI. Conclusion

Heilsgeschichte, as the evidence demonstrates, no longer undergirds Catholic religious education in the United States as it did during the mid-1960s. No one can ascertain precisely the causes of its demise, but if the foregoing analysis is correct, then an intriguing development appears. *Though the very theological foundations of salvation history were shaken to the core, it would appear that broader cultural, educational, and catechetical factors had far more to do directly with its downfall.* Such a phenomenon naturally raises the question of what the dénouement of salvation history says about the nature of religious education. The fourth chapter will offer a forum for reflection on this critical question.

NOTES

1. C. E. Braaten, *History and Hermeneutics* (Philadelphia: Westminster, 1966) 16.

2. Term from T. F. O'Meara, "Toward a Subjective Theology of Revelation," *TS* 36 (1975) 401. Among important recent studies on revelation, cf.: E. Schillebeeckx *(Revelation and Theology,* 2 vols. [New York: Sheed and Ward, 1967–68]); A. Dulles *(Revelation Theology: A*

History [New York: Herder and Herder, 1969]); R. Latourelle *(Theology of Revelation* [Staten Island: Alba House, 1966]); J. Moltmann *(Revelation as History* [New York: Macmillan, 1968]); J. Macquarrie *(Principles of Christian Theology,* 2nd ed. rev. [New York: Scribner's Sons, 1977] 7–10 and 84–103).

3. L. Gilkey, "Cosmology, Ontology and the Travail of Biblical Language," *JR* 41 (1961) 194–205.

4. *Ibid.,* 202.

5. *Ibid.,* 203.

6. L. Gilkey, *Naming the Whirlwind* (Indianapolis: Bobbs-Merrill, 1969).

7. L. Gilkey, *Reaping the Whirlwind* (New York: Seabury, 1976).

8. J. Barr, "Revelation through History in the Old Testament," Martin E. Marty and Dean G. Peerman, eds., *New Theology No. 1* (New York: Macmillan, 1964) 60–74. Brevard Childs *(Biblical Theology in Crisis* [Philadelphia: Westminster, 1970] 65–66) regarded this lecture as the "final blow" in the cracking of the walls of biblical theology.

9. J. Barr, *Biblical Words for Time,* 2nd rev. ed. (London: SCM, 1969). See Cullmann's response in the addendum to *Christ and Time,* rev. ed. (Philadelphia: Westminster, 1964) xxx–xxxi. See the discussion of this edition in Chapter I of this study.

10. Barr, *Biblical Words* 84.

11. J. Barr, *Old and New in Interpretation* (London: SCM, 1966).

12. J. Barr, "Trends and Prospects in Biblical Theology," *Journal of Theological Studies* XXV (October 1974) 265–282. The usage of this idea had appeared earlier in his *Old and New in Interpretation,* 98–99, and is noted also in the 1969 essay, "Postscript and Retrospect" that appeared in the 2nd rev. ed. of *Biblical Words for Time,* 172.

13. B. Albrektson, *History and the Gods* (Lund, Sweden: CWK Gleerup, 1967) 114. Albrektson concluded that events alone were incapable of expressing those ideas of Hebrew religion which might be truly distinctive, and claimed that the Old Testament view of the divine deed was not possible without the divine word (122), a notion implicit in Barr's 1962 Princeton lecture.

14. Barr, "Trends and Prospects in Biblical Theology," 272.

15. J. Barr, "Story and History in Biblical Theology," *JR* 56 (1976) 1–17.

16. H. Frei, *The Eclipse of Biblical Narrative: A Study in Eighteenth and Nineteenth Century Hermeneutics* (New Haven: Yale, 1974).

17. Frei, 130.

18. Frei identified this view with nineteenth-century theologians Gottfried Menken, Johann Tobias Beck, and, most important, J. C. K.

von Hofmann and the Erlangen confessional school. He traced their influence—ambiguities and all—to the biblical theology that characterized twentieth century neo-orthodoxy (173,181).

19. Frei, 181.

20. *Ibid.*, 135.

21. H. Frei, *The Identity of Jesus Christ: An Inquiry into the Hermeneutical Bases of Dogmatic Theology* (Philadelphia: Fortress, 1974).

22. See, for instance, reviews in *TS* 36 (1975) 155–158; *T Today* 31 (1975) 367; *JR* 55 (1975) 494; and *Religious Education* 70 (1975) 571–572.

23. G. Moran, *Theology of Revelation* (New York: Herder and Herder, 1966) and *Catechesis of Revelation* (New York: Herder and Herder, 1966). Henceforth abbreviated as *TR* and *CR,* respectively. Cf. his first publication, *Scripture and Tradition* (New York: Herder and Herder, 1963).

24. *CR,* 24.

25. *Ibid.*, 28; cf. *TR,* 37.

26. *TR,* 54.

27. *Ibid.*, 93.

28. *Ibid.*, 120.

29. *CR,* 34.

30. *Ibid.*, 44.

31. *Ibid.*, 45 and 51.

32. *Ibid.*, 53.

33. *Ibid.*, 86. Cf. also 85, where Moran cites *Dei Verbum* IV, #15.

34. *Ibid.*, 87.

35. *TR,* 58.

36. G. Moran, "Where Now, What Next" in P. O'Hare, ed., *Foundations of Religious Education* (New York: Paulist, 1978) 103.

37. G. Moran, *Design for Religion* (New York: Herder and Herder, 1971), abbreviated herein as *DR.* Moran had published two studies in the interlude since *TR* and *CR (Experiences in Community* [New York: Herder and Herder, 1968], which had been coauthored with Maria Harris, and *The New Community* [New York: Herder and Herder, 1971]). See also his autobiographical essay, "People, Places and Metaphors," in G. Baum, ed., *Journeys* (New York: Paulist, 1975) 236–254.

38. *DR,* 38–44.

39. *Ibid.*, 44.

40. *Ibid.*, 85.

41. *Ibid.*, 91.

42. *Ibid.*, 63–64. The entire chapter from which these citations are

taken, "An Educational Anthropology" (49–71), is crucial for Moran's argumentation.

43. *Ibid.*, 69–70.

44. G. Moran, *The Present Revelation* (New York: Herder and Herder, 1972). Hereafter *PR*.

45. Moran, "Where Now, What Next," 103.

46. *PR*, 17. Because of the abundance of references to this seminal work in the next pages, citations will simply be given in parentheses within the text.

47. Cf. G. Moran, *Religious Body* (New York: Seabury, 1974) 31–68, and "Two Languages of Religious Education," *Living Light* 14 (1977) 7–15; cf. "Where Now, What Next," 104.

48. Although Moran noted that he was not as concerned with the Old Testament as he was with the Jewish community that arose in ancient times and is still very much alive (240), his brief comments about the OT are significant in view of his earlier assertions in *CR*. His claim in *PR* (263) was: "The denigration of the 'Old Testament' not only means that a part of Christian heritage is lost. It also means that the part which is salvaged is badly distorted."

49. Cf. A. Dulles, "The Problem of Revelation," *CTSA* 29 (1974) 77–106; M. Bourke, "Response to Professor Dulles I," *CTSA* 29 (1974) 107–116; G. Moran, "Response to Professor Dulles II," *CTSA* 29 (1974) 117–123.

50. Macquarrie, *Principles of Christian Theology*, 7.

51. Augustine, "Reply to Faustus the Manichean," *A Select Library of Nicene and Post-Nicene Fathers* IV (Buffalo: Scribners, 1887) 186–188.

52. See A. Suelzer, "Modern Old Testament Criticism," *JBC* 70: 19–21.

53. W. Vischer, *Das Christuszeugnis des AT* (English translation, *The Witness of the Old Testament to Christ* [London: Lutterworth, 1949]). Vischer envisioned Jesus as the "hidden meaning of the OT writings"; G. Hasel *(Old Testament Theology: Basic Issues in the Current Debate*, rev. ed [Grand Rapids: Eerdmans, 1975] 112) cites his 1947 *Die Bedeutung des AT für das christliche Leben:* "All movements of life of which the OT reports move from his [Jesus] and towards him. The life stories of all these men are part of his life story. Therefore they are written with so little biographical interest for the individual persons. What is written about them is actually written as a part of the biography of the One through whom and towards whom they live." Such a point of view is not far from the second century allegorical methodology of Origen.

54. See R. Bultmann, "Promise and Fulfillment" in *Essays on Old*

Testament Hermeneutics, ed. C. Westermann (Richmond, Va.: John Knox, 1963) 50–76 and especially his "The Significance of the Old Testament for the Christian Faith" in *The Old Testament and Christian Faith,* ed. B. Anderson (New York: Herder and Herder, 1969) 8–35. For a similar perspective, see F. Bäumgartel, "The Hermeneutical Problem of the Old Testament" in *Essays on Old Testament Hermeneutics,* 134–159; also, in the same volume, F. Hesse, "The Evaluation and Authority of Old Testament Texts," 285–313. Hesse maintains that the OT man in the "existential sense" is the one addressed by God but not yet participating in full salvation, the one called to faith but not yet believing fully, the one under promise and under law; whereas, on the other hand, the NT man is the "one who has spoken his 'yes' to the full self-disclosure of God in Christ." The Anderson volume consists entirely of scholarly responses to the issue of the relationship of the testaments.

55. "Increasingly it has become plain that issues which seemed at one time capable of being dealt with as prolegomena belong to the very center of the theological interpretation of the Old Testament. Questions regarding its basic unity, its relationship to the New Testament and to Judaism, and its relevance to the modern world, are not matter for a cursory treatment in a preface, but belong to the heart of what an Old Testament theology should be." (R. E. Clements, *One Hundred Years of Old Testament Interpretation* [Philadelphia: Westminster, 1976] 138.)

56. For discussion of Barr, see chapter 2. Cf. D. S. Russell, *Between the Testaments* (Philadelphia: Fortress, 1960).

57. The term "late Judaism" is frequently used to denote the religion that grew out of this intertestamental period, and is so employed by Barr. Mention needs to be made, however, that it has also been attacked by some scholars as offensive, implying that this was something of an aberration or unfortunate development in the history of Judaism. See W. Wink, *The Bible in Human Transformation* (Philadelphia: Fortress, 1973) 7. The term "early Judaism" is to be preferred; see M. J. Cook, "Judaism, early rabbinic," *IDB Sup* (Nashville: Abingdon, 1976) 499–505.

58. Barr, *Old and New in Interpretation,* 156.

59. See P. Perkins, *Reading the New Testament* (New York: Paulist, 1977) 50–55.

60. Barr, *Old and New in Interpretation,* 124.

61. On Matthew's use of OT to enhance his message, see R. E. Brown, *The Birth of the Messiah: A Commentary on the Infancy Narratives in Matthew and Luke* (New York: Doubleday, 1977) 213–225.

62. Barr, *Old and New in Interpretation,* 126.

63. *Ibid.,* 128.

64. *Ibid.,* 129.

65. See P. Chirico *(Infallibility: The Crossroads of Doctrine* [Kansas City: Sheed Andrews and McMeel, 1977] 28): ". . . the great texts are an endless source of new acts of understanding and love. The broader a man's experience, the more open his heart, and the richer his field of understanding, the more will a great text tend to be for him a catalyst of new thoughts, desires and actions." To this statement, Chirico adds this note (n. 21, 301–302): "It is this process that accounts for the continuing reinterpretation in Scripture that is evidenced in Scripture itself. The New Testament is not simply a drawing out of the implications of the Old Testament. It uses the Old Testament with a liberty that goes beyond the attempt to find the exact understanding of the original author."

66. Barr, *Old and New in Interpretation,* 139.

67. *Ibid.,* 140–141. Barr later comments: "Perhaps the single most cogent argument which serves to relate the OT to the Church is not strictly a guide to interpretation at all, but the argument of Ephesians that in the Church Jew and Gentile are made into one body and thus bring and show forth reconciliation to all. This reasoning must, if it is taken directly, lead to the eagerness to hear the OT in the Church, and therefore, indirectly to the will to use it and interpret it" (165).

68. *Ibid.,* 141.

69. *Ibid.,* 153–154; R. E. Murphy, "Christian Understanding of the Old Testament," *TD* 18 (1970) 327.

70. J. Fitzmyer, "The Use of Explicit Old Testament Quotations in Qumran Literature and in the New Testament," *NTS* 7 (1960–61) 297–333 and reprinted in his collection, *Essays on the Semitic Background of the New Testament* (Missoula, Mont.: Scholars Press, 1974) 3–58. See also in the same volume " '4Q Testimonia' and the New Testament," 58–59.

71. R. Longenecker, *Biblical Exegesis in the Apostolic Period* (Grand Rapids, Mich.: W. B. Eerdmans, 1975). See however the review by J. A. Sanders and S. Skiles, *Int* 30 (1976) 212–213.

72. Fitzmyer, *Essays on the Semitic Background of the New Testament,* 30–31.

73. G. Vermes, "The Qumran Interpretation of Scripture in its Historical Setting," *ALUOS* VI (1966–68) 95.

74. On these presuppositions and practices, see Longenecker, *Biblical Exegesis in the Apostolic Period,* 19–50.

75. Longenecker, 211–212.

76. J. A. Sanders, "Torah and Christ," *Int* 29 (1975) 372–390.

77. Sanders claims that this intermingling is true whether Torah means simply the Pentateuch, divine revelation, or the symbol for the identity of Jews. Regarding this latter usage, he later writes: "Torah means the Jewish gospel which, in dialogue with the on-going believing communities of Jews wherever they might be, gives Jews both identity and a basic understanding of obedience. . . . Being indestructible and portable it provides the mythic power for life which a dispersed and beleaguered people have had" (*ibid.*, 388–389).

78. *Ibid.*, 379.

79. *Ibid.*, 382.

80. *Ibid.*, 383.

81. On Pharisaism, see E. Rivkin, *The Shaping of Jewish History: A Radical New Interpretation* (New York: Scribner's Sons, 1971) 42–83; L. Finkelstein, *The Pharisees*, 2 vols. (Philadelphia: Jewish Publication Society, 1964); J. Neusner, *From Politics to Piety: The Emergence of Pharisaic Judaism* (Englewood Cliffs, N. J.: Prentice-Hall, 1973), and the following articles by J. Pawlikowski, "The Minister as Pharisee," *Commonweal* 95 (1972) 369–373; "Jesus and the Revolutionaries," *The Christian Century* 89 (1972) 1237–1241; "On Renewing the Revolution of the Pharisees," *Cross Currents* 20 (1970) 415–434.

82. Sanders, "Torah and Christ," 385.

83. *Ibid.*, 389.

84. R. Ruether, *Faith and Fratricide* (New York: Seabury, 1974) 64.

85. *Ibid.*, 94.

86. *Ibid.*, 234.

87. *Ibid.*, 240.

88. See the angry and devastating review, J. M. Oesterreicher, *Anatomy of Contempt* (Seton Hall, N.J.: Institute of Judaeo-Christian Studies, n.d.). Oesterreicher takes issue in particular with what he perceives to be Ruether's depreciation of christology and also accuses her of oversimplifying the scriptural and patristic material. While the tone of his review is unfortunate and beyond the bounds of scholarly disagreement, I concur in general with much of his critique, particularly in regard to her handling of the NT. Nonetheless, Ruether's insistence on the imperialism that has accompanied much christology remains a substantial contribution that ought not to be overlooked. An essay which indirectly refutes, or at least places in broader perspective, some of Ruether's contentions is K. Stendahl's "Judaism and Christianity: A Plea for a New Relationship" (F. E. Talmage, ed., *Disputation and Dialogue: Readings in the Jewish-Christian Encounter* [New York: KTAV and Anti-Defamation League, 1975] 330–342).

89. K. Stendahl, "Judaism and Christianity," 339. Cf. J. D. Smart, *The Interpretation of Scripture* (Philadelphia: Westminster, 1961) 79–80.

90. H. Küng, "Introduction: From Anti-Semitism to Theological Dialogue," *Christians and Jews,* ed. H. Küng and W. Kasper (New York: Seabury, 1974) 12. In the same volume see also K. Hruby ("The Future of Jewish-Christian Dialogue: A Christian View," 87–92), who considers the present existence of the Jewish people as a necessity for Christianity.

91. S. Terrien, *The Elusive Presence: Toward a New Biblical Theology* (Religious Perspectives Series #26, ed. R. N. Anshen; New York: Harper and Row, 1978) 26.

92. Cf. D. R. Hillers, *Covenant: The History of a Biblical Idea* (Baltimore: Johns Hopkins, 1969); M. Weinfeld, "Covenant, Davidic" *IDBSup* 188–192; P. A. Riemann, "Covenant, Mosaic" *IDBSup* 192–196.

93. Terrien, *The Elusive Presence,* 23–26.

94. *Ibid.,* 62–409.

95. *Ibid.,* 31.

96. R. E. Brown in *Vatican II: An Interfaith Appraisal,* ed. J. H. Miller (Notre Dame: University Press, 1966) 94–95. See also R. E. Murphy, "Vatican III—Problems and Opportunities of the Future: The Bible" in *Toward Vatican III,* eds. D. Tracy, H. Küng, J. Metz (New York: Seabury, 1978) 25–26.

97. See V. Zamoyla, ed., *The Theology of Christ: Sources* (Beverly Hills, Cal.: Benziger, 1967).

98. K. Rahner, *Theological Investigations 6: Concerning Vatican II* (London: Darton, Longmann and Todd, 1969) 395. See also A. Röper, *The Anonymous Christian* (New York: Sheed and Ward, 1966); D. Maloney, "Rahner and the Anonymous Christian," *America* 123 (1970) 348–350.

99. C. Davis, *Christ and the World Religions* (London: Hodder and Stoughton, 1970) 124–132.

100. W. M. Thompson, "Risen Christ and World Religions," *TS* 37 (1976) 381–409. Cf. R. R. Niebuhr, *Experiential Religion* (New York: Harper and Row, 1972).

101. *Ibid.,* 391–393.

102. *Ibid.,* 408. Thompson's essay is now developed in his book *Christ and Consciousness: Exploring Christ's Contribution to Human Consciousness* (New York: Paulist, 1977).

103. J. P. Schineller, "Christ and Church: A Spectrum of Views," *TS* 37 (1976) 545–566.

104. In his latest work (*The Resilient Church: The Necessity and Limits of*

Adaptation [New York: Doubleday, 1977]), Dulles takes issue with Tracy's christology in his *Blessed Rage for Order* (New York: Seabury, 1975). See the debate in *National Catholic Reporter* 14 (4 November 1977) 9-10 and 15-16.

105. J. Hofinger, *The Art of Teaching Christian Doctrine*, rev. ed. (Notre Dame: University Press, 1962) 11.

106. J. Daniélou, *The Lord of History* (Chicago: Henry Regnery, 1958) 17, 26.

107. Terrien, *The Elusive Presence*, 6.

108. H. Richards, "Christ and the History of Salvation," in P. De Rosa, ed., *Introduction to Catechetics* (Milwaukee: Bruce, 1968) 51.

109. *Ibid.*, 52.

110. C. Klein, *Anti-Judaism in Christian Theology* (Philadelphia: Fortress, 1978).

111. *Ibid.*, 7.

112. G. F. Moore, "Christian Writers on Judaism," *HTR* 14 (1921) 197-254.

113. Klein, *Anti-Judaism in Christian Theology*, 142. Klein adds a chapter on British and American authors for the English edition which, in general, exculpates these authors from the biases so evident on the Continent.

114. *Ibid.*

115. E. P. Sanders, *Paul and Palestinian Judaism: A Comparison of Patterns of Religion* (Philadelphia: Fortress, 1977).

116. Sanders remarks that their works "proceed from wrong premises, they misconstrue the material, and they are, like those Jews who cast off the yoke, beyond redemption" (*ibid.*, 234).

117. *Ibid.*, 75. Sanders's usage of *pattern* is to be distinguished from the proposal that the *trajectory* of religious movements be studied (J. M. Robinson, "Introduction: The Dismantling and Reassembling of the Categories of New Testament Scholarship," in J. M. Robinson and H. Koester, *Trajectories through Early Christianity* [Philadelphia: Fortress, 1971] 1-19). Sanders (pp. 20-24) considers Robinson's term "trajectory" as implying sequential development and implicit goal; he denies that the developmental sequence can always be demonstrated. J. C. Beker ("Review of Paul and Palestinian Judaism," *T Today* 35 [April 1978] 110) takes issue with Sanders's "holistic pattern" approach.

118. Sanders, *Paul and Palestinian Judaism*, 75.

119. *Ibid.*, 57. For another discussion of the retrojection of Reformation debate, see K. Stendahl *(Paul among Jews and Gentiles* [Philadelphia: Fortress, 1976] 78-96).

120. Sanders, *Paul and Palestinian Judaism*, 82.

121. *Ibid.*, 205, 211.

122. *Ibid.*, 422.

123. *Ibid.*, 419.

124. *Ibid.*, 427.

125. *Ibid.*

126. See particularly the review essays by N. A. Dahl and S. Sandmel *(Rel S Rev* 4 [July 1978] 153–160), and the review by A. J. Saldarini (JBL 98 [June 1979] 299–303).

127. S. Ben-Chorim in J. Moltmann, "Messianic Hope in Christianity," in *Christians and Jews*, 62.

128. R. Ruether, *Faith and Fratricide* is discussed above; also Ruether "An Invitation to Jewish Christian Dialogue: In What Sense Can We Say That Jesus Was 'The Christ'?" *The Ecumenist* 10 (1972) 17–24, and "A New Church," *Commonweal* 90 (1969) 64. See also S. Sandmel, *Anti-Semitism in the New Testament* (Philadelphia: Fortress, 1978).

129. M. B. McGarry, *Christology after Auschwitz* (New York: Paulist, 1977).

130. Cf. Eckardt, *Elder and Younger Brothers: The Encounter of Jews and Christians* (New York: Scribner's, 1967). McGarry incorrectly refers to this on p. 62 as *Elder Brother, Younger Brother*.

131. McGarry includes the following among the major proponents of the christologies of discontinuity: J. Jocz (*The Jewish People and Jesus Christ* [London: SPCK, 1958]); G. Knight ("Beyond Dialogue" in *Jews and Christians: Preparation for Dialogue*, ed. Knight [Philadelphia: Westminster, 1965]); J. Daniélou (*Dialogue with Israel* [Baltimore: Helicon, 1966]); H. von Balthasar (*Church and World* [New York: Herder and Herder, 1967]).

132. On Cullmann and Daniélou, see chapter 2.

133. Among the major proponents of the christologies of continuity, McGarry includes the following: P. Chirico ("Christian and Jew Today from a Theological Perspective," *JES* 8 [1970] 744–762); E. M. Fleischner (*Judaism in German Christian Theology since 1945: Christianity and Israel Considered in Terms of Mission* [Metuchen, N.J.: Scarecrow Press, 1975]); J. Parkes (*Prelude to Dialogue: Jewish-Christian Relationships* [New York: Schocken, 1969]); J. C. Rylaarsdam ("Jewish-Christian Relationship: The Two Covenants and the Dilemmas of Christology," *JES* 9 [1972] 249–270); and M. Hellwig ("Christian Theology and the Covenant of Israel," *JES* 7 [1970] 37–51). Of course, McGarry also includes in this category R. R. Ruether, G. Baum, and

J. Pawlikowski; see the following notes for citations to their works. For an important study in relation to religious education, see E. Fisher, *Faith without Prejudice* (New York: Paulist, 1977).

134. G. Baum, "Introduction," *Faith and Fratricide*, 1–22. McGarry quoted from a paper by A. Roy Eckardt ("Comments at Israel Study Group Meeting," April 5, 1975) which holds a "basic inconsistency between the viewpoint of the major author and that of Gregory Baum . . ." See McGarry, 82, n. 56. For other statements by Baum, see his "The Jews, Faith and Ideology," *The Ecumenist* 10 (1971–72) 71–76, and "Theology after Auschwitz," *The Ecumenist* 12 (1974) 65–80.

135. Baum, "Introduction," 14. Baum, it may be noted, also contributes the foreword in C. Klein, *Anti-Judaism in Christian Theology.*

136. McGarry, *Christology after Auschwitz*, 82–83.

137. J. Pawlikowski, "The Contemporary Jewish-Christian Theological Dialogue Agenda," *JES* 11 (1974) 604.

138. J. Moltmann, "Messianic Hope in Christianity," 65. See also his *The Crucified God* (New York: Harper and Row, 1974).

139. E. Wiesel, *Ani Maamin* (New York: Random House, 1975) 71.

140. O. Cullmann, *Christ and Time* (rev. ed.; Philadelphia: Westminster, 1964) 146–147.

141. *Ibid.*, 151.

142. J. Hofinger, "Our Message," *Lumen Vitae* 5 (1950) 270.

143. J. Hofinger, *The Art of Teaching Christian Doctrine* (Notre Dame: University Press, 1957) 122.

144. Y. Congar, *Lay People in the Church* (Westminster, Md.: Newman, 1957) 39.

145. A. Dulles, "The Church as Eschatological Community" in J. Papin, ed., *The Eschaton: A Community of Love* (Villanova University Symposium 5; Villanova, Pa.: Villanova University, 1971) 76–77.

146. J. L. Moltmann, *Theology of Hope* (New York: Harper and Row, 1967) 75.

147. Dulles, "The Church as Eschatological Community," 70.

148. R. McBrien, *Church: The Continuing Quest* (New York: Newman, 1970).

149. *Ibid.*, 11.

150. *Ibid.*, 44.

151. R. McBrien, *The Church in the Thought of Bishop John Robinson* (Philadelphia: Westminster, 1966); *Do We Need the Church?* (New York: Harper and Row, 1969); and *The Remaking of the Church* (New York: Harper and Row, 1973). For recent, excellent theological analyses of Jesus and the kingdom of God, see W. Kasper (*Jesus the*

Christ [New York: Paulist, 1976] 72-88) and G. Aulén (*Jesus in Contemporary Historical Research* [Philadelphia: Fortress, 1976] 99-120, 135-152).

152. McBrien, *Church: The Continuing Quest,* 84.

153. *Ibid.,* 73.

154. *Ibid.,* 85.

155. Foremost, of course, in shaping the renewed thought on the church was Vatican II. Clearly the texts differentiate between church and kingdom; for example: "Its (the church's) goal is the kingdom of God, which has been begun by Himself on earth, and which is to be further extended until it is brought to perfection by Him at the end of time" (*Lumen Gentium* #9; W. Abbott, ed., *The Documents of Vatican II* [New York: America Press, 1966]). In the United States, a pastoral message on Catholic education issued by the National Conference of Catholic Bishops (*To Teach As Jesus Did* [Washington, D.C.: United States Catholic Conference, 1973] 3-8) focused attention on the threefold mission of message, community, and service.

156. *Justice in the World* (Washington, D.C.: United States Catholic Conference, 1972) 34.

157. Dulles, "The Church as Eschatological Community," 97.

158. *Ibid.,* 98.

159. *Ibid.,* 99.

160. See also H. Küng, *The Church* (New York: Sheed and Ward, 1968) 93.

161. *Sharing the Light of Faith* (Washington, D.C.. United States Catholic Conference, 1979)

162. See chapter 2.

163. b. Sabb. 13b.

164. H. Ibsen, quoted in E. Cassirer, *An Essay on Man* (New Haven: Yale, 1944) 52.

165. This phrase is taken from Theodore Roszak's analysis of the "Aquarian Frontier" (*Unfinished Animal* [New York: Harper and Row, 1975] 13), in which he maintains that spiritual intelligence is imperative at this point in history to discriminate among the countless options in the psychospiritual realm. This means the "power to tell the greater from the lesser reality."

166. See M. McLuhan, *Understanding Media* (New York: McGraw Hill, 1964). There is of course an extensive corpus of literature both by Teilhard and about him; see particularly P. Teilhard de Chardin, *The Phenomenon of Man* (New York: Harper, 1959) and *The Future of Man* (New York: Harper, 1964); also C. Mooney, *Teilhard de Chardin and the Mystery of Christ* (Garden City: Image Books, 1968).

167. See T. Roszak's *The Making of a Counter Culture: Reflections on the Technocratic Society and Its Youthful Opposition* (Garden City: Anchor Books, 1969). Also J. Ellul, *The Technological Society* (New York: A. A. Knopf, 1964); C. Reich, *The Greening of America* (New York: Random House, 1970).

168. C. D. Bryan, *Friendly Fire* (New York: Bantam, 1976).

169. G. Vahanian, *The Death of God: The Culture of our Post-Christian Era* (New York: George Grayella, 1961). See also T. J. J. Altizer and W. Hamilton, *Radical Theology and the Death of God* (Indianapolis: Bobbs-Merrill, 1966).

170. Niebuhr, *Experiential Religion*, 3–4.

171. *Ibid.*, 13.

172. D. Berrigan, "On 'The Dark Night of the Soul,'" *New York Review of Books* (22 October 1970). The phrase "nation with the soul of a church" originally was coined by G. K. Chesterton (see *The Man Who Was Chesterton*, Raymond T. Bond, ed. [Garden City, N.Y.: Doubleday Image Books, 1960] 131) but made famous by historian Sidney E. Mead ("The Nation with the Soul of a Church," *Church History* 36[1967] 262–283).

173. D. O'Brien, *The Renewal of American Catholicism* (New York: Paulist, 1972) 205.

174. W. B. Yeats, "The Second Coming," in *The Oxford Book of Twentieth Century English Verse*, ed. P. Larkin (Oxford: Clarendon, 1973) 79.

175. See J. Schwab, *The Practical: A Language for Curriculum* (Washington, D.C.: Center for the Study of Education, National Education Association, 1970). Cf. D. Huebner, "The Moribund Curriculum Field: Its Wake and Our Work" (Invited Address, Division B, American Educational Research Association, San Francisco, April 1976).

176. F. W. Taylor, *The Principles of Scientific Management* (New York: Harper, 1911).

177. E. P. Cubberly, *Public Administration* (Boston: Houghton Mifflin, 1916) 338. See L. A. Cremin, *The Wonderful World of Ellwood Patterson Cubberly* (New York: Teachers College Press, 1965).

178. J. F. Bobbitt, "The Elimination of Waste in Education," *The Elementary School Teacher* 12 (1912) 269. For a thorough critique, see R. Callahan, *Education and the Cult of Efficiency* (Chicago: University of Chicago Press, 1962).

179. See E. L. Thorndike, *Educational Psychology* (3 vols.; Westport, Conn.: Greenwood Press, 1913–1914). See also C. J. Karier's critique ("Testing for Order and Control in the Corporate Liberal State" in C. J. Karier, P. Violas and J. Spring, eds., *Roots of Crisis: American Edu-*

cation in the Twentieth Century [Chicago: Rand McNally, 1973] 108–137).

180. See J. F. Bobbitt, *How to Make a Curriculum* (Boston: Houghton Mifflin, 1924).

181. M. L. Seguel, *The Curriculum Field: Its Formative Years* (New York: Teachers College, 1966) 101–103.

182. A. Molnar and J. A. Zahorik, "Introduction," in Molnar and Zahorik, eds. *Curriculum Theory* (Washington, D.C.: Association for Supervision and Curriculum Development, 1977) 3.

183. R. W. Tyler, *Basic Principles of Curriculum and Instruction* (Chicago: University of Chicago, 1950).

184. See H. Taba, *Teaching Strategies and Cognitive Functioning in Elementary School Children* (San Francisco: San Francisco State College, 1966); idem, *Curriculum Development, Theory and Practice* (New York: Harcourt, Brace and World, 1962). For an appraisal of her research, see M. J. Dunkin and B. J. Biddle *(The Study of Teaching* [New York: Holt, Rinehart and Winston, 1974] 256–271). For an application of her work to a specific teaching model, see B. Joyce and M. Weil *(Models of Teaching* [Englewood Cliffs, N.J.: Prentice Hall, 1972] 123–136).

185. See J. Goodlad with M. N. Richter, Jr., *The Development of a Conceptual System for Dealing with Problems of Curriculum and Instruction* (Los Angeles: University of California, 1966).

186. See R. F. Mager, *Preparing Instructional Objectives* (Palo Alto: Fearon, 1962).

187. H. M. Kliebard, "Persistent Curriculum Issues," in W. Pinar, ed., *Curriculum Theorizing: The Reconceptualists* (Berkeley: McCutchan, 1975) 45.

188. See W. E. Hug, ed., *Strategies for Change Information Programs* (New York: R. R. Bowker, 1974).

189. C. A. Bowers ("Emergent Ideological Characteristics of Educational Policy," *Teachers College Record* 79[1977] 50) observes: "When compared to competency-based education, behavior modification is the John the Baptist to the new reality." See the following: AACTA Committee on Performance-Based Teacher Education, *Achieving the Potential of Performance-Based Teacher Education: Recommendations* (Washington, D.C.: American Association of Colleges for Teacher Education, 1974); AACTA Teacher Education and Media Committee, *Professional Teacher Education* (Washington, D.C.: American Association of Colleges for Teacher Education, 1968); B. Joyce, J. F. Soltis and M. Weil, *Performance Based Teacher Education Design Alternatives: the Concept of Unity* (Washington, D.C.: American Association of Colleges for Teacher Education, 1974); P. Nash, *A Humanistic Approach to Performance Based Teacher Education* (Washington, D.C.:

American Association of Colleges for Teacher Education, 1973); D. Huebner, "Humanism and Competency—A Critical and Dialectical Interpretation" (Paper presented to the Teachers College, Columbia University, Conference on Humanism/Competency, 5 October 1974). While the teacher competency movement is the focus of this discussion, integrally related is "competency-based education" in which state laws establish minimum competency requirements for promotion or graduation. (As of September 1977, twenty-six states had such laws.) See the extensive discussion in numerous articles of *Educational Leadership* 35 (1977) 83-133.

190. B. F. Skinner, *Science and Human Behavior* (New York: Macmillan, 1958); *Walden Two* (New York: Macmillan, 1948); *Beyond Freedom and Dignity* (New York: Knopf, 1971); and *The Technology of Teaching* (New York: Appleton-Century-Crofts, 1968).

191. H. M. Kliebard, "Reappraisal," in *Curriculum Theorizing*, 81.

192. See C. Silberman, *Crisis in the Classroom: The Remaking of American Education* (New York: Vintage, 1971) 168-171.

193. See D. Tanner and L. Tanner, *Curriculum Development: Theory into Practice* (New York: Macmillan, 1975) 407.

194. J. S. Bruner, *The Process of Education* (Cambridge: Harvard, 1960).

195. *Ibid.*, 33.

196. P. H. Phenix, *Realms of Meaning* (New York: McGraw-Hill, 1964).

197. *Ibid.*, 4-5.

198. A. R. King and J. A. Brownell, *The Curriculum and the Disciplines of Knowledge* (New York: John Wiley, 1966). Another variant is J. J. Schwab, "Structure of the Disciplines: Meanings and Significances," in G. W. Ford and L. Pugno, eds., *The Structure of Knowledge and the Curriculum* (Chicago: Rand McNally, 1964).

199. See B. S. Bloom, ed., *Taxonomy of Educational Objectives, Handbook I: Cognitive Domain* (New York: David McKay, 1956); D. R. Krathwohl, B. S. Bloom and B. B. Masia, *Taxonomy of Educational Objectives, Handbook II: Affective Domain* (New York: David McKay, 1964); and A. J. Harrow, *Taxonomy of the Psychomotor Domain* (New York: David McKay, 1972).

200. N. M. Sanders, *Classroom Questions* (New York: Harper and Row, 1966).

201. J. Piaget and B. Inhelder, *The Psychology of the Child* (New York: Basic Books, 1969). Piaget's schema has been the prime influence in the work of Ronald Goldman investigating the development of religious concepts; see his *Religious Thinking from Childhood to Adolescence* (New York: Seabury, 1968) and *Readiness for Religion: A*

Basis for Developmental Religious Education (London: Routledge and Kegan Paul, 1965).

202. Cited in Tanner and Tanner, *Curriculum Development*, 132. But see W. E. Doll, "The Role of Contrast in the Development of Competence" in Molnar and Zahorik, *Curriculum Theory*, 50–64.

203. F. Perls, R. Hefferline, and P. Goodman, *Gestalt Therapy* (New York: Delta Books, 1951). Cf. Roszak, *The Making of a Counter Culture*, 178–204.

204. A. Maslow, *Religions, Values and Peak Experiences* (New York: Viking, 1970).

205. W. Glasser, *Reality Therapy* (New York: Harper and Row, 1965) and *Schools without Failure* (New York: Harper and Row, 1968).

206. See D. Katz and R. Kahn *(The Social Psychology of Organization* [New York: J. Wiley and Sons, 1968] 406–451) on the NTL model. See also W. C. Schutz, *Joy* (New York: Grove, 1967) and *TIRO: A Three Dimensional Theory of Interpersonal Behavior* (New York: Holt, Rinehart and Winston, 1958).

207. C. R. Rogers, *Client-Centered Therapy* (Boston: Houghton & Mifflin, 1951); *On Becoming a Person* (Boston: Houghton & Mifflin, 1961); *Freedom to Learn* (Columbus, Ohio: Merrill, 1969).

208. Rogers, *Client-Centered Therapy*, 427.

209. *Ibid.*, 389–390.

210. *Ibid.*, 387–388.

211. See "The Case of the New English Primary Schools," in Silberman, ed., *Crisis in the Classroom*, 207–264. Also E. B. Nyquist and G. R. Hawes, eds., *Open Education: A Sourcebook for Parents and Teachers* (New York: Bantam Books, 1972); J. T. Evans, *Characteristics of Open Education* (Newton, Mass.: Educational Development Center, 1971).

212. See L. E. Raths, M. Harmin and S. B. Simon, *Values and Teaching* (Columbus, Ohio: Charles E. Merrill, 1966); S. B. Simon, L. W. Howe and H. Kirschenbaum, *Values Clarification* (New York: Hart Publishing, 1972). For a radically different approach to value education see L. E. Metcalf, ed., *Values Education: Rationale, Strategies and Procedures* (Forty-first yearbook; Washington, D.C.: National Council for the Social Studies, 1971). See also J. Holt, *How Children Fail* (New York: Pitman, 1964); P. Goodman, *Compulsory Mis-Education* (New York: Horizon, 1965); E. Z. Friedenberg, *Coming of Age in America* (New York: Random, 1964).

213. See especially G. B. Leonard, *Education and Ecstasy* (New York: 1968).

214. G. B. Leonard, *The Transformation: A Guide to the Inevitable Changes in Humankind* (New York: Dell, 1972) 36.

215. *Ibid.*, 37.

216. *Ibid.*

217. *Ibid.*, 109.

218. *Ibid.*, 199.

219. See G. I. Brown, *Human Teaching for Human Learning: An Introduction to Confluent Education* (New York: Viking, 1971).

220. T. Yeomans, "Confluent Education: The Dynamics of Wholeness" (unpublished paper, Palo Alto, n.d.) 2. I am indebted to Dianne LaGrandeur, a graduate of the confluent education program of the University of California at Santa Barbara, for this and the following reference.

221. G. I. Brown, cited in M. Phillips, "The Application of Gestalt Principles in Classroom Teaching," *Group and Organization Studies* 1 (1976) 84.

222. *Ibid.*, 85–86.

223. *Ibid.*, 86–91.

224. Brown, *Human Teaching*, 41–42.

225. See the fine analysis by C. A. Bowers ("Educational Critics and Technocratic Consciousness: Looking into the Future through a Rearview Mirror," *Teachers College Record* 80 [1978] 272–287). Bowers analyzes the revisionist stance from a philosophical and sociological vantage point very similar to that of the reconceptualists.

226. On the origins and work of the Frankfurt School, see M. Jay (*The Dialectical Imagination* [Boston: Little, Brown and Co., 1973]).

227. I. Illich, *Deschooling Society* (New York: Harper and Row, 1970).

228. I. Illich in a lecture at Yale University, February 18–19, 1970, cited in J. Spring, "Deschooling as a Form of Social Revolution," in *Roots of Crisis,* 144.

229. "Introduction," *Roots of Crisis,* 5.

230. C. J. Karier, "Business Values and the Educational State," *Roots of Crisis,* 6–29.

231. C. J. Karier, "Liberal Ideology and the Quest for Orderly Change," *Roots of Crisis,* 84–107.

232. C. J. Karier, "Testing for Order and Control in the Corporate Liberal State," *Roots of Crisis,* 108–137.

233. P. C. Violas, "Jane Addams and the New Liberalism," *Roots of Crisis,* 66–83.

234. J. Spring, "Education as a Form of Social Control," *Roots of Crisis,* 39.

235. D. Ravitch, *The Revisionists Revised: A Critique of the Radical Attack on the Schools* (New York: Basic Books, 1978).

236. See also J. Featherstone, "The Politics of Education," *New York Times Book Review* (18 June 1978) 9, 26–27.

237. Ravitch, 36.
238. *Ibid.*
239. *Ibid.*, 37.
240. *Ibid.*, 41.
241. *Ibid.*, 44.
242. *Ibid.*, 47.
243. *Ibid.*, 57.
244. *Ibid.*, 73.
245. *Ibid.*, 100.
246. Featherstone, "Politics of Education," 9.
247. P. Freire, *Pedagogy of the Oppressed* (New York: Seabury, 1974).
248. *Ibid.*, 71. See also D. Collins, *Paulo Freire: His Life, Works and Thought* (New York: Paulist, 1977); S. M. Grabowski, ed., *Paulo Freire: A Revolutionary Dilemma for the Adult Educator* (Syracuse, N.Y.: Syracuse University and ERIC, 1972); J. L. Elias, "Paulo Freire: Religious Educator," *Religious Education* 71 (1976) 40–56; and M. Clasby, "Education as a Tool for Humanization and the Work of Paulo Freire," *The Living Light* 8 (1971) 48–59. Cf. R. L. Howe on dialogue *(The Miracle of Dialogue* [New York: Seabury, 1963]).
249. J. B. Macdonald, "Curriculum and Human Interests," in *Curriculum Theorizing: The Reconceptualists*, 290. See J. Habermas, *Knowledge and Human Interests* (Boston: Beacon, 1971) 301–317.
250. W. Pinar, "Preface" in *Curriculum Theorizing: The Reconceptualists*, x xi. See also W. Pinar, ed., *Heightened Consciousness, Cultural Revolution and Curriculum Theory* (Berkeley: McCutchan, 1974).
251. J. S. Mann, in *Curriculum Theorizing*, 132.
252. P. Phenix, in *Curriculum Theorizing*, 321.
253. J. B. Macdonald, "A Transcendental Developmental Ideology of Education," in *Heightened Consciousness*, 89.
254. Macdonald's view is filled in thoroughly by C. A. Bowers ("Educational Critics and Technocratic Consciousness").
255. Macdonald, "Curriculum and Human Interests," 283–294. Cf. J. B. Macdonald, "Curriculum Theory As Intentional Activity" (Paper delivered to the Curriculum Theory Conference, Charlottesville, Va., October 1975).
256. See M. Greene, "Curriculum and Consciousness," in *Curriculum Theorizing*, 299–320; J. J. Schwab, *The Practical: A Language for the Curriculum*.
257. D. E. Huebner, "The Thingness of Educational Content" (Paper delivered at the Conference on Reconceptualizing Curriculum Theory, Cincinnati, Ohio, 18 October 1974) 5.
258. "Toward a Remaking of Curricular Language," in *Heightened Consciousness*, 49.

259. D. E. Huebner, "Curriculum as Concern for Man's Temporality" (Paper delivered to the Colloquium on Curriculum Theory Frontiers, Ohio State University, 5 May 1967) 10.

260. Huebner, "Toward a Remaking of Curricular Language," 37.

261. Huebner, "The Thingness of Educational Content," 8.

262. On the hidden curriculum see P. Jackson (*Life in Classrooms* [New York: Holt, Rinehart and Winston, 1968]); R. Dreeben (*On What is Learned in School* [Reading, Mass.: Addison-Wesley, 1968]); M. Apple ("The Hidden Curriculum and the Nature of Conflict," in *Curriculum Theorizing*, 95–117).

263. Freire, *Pedagogy of the Oppressed*, 77.

264. J. B. Macdonald, "Values and Curriculum Theory," in *Curriculum Theory*, 20.

265. D. E. Huebner, "Language and Teaching" (Mimeographed paper, December 1968) 11.

266. D. E. Huebner, "Education in the Church," *ANQ* 12 (1972) 126.

267. Bowers, "Educational Critics and Technocratic Consciousness," 285.

268. See M. Donnellan, "Bishops and Uniformity in Religious Education, Vatican I to Vatican II," *Living Light* 11 (1963) 237–248.

269. See N. McCluskey, *Catholic Education in America: A Documentary History*, Classics in Education, No. 21 (New York: Teachers College, 1964). For a thorough analysis of the genesis of the Baltimore Catechism, see M. C. Bryce ("The Influence of the Catechism of the Third Plenary Council of Baltimore on Widely Used Elementary Religion Textbooks from Its Composition in 1885 to Its 1941 Revision" [Ph. D. Dissertation, Catholic University of America, 1970]).

270. That is not to deny the pervasive presence of the Baltimore Catechism: some 250,000 copies were sold in 1970.

271. Lee prefers the term "religious *instruction*" (the process by and through which learning is caused in an individual in one way and another) to "religious education." The latter term, which he finds more accurate than either "catechetics" or "Christian education," nevertheless is broader than instruction (for Lee, all of one's experiences are in some sense educational) and hence not specific enough for his purposes. See J. M. Lee, *The Shape of Religious Instruction* (Dayton, Ohio: Pflaum, 1971) 6–9, abbreviated henceforth as *Shape*.

272. *Ibid.* Also J. M. Lee, *The Flow of Religious Instruction* (Dayton: Pflaum, 1973), abbreviated henceforth as *Flow; The Content of Religious Instruction* (Birmingham, Ala.: Religious Education Press, forthcoming).

273. Lee, "The Teaching of Religion," in J. M. Lee and P. C. Rooney, eds., *Toward a Future for Religious Education* (Dayton: Pflaum, 1970) 56–58.

274. *Ibid.*, 62.

275. J. M. Lee, "Foreword," in *Toward a Future for Religious Education,* 1.

276. Lee, "The Teaching of Religion," 67.

277. *Ibid.*, 69.

278. *Ibid.*, 70; cf. *Shape*, 59.

279. See H. W. Burgess, *An Invitation to Religious Education* (Birmingham, Ala.: Religious Education Press, 1975) 127–165; D. J. Piveteau and J. T. Dillon, *Resurgence of Religious Instruction* (Birmingham, Ala.: Religious Education Press, 1977) 139–151.

280. *Shape*, 10–47.

281. *Shape*, 28–30; 45 n. 42.

282. See *Flow*, 28 where Lee notes: "This notion of educational practice as process content will be a theme which will undergird and permeate much of this book." Cf. "Teaching of Religion," 76–78.

283. *Shape*, 33.

284. *Ibid.*, 34.

285. *Ibid.*, 186 and 210.

286. *Ibid.*, 190.

287. *Ibid.*, 196.

288. *Flow*, 149–205.

289. *Ibid.*, 190.

290. *Ibid.*, 192–193.

291. R. H. Stein *(The Method and Message of Jesus' Teachings* [Philadelphia: Westminster, 1978]) attempts to describe the form and content of Jesus' teachings. Largely indebted to the work of Joachim Jeremias, Stein himself does not distinguish the redactional level and hence would be open to criticism from exegetes working out of a more form critical mode.

292. In a personal communication to the author dated 7 March 1979.

293. See n. 279.

294. See the debate between Lee and Michael Warren (Lee, "Behavioral Objectives in Religious Instruction," *Living Light* 7 [1970] 12–19; Warren, "All Contributions Cheerfully Accepted," *Ibid.*, 20–30; Lee, "Toward a Dialogue in Religious Instruction," *Living Light* 8 [Spring 1971] 109–121). See also C. E. Nelson, "Review of *The Flow of Religious Instruction,*" *Living Light* 11 (Spring 1974) 146–148; P.

O'Hare, "The Image of Theology in the Educational Theory of James Michael Lee," *Living Light* 11 (Fall 1974).

295. This contention is an important one in evaluating Lee's work. In claiming that social science is value free, he asserts that it is an impartial investigation and explanation of phenomena without regard for any system of thought or group of people which would assign value judgements either to the phenomena themselves or to conclusions of research. Value-oriented words such as "good" or "excellent" are replaced by terms such as "effective," "fruitful," or "useful." Value-free social science is not normative; it simply makes statements about what is, as discovered from empirical observation and testing of phenomena. In this respect it differs from theology. Nevertheless, Lee maintains that the social scientist does accept certain "benchmark" values as a necessary framework within which it operates in a value-free way *(Shape,* 142–143). For a lively discussion of this point and others regarding Lee's basic contentions, see P. O'Hare, ed. *(Foundations of Religious Education* [New York: Paulist, 1978] 112–120). For analysis of the distinctiveness of social science, see P. Starr ("The Edge of Social Science," *Harvard Educational Review* 44[1974] 393–415).

296. P. Babin, *Options* (New York: Herder and Herder, 1967) 89.

297. See Babin, *The Crisis of Faith: The Religious Psychology of Adolescence* (New York: Herder and Herder, 1963).

298. M. van Caster, *The Structure of Catechetics* (New York: Herder and Herder, 1965) 19–20.

299. M. van Caster and J. LeDu, *Experiential Catechetics* (New York: Paulist, 1969); van Caster, *Values Catechetics* (New York: Paulist, 1970).

300. *Living with Christ 3,* Book 2 (Winona, Minn.: St. Mary's College Press, 1969).

301. R. J. Heyer and R. J. Payne, eds., *Discovery Patterns Book 2: Patterns of Dynamics and Strategies* (New York: Paulist, 1969) 9.

302. P. Kennedy, *Ultimate Concern: Teacher's Manual* (Chicago: Argus, 1968) 5.

303. Heyer and Payne, *Discovery Patterns,* 49–56.

304. *Ibid.,* 50.

305. *Ibid.*

306. *Ibid.,* 54–56.

307. F. Gray, "For Lycidas Is Dead," *New York Times Book Review* (19 June 1977) 38.

308. *Sharing the Light of Faith: National Catechetical Directory for Catholics of the United States* (Washington, D.C.: United States Catholic

Conference, 1979). Thorough analysis of the National Catechetical Directory is not possible herein; of special note, however, is the document's attention to the U.S. culture, to human development, and to justice issues.

309. Moran, *Design for Religion*, 51.

310. *Ibid.*, 68.

311. G. Moran, *Religious Body* (New York: Seabury, 1974). Moran identifies the second chapter of *Religious Body* as the most important piece he has ever written ("Where Now, What Next?" *Foundations of Religious Education*, 102).

312. Moran, *Religious Body*, 150.

313. *Ibid.*, 152–153.

314. *Ibid.*, 186.

315. *Ibid.*, 184.

316. G. Moran, "Two Languages of Religious Education," *Living Light* 14 (1977) 7–15.

317. *Ibid.*, 11–15.

318. Moran, *Religious Body*, 147.

319. He notes that the *NCD* reflects both the strengths and limitations of the church. Moran praises its inclusive language, ecumenical awareness, and sections on liturgy, social ministry, and human development; he questions its explanation of revelation and of adult catechesis *(National Catholic Reporter* 15 [1 June 1979] 18).

320. G. Moran, *Education toward Adulthood* (New York: Paulist, 1979) 147.

321. See T. H. Groome, "Shared Christian Praxis: A Possible Theory/Method of Religious Education," *Lumen Vitae* 31 (1976) 186–208; "Christian Education and the Task of Prophecy," *Religious Education* 72 (1977) 262–273; "The Crossroads: A Story of Christian Education by Shared Praxis," *Lumen Vitae* 32 (1977) 45–70; and "Christian Education: A Task of Present Dialectical Hermeneutics," *Living Light* 14 (1977) 408–422. Groome is presently completing a major statement on the praxis approach, *Christian Religious Education: Sharing Our Story and Vision* (New York: Harper and Row, forthcoming).

4. The Significance of the *Heilsgeschichte* Hermeneutic for Religious Education

The late southern writer Flannery O'Connor spoke of the fiction writer's need to possess a "certain grain of stupidity." By this she meant "the quality of having to stare, of not getting the point at once"; the result of the staring was that the longer one looked at an object, the more of the world could be seen in it.[1]

That "certain grain of stupidity" is likewise a prerequisite for this concluding section on *Heilsgeschichte*. Earlier chapters have identified its roots in biblical theology, traced its rapid rise into Catholic religious education in the United States in the mid-1960s, and sought to account for its equally rapid demise. The task herein is to step back, "to stare," as O'Connor put it; by so doing, one presses the question of significance. Of what consequence is *Heilsgeschichte*? What does the ascent-descent of the salvation history hermeneutic say about Catholic religious education in the United States? What does it say about Catholic religious education and the study of Scripture?

There can, of course, be no absolute assurance that one's vision is without its blindness, no matter how prolonged the stare. The reflections of this chapter are nonetheless this writer's attempt to know what she sees rather than merely see what she knows.[2] It is intended as a concluding chapter that is at once a retrospective and an invitation to dialogue.

I. The Status of Heilsgeschichte as a Hermeneutical Principle

As the fourfold theological analysis of the preceding chapter has indicated, recent studies have cast a long shadow of doubt on salvation history as the primary principle of biblical interpretation. It has, of course, not totally receded from preeminence; a leading evangelical exegete, George E. Ladd, still contends that his own understanding of NT theology is "distinctly *heilsgeschichtlich*," even if it appears rash "to espouse a theological stance which is out of favor today."[3] Yet such a position, as Ladd himself admits, represents a minority opinion in the present theological spectrum.

The more prevalent view suggests that *Heilsgeschichte* is no longer tenable as an exclusive or overarching principle for interpreting the biblical accounts. The salvation history approach glosses over the important revelation debate, inadequately conceptualizes the relationship between OT and NT, simplistically and narrowly asserts christocentrism and (among many Catholics) equates the kingdom of God with the church. In short, *Heilsgeschichte* has not proven sufficiently strong to carry the theological weight it was made to bear; its methodological flaws are too numerous, its dogmatic interests too deterministic.

But if salvation history has proven inadequate as a single interpretative principle, it would be theologically irresponsible to consign it to oblivion. After all, as James Barr has affirmed, there really is a *Heilsgeschichte* which does indeed thematize the biblical events. But, he cautions, it is only one among a number of equally pervasive and significant axes through the biblical material; Barr's asseveration that there exists a "plurality of centers" is echoed by Gerhard Hasel's argument for a "multiplex and multiform" approach to the study of Scripture.[4]

In other words, some of the biblical traditions, particularly the exodus accounts and Luke-Acts, rather clearly manifest a perspective that a later age can classify as *Heilsgeschichte*. When Israel recites the litany of what God's steadfast love has done (Ps. 136), she is obviously mindful of a salvation history. Similarly, the early church, reading the Hebrew Scriptures with "christological eyes," sees a plan of God come to fulfillment in Jesus of Nazareth. In fact, it was in large measure this distinctive way of reading the OT which set the "followers of the Way" apart from other Jews.

The *Heilsgeschichte* hermeneutic not only has a basis in Scripture; it also has answered both apologetic and pastoral needs, particularly in the Erlangen theology of Johann C. K. von Hofmann and in the catechetical work of Josef Jungmann. The Erlangen School, it should be recalled, exercised a certain mediational function as it sought to reconcile conflicting claims about Christ and culture; here the notion of God's self-revelation in history permitted a breakthrough against the orthodox reluctance to deal with divine actions in historical terms and against the rationalist refusal to acknowledge a divine presence in human history. Just as in the early centuries of the church allegory had offered emancipation from a literal rendering of the text and had made possible an understanding of the gospel in a Greek culture, so also did salvation history provide a means for nineteenth and twentieth century followers of Herder, Hegel, and Schleiermacher to make sense of the Bible in contemporary terms.[5]

Moreover, it is strikingly characteristic that all of the scholars of the salvation history school shared a profound regard for the Bible as a book of faith. Kähler's eloquent plea—"what is present only for scholars . . . has no power to awaken and establish faith"—is powerfully reiterated in Jungmann's concern that the substance of faith not be split up by academicians. In stressing the continuity of the testaments and "smoothing" the accounts into "one, all-embracing salvific plan of God," Jungmann sought only to show an "unchanging background and fixed framework for the multifarious searchings and struggles that pass across the stage of life." His concern that the kerygma not be "overburdened" with things of "second and third rank" reveals his pastoral hierarchy: *Heilsgeschichte* may have had its origin in the nineteenth century, the "century of history," but it was always a *history in the service of faith.*[6] Salvation history was clearly directed toward helping people to come to a greater appreciation of Scripture.

Ultimately, however, the apologetic and pastoral interests proved too dominant. An excess of enthusiasm had led to oversimplification: the Bible is *not simply* the story of our salvation, the OT is *not merely* a preparation for the NT, and Jesus *not only* the one in whom God's promises are kept. To avoid such an oversimplification, it seems imperative that *Heilsgeschichte* be regarded contextually: *it should neither be isolated from, nor ele-*

vated above, other hermeneutical guides. If this stricture is not heeded, then the potential result is what NT scholar Dominic Crossan terms "salvation history on the model of Detroit's assembly line with God as Supreme Mechanic."[7] In place of the neatly diagrammed "redemptive line," a more adequate image needs to be found.

Crossan suggests that God's presence in history:

> might well be like that of Art, something ever active but without plan or consummation, without clear development or steady improvement. We might be dealing with what should be visualized as neither static circle nor ascending line, but rather as spokes coming out from a wheel's core.[8]

God's ways are more inexplicable than salvation history (particularly as popularized in Catholic religious education) led its adherents to believe. Nonetheless, *Heilsgeschichte* was not without its value; but by itself it proved an inadequate guide through the unmarked terrain of twentieth century theology.

A further matter, however, lurks in the background: if *Heilsgeschichte* proved inadequate theologically, then its educational viability may be likewise vulnerable. What message might the kerygmatic era voice for contemporary religious education?

II. Heilsgeschichte and Catholic Religious Education in the United States

In the latter portion of the preceding chapter, it was argued that the dénouement of *Heilsgeschichte* as a hermeneutical principle in Catholic religious education must be understood against a broadened horizon. Not only had theological refinements made the fundamental tenets of salvation history problematic, but, in the latter 1960s, Catholic religious education had assimilated various aspects of certain cultural and educational developments. The pluralism which resulted meant that salvation history lost its force as a motif of singular importance. Especially important in dislodging the kerygmatic approach from its position of hegemony were the humanistic trends in the culture as a whole, but mirrored particularly in education. This humanism, in league with the mid-1960s publications of Gabriel Moran, combined to constitute a "double-layered formation" which, from the present vantage point, appears to be the single most significant factor responsible for the demise of the *heilsgeschichtliche* approach.

This sharing in the cultural and educational milieux illustrates the interdisciplinary character of religious education. In the popular imagination, however, as well as in much of the literature, it is generally presumed that religious education is merely a "delivery system" for theology, or, alternatively, for the doctrine of the church. This understanding of religious education as a popularized and simplified theology or doctrine accounts in some measure for its image as an endeavor prone to bandwagons, bandages and gimmicks, a field without much historical sense, self-definition, or reputation as a scholarly discipline. In short, it reflects the lack of consensus about the very nature of religious education.

A. The Interdisciplinary Nature of Religious Education

Religious education, it may be said, has had a long past but a short history. Its foundational literature is still in primitive form, as there presently exists no classic historical account and relatively few volumes attempting to delineate the content and method of religious education as its own enterprise.[9]

Among other issues as yet unsettled, the relationship of theology to religious education has not been adequately articulated.[10] J. M. Lee was among the earliest in arguing that theology should not dominate religious education; he claimed that for centuries theologians had treated the latter as a sort of "messenger boy by whom the wisdom and understandings acquired by theological science are delivered to the multitude."[11] He, on the contrary, posited the two as being "ontologically distinct": "Religious instruction is a compound, not a mixture, formed from theology and life experience."[12]

Despite reservations about Lee's understanding of both theology and education, it seems to this writer that his point in this regard is nevertheless fundamentally accurate. Religious education is more than a vehicle for popularizing theology, and Lee's attempt to construct an overarching schema for religious instruction as an enterprise with its own legitimacy must be regarded as a pioneering venture. Moreover, his contention that religious instruction is a "compound" seems verified by the story of the salvation history era: the *heilsgeschichtliche* hermeneutic would seem to have disappeared from prominence in religious education not because of its theological inadequacies but primarily because of the combination of cultural and educational factors described in the second half of Chapter 3. This suggests that any attempt to come to terms with religious education necessarily implies attending to its interdisciplinary character.

Perhaps it might be best, in these early days of establishing a foundational literature, to speak tentatively of religious education as a "configuration" of disciplines. Configuration means that because education ("the deliberate, systematic and sustained effort to transmit, evoke or acquire knowledge, attitudes, skills or sensibilites, as well as any outcome of that effort") happens in many settings beyond the confines of the schoolhouse,[13] attention needs to be directed toward the educational dimension of a variety of agencies and institutions. Particularly in reference to religious education, the notion of con figuration suggests a systematic pattern rather than an eclectic collection; as an interdisciplinary endeavor, religious education is a confluence, not a smorgasbord.

To understand the notion of religious education as a "configuration of disciplines," it is necessary to examine the outcome of a particular theological stance as it intersects with a particular educational approach. An especially clear example is evident in the work of George Albert Coe. As a colleague of John Dewey and as a proponent of the social gospel, Coe exemplified an understanding of religious education shaped by the dual forces of liberalism and progressivism.[14]

In reaction to the nineteenth century "ecology" of institutions of Protestant religious education—tract societies, revivals, Sunday schools, missionary alliances, temperance unions—Coe transposed religious symbols into social and ethical imperatives.[15] As heir of the liberal theology of Adolf von Harnack, who had reduced Christianity to an essential core and denied the legitimacy of dogmatic meanings, Coe developed a religious system devoid of dogma or mysticism. Infatuated with empirical, scientific methods and filled with the immanentist spirit of the post-Darwinian epoch, he castigated authoritarian systems. Salvation in this era of progressivism was by education; religious education dealt not with doctrine but with *growth* (a key term for Dewey) and the transformation of values. As Coe defined religious education:

> It is the systematic, critical examination and reconstruction of relations between persons, guided by Jesus' assumption that persons are of infinite worth, and by the hypothesis of the existence of God, the great Valuer of persons.[16]

In contrast to Coe's liberalism and progressivism, H. Shelton Smith combined a neo-orthodox theology with a more traditional approach to education: "Religious education must reckon with the Barthians."[17] The kerygmatic theology of Josef Jungmann, not unlike neo-orthodoxy in content but different in function,[18] similarly merged with an understanding of education that, if largely implicit, was also basically traditional. Lumen Vitae theorist Marcel van Caster, in a variant configuration, joined his essentially kerygmatic theology with an educational approach shaped by developmental and psychological categories. The later Gabriel Moran tends to work from a liberal theological stance, but is more influenced by a progressive view of education undergirded by a philosophical anthropology.

While only an outline of religious education as a "configuration of disciplines" is being sketched here, it is obvious that such an approach helps to give *order* to the widely divergent theological and educational understandings that lie at the foundation of religious education. To develop fully the configuration schema would also entail making a judgment as to the *relative importance* given by a particular theorist to theology in relation to education (and vice versa); a further step would involve a decision in regard to *congruence,* since a particular theological view (e.g., evangelicalism) may not "fit" a specific educational stance (e.g., progressivism).

A more complete explication of this concept of configuration constitutes part of an agenda for further work; its significance in relationship to this study lies in its attempt to identify more precisely the interdisciplinary character of religious education.

Such attempts to think through foundational issues are necessitated by the lack of attention to them in the past. Certainly the era of the "reign" of *Heilsgeschichte* as the primary hermeneutical principle is vivid testimony to the tendency for religious education to expand its categories rather than attend to its fundamental tenets. The humanist influence, for instance, had contributed significantly to making the term "salvation history" passé; yet, as this humanism was appropriated in religious education in the 1960s, it proceeded from the same kerygmatic emphases which were rooted in *Heilsgeschichte*. A similar lack of attention to foundational issues is evident in the rapid shifts from the kerygmatic to the anthropological to the political categories. This tendency suggests that religious education may be entirely too susceptible to panaceas. Goodwill and sensitivity to the human situation do not dispense one from the obligation to engage in an analytic and rigorous pursuit of complex issues. Heschel's admonition to religious educators that "our generation does not know how to study, how to relate itself to the classical sources of our tradition" is pertinent here.[19]

What seems to have happened in the early-to-mid-1960s in Catholic religious education in the United States is that *emphasis on the proclamatory obscured the interpretative. Religious education was viewed as "handing on the good news." Pedagogically, this generally meant that teaching was equated with telling. Though an understanding of the message had evolved since the Baltimore Catechism era, the methodology was basically identical.*

When the shift occurred in the latter part of the decade to more anthropological categories (from "preaching" to "relating"), the emphasis on the proclamatory mode of education was replaced with a focus on the dialogical and therapeutic. Subsequently, in the political phase, the Rogerian notion of dialogue between teacher and student gave way to an emphasis on mutual action and service. *But in none of these was there systematic attention to facilitating the individual's hermeneutical skills or to developing a critical faith.*

B. A Stipulative Definition of Religious Education

Religious education, it has been argued, is characteristically interdisciplinary; one fruitful way to analyze the definitions of various theorists lies in the identification of particular configurations formed by the intersection of theology and education.

A complementary way of grappling with this interdisciplinary character is the stipulation of an alternative definition: *religious education is the making accessible of the traditions of religious communities and the making manifest of the intrinsic connection between tradition and transformation.*[20]

The definition needs, first of all, to be situated historically. The "conclusion theology" endemic to nineteenth century Catholicism and its pedagogical equivalent in the catechism, had, for all practical purposes, meant the transmission of a "completed faith." It was this type of religious education ("the very antipodes of the aspiration for a democracy of God") in both Catholicism and Protestantism that led George Coe to advocate "creative" over "transmissive" education.[21]

Coe's advocacy rested on what is, in this author's view, ultimately a false dichotomy. Yet even Josef Jungmann, certainly working out of a very different theological framework, stands in implicit agreement with Coe in contending that neither the handing on of "hereditary formulas" nor the intensive exercise of "customs, devotions, pious thoughts and practices" constitutes an adequate approach to religious education.

Historically, one might then justly regard a religious education that "hands on" traditions as the antithesis of religious education that transforms the world. But such a bifurcation cannot be long maintained; as the neo-orthodox critics made evident to the liberals, transformation of society will be inadequate without a grounding in the traditions of faith. The liberals had seen that traditions could become absolutized and empty of vitality; the neo-orthodox saw that preoccupation with changing the world can easily degenerate into an uncritical exaltation of the present moment and into nonreflective practice. Relevance, as George Tavard has so aptly commented, is but the "surface texture of thought"; without traditions, there is no basis upon which to change the world.[22] Traditions and transformation, therefore, need to be held in a fruitful tension.

The dynamic of this relationship becomes more understandable when the meaning of *tradition* is elaborated upon: *biblical theology in particular offers a promising analogue for redeeming the term.* In OT studies, for instance, much discussion centers on how Israel's faith came to expression through a long and complex process of development; how memories precious to one region (Jerusalem, Bethel, Shechem) or group (priests, wise men, Levites, prophets, court officials) were shaped, applied, and passed on; and how these "streams of tradition" ultimately flowed together to form a sacred literature. The traditions of Israel, as von Rad vividly describes, are not a series of hard and fast rules, but living memories which *narrate, instruct, regulate, inform,* and *interpret* the experience of Israel.[23]

Jesus, too, recognized the diversity of traditions. He judged some of them unacceptable because they did not witness to the kind of kingdom he envisioned: "How well you set aside the commandment of God in order to maintain your tradition!" (Mark 7:9; cf. Mark 7:1, 15). Some traditions Jesus reinterpreted: "You have learned that our forefathers were told. . . . But what I tell you is this. . ." (Matt. 5:21, 27, 33, 38, 43). Others he appropriated more in the mainstream of Jewish tradition (on the greatest commandment, Mark 12:29 and par.), or in a fashion similar to the traditions of the Essenes (such as in his *pesher* ["this is that" fulfillment motif] exegesis, e.g., the usage of Isa. 61:1–2 in Luke 4: 16–20).

The methodologies of form and redaction criticism seek to account for the way the materials of the Christian tradition were preserved, interpreted, and modified. As with their sister endeavors in OT studies, they represent tentative and, at times, hypothetical reconstruction. But the conjectural aspects of form and redaction criticism need not obscure their fundamental portrayal of the primitive church as a Spirit-filled group of men and women who remembered the words and deeds of Jesus in such a way that their memories both shaped and were shaped by the exigencies of daily life.

At issue here is not an *apologia* for biblical criticism but simply a demonstration that the tools of criticism provide insight into the fascinating and complex process by which the traditions of the Jewish and Christian communities were remembered and reactualized. Form and redaction criticism provide a perspective on the malleability and vitality of traditions and a view of the various interests which catalyzed the preservation and adaptation of traditions.

Tradition, then, provided the very "stuff" out of which new was drawn from old (see Matt. 13:51). It was made accessible in ever creative and diverse ways: what was handed on was done with care and creativity, lest the *living* nature of tradition be lost. As Klaus Koch has remarked: "The biblical word has proved to be not truth in a fossilised, unchanging sense, but truth which is constantly adapting itself to the circumstances of the time."[24]

Contemporary biblical scholarship thus serves as a prime exemplar in reevaluating the place of tradition in religious education. C. Ellis Nelson's book, *Where Faith Begins*, proposes a substantially similar understanding of tradition.[25] Moreover, refinements in biblical scholarship since the publication of that work now make it possible to see that an understanding of tradition gives religious education a basis not only in the literature of socialization (Nelson's perspective), but also grounds it in the sociology of knowledge, in which interests of various communities can be identified through the traditions they have preserved.[26]

The ramifications of this enriched understanding of tradition become evident in examining the complementary foundational element, *transformation*. Above all else, transformation is the acknowledgment that tradition is to be acted upon. The history of Israel and of the early church are paradigmatic in this respect: traditions were reactualized *for the sake of living a relationship with God and neighbor*. The stories and sayings passed on from generation to generation were not for entertainment, but for the edification (in the literal sense of "building") of the community; it is this that Letty Russell calls the search for a "usable past."[27] Traditions, derived from living, provided the reflective basis for action. Practice, in turn, shaped the preservation of tradition.

One of the best known features of semitic anthropology is that it does not separate knowing from doing or feeling from willing. The verb *yada'*, "to know," refers not merely to cognitive comprehension but to intimate experience, and is used in some cases to refer to sexual intercourse. Likewise, *leb*, "heart," encompasses characteristics that Western thought has generally ascribed to the mind (reason, insight, memory, perception, knowledge, judgment, discernment); the heart is the place of decision, the organ symbolic of understanding and will. To be given a new heart (Ezek. 36:26) is to be given new insight and will for change.[28]

Word studies may, of course, be granted undue importance. The point at issue here, however, is not an extended theological treatise on biblical vocabulary, but an indication of the essential unity in the Jewish and Christian traditions: to know God is to do God's will. To be granted a heart renewed is to be graced with the possibility of living differently.

This is by no means an original insight and undoubtedly not a controversial one as long as it remains on the level of abstraction. The rub occurs in reaching agreement on the implication. That is, what does it actually mean in concrete, specific terms to know God's will and thereby do it?

It is because of the difficulty of this question that the understanding of religious education as a *making accessible* and as a *making manifest* becomes particularly important. To give access is not to impose or to indoctrinate, but to open doors and to erect bridges. Accessibility is best understood in terms of its exemplars: making metaphors, building highways, providing introductions and commentaries, translating foreign terms, map-making and ice-breaking (both literally and figuratively) are all instances. On occasion, the only way to provide access is to destroy; demolition experts, for instance, use radical means in a controlled fashion as the initial step in establishing access.

Religious education is the discipline in which attention is directed toward the most appropriate ways a community's traditions can be made accessible to diverse peoples.

Correlatively, to speak of religious education as a making manifest of the intrinsic connection between tradition and transformation recognizes the educator's need to respect the primacy of divine grace and human freedom. The religious educator's responsibility is to show (and not only with words but to witness with one's life) that transformation is the *telos* of tradition and that orthopraxy takes precedence over, but does not neglect, orthodoxy. As Edward Schillebeeckx has written, "Christianity is not a purely hermeneutic undertaking or a question of pure *theoria;* it is ultimately a question of action in faith."[29] But, and this is a crucial distinction, it is not the religious educator's role to specify the precise actions flowing from a person's faith.

Admittedly, the subtlety of the distinction must be recognized, lest the essential unity between tradition and transformation be obscured. It is not to suggest that religious educators avoid pressing crucial questions of significance or probing for the ethical and political ramifications of the traditions. Christians, for instance, cannot project the "glad tidings" of the gospel into an other-worldly happiness, or they have missed the meaning of the incarnation. If God saw fit to "pitch a tent" in the ordinary, workaday world, Christian religious educators can hardly do otherwise.

But, on the other hand, educators must submit their own visions and convictions to an "asceticism of negativism," a process of continual questioning of presuppositions and standpoints.[30] Not only may it be as idolatrous to equate the diversity of traditions with any single economic or social system as it is to worship a God who makes no demands,[31] but a distorted emphasis on the religious educator as the one who sets the standards of behavioral change in others masks the educator's own standpoint. The language of "readiness for learning" and the attention to developmental stages obviously have their place. But, characteristically, little or no attention is directed toward examining the educator's own readiness and development; in this light, Dwayne Huebner terms the developments in the behavioral sciences the source of a "false optimism."[32]

Huebner points out that, as development and learning can be more precisely explained and learning experiences more effectively designed, educators have an excuse for "not attending to how we live with young people"; that, as stages of thinking can be identified and better materials and teaching techniques can be designed, educators can avoid listening and conversing more carefully with children; that, as the social structure of schools can be more accurately described, the goals of education more clearly specified, and the content of schools more efficiently organized, educators hide the political control of knowledge and thus escape the responsibility to "rethink and reshape institutions within which people dwell together."[33]

Huebner challenges religious educators to penetrate into their own foundations and to live within their doubts rather than to escape into the "pseudo-assurance" of the secular educator. His mandate to engage in critical reflection about origins and alternatives shifts the burden of responsibility from the young to the adult, lest the "mote in the adult's eye" be the idolatrous life form he or she imposes upon the powerless child, a neophyte in an established community.[34]

A similar challenge is voiced by Bernard Lonergan; in affirming that there are basic theological questions "whose solution depends on the personal development of theologians," Lonergan relates an ancient notion of the term *praxis* (the conduct and doing that results from deliberation and choice under the guidance of practical wisdom) to the growth of the theologian.[35] Utilizing Eric Voeglin's distinction between revelation and information, Lonergan speaks of the importance of the theologian's being one who "habitually dwells in the world mediated by meaning and motivated by values." Such a theologian has moved from the "horizon of ocular vision" to the "horizon of being" in which one discovers and follows up on significant questions.[36] Lonergan argues that, though a distinction may be made between a theologian's spiritual life and professional activities, a separation of the two is false.

This essay, together with his understanding of intellectual conversion as sublated (preserved and carried forward to a fuller realization within a richer context) by the moral and religious conversions, suggests that much emphasis in religious education may be misplaced.[37] Rather than the continual talk of "readiness for learning," should not there be equal attention to "readiness for teaching"? Then, in Huebner's phrase, education grounded in religion will not be a "vehicle of control," but rather an "opportunity for reflection about the meaning and significance of the life styles of educator and educatee."[38]

In sum, "to make accessible" and "to make manifest" focus not on changing the other but on the educator's dual responsibility to (1) present the traditions in all their luminosity and significance; and (2) allow individuals to appropriate freely those traditions as they are helped to interpret, evaluate, and reactualize them according to their own graced development. The first responsibility demands that religious educators themselves have a sense of the inner coherence of the traditions, that is, that they possess a competence born of a deep understanding and insight.[39] The second suggests how religious educators should make manifest the transformational character of tradition: to utilize a dialogical mode which summons participants to their own analysis and decision rather than to impose some sort of revivalist diatribe which demands conversion according to the program of the preacher.

C. Implications of the New Definition

This concept of religious education necessitates making some changes from the days of the reign of salvation history, and even from the post-*heilsgeschichtliche* era. First, it entails a willingness to make the traditions accessible in all their ambiguities and ambivalences. While, for instance, the salvation history adherents did Catholics the favor of opening up the world of the Old Testament, they reductionistically flattened out the long struggle for monotheism mirrored in the biblical texts, and eliminated much of the diversity and contradiction in the various layers of traditions. As a consequence, only a superficial comprehension of the Scriptures was fostered. Both in the handing on of specific biblical texts and in the presentation of the overall salvific plan, little indication was given of the developing character of traditions, that is, of how traditions emerge out of a process in which believers interpret the memory of the past as normative for the faith of the future. The nearly exclusive concentration on proclamation tended to result in a certain glibness about God's "plan of salvation." Underemphasized was the necessity of bringing interpretative powers to bear on issues not easily resolved even in the light of the Bible and of traditional church teaching.

By recognizing the nexus of traditions and stressing the importance of responsible freedom in appropriating them, the proposed definition may facilitate an expanded notion of faith. During the salvation history period, education in faith was of profound significance; Jungmann, it may well be remembered, had proposed a pastorally-oriented approach as a critique of the desiccated theology of the schoolmen. But though the concern of the kerygmatics for faith was genuine, their notion of faith left little room for doubt: *Heilsgeschichte* was a positivistic schema.

What is needed, particularly in Catholicism, is an understanding of religious education that facilitates the development of a faith which encompasses a critical sense. Langdon Gilkey rightly criticizes the life of the Catholic community, otherwise rich in learning, intelligence, and devotion, as more "archaic, trivial and defensive" than it might have been had not its traditions been de-historicized and absolutized.[40] Catholicism had characteristically prized rational reflection and thereby held faith and reason in mutuality; but, as Gilkey so insightfully comments, the speculative rather than the critical powers of reason held sway in it.[41]

Welcome, then, is the contention of Avery Dulles that the chief task of faith may well be "to preclude superficial and premature answers, which give the impression of having mastered the unfathomable."[42] One of the principal implications of the definition stipulated herein is that it acknowledges this type of faith. To educate religiously is not simply to evangelize or to socialize; it is not to indoctrinate with ready-made answers, but to draw forth questions and to direct and encourage the search engendered by questioning; it is not to manipulate with Skinnerian conditioning, but to make traditions accessible for the transformation of the world.

A third change must occur if religious education is to be

enhanced by lessons from its own history: religious education must value and seek to develop the individual's responsibility to learning. The era of the dominance of *Heilsgeschichte* reflected the persistence of anti-intellectualism that has long plagued religious education. In the United States, Catholics not only shared in the general anti-intellectualism of the pioneer nation, but had their own further causes. The huge number of relatively uneducated immigrants (the church absorbed nearly 9,317,000 immigrants in the period from 1820 to 1920), the absence of any prominent intellectual tradition among American Catholics, the emphasis on the school as an agency for moral development,[43] and a spirituality which cautioned against the pride of the intellectual while exalting the humility of the unlettered all served to undermine any legitimation of a learned, doubt-encompassing faith for other than a small elite. And even that elite were prevented from full freedom in their scholarly pursuits because of the "siege mentality" associated with the modernist era from which the church has only slowly emerged.

Moran's contention, cited earlier, that the great crisis in religious education was *not* the disappearance of the catechism or theology manual but the naive hope that Christianity could be passed on in "an incredibly complex world" with "a bit of Scripture and liturgy and much sincerity and good will," is appropriate here.[44] The sort of sustained inquiry Moran has called for stands in stark contrast to the anti-intellectualism so pervasive in Catholic religious education. In particular his remarks may be read as a critique of the kerygmatic proclivity to reduce the Scripture to an easily schematized plan of God.

Moran's own reconsideration of the meaning of the intellectual life provides a rich alternative. He considers intelligence to be the human capacity to deal with life as a whole, including within itself the entire spectrum of human affectivity:

Although feeling may not include intelligence, intelligence always subsumes feeling within itself. . . . Intelligence not only sees life as it is but as it can be. . . . The aim of intelligence is to understand life rather than oppose it, not to suppress spontaneity but to enlarge it. . . . In my use of the word, it is simply impossible to be too

intellectual, that is, too interested in persons perceiving, symbolizing, understanding and directing experience.[45]

In Moran's perspective, the intellectual life signifies a prizing of
the distinctively human capacity to understand one's life; it, he
stipulates, is a "transcending of reason" which is possible only
by discipline and communion.[46]

Fourthly, the definition of religious education being proposed here suggests the need to reconsider the role of doctrine
in Catholic religious education. As noted at numerous points in
earlier chapters, *Heilsgeschichte* as a hermeneutical principle is
closely aligned with doctrinal interests, a not surprising phenomenon in view of its popularity in Lutheranism and Catholicism. But it reflects a one-dimensional and reified notion of
doctrine, particularly in the kind of ecclesiology characteristic
of Catholic salvation-history adherents. The *Heilsgeschichte*
hermeneutic too easily served to deliver people from their own
obligation to think by prematurely claiming "the church
teaches," thus by implication suggesting that the tradition is
ready-made and finished, rather than vital and accumulative.
Because of this, the correlative to the church as teacher—that
is, the "church as learner"—was seldom, if ever, emphasized.
The concept of the church as learner would be an acknowledgment of the church's obligation to pursue the meaning and
significance of the gospel in every age, and hence be a catalyst
for religious education.

Such criticism should not be construed as a desire to remove
doctrine from Catholicism or, more particularly, to absolve the
religious educator from any responsibility to teach doctrine. On
the contrary, the doctrinal emphases are among the most distinct characteristics of the Catholic tradition of education and,
hence, are of great significance. At its best, Catholicism's concern
for doctrinal formulation reflects the insistence on interpretation and serves as a counter to the dangers of individualism
and privatization. Doctrine facilitates unity and identity and
suggests the respect given to inquiry.[47] That it all too often falls
short ought not to be taken as a reason for a romantic emphasis
on feeling to the exclusion of sustained questioning. The catechism mentality handed on simplistic formulations. The keryg-

matics repeated the biblical formulas, and the experiential catechists virtually ignored doctrine. None of these is an adequate *modus operandi.*

Baum's admonition that the "traditioning" of the gospel is neither the repetition of an ancient formula nor the reiteration of biblical sayings points to the deficient conceptualization of doctrine in the *Heilsgeschichte* hermeneutic.[48] It too easily led to "indoctrination" (in which the church is a surrogate parent and critical inquiry is not facilitated) rather than to a teaching that made traditions *accessible.* The latter mode of teaching reflects the malleability of traditions and accepts the complexity and paradoxes of the religious journey while accepting the church's role as a unifier of vision. Ironically, indoctrination is insufficiently conservative:

> That the Church cannot be faithful to the Gospel by repeating the original message but that, in order to preserve it, she may have to reformulate and, hence, change it, is acknowledged in the Catholic doctrine of "divine tradition" . . . We cannot protect the Gospel by repeating the ancient formulas. If we insist on repeating them without qualification, we may actually announce another message and hence fail to mediate the divine self-communication to men.[49]

The kerygmatic movement rooted in *Heilsgeschichte* had, as Jungmann so painfully discovered when his *Die Frohbotschaft* was banned, once been a prophetic moment in church renewal. But its content was too simplistic, too locked into ancient formulas to sustain the depths of Catholic tradition and to reflect the richness of the Scriptures. It was not, in short, an adequate base in which religious education theory and practice could be grounded.

It is, of course, not so difficult to reach such conclusions from the present vantage point, the adage about hindsight again being verified. But the issue at hand is that of *insight,* which in this instance means reflecting ("staring" at) on the era of the supremacy of *Heilsgeschichte* for the sake of what it reveals about the present. There is no intention in these pages of arrogantly dismissing that period in Catholic religious education as if it were of little consequence or of angrily condemning its inadequacies.

But, as the decade of the sixties so well manifested, religious education, like education in general, had shifted from one movement to another without seriously and systematically examining the ground from which its roots are nourished. This critical perspective on *Heilsgeschichte* is, in fact, testimony to the value of that era precisely because it uncovers so much about religious education.

What, then, in summary, does the rapid rise and fall of salvation history as a hermeneutical principle say about Catholic religious education in the United States? It illustrates the interdisciplinary nature of that endeavor, in contrast to the more common understanding of religious education as a "delivery system" for theology. Secondly, it reflects the proclivity to panaceas that has characterized recent ventures and mirrors the anti-intellectualism of much of American Catholicism, thereby divorcing theory from practice and glossing over the roots of the present pluralism. Thirdly, it demonstrates the inadequacy of religious education as proclamation.

Analysis of the history of this significant period in religious education has generated a definition that attempts to remedy, at least in part, those defects. By speaking of religious education as making accessible the traditions of the religious community and making manifest the intrinsic connection between tradition and transformation, the author hopes to learn from the story of the salvation history era and to contribute to the literature of an emerging discipline.

The proposed definition does not deftly or definitively solve the complexities of religious education. It presents, rather, an agenda for further study. What, for instance, is the pedagogical shape of a religious education in the interpretative mode? How can faith and intelligence be shown to be "friends"?[50] What is the developmental framework for a critical faith?[51] How might religious educators engender the reactualization of the traditions of the religious community? These, and numerous other questions, are part of the task of a lifetime, and necessarily go far beyond this brief retrospective. But they are reflections drawn from the narrative of the previous chapters: *Heilsgeschichte* as a hermeneutical principle in religious education has proved to be an instructive phenomenon.

III. *Religious Education and Contemporary Biblical Scholarship*

By "staring" at the salvation history hermeneutic in Catholic religious education in the United States, one may derive both an understanding of its interdisciplinary character and a reformulated definition. Further probing into the meaning of the kerygmatic era uncovers an obligation too easily glossed over in current concerns: the special responsibility and role of religious educators in regard to modern study of Scripture. Because the discipline of religious education is formed at the juncture of specific theological and educational approaches, its professionals necessarily utilize theology and education in their task of making accessible traditions and making manifest their transformational character. To utilize theology demands both an intelligent comprehension of the methodology and meaning of modern biblical scholarship and a sensitivity to its enormous pastoral implications. The simple fact is that the advent of historical criticism has revolutionized the study of Scripture: religious educators ignore this revolution at their own peril and at the peril of their communities.

A. *A New Attitude toward the Bible*

There can be little doubt that people today do not approach the Bible as did people of a previous era. In the past, as Dennis Nineham writes, people were universally convinced that God produced the Bible and that, therefore, the text could be taken at face value, because it meant precisely what it said. Consequently, little attention was directed toward an author's historical situation or the context of a passage. Each passage had an evident meaning; its references, moreover, were factual: if the NT spoke of Christ expelling demons or proclaimed the coming of the messiah, then it was assumed that demons actually existed and that a person called the messiah had come into the world.[52]

The modern *Weltanschauung*, however, leads to a different set of interests and questions in biblical interpretation, particularly in the Western world.[53] Rather than automatically accepting a passage at its face value, persons today might much more readily probe into "what really happened?" Moreover, for many contemporary persons the cultural distance seems very great indeed, so that a further query arises: what might all this mean today?

To categorize contemporary perspectives, five related sets of concerns may be identified as undergirding the modern's approach to the Bible.[54] The first centers around *relevance*. Obviously a number of the issues of biblical times—such as the controversy in the early church regarding circumcision and dietary laws—are simply not at stake today. How can the Bible, an ancient document, speak to current concerns? A second matter involves the factor of *communicability*. Given the tremendous cultural gulf, how does one grasp what an earlier age with a different mentality thought? As American literary critic Lionel Trilling once wrote:

> To suppose that we can think like men of another time is as much of an illusion as to suppose that we can think in a wholly different way. . . . It ought to be for us a real question whether, and in what way, human nature is always the same. I do not mean that we ought to settle this question before we get to work, but only that we insist to ourselves that the question is a real one. What we certainly know has changed is the *expression* of human nature, and we must keep before our minds the problem of the relation which expression bears to feeling. . . . The problem . . . is a very difficult one, and I scarcely even state its complexities, let alone pretend to solve them. But the problem with its difficulties should be admitted, and simplicity of solution should always be regarded as a sign of failure.[55]

Trillings's contention that "simplicity of solution should always be regarded as a sign of failure" stands as a warning signal to those who impatiently demand instant application of biblical matters to contemporary complexities. The insistence on relevance so characteristic of the present era reflects a genuine need to create a "usable past," but the alacrity and simplicity with which the relevant is determined may well distort the past. Perhaps what is truly relevant can be ascertained only after confronting the distance between past and present.

Thirdly, legitimate questions exist about the *limitations* of the Bible. Its literature encompasses a limited segment of time and people. How can its insights be decisive for all times and people? In what sense do biblical injunctions and stories transcend their particularity? Fourthly, how does this era articulate the *normativity* of the Scriptures, and what is the status of the Bible vis-à-vis other norms? If the Bible is the *norma normans non normata,* then how does its authority function in theology and ethics?[56] How, for instance, is the teaching of Jesus on marriage and divorce authoritative for the present culture? Or what is the authority of the Bible in regard to issues such as genetic engineering or nuclear power—complex matters simply outside the scope of the biblical authors?

A fifth crucial question revolves around the *obligation of Christians and Jews to speak to the world in terms it can hear and understand* rather than merely to repeat biblical formulations. How can the power of the Word be heard anew in the twentieth century?

The pastoral import of these and related questions cannot be underestimated. Schillebeeckx suggests that believers, if they are to be faithful to the gospel, must undergo the "ordeal of a new interpretation" of faith.[57] Biblical scholars and religious educators themselves are, of course, not exempt from such a "passage through fire," and it may be the case that much of their work derives from their own need to reinterpret their understanding of faith in an increasingly pluralistic world. Yet, though they hold in common many of the same questions and concerns, the last decade in particular has witnessed a widening gulf between biblical scholars and religious educators. It is necessary to identify possible reasons for such a chasm because the pastoral ramifications of modern biblical study are crucial for the work of both groups.

B. *The Chasm between Religious Education and Biblical Scholarship*

Whatever can be learned from the salvation history era is of great importance, since the literature otherwise offers an embarrassing testimony of silence in regard to the relationship of the two. It is obvious from the narrative of the third chapter that *Heilsgeschichte* was abandoned by biblical scholars in general before it fell out of favor for a different set of reasons among religious educators. In the first generation of twentieth century Catholic biblical scholarship (that is, in the years following the 1943 publication of *Divino Afflante Spiritu*), North American scholars such as David Stanley had promulgated salvation history along the lines of Cullmann, while French scholars, exemplified in Jean Daniélou, propounded it with a greater emphasis on the typological. The popularity of Stanley's 1959 essay, "The Conception of Our Gospels As Salvation History," testified to the eagerness with which Scripture studies were received by religious educators.[58] Moreover, the institution of *Worship's* regular column on Scripture in 1955, the inauguration of a popular, nontechnical magazine, *Bible Today*, in 1963, and the publication of C. Luke Salm's 1964 anthology *(Studies in Salvation History)* were but three examples of the flood of Scripture materials readily available to Catholics for the first time. In the biblical renewal engendered by *Divino Afflante Spiritu* and fostered by Vatican II, Catholics had a hitherto unknown hunger for an understanding of Scripture. For many, emphasis was on *Heilsgeschichte* as the primary hermeneutical principle. Such was the tale of the second chapter of this study.

But what originally appeared to be a strong linkage between biblical scholars and religious educators—albeit one in which religious education was clearly a "delivery system" for biblical scholarship—soon changed. It is difficult to assert with confidence precisely what happened, but at least three causes can be readily identified. First, many religious educators discovered, after their initial flush of enthusiasm, that "proclaiming the Good News" along the salvation-history line did not long assure them of a captive audience. It was, to be sure, a refreshing improvement over the catechism, but it did not seem to touch deeply the lives of those who heard it. Thus they moved from the kerygmatic to the relational in hopes that questions such as "What does King David have to do with me?" would be answered by discussion and "experience." (Alas! usually collage construction!)

Secondly, Catholic biblical scholarship was rapidly developing and reaching a new level of maturity. The proliferation of knowledge made possible by philological refinements and by new finds such as at Qumran and Nag Hammadi meant that studies grew more technical and specialized.[59] As the guild of biblical scholars expanded, it necessarily engaged in its own level of communication, utilizing the vocabulary proper to its own growth. But what facilitated discussion among scholars alienated nonspecialists. To the neophyte, the typical Scripture article or book read like a manual of glossolalia.

Closely related to this was a third factor: as biblical scholars more and more skillfully employed the tools of biblical criticism, religious educators and other nonspecialists grew correspondingly more and more bewildered. In earlier days, the scholars had opened the treasures of Scripture to a hungry public; it seemed now as if they were trying to destroy those treasures. Popular journals such as *Time* and *Newsweek* reported just enough of scholarly debates about the "New Quest of the Historical Jesus," the creation story, virgin birth, and infancy narratives to make that public either suspicious about biblical scholars or about the veracity of Scripture—or both. It is no exaggeration to claim that the relatively sudden advent of biblical criticism in Catholic scholarship set off a crisis in Catholic renewal exacerbated by the accompanying "aftershocks" of Vatican II.[60] The meaning and role of the Bible in religious education accordingly became very problematic.

Added to this bewilderment was what appeared to be the negative function of historical criticism (termed the "destruction-sophistication complex" by Monika Hellwig) for the devotional life of many believers.[61] The immediate outcome of much of the scholarly work to date has been to clear away misunderstandings and oversimplifications (such as the popular misconception that, in calling Jesus the Son of God, the NT writers were affirming the same philosophical propositions as did the later councils). This apparently "destructive" work is more of the nature of pruning, because it ultimately has produced many fruitful new understandings, but the positive contribution of historical criticism has not always been evident to nonspecialists and thus has been received with antagonism or ambivalence.

A further "fly in the ointment" has been an arrogance that has at times infected certain practitioners of historical criticism. NT exegete Leander Keck reports an attitude of pseudo-liberation among beginning scholars; he suggests that their prayer of thanksgiving might be something like:

> Lord, I thank thee that I am no longer the pious conservative I once was. I know that some psalms were composed for the enthrone-ment festival borrowed from Mesopotamia. I know that II Corin-thians is a compilation of at least four letter fragments. I know that most of the Fourth Gospel does not accurately report Jesus' words. Above all, I am thankful that I have been liberated from my past by what I know.[62]

The gap between biblical scholar and nonspecialist (including most religious educators) is a serious and potentially harmful divide. The Bible is above all else the church's book: it is not the exclusive property of a professional guild of scholars. When Joseph Parker asked in the nineteenth century, "Have we to await a communication from Tübingen or a telegram from Oxford before we can read the Bible?" he was posing a question that remains unanswered today.[63]

Three matters are at stake here. One involves the increased dependence upon professionals and specialists with the con-comitant devaluation of "lay" opinion. Sociologist John Cole-man proffers the opinion that the split in the church today is not between clergy and laity, but between professionals and laity. As a result, there is what Ivan Illich calls a "professional monopoly"; accordingly, the social structure of the church is stratified into a new hierarchy: "professionals have a penchant for turning co-participant *peers* into *clients.*"[64] Allied with this is Paul Minear's concern that academe rather than the church will claim the interests and energies of biblical scholars and theolo-gians in the future.[65]

A second matter of concern is that the division between scholar and nonspecialist will obscure the positive contribution of historical criticism. Without doubt, historical criticism has made the Bible more difficult to read; no longer is it possible to treat Scripture as a source of timeless truths addressed to the world at large. But if a certain pseudo-innocence has been lost, the gains are enormous.[66] Biblical criticism functions *apologetically* in the church; it is an intellectually honest tool in the contemporary mode. Perhaps most illustrative of this is the rapprochement between science and religion made possible in part by a historical-critical reading of the creation narratives of Genesis; no longer need one find the Bible incompatible with evolutionary theory. Moreover, biblical criticism offers the church a *tool for discernment* in arbitrating between conflicting interpretations. By its attention to the original meaning of a passage in its historical and literary contexts, biblical criticism serves to correct oversimplifications that, especially when hardened into ideologies (such as the linkage of the messiahship of Jesus with Christian imperialism which resulted in persecution of Jews) or used as warrants for moral crusades (such as witch hunts legitimated by reference to Exod. 22:18) that have done untold harm. The ecumenical import of this corrective tool is obvious.

In addition, biblical criticism offers a *paradigm for theological reflection* in the church. Redaction criticism, in particular, by its attention to the development, diversity, and modification of traditions, provides insight into ways the contemporary church might similarly adapt the teachings of Jesus to new situations. Such a possibility has, for instance, been proffered by Joseph Fitzmyer in his study of the divorce texts in Matthew's gospel.[67] Fitzmyer raises the question whether the Catholic church today might not find a warrant for rethinking its teaching on divorce by following the model of the Matthean church which, in its concern for Gentiles who had married within a degree of kinship closer than that permitted by Jewish law (Lev. 18:6–18), modified Jesus' absolute prohibition against divorce (Matt. 5:31–32; 19:3–9).

By enabling reinterpretation of ancient texts, modern biblical scholars, utilizing the full range of their critical tools, offer the church fruitful ways of listening anew to its Scripture. But precisely at this juncture, a third matter of concern arises: however invaluable is the contribution of modern scripture scholars, their work suffers the limitation of a Western, first-world (and generally white, male) reading of the text. One who is hungry or denied other fundamental human rights may well approach the Bible with a very different set of interests. If the value of biblical criticism is to be recognized, then its limitations must also be recognized.

Spanish exegete Luis Alonso-Schökel has best posed the issue:

> Scientific exegesis is a Western product today; indeed, when it comes to the Old Testament, it is not merely Western but almost exclusively German and Anglo-American. So it is no use talking about some abstract, hypothetical exegesis; one has to take the one in existence; and so the question today has to be posed in these terms: "Does a Chinaman need German scientific exegesis to understand Scripture? Does an African need Anglo-American exegetical knowledge?"[68]

Alonso-Schökel, following up his own query, suggests that scientific exegesis is justified only insofar as it offers a "necessary or useful service to the ecclesial community and to the degree that this service is necessary or useful."[69] Specifically, he identifies four means of service exegetes may contribute to the universal church: (1) the service of translation; (2) linguistic service—helping people penetrate the major concepts, symbols, formulas, and structures of the Bible; (3) the service of a rigorous, analytical training and methodology; and (4) the service of revealing hidden riches in a text. He sees the translation and linguistic services as possessing a universal and permanent validity. Scientific exegesis, moreover, has a legitimate function in criticizing the "multiplicity of traditions which have grown up without sufficient discipline or accountability," but he cautions:

> Scientific exegesis can deal with questions conditioned by the tastes of the age or region, but must avoid the dangers of concentrating on irrelevant problems, of gratuitously complicating what is simple, and of replacing deep understanding with erudition. It will be able to avoid these dangers only by keeping in contact with Christian experience and retaining a living understanding of Scripture.[70]

Alonso-Schökel's conviction that "Christians who belong to critical, scientific cultures cannot renounce the use of acquired knowledge,"[71] and his concern that exegetical expertise must be brought to bear on truly important issues is amply fulfilled by Raymond E. Brown's attempt to wrestle with biblical criticism in the life of the North American church. Brown offers two theses in response to his own question as to why NT criticism does not more adequately "leaven" the discussion of American Catholics, particularly in regard to sensitive issues of church doctrine and life.[72]

The first argument he proposes is that Catholic NT scholarship, because of its origin (no first-class American Catholic graduate biblical school) and history (a misunderstanding that Vatican II had provided an "advanced" level of NT scholarship, and antiquated views about NT scholarship and dating), has generally been "mild and somewhat slow to come to grips with sensitive areas that crucially affect christology and ecclesiology."[73] A prime example is the failure to understand the gospel inclusion of postresurrection sayings of Jesus as a distillation from the first century experience of the early church. Many, if not most, American Catholics do not have the conceptual framework, for example, to understand Matt. 16:18 ("You are Peter") as a postresurrectional saying. Thus they operate out of a "blueprint ecclesiology," presuming that Jesus specified a precise plan for his church.[74] As a result, subsequent generations have "no real possibility for changing church structure."[75]

A second thesis follows: American Catholics are still affected by a wrong understanding of how to relate biblical criticism to church teaching. Brown cites three examples in support of this. First, there is the attempt to solve modern critical problems on the basis of dogmatic statements formulated in precritical eras. An obvious instance is the assertion that "Christ founded the church," a statement that modern criticism would regard as a distillation from the entire NT picture and from the whole of first century history rather than as an observable action by Jesus during his historical ministry. Secondly, Catholics have a tendency to interpret the silence of the NT in the light of later dogmatic interests; witness the claim that only a male ordained by a bishop by means of imposition of hands can validly preside at the eucharist and the implicit expectation that this can be proved by the NT. Thirdly, Catholics tend to neglect or underplay texts which do not accord with later dogmatic positions; a vivid example is the refusal to acknowledge the unfavorable view of the natural family of Jesus (including, of course, Mary) in Mark 3:21–35 and 6:1–6, and instead to harmonize the Marcan position with later emphases in Matthew and Luke.[76] Brown concludes:

> There are those in the Church who charge that biblical criticism is barren and that we need a more spiritual reading of the Bible. Criticism may be barren in the hands of certain practitioners, but some who make the charge would dearly like to distract Catholics from a frank and honest discussion of the origins of Christianity and the challenging implications of those origins for bringing about change in the Church of today.... In particular, American Catholic NT criticism, as it begins to be more trenchant than was possible in the period of the Council, must draw out honestly the implications of its observations for theology and ecclesiology and ecumenism.[77]

C. *Proposals for Collaboration*

Brown's theses may, in this author's view, be amplified by a third contention: biblical criticism will not permeate church life until religious educators collaborate with Scripture scholars.[78] Foundational to such collaboration is an understanding of the other's constitutive responsibility. Perhaps the confusions over foundational categories endemic to religious education have blinded biblical scholars to its importance, just as their tendency to obscurantism has shrouded the power of biblical criticism from religious educators. Both are necessary: whereas biblical theologians utilize their research skills to illumine the nature and content of the biblical traditions, religious educators utilize their educational expertise to make accessible those traditions. Insofar as both groups function as part of a community of believers, they share a pastoral obligation to manifest the transformational power of the traditions.

1. The Formation of Religious Educators.   Analysis of the kerygmatic era reveals a chasm rather than collegiality. As Catholic biblical scholarship in the 1960s and 1970s grew more technical and trenchant, religious educators became less able to utilize it in their work. There is no evidence to suggest opposition on their part to the developing maturity of biblical studies; rather only bewilderment and lack of comprehension. *To study the ascent-descent of Heilsgeschichte in Catholic religious education in the United States is to see the need for serious and systematic preparation of religious educators in the premises and practices of modern biblical scholarship.*

Implicit, of course, in this proposal is the assumption that the formation of religious educators will be grounded in *sustained study of the Scripture itself,* including some schooling in exegetical methodology and in biblical theology. Nothing can or should substitute for this.

But a necessary complement to a first-level encounter with the text is an understanding of the nature and significance of biblical scholarship; explicit attention to this will foster the background necessary for collaboration with Scripture scholars and facilitate the development of a context for utilizing the results of biblical criticism. Religious educators who understand the fundamental processes, the meaning, and the limitations of contemporary biblical studies will be better able to make intelligent decisions about when and how to appropriate the contributions of those studies.

Two areas, the *history of biblical interpretation* and *interpretation theory* itself, seem especially promising in leading to a deepened grasp of biblical scholarship. The first provides a panoramic view of the varied modes by which the Bible has been understood over the centuries. To examine the way the NT authors read the Hebrew Scriptures with "christological eyes" helps to nuance and to place in context the assertion that the OT is fulfilled in the NT. To study interpretation in the early church permits one to see the apologetic function of allegory as well as to become aware of its extravagant excesses.

Likewise, some familiarity with interpretation in the early Middle Ages provides insight into the results of a preoccupation with a spiritual rather than a literal reading of a text and into the retardation caused by excessive adherence to past interpretations. A review of the later Middle Ages manifests biblical interpretations as popularized in cathedral windows, mystery plays, illustrated Bibles, and poetry.

Particularly important is the transition from "precritical" to "critical" interpretation during the Enlightenment period, for which the Reformation and Renaissance served as underlying causes, and Deism and textual criticism the more immediate causes. The shift was completed during the nineteenth century, an era which decisively shaped the agenda for twentieth century scholarship because of its great scholars, such as Ferdinand Baur, David Strauss, Julius Wellhausen, and Herman Gunkel. Against this horizon the developments and dilemmas of contemporary scholarship become clearer. The historical perspective is invaluable; elsewhere I have indicated in detail how it might be obtained by religious educators.[79] Care needs to be taken, however, neither to dwell on history to the exclusion of the biblical texts themselves, nor to lose sight of the way in which interpretation spills over into action. Thus it is appropriate that one specific text be utilized as a focal point over the spectrum of interpretations. By so doing, one sees not merely the history of interpretation, but also something of how a given passage functions in the life of a community.

A text that has proven particularly luminous in this regard is the narrative of Abraham's sacrifice of Isaac (Gen. 22:1–19). God's command to Abraham to take his son, his only son Isaac, whom he loves, to Mount Moriah and offer him there as a burnt offering, continues to evoke awe in modern readers, just as it did in earlier interpreters. Its enigmatic, mysterious nature suggests rich possibilities for interpretation.

For both Jews and Christians, Abraham is a model of faith; nevertheless, the story of his sacrifice has functioned very differently in the life of their respective communities. Precisely because, as Judah Goldin has so aptly expressed it, "text and personal experience are not two autonomous domains" but are, on the contrary, "reciprocally enlightening," the differing experiences of Jewish and Christian communities have shaped their hearing and usage of the text.[80]

Without going into extensive detail, the general contours of their respective traditions of interpretation can be expressed as follows: for Jews the binding of Isaac (the *Akedah,* from the

verb in Gen. 22:9, ʿkd, to bind) has served as a story of martyr-
dom and survival, and thus as a paradigm of their own slaugh-
ter and endurance. For Christians, it has served as a type of the
crucifixion, and hence as a way of understanding the meaning
of the death of Jesus. Within these basic points of view, of
course, there are numerous variations; these variants are, to a
large extent, understandable in terms of the major interpretative patterns.

In Jewish literature, the Book of Jubilees (ca. 150–125 B.C.)
most likely represents the earliest commentary on Gen. 22:1–
19; its rendition is quite close to the original, except in its as-
signment of the 15th Nisan as the date of the sacrifice. Philo of
Alexandria, whose architectonic schema of allegory enabled
him to "transform Scripture into the nature and experience" of
every person,[81] recounts the narrative with substantial accu-
racy, only to add:

> But the story here told is not confined to the literal and obvious
> explanation, but seems to have in it the elements of a further
> suggestion, obscure to the many but recognized by those who pre-
> fer the mental to the sensible and have the power to see it. It is as
> follows. The proposed victim is called in Chaldaean Isaac, but, if
> the word is translated into our language, Laughter. But the laugh-
> ter here understood is not the laughter which amusement arouses
> in the body, but the good emotion of the understanding, that is joy.
> This the Sage is said to sacrifice as his duty to God, thus showing in
> a figure that rejoicing is most closely associated with God alone. For
> mankind is subject to grief and very fearful of evils either present
> or expected, so that men are either distressed by disagreeables close
> at hand or are agitated by troublous fear of those which are still to
> come. But the nature of God is without kind, and alone partakes of
> perfect happiness and bliss. The frame of mind which has made
> this true acknowledgement of God, Who has banished jealousy
> from His presence in His kindness and love for mankind, fitly
> rewards by returning the gift in so far as the recipient's capacity
> allows.[82]

Allegory permitted Philo to bring together his Jewish heritage with Hellenistic modes of thought. For the historian
Flavius Josephus, Abraham's offering of Isaac at the age of
twenty-five is regarded as a means by which the son will be
placed nearer God, thus able to be a succorer and supporter for

his father's old age. Such a thought causes pleasure to Isaac who proceeds immediately to the altar to be sacrificed.[83]

This view of Isaac as hero is somewhat simplified in the *Biblical Antiquities of Pseudo-Philo* and in 4 Maccabees, wherein Isaac is viewed as the exemplary martyr—a notion no doubt related to the persecution being suffered during the period of the composition (ca. 70–135 A.D.). In the Palestinian Targums, however, not only is Isaac an exemplary martyr ("Bind me properly that I may not kick you and your offering be made unfit . . ."), but he is also an intercessor:

Abraham worshipped and prayed the name of the Word of the Lord, and said: (O Lord, you are He that sees and is unseen!) I pray by the mercy which comes forth from you: all is revealed before you. It is known before you that there were no divisions in my heart the first time (at the time) when You told me to offer Isaac my son, and to make him dust and ashes before You. But I departed immediately in the morning and did Your word with joy and fulfilled Your decree (it). (Now) I pray for mercy before you, O Lord God, that when the children of Isaac come to a time of distress (when they offer their sacrifices in a time) you may remember on their behalf the binding of Isaac their father, and listen to the voice of their prayer and answer them (and loose them and forgive their sins) and deliver them from all distress, so that the generations which follow him may say: In the mountain of the Temple of the Lord, Abraham offered Isaac his son, and in this mountain—of the Temple—the glory of the Shekinah of the Lord was revealed to him.[84]

Another Targum, most likely a post-70 A.D. synagogal commentary, expresses Isaac's intercessory power in this manner:

After this (viz., the birth of Isaac), the lamb was chosen to recall the merit of the one man who was bound upon a mountain as a lamb for a burnt offering upon the altar. God delivered him in His merciful goodness, and when his (Isaac's) children pray in the time of their distress and say, as they are obliged to say, "Answer us and listen to the cry of our prayer." He agreed to remember on our behalf the Binding of Isaac our father.[85]

In the midrashic commentaries of the Amoraim (Talmudic masters, A.D. 200–500) Isaac is more mature (37 years old, an age apparently computed by the linkage of Sarah's death at age 127 [Gen. 23:1] with the sacrifice), and aware of the cost of God's command: "Isaac put his hands to his head and began to cry out, and wept bitterly."[86] This anguish is echoed and magnified in the late Middle Ages when Jewish communities, suffering from the onslaught of the Crusaders, asked: "When were there ever a thousand and a hundred sacrifices in one day, *each and every one of them like the Akedah of Isaac son of Abraham?*"[87] As one synagogue poem plaintively puts it:

O Lord, Mighty One, dwelling on high!
Once, over one *Akedah,* Ariels cried out before Thee.
But now how many are butchered and burned!
Why over the blood of children did they not raise a cry?
Before that patriarch could in his haste sacrifice his only one,
It was heard from heaven: Do not put forth your hand to destroy!
But now how many sons and daughters of Judah are slain—
While yet He makes no haste to save those butchered nor those cast on the flames.
On the merit of the *Akedah* at Moriah once we could lean,
Safeguarded for the salvation of age after age—
Now one *Akedah* follows another, they cannot be counted.[88]

The function of the *Akedah* in Jewish life has been magnificently chronicled in Shalom Spiegel's classic volume, *The Last Trial.* In his expansive commentary on a twelfth century liturgical poem, "The Akedah" by Rabbi Ephraim ben Jacob, Spiegel shows how continual reinterpretation of the narrative of Genesis 22 sustained Jews in their darkest moments. In the mystery of Abraham, both bound to God in a knot of love and bound up in Isaac's life, yet commanded to bind him "hand and foot like the perpetual offering," Jews saw the deliverance of their own "bound flock":

Recall to our credit the many Akedahs,
The saints, men and women, slain for Thy sake,
Remember the righteous martyrs of Judah,
Those that were bound of Jacob.[89]

Within this tradition of reinterpretation is Elie Wiesel's contemporary reading in light of his own experience of the Holocaust. Wiesel invokes the merit of the *Akedah* in creating this dialogue between God and Isaac:

> When Abraham heard the celestial voice ordering him to spare his son Isaac, he declared: I swear I shall not leave the altar, Lord, before I speak my mind.—Speak, said God.—Did You not promise me that my descendants would be as numerous as the stars in the sky?—Yes, I did promise you that.—And whose descendants will they be? Mine? Mine alone?—No, said God, they will be Isaac's as well.—And didn't You also promise me that they would inherit the earth?—Yes, I promised you that too.—And whose descendants will they be? Mine alone?—No, said God's voice, they will be Isaac's as well.—Well then, my Lord, said Abraham unabashedly, I could have pointed out to You before that Your order contradicted Your promise. I could have spoken up, I didn't. I contained my grief and held my tongue. In return, I want You to make me the following promise: that when, in the future, my children and my children's children throughout the generations will act against Your law and against Your will, You will also say nothing and forgive them.—So be it, God agreed. Let them but retell this tale and they will be forgiven.[90]

Precisely because of this, Wiesel claims, Abraham's name has become synonymous with *hesed:* "Indeed he was charitable, not so much with Isaac as with God. He could have accused Him and proved Him wrong; he didn't."[91] Isaac remains Israel's *Melitz-Yosher,* defender of his people, pleading their cause and entitled to say whatever he likes to God:

> Because he suffered? No. Suffering, in Jewish tradition, confers no privileges. It all depends on what one makes of that suffering. Isaac knew how to transform it into prayer and love rather than into rancor and malediction. This is what gives him rights and powers no other man possesses.[92]

Christian interpretation of the same text has moved in quite another direction: Isaac as a type of Christ. Whereas this is not explicitly stated in the NT, Rom. 8:32 provides the implicit linkage by its similarity in wording to the LXX of Genesis 22: "He

who did not spare his own Son but gave him up for us all, will
he not also give us all things with him?"[93] The typology, however, is amply laid out in the Fathers. For Tertullian, Isaac's
carrying of the wood serves as a type fulfilled by Christ's carrying of the cross.[94] Irenaeus extends the typology to the Christian community:

> Righteously also the apostles, being of the race of Abraham, left the
> ship and their father, and followed the Word. Righteously also do
> we, possessing the same faith as Abraham, and taking up the cross
> as Isaac did the wood, follow Him. For in Abraham man had
> learned beforehand, and had been accustomed to follow the Word
> of God. For Abraham, according to his faith, followed the com-
> mand of the Word of God, and with a ready mind delivered up, as a
> sacrifice to God, his only-begotten and beloved son, in order that
> God also might be pleased to offer up for all his seed His own
> beloved and only-begotten Son, as a sacrifice for our redemption.[95]

Clement of Alexandria (ca. 150–250 A.D.), undoubtedly influenced by his predecessor Philo, transforms the typology into
allegory:

> Again, "Abraham, when he came to the place which God told him
> of on the third day, looking up, saw the place afar off." For the first
> day is that which is constituted by the sight of good things; and the
> second is the soul's best desire; on the third, the mind perceives
> spiritual things, the eyes of the understanding being opened by the
> Teacher who rose on the third day. The three days may be the
> mystery of the seal, in which God is really believed. It is con-
> sequently afar off that he sees the place. For the region of God is
> hard to attain; which Plato called the region of ideas, having
> learned from Moses that it was a place which contained all things
> universally. But it is seen by Abraham from afar off, rightly, be-
> cause of his being in the realms of generation, and he is forthwith
> initiated by the angel. Thence says the apostle: "Now we see as
> through a glass, but then face to face," by those sole pure and incor-
> poreal applications of the intellect. . . .[96]

This allegorical usage is taken up by Gregory of Nyssa, for
whom "the whole mystery of faith can be seen in the story of
Isaac":

The lamb is fixed to the tree, suspended by its horns: the first-born carries upon him the wood for the sacrifice. He, then, who upholds the universe by the word of his power, is the same who bears the burden of our wood, and is hung up on the wood, upholding as God and carried as the lamb, the Holy Spirit having in figure divided the mystery between the two, the only son and the lamb who appears at his side. In the lamb is revealed the mystery of death and in the only son the life which will never be cut short by death.[97]

Augustine's allegory even permits the interpreter to see the church prefigured in the sacrifice of Isaac.

He [Abraham] who had obeyed in striking, obeyed in sparing: obedient in all things, timid in nothing. But in order that the sacrifice might be completed, and that he might not depart without a blood of offering, a ram appeared caught by its horns in a thicket; Abraham immolated it, and the sacrifice was consummated. What is the underlying meaning? The story is a figure of Christ shrouded in mystery. So we are discussing it in order to throw light on Him, we are studying it in order to see Him, so that what is concealed may be revealed. Isaac is the one beloved son typifying the Son of God, bearing the wood for himself, just as Christ bore His cross. Lastly the ram itself was a type of Christ. For what is being caught by the horns except, after a fashion, being crucified? This figure denotes Christ. But the Church must be predicted; once the Head has been foretold, the Body must be foretold also. The Spirit of God, or rather God himself, began to foretell the Church to Abraham and dropped the imagery. . . .[98]

Underlying the topology and allegory was, of course, the notion expressed by John Chrysostom, "The type carries us a long way, but how much further does the reality go."[99] Typology enabled the Fathers both to preserve the unity of the two testaments and to wrestle with the meaning of the violent death of Jesus. Their allegory, however fanciful, enabled Christians to transpose their Semitic origins to a Greek culture and thus played an essentially apologetic function.[100] It also fostered the development of an identity separate from Judaism.

The patristic interpretation dominates the Middle Ages, even to the extent of an "inordinate reverence for the antiquity and authority of the writings of the Greek and Latin Fathers of the Church."[101] Their sense of the NT being concealed in the OT is vividly portrayed in a soliloquy given by Abraham in a twelfth century religious drama:

> Abraham, I; such is my name.
> Hear, now, the message I proclaim;
> Whose hope is on God's promise stayed,
> Let him keep faith and trust unswayed;
> Whose faith is fixed in God, for aye
> Will God be with him. This I say
> Through knowledge; God my faith did test;
> I did his will, obeyed his test;
> For him, mine own son had I slain,
> But God's hand did my hand restrain.
> The unfinished offering did he bless,
> 'Twas counted me for righteousness.
> God promised me—'tis truth, indeed,—
> An heir shall issue from my seed
> Who shall subdue his every foe,
> And strong and mighty shall he grow;
> Their gates possessing, ne'er shall he
> A menial in their castles be.
> E'en such an one, sprung from my root,
> Shall all our punishment commute;
> By him the world shall ransomed be,
> And Adam from his pain set free;
> And men, of every race and kind
> On earth, through him shall blessing find.[102]

The *Sitz im Leben* of the drama is more evident when one sees that the play begins with this chorus: "You, I say, do I challenge, O Jews."[103] After each of the OT characters speaks, he is carried off to hell. Other mystery plays of the era treat Abraham more sympathetically, emphasizing the pathos of his dialogue with Isaac and stressing the patriarch's obedience to God despite his fear.[104] Nonetheless, it is abundantly clear that for some Christians, Gen. 22:1–19 was incorporated into their polemic with the Jews. Typology and allegory, when linked with cultural domination, functioned to legitimate persecution and thus to betray the interpretative task of Scripture.

Martin Luther, for whom the allegorical tradition of the church appeared to be an imposition of meaning from outside the text, effected a major shift in biblical hermeneutics: the sense of Scripture was to be explained by Scripture itself.[105] Thus primacy was bestowed on the literal meaning, as is evidenced by his restrained (in comparison with the Fathers) commentary on Genesis 22. Nevertheless, Luther's larger theological agenda permeated his reading of the narrative. Abraham and Isaac are held up as "examples of true believers whose faith is never without good works"; Abraham's deed was one of great faith because it was done in obedience to God's word. In contrast, papists and Turks have a "fictitious faith and sheer arrogance" because their faith does not rest upon the divine word.[106] Interestingly, Luther's Abraham is a model of "perfect Christian obedience."[107]

The hermeneutical divide inaugurated by the Reformation and refined by the Enlightenment is abundantly evident in nineteenth and twentieth century commentaries on the saga of Abraham and Isaac. Now attention is directed to the compositional elements (the attribution of vv. 1–14 to E, of vv. 15–19 to the J redactor, and of v. 11 and v. 19 to the redactor), the literary genre ("saga," narration of the history of a people by way of the history of an individual and his family which reflects manifold experiences over long periods of time and is handed down orally for centuries), the aetiological origins (the motif of the substitution for human sacrifice), and the *Sitz im Leben* (Israel's "testing" by God during the exile).[108]

Biblical criticism in the twentieth century mode obviously counters the excesses of typology and allegory with attention to historical context; it is also more bound to the actual text than is midrashic commentary. Yet other interpretational considerations may well contribute to the meaning of the text. One seldom dealt with in any depth concerns the developmental aspect; at issue here is the appropriate time for an individual (and, by extension, a community) to hear the text on its own terms. Psychologist André Godin has found, for instance, that children (especially boys) tend to identify with Isaac, and that this sense of identification is increased in children suffering from severe anxiety.[109] His work, though based on a small sample (seventy children), certainly raises the issue of the way immaturity or traumatic experience could cause a misreading or distortion of a passage. Another consideration for modern interpretation is the liturgical function of a text. A vivid example is the lectionary usage of Gen. 22:1-14 in Roman Catholicism: by juxtaposing this passage with Rom. 8:31-34 and Mark 9:2-11 (the Transfiguration), a certain interpretational frame is established.[110]

In sum, by viewing the history of interpretation through the lens of a single passage, one sees not simply the progression from precritical to critical to postcritical (integrating biblical criticism into the life of faith) methods, but also the way interpretation functions in the Christian and Jewish communities for which it is Sacred Scripture.

Another means of looking at the way interpretation functions is suggested by James A. Sanders in an article laying out the principles and rules for *canonical hermeneutics* ("the means whereby early believing communities pursued, and later believing communities may yet pursue, the integrity [oneness of God, both ontological and ethical"]).[111] His basic norm is that of *discernment of context in both past and present:* "The greater the knowledge we have of the ancient contexts, the clearer becomes the impact (the words of the) text had; and the greater the discernment of current contexts, the clearer one's choice of hermeneutics for transmitting the point originally made."[112]

Some specific principles enflesh this general precept. Primary for Sanders is the matter of discerning the contemporary context so as to determine whether the message of constitutive support (utilizing the tradition in a consoling way) or of prophetic challenge (utilizing the tradition in a confrontative way) is needed. Underlying this principle is Sanders's assumption that "to derive consolation from the Torah story of God's gracious acts, without also deriving the obligations of the covenant relationship, is falsehood."[113] Secondly, Sanders makes a case for biblical interpretation fittingly being done *from within* the covenant community. Closely allied is his third principle: the hearing of the word is characteristically an act of *remembrance* of God's mighty acts; but, fourthly, they must be remembered in terms of the principle of *dynamic analogy:*

If a prophet challenged ancient Israel, or if Jesus challenged his own Jewish, responsible contemporaries, then a prophetic reading of the Bible today should challenge those dynamically equivalent to those challenged in the text: if the priests and prophets of Hosea's day or the Pharisees in Jesus' day, then the church establishment today, since prophets, priests, and Pharisees represented the responsible church leaders and groups of their time. Dynamic analogy also means that one reads the text for oneself and not only for others. It should not be read to identify false prophets and Pharisees with another group or someone else, but with one's own group and with oneself, in order to perceive the right text in the right context.[114]

A fifth principle emerges from the preceding one: biblical texts need to be read in terms of the *ambiguity of reality* which any situation has. Related to this are Sanders's sixth and seventh principles: biblical texts are generally to be read not as models for morality but as *mirrors for identity* and, therefore, the Bible should be read *theologically* before it is read morally. This involves searching for the full canonical context by first theologizing—recognizing that the "primary means of redemption is that God has caught up human sinfulness into his plans and made it part of those plans"[115]—and only then asking what the implications are for obedience or for lifestyle.

Because, as Sanders maintains, the Bible itself gives indications of how to make again today the points made originally, exegetes can be particularly valuable in sifting through the layers of history to those indicators. But they alone cannot answer the two-pronged query with which believing communities approach their Scripture: who are we and what are we to do? In Sanders's terminology, the Bible, "Read as a paradigm of the verbs of God's activity," permits us to "conjugate in our own contexts the verbs of his continuing activity."[116] His rules for conjugation suggest that the full range of the Word's function in the life of believers past and present become a model for interpreting texts today. Such is the understanding of the history of interpretation being proposed in these pages also.

An important supplement to the history of interpretation is a basic grasp of *interpretation theory* itself. As a second recommended area of study, interpretation theory provides a basis for religious educators to develop alternatives to a proclamatory mode of education. In addition, some exposure to recent hermeneutics offers a way of understanding and honoring the complexity of meaning in texts by relativizing historical criticism.

The need for interpretation theory is illustrated by the current situation in which many in the church presume that experts, with their command of history, philology, research literature, and comparative texts, can thereby determine *the* meaning of the Bible. Thus a hierarchy is created: specialists have only to communicate *the* meaning to the public. In such a social structure, religious educators function largely as popularizers who hand on the predetermined meanings in a simplified form.[117]

At the root of this situation is the notion that the biblical texts have a single meaning that excludes all others. But interpretation is more complex than that misconception judges it to be. Nineham again draws upon the literary criticism of Trilling: "De Quincy's categories of *knowledge* and *power* are most pertinent here; the traditional scholarship, in so far as it takes literature to be chiefly an object of knowledge, denies or obscures that active power by which literature is truly defined."[118] Continues Nineham himself:

> Our approach to the Bible in recent years has been predominantly one which has sought to use the Bible as a source of knowledge—knowledge of historical facts and circumstances, and so knowledge of exceptional divine acts. Has it not, for all its value, prevented the immense power the Bible possesses from making its full impact upon us? If we could let go our almost compulsive hold on the historian's—and to some extent the philosopher's—hand, we should be in a position to take the hands of psychologists, literary critics and others skilled in exploring the full meaning of words and images. With their help, and using their methods, we should be able to let the Bible be the Bible, make its full impact on us, including its imaginative and emotional impact, and reveal to us the profound depths and power of many of its stories and images.[119]

Nineham argues that a text has a *totality* of meanings, even if they were neither directly intended nor recognized by the original author. Consequently, a shift in attitude is called for; rather than approaching the biblical text with the anticipation of immediately discovering *the* meaning, readers (particularly nonspecialists) might instead approach the text in a more relaxed spirit by distancing it and first allowing for its "pastness." To regard a text in this spirit is not to denigrate historical criticism but to make it relative. Historical criticism is absolutely invaluable and foundational; however, it ought not to dominate totally the act of interpretation, as is made clear in the work of Paul Ricoeur.

Ricoeur speaks of the "semantic autonomy" of the text: the verbal meaning of a text no longer coincides with the author's meaning or intention, which is beyond the reader's reach. Thus:

> The text is mute. An asymmetric relation obtains between text and reader, in which only one of the partners speaks for the two. The text is like a musical score and the reader like the orchestra conductor who obeys the instructions of the notation. Consequently, to understand is not merely to repeat the speech event in a similar event, it is to generate a new event beginning from the text in which the initial event has been objectified.[120]

Consequently, textual interpretation begins with "guessing"— "in the beginning understanding is a guess"—[121] and moves to explanation or validation. Validation, however, is not synonymous with verification, because "to show that an interpretation is more probable in the light of what we know is something other than showing that a conclusion is true."[122] Ricoeur, however, makes a firm distinction between the dual movement of guess-validation and mere guesswork that would have the text mean anything the reader desired it to mean:

> . . . If it is true that there is always more than one way of construing a text, it is not true that all interpretations are equal. The text presents a limited field of possible constructions. The logic of validation allows us to move between the two limits of dogmatism and scepticism. It is always possible to argue for or against an interpretation, to confront interpretations, to arbitrate between them and to seek agreement, even if this agreement remains beyond our immediate reach.[123]

Another movement then follows, from explanation to comprehension, in which the reader seeks to "grasp the world-propositions opened up by the reference of the text," following the movement from "sense" to "reference," from what the text "says" to what it "talks about." Interpretation thus does not focus on the author but on the text as a "new way of looking at things, as an injunction to think in a certain manner."[124]

In sum, Ricoeur contends that what is to be understood and appropriated in a text is *not* the author's intention, *not* the historical situation common to the author and his or her original readers, *not* the expectations or feelings or self-understandings of the original readers, but the "meaning of the text itself, conceived in a dynamic way as the direction of thought opened up by the text." Because the reader is distanced from the original author:

> The meaning of a text is open to anyone who can read. The omni-temporality of the meaning is what opens it to unknown readers. Hence the historicity of reading is the counterpart of this specific omnitemporality; since the text has escaped its author and his situation, it has also escaped its original addressee. Henceforth it may provide itself with new readers.[125]

Ricoeur's claim that a text carries a "surplus of meaning" best catches in a single phrase his work on interpretation. Precisely because each text has a *surplus of meaning* beyond what the author may have intended, knowledge of the author's intention is important to the process of *validation* but is not the sole criterion of valid *interpretation*.

Ricoeur's interpretation theory, much indebted to the structuralist school though not controlled by it, implicitly suggests that, while historical criticism may be highly significant in the process of validation, it alone does not determine interpretation. George Montague questions whether Ricoeur's theory (with which Montague substantially agrees) actually assures that the reader who finds in the text "a new way of looking at things" has in fact been changed for the better. One could, for instance, be inspired by Mark 16:18 to give God glory by handling snakes or drinking cyanide, or, conversely, be moved by the eschatological expectation of the Sermon on the Mount to tighten around one's neck the "reins of neo-legalism."[126]

Montague accordingly suggests two correctives: biblical interpretation should take place in the context of a faith community and it should be lived. Interpretation within the context of community (including liturgical celebrations) does not in itself guarantee correct interpretation, but at least seems to be a lesser risk than the solipsism which the isolated individual runs "even when having some objective linguistic controls."[127] "Hearing the Word," moreover, has been traditionally subordinated to "doing the Word." In this light, Montague quotes David Lochhead:

> We have a "problem" of private interpretation because we see hermeneutics as a primarily individualistic activity. Under the impact of the dominant liberal ideology of Western society, the insistence of the reformers on the freedom of conscience of the interpreter has led to a view of hermeneutics in which an interpretation is a matter of opinion of the individual and in which one opinion is as good as another.
>
> Against this we need to insist that interpretation is not a matter of "opinion" but of *praxis*. Interpretation does not end when we draw the "moral" of a text, but when we act upon it. Secondly, the *praxis* which is the end of interpretation is not individual but corporate. In the last analysis, it is the involvement of the interpreter in a community of interpretation, in a community of *praxis*, which makes interpretation a meaningful activity.[128]

The many complexities of hermeneutics mean, of course, conflicting views among the various theorists. But a lack of unanimity among theorists need not deter religious educators from being informed by their discussion. Among the most pertinent ramifications is the realization that the "great texts are an endless source of new acts of understanding and love"; the broader people's experience, the more open their hearts and the richer their field of understanding, the more will a great text be for them a "catalyst of new thoughts, desires and actions."[129]

Because of this "surplus of meaning," a new attitude toward the text is possible. Interpretation is not restricted to analysis, in which the reader is totally dependent upon an expert analyst, but encompasses understanding as well:

> Understanding is most open when it is conceived of as something capable of being seized by being rather than as a self-sufficient grasping consciousness. An interpretive act must not be a forceable seizure, a "rape" of the text, but a loving union that brings to stand the full potentialities of interpreter and text, the partners in the hermeneutical dialogue.[130]

If such is the case, then readers need not prize only exegetical expertise but also the ability to listen, even to the extent of going "behind the text to find what the text did not, and perhaps could not, say."[131] Thus it is that nonspecialists may indeed bring very special gifts to biblical interpretation. Listening is an art not learned primarily in graduate schools, but in the give-and-take of everyday life. Those who work with children, the elderly, or the physically and mentally handicapped may well have refined this ability far beyond the most learned, articulate scholar. Likewise, the skill of questioning is not the exclusive possession of those trained in dialectic; those who approach the biblical text from the horizon of their own life experience, often unaware of the technicalities of scholarly debate and perhaps wary of institutional religion, may pose insightful, powerful questions to the text. The call to conversion in the biblical texts can be understood by all; such is the burden of contemporary interpretation theory.

Familiarity with this theory and with the history of interpretation gives religious educators a basis for collaboration with their colleagues in biblical studies. It also provides the appropriate point of transition from which one can assess the unique contributions religious educators can make to biblical studies.

2. The Contributions of Religious Educators.   If, as has been proposed in the preceding pages, religious education is a compound constituted by the convergence of theology and education and is thus a configuration of disciplines, then it follows that its professionals ought to be able to work at the point of confluence. More specifically, this means that their skills should primarily lie in the ability to synthesize. Religious educators make their unique contribution by engaging in decisions about the educational ramifications of particular theological under-standings, as well as by scrutinizing educational views for their religious and theological underpinnings. Thus the expertise of the religious educator consists not simply in having a sense of theological content and methodology, but also in being able to educate.

Perhaps that is to say the obvious. Yet, as Moran and Lee have both long pointed out (albeit from widely divergent perspectives), religious educators have been so dominated by theology that they have never claimed fully the educational dimension of their task.[132] Yet education has its own integrity and exercises its own demands. Its meaning is not self-evident, as the differences delineated in the typology of the third chap-ter make plain. Religious educators, therefore, need first of all to possess the theoretical competence to recognize the funda-mental assumptions and attitudes undergirding specific prac-tices.

This, of course, can only happen when they resist the equa-tion of education with schooling. Because the two are synony-mous in the minds of many, particularly in ecclesiastical or synagogal circles, an awareness that the life of faith is enhanced by lifelong learning has been lost. Likewise, the equation has hidden from view—and thus from analysis and critique—the educational component of preaching, counseling, working for social justice, presiding at liturgy, and so forth. Similarly, by restricting the understanding of curriculum to a written course of study, the religious curriculum embedded in the midst of everyday life has been overlooked, as has been the hidden cur-riculum of church policies and practices. On the contrary, to understand curriculum as the design of educational environ-ment facilitates the recognition that religious education hap-pens in a variety of settings and through a multiplicity of in-stitutions.[133] It also fosters the recognition that decisions re-garding budget, materials, and personnel impinge on the edu-cational life of the church.

If, in fact, one takes such a broad notion of curriculum, then the contours of the religious educator's distinct contribution to biblical studies become clearer. Fundamental are decisions about how to utilize the Bible in making a particular religious community's traditions accessible and about which biblical traditions are most appropriate in view of the people, time, and occasion; a prime criterion for these decisions is the extent to which the biblical traditions point to transformation. Still another basic consideration revolves around how religious educators ought to utilize the Bible to help people to reconstruct their experience.

More specifically, these basic curricular questions can be looked at by means of a tripartite schema of goods, services, and social-political relationships. The first, goods, involves the production and usage of materials by which people can get a hold on the meanings of the biblical texts. Here the question is twofold: what "stuff" (written materials, tapes, films) best materializes biblical traditions and also best fosters creative participation (rather than passive comprehension)?[134] The educator's concerns center around providing experiences and exercises that, by embodying abstract, complex ideas, will provide access to the wealth of the community's interpretation of the Bible.

Related to this, of course, is the matter of teaching (services). The immense value of teaching in biblical studies has been well expressed by Montague, who, in contending that teaching is more than an exercise in communication, claims that it has a vital heuristic rebound and hermeneutical function:

> To teach is to expose oneself to questions one had not thought of in one's own research, questions deriving often from a world different from ours. If some of these questions are requests for completion of the hermeneutical circle opened by the exposition of the text, others are often pointers to meanings in the text itself which we may have overlooked. Thus the moment of teaching may prove to be a precious one even in the process of understanding the text. And so the pedagogical question may in the long run be as important to our profession as the road performance of an automobile is to the engineering theory on which it is based.[135]

Montague's admission of the important role of pedagogy is welcome particularly because it was made in the course of his presidential address to the Catholic Biblical Association in

1978. Yet, at least from the religious educator's perspective, his remarks are incomplete. *The fact is that not every way of teaching leads to new questions or to a heuristic rebound.* Paulo Freire's metaphor of banking education superbly captures that style of teaching which deposits information and delivers answers. In banking education, the teacher teaches and the students are taught; the teacher knows everything and the students nothing. The teacher talks while the students listen; the teacher makes decisions and enforces them while the students comply. The teacher chooses the program content, and the students adapt to it. It is the teacher who is the subject of the learning process and the students who are mere objects.[136]

Freire juxtaposes this pedagogical mode with his own problem-posing education, in which the teacher rejects communiques and establishes dialogue. Freire's alternative is helpful in providing the broad outline of a more liberating pedagogy, but it too is insufficient. To teach dialogically, as both Montague and Freire desire, demands attention to specific pedagogical strategies; it is not enough simply to proclaim that one's educational style is humanistic. Because there is more to teaching than verbalizing, it is imperative to hold together theory and practice. Well-trained teachers will possess a repertoire of strategies which they select from and modify according to the demands of both students and subject matter.

Teaching involves intelligent decision making, reflects demonstrable skills, and involves application of philosophical and psychological understandings. *Skilled teaching is as fundamental and as significant to the religious educator as linguistic proficiency is to the exegete, and just as exacting.*

The precision necessary for teaching is best illustrated in the joint work of Bruce Joyce and Marsha Weil detailing models of teaching according to four major groupings. *Social interaction* models of teaching emphasize the processes by which reality is socially negotiated and provide viable alternatives to the shared-ignorance mode of discussion. *Information processing* models are oriented toward assisting students to give order to the vast amount of factual and conceptual knowledge with which they are inundated. The *personal models* are grounded in counseling theory and hence are directed toward an individual's construct of reality. The final family of models, drawn from Skinnerian psychology, emphasize *behavior modification* and are not developed by Joyce and Weil in their later work.[137]

The value of models of teaching is twofold: they demonstrate the broad range of alternatives a teacher may utilize, and they make operational significant and diverse teaching theories. The models are not a collection of simple recipes, but a systematic exposition of theory in practice. Religious educators familiar with models of teaching, or other work on teaching strategies (such as micro-teaching) can help to give substance to the desire to teach humanistically.

The advocacy of these models is not intended to suggest that teaching is merely the skilled application of sound theory. It is that, of course, but more besides. Because teachers work with human beings, their work has a transcendent quality that should be characterized by hope, creativity, awareness, faithful doubt, wonder, awe, and reverence. The Joyce-Weil models, with their carefully designed strategies, certainly do not preclude an understanding of teaching as an artistic, mystery-laden endeavor. Teaching is meant to be inspiring, enabling diverse persons to "break through the cotton wool of daily life and to live more consciously."[138] That is why, as Josiah Royce advised teachers in 1891:

> You will degrade science,—not help your children,—if you persist in seeing only the "scientific" aspects of your pedagogy. True pedagogy is an art. . . . It is abstraction that simplifies; and abstraction is invaluable to science. But he who returns from science to life is a poor pupil if he has not learned the art of forgetting his formulas at the right moment, and of loving the live thing more than the describable type.[139]

Royce's admonition—"when you teach you must know when to forget formulas; but you must have learned them in order to be able to forget them"—[140] aptly summarizes the way religious educators might draw upon the models of teaching for their work. Thus grounded in the theory and practice of teaching, they might also re-mediate teaching skills for their colleagues in biblical studies. Perhaps then this mutual attention to the art and science of teaching will engender the type of heuristic rebound envisioned by Montague.

Teaching, of course, does not exist in isolation from the other elements of curriculum. The kinds of materials employed are obviously crucial to teaching. Of similar significance are matters concerning social and political relationships, which focus primarily on the control of the goods and services.

At issue here are some economic matters, such as the allocation of funds by a given institution or agency for the education of its members. For instance, a parish which decides to devote its funding and staff resources almost entirely to the sacramental preparation of young children has thereby effectively forestalled any systematic and sustained immersion in the biblical traditions for its adolescent and adult members. On the other hand, a decision such as that by the Roman Catholic diocese of Memphis, Tennessee, to focus its entire educational efforts in a 1976 "Matthew Year" involved assigning a certain budgetary priority to Scripture.[141] Also at stake are some political matters involving the decision-making processes employed in the formulation of policies and development of written curriculum. Another political and social issue is that of control of work. Biblical scholars are often employed by colleges and universities which provide them with academic freedom and, to a certain extent, job security (depending on the exigencies of tenure). But the academic freedom of religious educators is seldom addressed. To what extent should professional religious educators who work outside the university enjoy academic freedom? What is the relationship between such freedom and pastoral responsibility? And, most fundamentally, for whom do biblical scholars and religious educators work?

The difficulty of these questions ought not to obscure their necessary place in the educational life of the church. To take a broadened view of curriculum as the design of educational environment is to see that material resources, teaching services, and social-political arrangements exist in a single nexus. By possessing a working knowledge of curriculum, the religious educator will be able to help others in the religious community to identify ways biblical studies can become embodied in church life and to analyze situations and structures which may hinder their appropriation.

Admittedly, it is at present easier to see in greater detail what biblical scholarship can offer religious education than what the latter can bring to biblical studies. The lopsided character of the two proposals offered here testifies to the greater maturation of biblical studies and suggests the need to continue to attend more carefully to the educational dimension of the mission of the church.

IV. *Summary*

The primary concern of this final chapter has been with the significance of the rapid rise and equally rapid demise of salvation history in religious education. Accordingly, three issues were explored: the present status of *Heilsgeschichte* as a hermeneutical principle, the educational implications of the kerygmatic era, and religious education in relation to contemporary biblical scholarship.

1. Though *Heilsgeschichte* is no longer tenable as an exclusive or overarching principle of interpretation, it nonetheless does express one important aspect of biblical theology. In addition, its usage has consistently reflected both apologetic and pastoral concerns. When, however, those concerns were allowed to dominate to the exclusion of theological refinements, salvation history became isolated from, and elevated above, other hermeneutical guides. Consequently, it bore more theological weight than it could adequately sustain; *Heilsgeschichte* needs always to be placed in its proper theological context.

2. Because the dénouement of *Heilsgeschichte* as a hermeneutical principle in religious education appears to be more related to educational and cultural developments than to theological refinements, its demise reveals the interdisciplinary character of religious education.

   2.1 Religious education, a relative neophyte as a field of

study in its own right, may be regarded as a "configuration of disciplines," in which it serves as a point of
intersection of particular theological and educational
approaches.

2.2 Religious education may be more specifically defined
as the making accessible of the traditions of religious
communities and the making manifest of the intrinsic
connection between tradition and transformation.

2.3 The implications of this new definition of religious
education include a willingness to make the traditions
accessible in all their ambiguity and ambivalence, the
development of an expanded notion of faith, and a
reconsideration of the role of doctrine.

3. Further probing into the meaning of the kerygmatic era
uncovers an obligation seldom explicitly addressed: the
special responsibility and role of religious educators in
regard to modern study of Scripture.

3.1 The advent of biblical criticism has revolutionized
the study of Scripture. A new attitude toward the
Bible means that new educational and pastoral
modes of dealing with Scripture must be developed.

3.2 At present a chasm exists between biblical scholars
and religious educators; this divide in many respects
is the result of the ever-increasing complexity of biblical studies and the concomitant specialization it demands. But the Bible does not belong to just this guild
of scholars. It is imperative that biblical criticism more
adequately permeate the life of the church.

3.3 In order for this to happen, religious educators must
collaborate with Scripture scholars. Prerequisite to
this collaboration is a threefold, systematic preparation of religious educators in knowledge of the Bible
itself, the history of interpretation, and interpretation
theory. Moreover, religious educators themselves can
contribute to the integration of biblical studies into
the life of the church by their expertise in curriculum
(the design of educational environments along the
lines of material resources, teaching services, and
social-political arrangements).

V. Conclusion

It may be most appropriate to conclude on a note laying out a brief agenda for the attention of both biblical scholars and religious educators. One item concerns the ability to read the biblical texts. Certainly the exegete is uniquely prepared to enhance that reading; but the ability to exegete a text is not the same as the ability to teach that text, or even to teach exegesis itself. Perhaps exegesis is, at one level, a specialized way of providing someone else with the tools to read for himself or herself; thus it would seem fitting that both exegetes and educators might on occasion join in team teaching so as to honor the philological, historical, religious, theological, and educational dimensions of reading the Bible.[142]

Moreover, if the collaborative team would document, assess, and publish its processes then both disciplines could profit from their experience. In so doing, a network of scholarship would be erected and the limitations of specialization transcended.

Not unrelated is a concern arising out of Leander Keck's observation that persons who do not bring a lifelong relationship to the Bible come to biblical criticism very differently. Criticism, Keck maintains, cannot of itself generate a "religiously significant relationship" to the Bible.[143] If this is the case, then how can biblical criticism be relativized and utilized so as to enhance faith? How should the riches of the Bible be made accessible to people previously unacquainted with it? How can the "surplus of meaning" in the biblical texts be drawn forth? How will biblical interpretation become an act of corporate praxis?

Questions such as these indicate that the work ahead should be a collaborative venture. *Heilsgeschichte* originated out of a pastoral concern that the meaning of the Bible be made accessible; whatever the deficiencies of this hermeneutical principle, its *raison d'être* remains relevant.

NOTES

1. F. O'Connor, *Mystery and Manners,* ed. S. and R. Fitzgerald (New York: Farrar, Straus and Giroux, 1957) 72.

2. A phrase borrowed from A. J. Heschel *(The Prophets* [New York: Harper and Row, 1955] xi)'.

3. G. E. Ladd, "The Search for Perspective," *Int* 25 (1971) 47.

4. See G. F. Hasel, *Old Testament Theology: Basic Issues in the Current Debate,* rev. ed. (Grand Rapids: Wm. Eerdmans, 1978) 204-220.

5. For a perspective on the significance of allegory in the history of biblical interpretation, see R. P. C. Hanson ("Biblical Exegesis in the Early Church," *Cambridge History of the Bible* 1, ed. P. R. Ackroyd and C. F. Evans [Cambridge: University Press, 1970] 412-453); B. Smalley *(The Study of the Bible in the Middle Ages,* 2nd ed. [Notre Dame: University of Notre Dame, 1964]); R. M. Grant *(The Letter and the Spirit* [London: S. P. C. K 1957] 1-23, 85-115).

6. On the "century of history," see A. Darlap and J. Splett, *Encyclopedia of Theology: The Concise Sacramentum Mundi,* ed. K. Rahner (New York: Seabury, 1975) 621.

7. D. Crossan, *In Parables* (New York: Harper and Row, 1973) 31.

8. *Ibid.*

9. But see the three-volume history by P. J. Marique *(History of Christian Education* [New York: Fordham University, 1924, 1926, 1932]), which best approximates a "classic" history. Also in recent years some important essays have appeared which grapple with the foundational questions. See D. Huebner, "Education in the Church," *ANQ* 12 (1972) 122-29; B. Marthaler, "A Discipline in Quest of an Identity: Religious Education," *Horizons* 3 (1976) 203-215; R. P. McBrien, "Toward an American Catechesis," *Living Light* 13 (1976) 167-181; C. J. Melchert, "What Is Religious Education?" *Living Light* 14 (1977) 339-353; P. O'Hare, ed., *Foundations of Religious Education* (New York: Paulist, 1978) and *Tradition and Transformation in Religious Education* (Birmingham, Ala.: Religious Education Press, 1979); John Westerhoff, ed., *Who Are We? The Quest for a Religious Education* (Birmingham, Ala.: Religious Education Press, 1978).

10. N. Thompson ("Current Issues in Religious Education," Presidential Address, Association of Professors and Researchers in Religious Education [St. Louis, 18 November 1977] 1-9) contends that this relationship is one of the three fundamental concerns in religious education. She further identifies five major expressions of the relation between theology and religious education: theology "behind the curriculum" (Randolph C. Miller); theology and religious instruction as "ontologically distinct" (James M. Lee); theology and religious education as "complementary languages" (Enrique Ahumada); religious education as "beyond theology" (Gabriel Moran); and religious education as an outgrowth of "theologizing" (Matthew Hayes). B. Marthaler ("Catechesis and Theology," *Proceedings of the Catholic*

Theological Society of America 28 [1973] 261–270) proposes that religious education be regarded as a "functional specialty," a proposal, of course, based on B. Lonergan *(Method in Theology* [New York: Herder and Herder, 1972] 125–369). See also S. Little, "Theology and Religious Education," in M. J. Taylor, ed., *Foundations for Christian Education in an Era of Change* (Nashville: Abingdon, 1976) 30–40.

11. J. M. Lee, *The Shape of Religious Instruction* (Dayton: Pflaum, 1971) 246.

12. *The Flow of Religious Instruction* (Dayton: Pflaum, 1973) 17.

13. L. A. Cremin, *Traditions of American Education* (New York: Basic Books, 1977) 134–143.

14. See the superb work on Coe by H. A. Archibald ("George Albert Coe: Theorist for Religious Education in the Twentieth Century" [Ph.D. Dissertation, University of Illinois at Urbana-Champaign, 1975]).

15. On the term "ecology" in this context, see R. W. Lynn, "Sometimes on Sunday: Reflections on Images of the Future in American Education," *ANQ* 12 (1972) 130–139.

16. G. A. Coe, *What Is Christian Education?* (New York: Scribner's, 1930) 296.

17. H. S. Smith, "Let Religious Educators Reckon with the Barthians," *Religious Education* 24 (1934) 45; reprinted in J. Westerhoff, ed., *Who Are We? The Quest for a Religious Education,* 98. See also H. S. Smith, "Christian Education: Do Progressive Religious Educators Have a Theology?" *America at the End of the Protestant Era,* ed., A. S. Nash (New York: Macmillan, 1951).

18. Because of the very different function that kerygmatic theology and catechetics played in Catholicism, it is misleading to group Jungmann, Hofinger, *et al.* with Protestant evangelicals under the rubric of the "traditional theological approach" as does H. W. Burgess *(An Invitation to Religious Education* [Mishawaka, Ind.: Religious Education Press, 1975] 21–58).

19. A. J. Heschel, "Idols in the Temple," in A. McBride, *Heschel: Religious Educator* (Denville, N.J.: Dimension Books, 1973) 126. Heschel's essay, with its rejection of "cliches buttered with sentimentality," might profitably be read by those who advocate a spirituality in which "feelings are in and thinking is out."

20. I am indebted to Prof. Dwayne Huebner for the identification of my definition as stipulative; see I. Scheffler *(The Language of Education* [Springfield, Ill.: Charles C. Thomas, 1960] 13), who identifies a stipulative definition as one which "exhibits some term to be defined and gives notice that it is to be taken as equivalent to some other

exhibited term or description, within a particular context." By "stipulating" a definition, I am declaring how I myself regard religious education, rather than looking to a "programmatic" or "descriptive" definition. My definition, however, has programmatic implications. In developing the definition I am also drawing upon my essay, "Access to Traditions and Transformation" *(Tradition and Transformation in Religious Education,* ed. P. O'Hare [Birmingham, Ala.: Religious Education Press, 1979] 9–39).

21. G. A. Coe, *A Social Theory of Religious Education* (New York: Scribner's 1917) 298.

22. G. Tavard, "Tradition in Theology: A Methodological Approach," *Perspectives on Scripture and Tradition,* ed. J. F. Kelly (Notre Dame: Fides, 1976) 107.

23. See D. A. Knight, *Rediscovering the Traditions of Israel,* rev. ed. SBLDS No. 9 (Missoula, Mont.: Scholars Press, 1975) 5–32. Also W. E. Rast, *Tradition History and the Old Testament* (Philadelphia: Fortress, 1972).

24. K. Koch, *The Growth of the Biblical Tradition: The Form Critical Method* (New York: Scribner's, 1969) 100.

25. C. E. Nelson, *Where Faith Begins* (Atlanta: John Knox, 1967).

26. See E. Schillebeeckx, *The Understanding of Faith* (New York: Seabury, 1974) 55–77 and 102–155.

27. L. M. Russell, "Handing on Traditions and Changing the World," *Tradition and Transformation in Religious Education,* 77.

28. See H. W. Wolff, *Anthropology of the Old Testament* (Philadelphia: Fortress, 1974).

29. Schillebeeckx, *The Understanding of Faith,* 59.

30. See A. Blum, "Positive Thinking," *Theory and Society* 1 (1974) 245–269.

31. See A. Dulles, "The Meaning of Faith Considered in Relationship to Justice," *The Faith That Does Justice,* ed. J. C. Haughey (New York: Paulist, 1977) 10–46.

32. Huebner, "Education in the Church," 122.

33. *Ibid.,* 122–123.

34. *Ibid.,* 127.

35. B. J. F. Lonergan, "Theology and Praxis," *Proceedings of the Catholic Theological Society of America* 32 (1977) 2.

36. *Ibid.,* 11.

37. See B. J. F. Lonergan, *Method in Theology,* 237–244; reprinted in part in W. E. Conn, ed., *Conversion: Perspectives on Personal and Social Transformation* (New York: Alba House, 1978) 3–22.

38. Huebner, "Education in the Church," 126.

39. See M. Hellwig, *Tradition: The Catholic Story Today* (Dayton: Pflaum, 1974).

40. L. Gilkey, *Catholicism Confronts Modernity* (New York: Seabury, 1975) 29.

41. *Ibid.*, 23.

42. See A. Dulles, *The Survival of Dogma* (Garden City: Doubleday, 1971) 139; see also P. Tillich *(Dynamics of Faith* [New York: Harper, 1959] 20-22), who claims that doubt is the consequence of the risk of faith; N. Lamm, *Faith and Doubt: Studies in Traditional Jewish Thought* (New York: KTAV, 1972) 1-40; and M. C. Boys, "Contending with God: The Meaning of Faith in Elie Wiesel," *NICM Journal* (1978) 75-85.

43. See the classic essay by J. T. Ellis, "American Catholics and the Intellectual Life," *Thought* 30 (1955) 353-386. Cf. R. Hofstadter, *Anti-Intellectualism in American Life* (New York: Vintage, 1963), who places this in broad perspective. It should be noted, however, that anti-intellectualism is a phenomenon correlated with economic status; the poverty of the immigrants, for instance, most often precluded their entrance into academic circles.

44. G. Moran, *Catechesis of Revelation* (New York: Herder and Herder, 1066) 34.

45. G. Moran, *Design for Religion* (New York: Herder and Herder, 1971) 68-69.

46. *Ibid.*, 71.

47. For an original and stimualting *apologia* for doctrine, see P. Chirico (*Infallibility: The Crossroads of Doctrine* [Kansas City: Sheed Andrews and McMeel, 1977] 114-124). See also R. E. Brown, "The Current Crisis in Theology As It Affects the Teaching of Catholic Doctrine," in *Biblical Reflections on Crises Facing the Church* (New York: Paulist, 1975) 3-19; K. Coughlin, "The Role of Doctrine in Religious Education," *Living Light* 11 (1974) 487-502; U. O'Neil "Perspectives on the Hierarchy of Truths," *Living Light* 14 (1977) 377-391; and R. P. McBrien, "Doctrine and Community: Problems and Solutions," in J. McCall, ed., *Dimensions in Religious Education* (Haverton, Pa.: CIM Books, 1973) 165-177. See also the important address by A. Dulles ("The Theologian and the Magisterium," *Catholic Mind* 75 [1975] 6-16), in which he proposes there to be two magisteria, one of pastors and one of theologians, which are complementary and mutually corrective. Perhaps one might consider the lived faith experience of the people as, at least in an analogous way, the third magisterium.

48. G. Baum, *Faith and Doctrine* (New York: Newman, 1969) 119-121.

49. *Ibid.*

50. A phrase appearing in a closing message of Vatican II spoke of faith as "this great friend of intelligence." See W. M. Abbott, ed., *The Documents of Vatican II* (New York: America Press, 1966) 731.

51. Mention here, of course, must be made of the pioneering work of James W. Fowler in exploring the developmental stages of faith. See especially J. W. Fowler, "Life Faith Patterns: Structures of Trust and Loyalty," in J. Berryman, ed., *Life Maps: Conversations on the Journey of Faith* (Waco, Tex.: Word Books, 1978) 14-101.

52. D. Nineham, *The Use and Abuse of the Bible* (London: Macmillan, 1976) 40-59.

53. This is a central argument of H. W. Frei, *The Eclipse of Biblical Narrative: A Study in Eighteenth and Nineteenth Century Hermeneutics* (New Haven: Yale, 1974).

54. The outline of the five points is derived from J. Barr *(The Bible in the Modern World* [New York: Harper and Row, 1973] 10). Barr, however, fails to recognize that these concerns are shaped by a largely white, middle-class perspective.

55. L. Trilling, *The Liberal Imagination,* as cited in Nineham, 39.

56. See D. H. Kelsey, *The Uses of Scripture in Recent Theology* (Philadelphia: Fortress, 1975) 182-216; Barr, 23-30; 89-111; C. Curran, *Catholic Moral Theology in Dialogue* (Notre Dame: Fides, 1972) 24-65.

57. Schillebeeckx, *The Understanding of Faith,* 3.

58. D. M. Stanley, "The Conception of Our Gospels As Salvation History," *TS* 20 (1959) 561-589.

59. Even biblical scholars themselves express frustration in this regard, as Brevard Childs reveals: "Yet who can control equally well the field of Semitic philology, ancient Near Eastern history, text and form criticism, rabbinics, New Testament, patristics, medieval and Reformation studies, philosophy and dogmatics?" *(The Book of Exodus* [Philadelphia: Westminster, 1974] ix-x).

60. Protestants, it should be remembered, had been dealing with biblical criticism for well over a century. As R. E. Brown *(Biblical Reflections on Crises Facing the Church,* ix) notes: "The Roman Catholic Church could not have made its advance in biblical criticism without Protestant aid. In the first third of the century the torch of biblical criticism was kept lighted by Protestant scholars; and when after 1943 Catholics lit their candles from it, they profited from the burnt fingers as well as the glowing insights of their Protestant confreres."

61. Hellwig, *Tradition,* 41. See in this context W. Wink *(The Bible in Human Transformation* [Philadelphia: Fortress 1973] 1-18) on the

"bankruptcy of the biblical critical paradigm." For some similarity in criticism, but a very different solution, see G. Maier (*The End of the Historical-Critical Method* [St. Louis: Concordia, 1974]).

62. L. Keck, *The Bible in the Pulpit: The Renewal of Biblical Preaching* (Nashville: Abingdon, 1978) 25.

63. Cited in W. Neil, "The Criticism and Theological Use of the Bible," in *The Cambridge History of the Bible* 3, ed. S. L. Greenslade (Cambridge: University Press, 1963) 286.

64. J. Coleman, "The Worldly Calling," *Commonweal* 105 (1978) 115-116.

65. Cited by R. Murphy, "Vatican III—Problems and Opportunities of the Future: The Bible," in *Toward Vatican III: The Work That Needs to Be Done*, eds. D. Tracy, H. Küng and J. Metz (New York: Seabury, 1978) 22.

66. See R. May, *Power and Innocence* (New York: W. W. Norton, 1972).

67. J. Fitzmyer, "Matthean Divorce Texts," *TS* 37 (1976) 197-226.

68. L. Alonso-Schökel, "Is Exegesis Necessary?" *Concilium* 70, ed. R. Murphy (New York: Herder and Herder, 1971) 32.

69. *Ibid.*, 38.

70. *Ibid.*

71. *Ibid.*, 35.

72. R. E. Brown, "Difficulties in Using the New Testament in American Catholic Discussions," *Louvain Studies* 6 (1976) 144-158.

73. Brown, "Difficulties in Using the New Testament," 145.

74. For a more complete explication, see R. E. Brown, "The Meaninig of Modern New Testament Studies for the Possibility of Ordaining Women to the Priesthood," in *Biblical Reflections on Crises Facing the Church,* 52-60.

75. Brown, "Difficulties in Using the New Testament," 151.

76. See another of Brown's essays in *Biblical Reflections,* "The Meaning of Modern New Testament Studies for an Ecumenical Understanding of Mary," 84-108. See also R. E. Brown, K. Donfried, J. Fitzmyer and J. Reumann, eds., *Mary in the New Testament* (New York: Paulist and Philadelphia: Fortress, 1978).

77. Brown, "Difficulties in Using the New Testament," 157. Brown's observation about the "challenging implications" of Christian origins is developed in a recent study of the Johannine epistles *(The Community of the Beloved Disciple: The Life, Loves and Hates of an Individual Church in New Testament Times* [New York: Paulist, 1974] in which he differentiates four phases of Johannine history and six religious groupings outside the community (see pp. 166-170).

78. By virtue of their collaborative work with Scripture scholars and their obligation to make accessible traditions and to make manifest the transformational character of the traditions, religious educators obviously exercise something of a mediational function. J. M. Lee *(The Flow of Religious Instruction,* 17–19, 21–23 and 300–301) also speaks of religious instruction as mediation, calling it the "active concrete process of existentially mediating theology and concrete reality" (17). His view, however, is in part derived from an understanding of theology not shared herein; Lee sees theologians as removed from the "hurly-burly" of the world, and thus claims a prophetic role for religious instruction, since its work consists in "here-and-now, deeply existential theologizing" (20).

79. M. C. Boys, "Religious Education and Contemporary Biblical Scholarship," *Religious Education* 74 (1979) 182–197.

80. J. Goldin, "Introduction," in S. Spiegel, *The Last Trial* (New York: Pantheon, 1967) xvi.

81. S. Sandmel, *Philo of Alexandria* (New York: Oxford University, 1979) 24.

82. *De Abrahamo,* 200–203.

83. *Jewish Antiquities* 1:13, 1–4.

84. A translation of the *Tg. Neof.,* Gen. 22:14 (with fragments in parentheses of *Frg. Tg.)* by G. Vermes and cited in R. Daly, "The Soteriological Significance of the Sacrifice of Isaac," *CBQ* 39 (1977) 51. Disagreement about the dating of the Targums as well as about the precise meaning of the term *Akedah* exists between Daly and P. R. Davies and B. D. Chilton ("The Aqedah: A Revised Tradition History," *CBQ* 40 [1978] 514–546), but their disagreement does not affect the points under discussion here.

85. Again, Vermes's translation of *Tg. Neof.,* Lev. 22:27, cited in Daly, 53.

86. In *Gen. Rab.* 56:11, cited in Davies and Chilton, 537.

87. Spiegel, *The Last Trial,* 20.

88. *Ibid.,* 20–21.

89. Rabbi Ephraim ben Jacob, cited in Spiegel, 152.

90. E. Wiesel, *Messengers of God: Biblical Portraits and Legends* (New York: Random House 1976) 92–93.

91. *Ibid.,* 93.

92. *Ibid.,* 97.

93. The LXX renders the MT's "only son" as "beloved son."

94. *Adv. Marc.* 3.18 and *Adv. Jud.* 13.

95. *Adv. Haer.* 4:5, 4

96. *Strom.* 5:11.

97. Gregory of Nyssa, *Hom. Res. 1,* cited in J. Daniélou, *From Shadows to Reality* (Westminster, Md.: Newman, 1960) 129.

98. Augustine, *Third Discourse on Psalm 30:9.*

99. John Chrysostom, *Hom. Gen.* 47:3, cited in Daniélou, 129.

100. See n. 5.

101. R. E. McNally, *The Bible in the Early Middle Ages* (Westminster, Md.: Newman, 1959) 11.

102. "The Mystery of Adam" in F. E. Talmage, ed., *Disputation and Dialogue: Readings in the Jewish-Christian Encounter* (New York: KTAV and Anti-Defamation League, 1975) 100–101.

103. *Ibid.,* 100.

104. See "Abraham" in M. Rose, ed., *Wakefield Mystery Plays* (New York: W. W. Norton, 1961) 107–116; "Abraham and Isaac," in A. C. Cawley, ed., *Everyman and Medieval Miracle Plays* (New York: E. P. Dutton, 1959) 52–68.

105. See R. Bainton, "The Bible in the Reformation," *Cambridge History of the Bible* 3, 1–37; J. S. Preus, *From Shadow to Promise: Old Testament Interpretation from Augustine to Young Luther* (Cambridge: Belknap Press of Harvard University, 1969).

106. M. Luther, *Commentary on Genesis* 2 (Grand Rapids: Zondervan, 1958) 13.

107. *Ibid.,* 10.

108. See B. Vawter, *On Genesis: A New Reading* (New York: Doubleday, 1977); G. von Rad, *Genesis: A Commentary,* rev. ed (Philadelphia: Westminster, 1972).

109. A. Godin, "Isaac 'at the Stake,'" *Lumen Vitae* 10 (1955) 65–92.

110. In the U.S. and Canada, Roman Catholics follow this juxtaposition of readings on the Second Sunday of Lent, Year B. It is also one of the readings during the Easter Vigil.

111. J. A. Sanders, "Hermeneutics," *IDB Sup* (Nashville: Abingdon, 1976) 404. See also his "Text and Canon," *JBL* 98 (1979) 5–29.

112. Sanders, "Hermeneutics," 404.

113. *Ibid.*

114. *Ibid.,* 405.

115. *Ibid.,* 406.

116. *Ibid.,* 407. See also J. A. Sanders, *God Has a Story Too: Sermons in Context* (Philadelphia: Fortress, 1979).

117. A result related to J. M. Lee's criticism of religious instruction as a "messenger boy" (see n. 11).

118. Trilling cited in Nineham, 194.

119. Nineham, 194.

120. P. Ricoeur, *Interpretation Theory: Discourse and the Surplus of Meaning* (Fort Worth: Texas Christian University Press, 1976) 75. See also J. D. Crossan, ed., *Paul Ricoeur on Biblical Hermeneutics* (*Semeia* 4; Missoula, Mont.: Scholars Press, 1975).

121. Ricoeur, *Interpretation Theory*, 74.

122. *Ibid.*, 78.

123. *Ibid.*, 79.

124. *Ibid.*, 87–88.

125. *Ibid.*, 93.

126. G. T. Montague, "Hermeneutics and the Teaching of Scripture," *CBQ* 41 (1979) 11.

127. *Ibid.*

128. *Ibid.*, 12.

129. Chirico, *Infallibility: The Crossroads of Doctrine*, 28.

130. R. Palmer, *Hermeneutics: Interpretation Theory in Schleiermacher, Dilthey, Heidegger and Gadamer* (Evanston: Northwestern University Press, 1969) 245.

131. *Ibid.*, 235.

132. See G. Moran, "Two Languages of Religious Education," *Living Light* 14 (1977) 7–15; J. M. Lee, *The Shape of Religious Instruction*, 225–257.

133. My debt to the curricular theory of Prof. Dwayne Huebner is obvious here.

134. A superb example of a book which makes form criticism understandable and invites participation is that of G. Lohfink *(The Bible: Now I Get It* [New York: Doubleday, 1979]).

135. Montague, 1–2. See his proposed paradigm for teaching, 13–16.

136. See P. Freire, *Pedagogy of the Oppressed* (New York: Seabury, 1974).

137. See the series of carefully laid out teaching strategies by M. Weil and B. Joyce (*Information Processing Models of Teaching* [Englewood Cliffs, N.J.: Prentice-Hall, 1978]; *Social Models of Teaching* and *Personal Models of Teaching* [Englewood Cliffs, N.J.: Prentice-Hall, 1978]). Their original one-volume work (*Models of Teaching* [Englewood Cliffs: Prentice-Hall, 1972]) has been thoroughly refined in the newer three-volume series.

138. M. Greene, *Landscapes of Learning* (New York: Teachers College, 1978) 185.

139. J. Royce, "Is There a Science of Education?" *Educational Review* 1 (1891) 15–25; and reprinted in M. L. Borrowman, ed., *Teacher*

Education in America (Classics in Education #24; New York: Teachers College Press, 1965) 109.

140. *Teacher Education in America,* 110.

141. See the commentary on the Gospel of Matthew written for diocesan usage, R. E. Obach and A. Kirk (*A Commentary on the Gospel of Matthew* [New York: Paulist, 1978]).

142. See *Lumen Vitae* 33 (1978), an issue on "Reading Texts and Events," with articles by both religious educators and biblical scholars.

143. Keck, 28.

Conclusion

The era of the dominance of *Heilsgeschichte* in Catholic religious education in the United States has come to an end. The theological deficiencies inherent in that hermeneutic could not sustain the significance given it, nor could its educational basis support the pluralism emerging in religious education. The age, however, is immensely instructive for present-day educators; a retrospective offers the possibility of reconstructing our experience and of building upon the past. As Winston Churchill once sagely observed: "The farther backward you can look, the farther forward you are likely to see."

During the early stages of my research and writing, I was acutely conscious of the theological and educational limitations of salvation history. Now, some three years later, I am no less aware of these problems, but I am also much more appreciative of its significance. Salvation history was, in its own way, to borrow a phrase from T. S. Eliot, "a raid on the inarticulate." It recognized that the Bible, a classic text and Sacred Scripture, must be interpreted anew in every era and that this interpretation must contribute to the vitality of the life of faith. If today our theological and educational views are more refined and pluralistic, we can, nevertheless, discover that the concerns lying at the heart of *Heilsgeschichte* are timeless.

Readers will, I believe, discover that many important questions about biblical interpretation emerge from this study. Good questions, as John Ciardi once commented, are not bolts to be tightened, but seeds to be planted toward the hope of "greening the landscape of an idea." It is my hope that the explorations engendered by good questions will bear fruit.

ACKNOWLEDGMENTS

Grateful acknowledgment is made to the following for use of copyrighted material:

America Press, Inc., for quotations from *The Documents of Vatican II*, © 1966. All rights reserved.

Augsburg Publishing House, for quotations from *Interpreting the Bible*, by J. C. K. von Hofmann, translated by Christian Preus, © 1959. Used by permission.

Darton, Longman and Todd, Ltd., for quotations from *Theological Investigations*, Vol. 6 by Karl Rahner published and © 1969. Used by permission of the publishers.

Houghton Mifflin Company, for quotations from *Client-Centered Therapy* byCarl Rogers et al. Copyright © 1951, renewed 1979, by Carl R. Rogers. Reprinted by permission of Houghton Mifflin Company.

McCutchan Publishing Corporation, for quotations from *Curriculum Theorizing*, ed. by William Pinar, 1974. Reprinted by permission of the publisher.

Orbis Books, for quotations from *Our Idea of God* by J. L. Segundo, © 1974. Used by permission.

Paulist Press, for quotations from: *A Survey of Catholic Theology 1800–1970* by T. M. Schoof, © 1970; *The Renewal of American Catholicisim* by David O'Brien, © 1972; *Discovery Patterns Book 2*, ed. by R. J. Heyer and R. J. Payne, © 1969; and *Church: The Continuing Quest* by Richard P. McBrien, © 1970.

Prentice-Hall, Inc. for quotations from *Studies in Salvation History*, ed. by Luke Salm, © 1964, p. xiii. Reprinted by permission of the publisher, Englewood Cliffs, New Jersey.

Religious Education Association, for quotations from the March April 1964 issue of the journal, *Religious Education*, by permission of the publisher, 409 Prospect Street, New Haven, CT 06510. Membership subscription available for $20.00 per year.

Temple University for quotations from the *Journal of Ecumenical Studies*, Vol. 11, © 1974.

Texas Christian University, for quotations from *Interpretation Theory* by Paul Ricoeur, © 1976.

Index of Biblical References

Index of Names

Abbott, Walter M., 11, 127, 263, 333
Ackroyd, Peter R., 329
Adam, Karl, 76, 130
Addams, Jane, 222
Adolphus, King Gustavus, 14
Agus, J. B., 136
Ahern, Barnabas, 112
Ahlstrom, Sydney E., 54, 56
Ahumada, Enrique, 326
Albrektson, Bertil, 145, 253
Alonso-Schökel, Luis, 301, 334
Altizer, Thomas, J. J., 264
Anderson, Bernhard W., 55, 256
Anshen, Ruth N., 259
Apple, Michael W., 270
Archibald, Helen A., 330
Auberlerlen, Carl August, 37
Aubert, R., 129
Augustine, of Hippo, 14, 52, 91, 94, 114, 115, 164, 204, 255, 311, 336
Aulén, Gustaf, 262
Austen, Jane, 128
Aymes-Coucke, Maria de la Cruz, 137

Babin, Pierre, 95, 239, 272
Bainton, Roland, 336
Balthasar, Hans von, 261
Barr, James, 43, 50, 61, 141, 143–146, 148, 161, 163, 165–169, 174, 178, 248, 253, 256–257, 275, 333
Barrosse, Thomas, 113
Barth, Karl, 16, 17, 35, 43, 55, 56, 75, 106, 196

Bartsch, Hans W., 57
Baum, Gregory, 191, 197, 241, 254, 261–262, 292, 332
Baumgärtel, Friedrich, 256
Baur, Ferdinand Christian, 16, 27, 65, 305
Beck, Johann Tobias, 30, 37, 56, 253
Beker, J. C., 260
Ben-Chorim, Schalom, 261
Bengel, Johann Albrecht, 15, 20, 54
Bengsch, A., 54
Berger, Klaus, 137
Berrigan, Daniel, 204, 264
Berrigan, Philip, 204
Berryman, Jerome, 333
Bett, H., 54
Biddle, Bruce T., 265
Billerbeck, Paul, 185–186
Bismarck, Otto von, 70, 75
Bloom, Benjamin S., 213, 266
Blum, A., 331
Bobbitt, J. Franklin, 207, 209, 211, 264, 265
Boman, T., 60
Bond, Raymond T., 264
Bongler, J., 135
Bornkamm, Günther, 196
Borrowman, M. L., 337
Bouillard, Henri, 129
Bourke, Myles, 112, 255
Bousset, Wilhelm, 185–186
Bowers, C. A., 230, 265, 268, 269–270
Bowles, Samuel, 223
Boys, Mary C., 331, 332, 335

343

Index of Subjects